A Concise Companion to
the Romantic Age

Blackwell Concise Companions to Literature and Culture
General Editor: David Bradshaw, University of Oxford

This series offers accessible, innovative approaches to major areas of literary study. Each volume provides an indispensable companion for anyone wishing to gain an authoritative understanding of a given period or movement's intellectual character and contexts.

Published

Chaucer	Edited by Corinne Saunders
English Renaissance Literature	Edited by Donna B. Hamilton
Shakespeare and the Text	Edited by Andrew Murphy
Shakespeare on Screen	Edited by Diana E. Henderson
Milton	Edited by Angelica Duran
The Restoration and Eighteenth Century	Edited by Cynthia Wall
The Victorian Novel	Edited by Francis O'Gorman
Modernism	Edited by David Bradshaw
Postwar American Literature and Culture	Edited by Josephine G. Hendin
Twentieth-Century American Poetry	Edited by Stephen Fredman
Contemporary British Fiction	Edited by James F. English
Contemporary British and Irish Drama	Edited by Nadine Holdsworth and Mary Luckhurst
Feminist Theory	Edited by Mary Eagleton
American Fiction 1900–1950	Edited by Peter Stoneley and Cindy Weinstein
The Romantic Age	Edited by Jon Klancher

A Concise Companion to
the Romantic Age

Edited by Jon Klancher

A John Wiley & Sons, Ltd., Publication

This edition first published 2009
© 2009 Blackwell Publishing Ltd

Blackwell Publishing was acquired by John Wiley & Sons in February 2007. Blackwell's publishing program has been merged with Wiley's global Scientific, Technical, and Medical business to form Wiley-Blackwell.

Registered Office
John Wiley & Sons Ltd, The Atrium, Southern Gate, Chichester, West Sussex, PO19 8SQ, United Kingdom

Editorial Offices
350 Main Street, Malden, MA 02148-5020, USA
9600 Garsington Road, Oxford, OX4 2DQ, UK
The Atrium, Southern Gate, Chichester, West Sussex, PO19 8SQ, UK

For details of our global editorial offices, for customer services, and for information about how to apply for permission to reuse the copyright material in this book please see our website at www.wiley.com/wiley-blackwell.

The right of Jon Klancher to be identified as the author of the editorial material in this work has been asserted in accordance with the Copyright, Designs and Patents Act 1988.

All rights reserved. No part of this publication may be reproduced, stored in a retrieval system, or transmitted, in any form or by any means, electronic, mechanical, photocopying, recording or otherwise, except as permitted by the UK Copyright, Designs and Patents Act 1988, without the prior permission of the publisher.

Wiley also publishes its books in a variety of electronic formats. Some content that appears in print may not be available in electronic books.

Designations used by companies to distinguish their products are often claimed as trademarks. All brand names and product names used in this book are trade names, service marks, trademarks or registered trademarks of their respective owners. The publisher is not associated with any product or vendor mentioned in this book. This publication is designed to provide accurate and authoritative information in regard to the subject matter covered. It is sold on the understanding that the publisher is not engaged in rendering professional services. If professional advice or other expert assistance is required, the services of a competent professional should be sought.

Library of Congress Cataloging-in-Publication Data

A concise companion to the Romantic age / edited by Jon Klancher.
   p. cm. — (Blackwell concise companions to literature and culture)
   Includes bibliographical references and index.
   ISBN 978-0-631-23355-8 (hardcover: alk. paper)
   1. English literature—18th century—History and criticism. 2. English literature—19th century—History and criticism. 3. Romanticism—Great Britain. 4. Literature and society—Great Britain—History—18th century. 5. Literature and society—Great Britain—History—19th century. 6. Great Britain—Intellectual life—18th century. 7. Great Britain—Intellectual life—19th century. I. Klancher, Jon P.

PR447.C59 2009
820.9'007—dc22
                                                                          2008031715

A catalogue record for this book is available from the British Library.

Set in 10/12.5pt Meridien by Graphicraft Limited, Hong Kong
Printed in Singapore by Utopia Press Pte Ltd

1   2009

Contents

List of Illustrations vii
Notes on Contributors viii

Introduction 1
Jon Klancher

1 Transfiguring God: Religion, Revolution, Romanticism 14
  Robert M. Maniquis

2 Romanticism and Empire 36
  Saree Makdisi

3 "Associations Respect[ing] the Past": Enlightenment and
  Romantic Historicism 57
  Anthony Jarrells

4 Nationalisms in Romantic Britain and Ireland: Culture,
  Politics, and the Global 77
  Miranda Burgess

5 "With an Industry Incredible": Politics, Writing, and
  the Public Sphere 99
  Paul Keen

Contents

6	Romantic Justice: Law, Literature, and Individuality *Mark Schoenfield*	119
7	Natural History in the Romantic Period *Noah Heringman*	141
8	Romantic Sciences: British and Continental Thresholds *Frederick Burwick*	168
9	Consumer Culture: Getting and Spending in the Romantic Age *Nicholas Mason*	189
10	The Romantic-Era Book Trade *Lee Erickson*	212
11	Visual Pleasures, Visionary States: Art, Entertainment, and the Nation *Gillen D'Arcy Wood*	232
12	What's at Stake? Kantian Aesthetics, Romantic and Modern Poetics, Sociopolitical Commitment *Robert Kaufman*	257
Index		283

List of Illustrations

Figure 1 "The Natural___ist." Anonymous engraving from "Simon Snip," *The Philosophical Puppet Show* (London, 1785) — 148

Figure 2 Mrs. Richard Brinsley Sheridan, c.1785–87 (oil on canvas) by Thomas Gainsborough (1727–88) — 234

Figure 3 "The Cornfield" by John Constable (1776–1837). Presented by subscribers, including Wordsworth, Faraday and Sir William Beechey, 1837 — 248

Figure 4 "The Exhibition Stare Case," c.1800 (engraving) by Thomas Rowlandson (1756–1827) — 251

Notes on Contributors

Miranda Burgess is Associate Professor of English at the University of British Columbia. She is the author of *British Fiction and the Production of Social Order, 1740–1830* (2000), a study of the uses of genre change in theorizing British nationhood, as well as essays on the histories of nationalism/transnationalism, genre and reading, and Irish and Scottish print culture. She is completing *Romantic Transport: Reading, Feeling, Literary Form, 1790–1830*, a book which examines the media contexts and literary outcomes of Romantic affect in relation to contemporary understandings of transnational exchange.

Frederick Burwick, Professor Emeritus at UCLA, is author and editor of 24 books and over a hundred articles. His research is dedicated to problems of perception, illusion, and delusion in literary representation and theatrical performance. His *Poetic Madness and the Romantic Imagination* (1996) won the Barricelli Book of the Year Award of the International Conference on Romanticism. He has been named Distinguished Scholar by the British Academy (1992) and the Keats–Shelley Association (1998). Recent publications include *Romantic Drama: Acting and Reacting* (2008) and his electronic edition of *The Theatre Journal of John Waldie* (2008).

Lee Erickson (1952–2008), Professor of English at Marshall University, specialized in nineteenth-century literary history and theory, with books including *Robert Browning: His Poetry and His Audiences* (1984), and the widely cited *The Economy of Literary Form: English Literature and the Industrialization of Publishing, 1800–1850* (1996). His recent research focused on the publishing history of poetry, addressing anonymous and pseudonymous authorship, the formats used for poetic works, editorial difficulties, and the problematic social decorum of reading in the nineteenth century. He also contributed an essay on the book trade to Blackwell's *A Companion to Victorian Poetry*.

Noah Heringman is an associate professor of English at the University of Missouri-Columbia. He has published *Romantic Rocks, Aesthetic Geology* (2004), an edited collection, *Romantic Science* (2003), and various articles and book chapters. He is currently completing a book entitled *Sciences of Antiquity* (forthcoming 2010), on the relationship between writing and fieldwork in the practice of antiquarianism and natural history.

Anthony Jarrells is Associate Professor of English at the University of South Carolina. He is the author of *Britain's Bloodless Revolutions: 1688 and the Romantic Reform of Literature* (2005) and the editor of a volume of selected prose tales from *Blackwood's Magazine* (2006). He is currently working on a project entitled "The Time of the Tale: Romanticism, Genre, and the 'Intermixing' of Enlightenment."

Robert Kaufman teaches in the Comparative Literature Department at the University of California, Berkeley. He is the author of *Negative Romanticism: Adornian Aesthetics in Keats, Shelley, and Modern Poetry* (forthcoming) and is at work on two related books: *Why Poetry Should Matter – to the Left*, and *Modernism after Postmodernism? Robert Duncan and the Future-Present of American Poetry*. His essays have appeared in numerous journals and collections, including *Critical Inquiry, October, American Poetry Review, PMLA, Modernist Cultures, Cultural Critique, New German Critique, Walter Benjamin and Art, The Cambridge Companion to Adorno, Adorno and Literature, Studies in Romanticism*, and *European Romantic Review*.

Paul Keen is Professor of English at Carleton University. He is the author of *The Crisis of Literature in the 1790s: Print Culture and the Public Sphere* (1999), editor of *The Radical Popular Press in Britain, 1817–1821* (2003) and *Revolutions in Romantic Literature: An Anthology of Print Culture, 1780–1832* (2004), and coeditor of *Bookish Histories: Books, Literature and Commercial Modernity, 1700–1900* (forthcoming).

Notes on Contributors

Jon Klancher teaches Romantic and Victorian literature, the sociology of culture, and the history of books and reading at Carnegie Mellon University. He has written widely on Romantic and nineteenth-century British literary and cultural history in such journals and collections as *ELH, Studies in Romanticism, MLQ, Romantic Metropolis, The Cambridge History of Literary Criticism, The New Historicism*, and *The Oxford Companion to the Romantic Age: British Culture 1776–1837*. Author of *The Making of English Reading Audiences, 1790–1832* (1987), he is currently completing a book, *Transfiguring "Arts & Sciences": Knowledge and Cultural Institutions in the Romantic Age*.

Saree Makdisi is Professor of English and Comparative Literature at UCLA. He is the author of *Romantic Imperialism* (1998); *William Blake and the Impossible History of the 1790s* (2003), and *Palestine Inside Out: An Everyday Occupation* (2008).

Robert M. Maniquis teaches in the English Department at the University of California, Los Angeles. He is the author of many essays on Enlightenment and Romantic literature as well as *Lonely Empires: Personal and Public Visions of Thomas De Quincey, the English Opium-Eater* (1976), and editor of such volumes as *British Radical Culture of the 1790s* (2002), *The Encyclopedie and the Age of Revolution* (with Clorinda Donato, 1992), *The French Revolution and the Iberian Peninsula* (with Oscar Marti and Joseph Perez, 1992), and *Defoe's Footprints* (with Carl Fisher, 2008).

Nicholas Mason is Associate Professor of English at Brigham Young University. In addition to editing scholarly collections on Romantic-era satire, *Blackwood's Edinburgh Magazine*, and Edward Kimber's *History of the Life and Adventures of Mr. Anderson*, he has published articles on nineteenth-century consumerism in *Modern Language Quarterly, Nineteenth-Century Literature*, and *Victorian Literature and Culture*. He is currently completing a book manuscript on the interrelationship of advertising and literature in the Romantic age.

Mark Schoenfield, an associate professor of English at Vanderbilt University, is the author of *The Professional Wordsworth: Law, Labor, and the Poet's Contracts* (1996) and *British Periodicals and Romantic Identity: The "Literary Lower Empire"* (2008). In both books as well as in articles on Byron, legal entails, wager of battle, and other topics, he has explored the intersection of law and literature and the contribution of their synergies and antagonisms to British Romantic culture.

Notes on Contributors

Gillen D'Arcy Wood is associate professor of English at the University of Illinois, Urbana-Champaign. He is the author of *The Shock of the Real: Romanticism and Visual Culture, 1760–1860* (2001), and a historical novel, *Hosack's Folly* (2005). His forthcoming book examines the intersections of British Romanticism and continental music culture in the period 1770–1840.

Introduction: A Concise Companion to the Romantic Age

Jon Klancher

What was Romanticism? How did the Romantic age, a pivotal moment of modernity, begin and end? What were its defining genres, languages, knowledges, conflicts over matters of politics, religion, or truth? Why has Romanticism persisted, well beyond its age of revolutions in the later eighteenth and early nineteenth century, to reappear in often unlikely places or forms, or at the most unexpected of times, ever since? Both basic and complex, these questions still lie at the center of studying Romantic writing or culture. They continue to provoke new thinking about Romanticism's place in modern culture, as the chapters in the present volume will do further. This companion to the age of Romanticism guides the reader to a shape-shifting Romantic period that may have had several different points of origin, and perhaps only a provisional ending (estimates have ranged from 1798–1830, to 1789–1832, or 1776–1837 among others). As we're now aware, to periodize is to construct an interpretive as well as historical frame of analysis; it should not surprise the student approaching Romanticism for the first time to learn that there is no certain or consensual dating of this nonetheless watershed cultural moment. Yet the accumulating cluster of varying temporal frameworks built by critics and scholars tells us something important about the complexity and unevenness of this extraordinary moment. No matter what particular dates we use to frame it, the Romantic age continues to have a special and sometimes hotly debated place in the literary and cultural history of Britain or Europe (if a somewhat different one in the United States).

Introduction

Chapters of this book largely concentrate on the wide range of writing, knowledge production, and visual imagining of that variably defined period (for our purposes here, about 1770–1840). Long-read Romantic writers – Byron, Wordsworth, Shelley, Keats, Blake, Coleridge – appear side by side with figures only now being studied as among the period's most significant cultural producers: Charlotte Smith, Robert Southey, Sir Joseph Banks, Sir Walter Scott, Anna Seward, John Galt, Jane Austen, Hannah More, William Cobbett, Francis Jeffrey, Humphry Davy, John Gibson Lockhart, Francis Burney, and others. Still, as the first and last essays emphasize with special force, it would be a mistake to think Romanticism was only a remarkable period of literary history. In various senses, essays in this volume show why Romanticism itself has so interestingly complicated our idea of what "history" is – as well as what culture, nation, religion, politics, justice, even nature, science, aesthetics, or knowledge are.

While this Companion cannot sort out all the meanings of "Romanticism" that have radiated through modern culture since the end of the eighteenth century, it can help the student of modern literature and cultural history to try to place this hugely influential cultural phenomenon in terms that make sense in the early twenty-first century. We try to accomplish that aim by focusing, not only on key topics or important questions that emerged in the Romantic age, but on their *relationships*. Thus a chapter on the volatile nature of religious beliefs in that period will also, of necessity, speak to the framing political and imaginative context of what Percy Shelley called "the master theme of the age," the French Revolution. The question of law or political canons of justice in this age of extremes must also engage the discourse of "poetic justice" and the period's great narrative experiments in representing legal cases and conflicts for inquiring readers. On a very different topic, the essay on the role of the book in the early nineteenth century accentuates publishing's intricate interdependence with the market economy and the power of publishers or editors to shape their contemporary culture.

Every essay in this volume situates a literary or cultural aspect of Romanticism – poetry, the novel, painting and theatrical performance, aesthetic theory, religion – in terms of a geopolitical, social, and volatile economic world. There is no single essay on poetry as such – a departure from traditional ways of representing Romanticism, to be sure – but poetry and poetics reappear as constant points of focus or interpretation for grasping religious controversy, empire and Orientalism, natural history, political debate, or aesthetic theory in the

Romantic era or since. The explosive growth and range of the novel or related fictional genres likewise become an ongoing focus in chapters on nationalism, historiography, law and justice, or consumer culture rather than a topic in itself. Yet each essay also takes pains to show why literary, visual, and cultural actions could transform political, social, or marketplace circumstances and ideas – and would continue to do so long after we usually say the Romantic age "ended."

To set the stage for what follows in this volume, it is important to recall that, variously celebrated or reviled in the nineteenth and early twentieth centuries, Romantic writing was never uncontroversial; indeed it was an explosive enough subject from the 1910s to 1940s – ideologically and aesthetically – for modern scholarly Romantic studies to begin developing systematically only in the decades after World War II. Certain critical monuments of that time are still required reading for anyone attempting to grasp the shape and protean philosophical, aesthetic, or cultural questions posed by the Romantic age – from *The Mirror and the Lamp* (Abrams 1953) or *Blake: Prophet Against Empire* (Erdman 1954) to *Culture and Society, 1780–1950* (Williams 1958) or *Wordsworth's Poetry 1787–1807* (Hartman 1964). Variously formalist or antiformalist (Abrams, Williams), philosophical or concretely historical (Hartman, Erdman), such works and many others initially defined the territory of debate, theory, and research that would mark the vitality of Romantic studies long afterward. By the time of Harold Bloom's collection *Romanticism and Consciousness* (1970) or Abrams's second major study, *Natural Supernaturalism* (1971), the field of Romanticism had become the most intriguing and perhaps consequential period of literary studies for the profession as a whole. It was also poised to be a staging ground for the powerfully debated transformations in literary and cultural studies about to commence.

The first of these – a "theory revolution" drawing on then-unfamiliar Continental philosophies rearticulated as structuralism, deconstruction, or poststructuralism – found in Romantic poetry and its interpretation a textual portal through which critics could begin to rethink long-held assumptions about language, textuality, temporality, and indeed literariness itself (de Man 1984, Rajan 1990). Later generations of more historically or culturally minded critics and scholars were often first weaned on this heady blend of rhetorical, textualist, and philosophical skepticism that performed "close reading" – no longer a property of the New Critics – with a vengeance, opening unsuspected gaps, contradictions, or abyssal spirals of uncertainty (*mise en abyme*) in the same texts or literary works long cherished for their Platonic, imaginative,

Introduction

or ontological idealisms. Yet such criticism, often trained in comparative literature and absorbing English Romanticism into Germanic as well as French philosophical languages, could also reinforce long-standing assumptions about the radical break Romanticism had made with the Enlightenment, claiming that instead it was the origin of our modernity as well as an important precursor to modernism.

The philosophical turn in Romantic studies did not simply come to an end when a new historical and cultural critique of both traditional literary history and newer kinds of theory emerged forcefully in the early 1980s. Historicist, cultural, and philosophical modes of critical reading and cultural history have tended rather to coexist (as anyone who attends conferences on Romantic questions knows) and they have often blended in Romanticist scholarship and debates. Yet it would be hard to overestimate the scope and (I believe) the irreversible effects of the successively historicist, feminist, Marxist, postcolonial, and other critical modes of rethinking the texts and contexts of Romantic-age cultural production or its aftermath. Early on, debates focused on what Jerome McGann called *The Romantic Ideology* (1983), or what Marilyn Butler (1981) pointed to as the extraordinary range of Romantic-age cultural production (in *Romantics, Rebels, and Reactionaries*). Other polemical criticism raised serious doubt about centering the Romantic period as an "age of Wordsworth" or construing its great poetry and other genres as mainly in terms of mind or imagination (Levinson 1986, Liu 1989, Chandler 1998). Canon revision, the reemergence of women writers and readers to modern view, new attention to print culture and its audiences, a turn toward the long-neglected novels of the era as key to grasping both what "literature" meant to the period and how rich a cultural matrix the narrative fictions produced then and afterward – all this should be now familiar and necessary territory for anyone pursuing Romantic studies today.

The following essays will not be starting from scratch on their topics, but assume some familiarity already with what's at stake in the history, study, and controversies attending Romanticism and the problems posed by defining a Romantic age in cultural history. They take for granted, for example, that what had long been called "English Romanticism" must now be approached as a complexly produced *British* mode of writing or visualizing that entails increasing attention to Scottish, Irish, or Welsh as well as specifically English sorts of cultural production. As the essays on nationalisms or Enlightenment and Romantic historicism will clarify, the uneven development of those national literatures and cultures – as influentially brought to the foreground of Romantic studies by James Chandler and others – effectively redraws the geographical landscape of a Romanticism that was grasped as oriented to Western Europe or isolated in England itself (see Trumpener 1997, Chandler 1998, Duncan 2007). The same geo-cultural awareness makes the East's impact on Romantic writing a matter of sometimes startling defamiliarization of old or long-disregarded writers or genres, as Robert Southey's role in the essay on empire and imperialism will suggest (Leask 1992, Makdisi 1998). Book history and print culture, meanwhile, can no longer be regarded as incidental matters, but in one way or another figure centrally in grasping the period's sciences or natural history, political argument or novelistic imaginations, poetries or religious quarrels.

Finally, the diversity and complexity of what both students of and experts in the study of Romanticism now confront in their field can produce very different styles of argument or presentation. Essays in this Companion are written in variously contextualist, empirical, interpretive, or philosophical ways. They attend to both historical and theoretical matters, shifting from close-ups that spotlight fine textual or historical grain, to wide-angle views engaged in broader cultural mapping. They echo across one another and give, I think, a richly multifaceted perspective – if necessarily, within the reach of one 12-essay volume, hardly a totalized picture – on the "Romantic" as both a period and an ongoing cultural and intellectual force.

The first six chapters place Romanticism in a spacious geographic and cultural matrix: West and East, nationalism and empire, religion and revolution, political controversy, narratives of historical change and fictional imagining, or matters of justice or interpreting the law. The next six essays focus on kinds of cultural production and disciplines of knowledge that would affect many genres of writing or visualization in the Romantic age and afterward: natural history, geographic exploration, and the sciences; economic behavior, consumerism, and publishing history; the visual and performing arts, poetics, and the aesthetic controversies that, long after the Romantic age itself, inflected the politics of Modernism and continue to demand rigorous reflection today.

In "Transfiguring God: Religion, Revolution, Romanticism," Robert Maniquis reminds us that *everyone* lived their lives in a deeply and inescapably religious culture at this time (even if they were atheists), one that was more sharply divided and decidedly political about their religious understandings than at any time since the religious and political struggles of the mid-seventeenth century. His essay crosses

Introduction

disciplinary boundaries to grasp the ferocity of religious arguments descending from the West's long history of Christendom that were inescapably political, as overtly political debates raged in often religious language. Modern readers still have difficulty sorting out the complex arguments between older and newer viewpoints held by Anglicans, Catholics, and all manner of dissenters (Methodists, Presbyterians, Calvinists, Unitarians, and the like). Clarifying these clashes in the late eighteenth century, Maniquis accentuates the "fragility of Enlightenment" that becomes apparent when religious passions surge into the public realm at crisis moments like the 1790s. He shows why the French Revolution would be seen to introduce a new kind of violence into modern life – not mass slaughter, which had been known for centuries and had been justified by precisely religious motives or rationales – but a violence without "meaning" of the kind religion had traditionally provided (for instance, in rituals of sacrifice). Rather, the Romantic writer's appropriation of "imagination" from its earlier eighteenth-century meanings is most telling – the idea of a reintegration of mind and body after the painful tearing apart that modernity's endless violence toward the past seemed to make irreparable.

Shifting from its struggles with the past of Western Christendom and the present of modernizing revolutions, Saree Makdisi's essay dates the Romantic age by two great shifts in the discourse on Empire and the East – when the linguist William Jones introduced the "poetry of Eastern nations" to Britain in 1772 and when the historian Thomas Macaulay authoritatively pronounced such matters of no further interest to the British in 1835. Makdisi uses these moments to frame the new fascination of the Orient and especially its literature to British and Romantic writers in a period that has sometimes been called the "second Oriental renaissance." What distinguished Romantic imperialism from the wider span of modern empire-building between the seventeenth and twentieth centuries for Makdisi is thus its peculiarly strong sense of relation between the archaic and exotic remainders of an ancient past the British thought they encountered in the East, as against a rapidly modernized, rationalized course of development all around them in the West. Nearly all Romantic poets engaged in this fascination with the East, not least Byron, Blake, and Wordsworth, but Makdisi pays special attention to a then popular, but long since disregarded, poet who is only today being reread with great interest again – Robert Southey, author of *Thalaba the Destroyer*, *The Curse of Kehama*, and other narrative verse epics that in the early 1800s thrilled and impressed British readers. In Makdisi's absorbing account,

Southey's verse typifies Romantic literary imperialism in many ways, particularly as it weaves distinctly Christian beliefs or phrases into the mouths of Muslim speakers, paradoxically calling in question England's own proud discourse of becoming modern and powerful. The sociocultural critique available within Southey's Orientalist epics also suggests why Whig historians like Macaulay would find a certain kind of Romantic poetic practice altogether too powerful – what Makdisi calls an "exhilarating, threatening, sublime spectacle of Oriental alterity" (p. 55).

The next two chapters address two long-standing ways of defining the Romantic age – its association with the rise of nationalism in Western Europe and its putative opposition to a preceding Enlightenment. In his essay on Enlightenment, Romanticism, and historicism, Anthony Jarrells shows why thinking about Romanticism more historically than in the past also complicates one of the oldest ways of defining it – as standing in stark contrast to the seventeenth- and eighteenth-century Enlightenment. Instead, recent scholarship has been discovering the complex continuities as well as swerves between Enlightenment and Romantic-age writing, most influentially in the work of Marilyn Butler, James Chandler, Katie Trumpeter, or Ian Duncan. Jarrells asks why it's been the case that thinking about Enlightenment and Romanticism in new ways would inevitably lead to a new cultural geography of the Romantic period as well – for instance, to the Scottish writers of both Edinburgh's high Enlightenment moment, from David Hume to Adam Smith and Dugald Stewart, or Romantic-age novelists like Walter Scott or tale-writers like John Galt. The epochal battle here lies in a more culturally activist Scotland that pitted Enlightenment arguments (in the *Edinburgh Review* and elsewhere) against those being imported from Germany by Coleridge or *Blackwood's Edinburgh Magazine*. Jarrells contributes a new reading of the relation between Romanticism and historicism by showing the paradoxical way in which Galt's fictional tales would, unlike Scott's historical novels, "intermix" two contrasting ways of representing history – Scotland's developmental (or "stadial") historicism, and Germany's relativist *historismus*.

In her essay on the rise of nationalism in this era, Miranda Burgess shows why modern concepts of nationalism do not easily fit the British case, especially its literatures as they emerge from the incommensurate national cultures of Ireland, Scotland, or England. She guides her reader through some recently influential accounts of nationalism – including those that emphasize a "reading nation" or "print capitalism" – by

Introduction

pointing to the great range of Irish, English, and Scottish fictional or polemical ways of representing nations to readers and to one another. Burke's *Reflections on the Revolution in France*, *Florence Macarthy* and *The Wild Irish Boy* by the Irish writers Sidney Owenson and Thomas Maturin, and Walter Scott's Waverley novels, particularly *The Antiquary*, make up part of the complicated terrain of national figurations Burgess helps us negotiate. Like Makdisi and Jarrells, she points us back out of the thicket of British national self or communal identifications and literary figures to the wider impact they would have on what we now see, in light of these Romantic-period works, as the cultural tensions of a global modernity.

The late eighteenth and early nineteenth century saw the emergence of national literatures across Europe as well as in Britain, but just what "literature" was coming to mean in the Romantic age is the focal point of the next two chapters on political debate and legal justice. Paul Keen's chapter on politics and the literary field shows why political ideas and print media were inextricably "bound up with one another" at a time when the literary field was still being defined as a broad public sphere of discursive genres, not yet a more specialized category of imaginary works. Keen focuses on three symptomatic moments of political debate (1792, 1802, 1818) when print media themselves put contemporary writing to the political tests of legal and national legitimacy, professional authority, and democratic recognition. From the impact of Paine's *The Rights of Man* and 1790s revolution debate to the innovation of the *Edinburgh Review*, writing in public altered political and literary understandings or alignments alike. For the Regency period, Keen's brief case study of the little-studied journal *Yellow Dwarf* illuminates the period's emerging tension between Enlightenment and Counter-Enlightenment categories of literary production, reminding us that a Romantic notion of literature as distantly removed from political life was as strongly disputed then as it has become again today.

Mark Schoenfield's chapter on law and literature turns from matters of political justice to the individual's increasingly perplexed status amidst the sweeping economic and legal changes that Karl Polanyi once called the Great Transformation. From property laws to those affecting personal behaviors, legal justice in the Romantic age became intriguingly entwined with fictional and literary means of coping with the unruly historical cases and outcomes of enacting or applying statutes to circumstances. Schoenfield takes his reader across the frontier of one of the oldest professions to the newly emerging profession of literary authorship – from Blackstone's authoritative

Commentaries to the poet Charlotte Smith, the novelist/lawyer Walter Scott, or the critic/lawyer Francis Jeffrey. But he also pays special attention to the paradoxical uses of "poetic justice" as an age-old ideal being put to new purposes in both the legal system itself and the emerging category of what post-Romantic readers would know as imaginative literature in the now-familiar sense. Thus Thomas De Quincey's famous case for a "literature of power" would distinguish it from a scientific or legal "literature of knowledge" by finding in the literary a kind of "justice that is more omnipotent over its own ends" than the messy, unequal outcomes of justice in the lived world (p. 124).

Modernity, according to Immanuel Kant's great schema, comes to us in three forms: Pure (the rational or scientific), Practical (ethical, political, or economic), and the Aesthetic (fine arts, literature). The next six chapters explore the complexity of these classifications and how they overlapped in the Romantic age. The "scientific," first of all, has long been taken to be antithetical to either the practical or the artistic. Noah Heringman's essay on natural history shows how one such scientific discourse could frustrate that neat division, since a richly diverse, contradictory "natural history" would ultimately remain unassimilable to later disciplinary practices instituted by the other sciences. Heringman demonstrates how truly strange its revelations could be, how fully it could articulate nature's past with British or imperial social and cultural histories, and how, beginning with Cook's Pacific voyages of exploration in the 1770s, natural history could become increasingly "a forum for critical engagement with institutionalized science" itself in the early nineteenth century (p. 141). Such "immunity to disciplinary stability," Heringman proposes, made natural history perhaps a more truly Romantic science than others, while also ultimately condemning its far-flung practices to the margins of specialist knowledge by the later nineteenth century. Vividly open to popular print and visual display (as the chapter's illustration "The Natural_ist" will suggest), natural history was also, of all scientific inquiries, the most accessible to print formats: encyclopedias, periodicals, or poems and books of verse like Erasmus Darwin's *The Botanical Garden* (1791). Heringman's special case of a powerful literary reworking of natural history, Charlotte Smith's *Beachy Head* (1807), shows how poetry could not only engage with, but actively help produce scientific knowledge and representation in the Romantic age.

That Romantic-age literary writing helped to produce as well as to question scientific discourse is a picture at serious odds with the more familiar modern sense that the literary and scientific have been at least

Introduction

"two cultures" apart. Frederick Burwick's chapter extends this newer way of rethinking the period's knowledge production by examining the interconnections between Romantic writing and early-nineteenth-century sciences that (unlike natural history) did result in stable modern disciplines: chemistry, astronomy, geology, physics, and medicine. Even as Britain, France, and other Continental nations went to ideological and military war between 1793 and 1815, Burwick notes, a different kind of "international dialogue became crucial in the sciences" (p. 00). This chapter thus invokes a comparative-literature framework for grasping the breadth and complexity of Western European exchanges over scientific and literary knowledges. At the same time, we become strongly aware of the problematic as well as enabling modes of translation and publication needed to make sense of scientific and literary interchange.

Meanwhile, Kant's practical reason embraced a great many discourses in the Romantic age – moral philosophy, political writing, and economic figuring. The next two chapters investigate the "practical" at what both then and today remains the bottom line – getting and spending, or the economic basis of cultural production. If there was still no such term as "consumer" in the early nineteenth century, Nicholas Mason's essay compares recent sociological and historiographic accounts of consumer society in the late eighteenth and early nineteenth century to the ways fashion-conscious, market-savvy men and women acted in Jane Austen's novels. Vividly a decade of conspicuous consumption, the Regency (1812–21) was simultaneously a time of war, social unrest, and hunger for many British subjects. Lord Byron encompassed that contradiction as one of the period's most dandyish yet outspokenly rebellious of poets; Jane Austen could be as prim as Byron could be cool, but her novels, as Mason argues, articulate British subjects' awareness of themselves as both citizens and consumers with unprecedented exactness. He examines the pleasures and tensions of market culture in relation to the more hostile critique of commercial society in writers like Coleridge, Wordsworth, and Shelley, who mingled classically republican suspicions of the marketplace with prophet-style denunciation.

The publishing world was especially open to economic volatility – and thus all intellectual, aesthetic, or popular discourse that was committed to print. From the spiraling price of new books and what book historians call the quasi-industrial "take-off" of the modern novel in about 1770–1825, to the fateful crash of the reading market in 1826, the Romantic age was both crowded with new print products (periodicals, anthologies, miscellanies of all kinds) and equally fascinated with the oldest of books. The notorious craze called the Bibliomania drove prices of rare fifteenth or sixteenth-century books to astronomical levels, even while the recent 1774 copyright law opened up cheap new publishing methods for reprinting selected older works now in the public domain. Lee Erickson shows how knowledges ranging from the scientific to self-help writing circulated around poems, novels, or plays in the last decades of the "hand press period" before the mechanization of printing novels, poetry, and periodicals by the steam press in the 1830s. The Romantic-era book market made book-buying extraordinarily expensive on the one hand, and the publishing trade unusually volatile, competitive, and profitable (or sometimes disastrously costly) on the other. This chapter, completed before Erickson's untimely death in May 2008, brings the cultural prominence of the literary and intellectual world into the nitty-gritty economic strategies of publishers and authors who struggled to make a living and simultaneously to make literary history while occupying a risky, marginal sector of the industrializing British economy.

As for the aesthetic part of Kant's categories, the Romantic age has often been misunderstood as dedicated mainly to a rarefied sense of the arts. Today the widening domain called "visual studies" increasingly opens up the range of painting, illustration, or engraving, theatrical performances, and public spectacles that also defined the explosive cultural productivity of the Romantic era. Gillen D'Arcy Wood's account of Romantic visual culture puts special emphasis on the hybrid character of an expanding arts-and-entertainments world of the early 1800s as at once "a language of private feeling *and* a mode of charismatic public performance" (p. 232). His essay ranges from landscape painting like Constable's to portraiture like Gainsborough's, to pleasure gardens and panoramas, theaters and exhibitions, whether as intimately encountered in London or vastly enlarged to phantasmatically prefigure the sense of "nation." Long a specialist's domain even within Romantic studies, the fine arts merge now in relation to the popular urban entertainments as well as to a great many writerly encounters in the work of Austen, Wordsworth, Charlotte Smith, Frances Burney, or Charles Lamb. This chapter embraces drama and theater as performing arts continuous with the plastic arts rather than its own literary or textual sphere, a view characteristic of the period rather than our own more separate categorizations.

This volume's final word goes to a question that has long preoccupied students and critics of Romanticism – the discourse on aesthetics and the problem of the "autonomy" of cultural practices like painting, poetry, theater, the novel, or the "literary" itself vis-à-vis the wider social world. Kant's *Critique of Judgment* (1790) remains the philosophical touchstone – however antithetically – of all subsequent efforts to articulate the relation of "art and politics" or "culture and society." Even recent sociological works on culture (like Pierre Bourdieu's 1984 *Distinction*) recur to Kant's argument and title to make their own quite different case for the social basis of cultural tastes. As Robert Kaufman argues in concluding this volume, the modern sociopolitical critique of aesthetic autonomy must deal with the fact that this critique was itself Romantic in origin (in Shelley, Blake, and elsewhere) – and that it is closely tied to the persistence of "Romanticism" in new, alien, or even hostile cultural environments ever since, including modernism and late modernist poetics. In a style that is necessarily more philosophical than most preceding essays require, Kaufman's chapter shows us why Marx's thinking about commodities or capital needed a corollary reflection upon "aesthetics" – and why writings of Walter Benjamin or Theodor Adorno, or the late-modernist works of poets like Robert Duncan, form essential mediations between Romanticism's questioning of art and politics and the increasingly complex nature of that relationship in twentieth- and twenty-first century arts and poetry.

References and Further Reading

Abrams, M. H. (1953) *The Mirror and the Lamp: Romantic Theory and the Critical Tradition*. New York: Norton.

Abrams, M. H. (1971) *Natural Supernaturalism: Tradition and Revolution in Romantic Literature*. New York: Norton.

Bloom, Harold (ed.) (1970) *Romanticism and Consciousness*. New York: Norton.

Bourdieu, Pierre. (1984) *Distinction: A Social Critique of the Judgment of Taste*, trans. Richard Nice. Cambridge, MA: Harvard University Press.

Butler, Marilyn. (1981) *Romantics, Rebels, and Reactionaries*. New York: Oxford University Press.

Chandler, James. (1998) *England in 1819: The Case of Romanticism and the Politics of the Literary Field*. Chicago: University of Chicago Press.

De Man, Paul. (1984) *The Rhetoric of Romanticism*. New York: Columbia University Press.

Duncan, Ian. (2007) *Scott's Shadow: The Novel in Romantic Edinburgh*. Princeton, NJ: Princeton University Press.

Erdman, David. (1954) *Blake: Prophet Against Empire*. New York: Doubleday.

Hartman, Geoffrey. (1964) *Wordsworth's Poetry, 1787–1807*. New Haven, CT: Yale University Press.

Keach, William. (2004) *Arbitrary Power: Romanticism, Language, Politics*. Princeton, NJ: Princeton University Press.

Klancher, Jon P. (1987) *The Making of English Reading Audiences, 1790–1832*. Madison: University of Wisconsin Press.

Leask, Nigel. (1992) *Romantic Writers and the East*. Cambridge, UK: Cambridge University Press.

Levinson, Marjorie. (1986) *Wordsworth's Great Period Poems*. Cambridge, UK: Cambridge University Press.

Liu, Alan. (1989) *Wordsworth: The Sense of History*. Stanford, CA: Stanford University Press.

Makdisi, Saree. (1998) *Romantic Imperialism*. Cambridge, UK: Cambridge University Press.

McGann, Jerome. (1983) *The Romantic Ideology*. Chicago: University of Chicago Press.

Rajan, Tilottama. (1990) *The Supplement of Reading: Figures of Understanding in Romantic Theory and Practice*. Ithaca, NY: Cornell University Press.

Siskin, Clifford. (1998) *The Work of Writing: Literature and Social Change in Britain, 1700–1830*. Baltimore: Johns Hopkins University Press.

Trumpener, Katie. (1997) *Bardic Nationalism: The Romantic Novel and the British Empire*. Princeton, NJ: Princeton University Press.

Williams, Raymond. (1958) *Culture and Society, 1780-1950*. New York: Harper & Row.

Acknowledgements

I wish to thank Aubrey Bowser, Thora Brylowe, David Cerniglia, Andrea Pfaff, and Jenny Roberts for various and invaluable help in the preparation of this volume. *JK*

Chapter 1

Transfiguring God: Religion, Revolution, Romanticism

Robert M. Maniquis

During the 1790s, the English looked across the Channel at a hurly-burly French Revolution that would sweep away a monarch's divine right, desecrate mighty cathedrals, and change the face of God. The English had under Henry VIII desecrated their own Catholic altars, would in 1649 decapitate King Charles I, and murder one another during the Civil War of 1640 to 1660. English religious fury, from the sixteenth to the seventeenth centuries, filled the ground with corpses and left upon the landscape many a ruined church or abbey to become an ivy-covered icon of poetry and chiaroscuro drawings. French revolutionary violence was not to be so pleasantly portrayed. The news in 1789 that aristocrats and priests were hanging from lampposts, at times with their severed genitals crammed into their mouths, was shockingly brutal. Some smugly thought that French barbarism simply arose from evil habits acquired in living for centuries under a bloody Catholic anti-Christ. But more disturbing than Papist spiritual corruption was the spectacle of the deist Robespierre, who, in fighting off both Catholics and atheists, convinced the National Assembly to vote the Supreme Being into existence. England, alarmed at such spiritual arrogance, would wage war against the French revolutionary government, as it would against Napoleon, its imperial heir. But both before and after fighting the impious French, in what some described as no less than a religious war, Britain underwent religious transformations as important as any that occurred across the Channel.

Those transformations, from roughly the 1770s through the 1870s, grew out of long-standing compromises of "Church" and "chapel," between those sworn to the doctrine of the Anglican Church and the Nonconformists, those seeking salvation outside the established church in plain or extravagant styles of "low" Protestant belief. Unlike radical dissent, Methodist enthusiasm spread everywhere within and without the Anglican Church – in the universities, in churches, chapels, in the unadorned "meeting-house," and in the open fields with English workers and peasants. Methodism, later organized evangelicalism, and Christian moralizing tracts may have absorbed political anger and saved England from revolutionary ruptures. The extent to which this was true is still a thorny historical question. Obviously many believers were less concerned with politics than with their personal fear of God's discontent. On the other hand, everything religious was political and everything political religious. Methodists celebrated the Good Shepherd, but they were not always sheeplike and sometimes showed something like Calvinist political fire. What Christian revolutionaries, reformists, and reactionaries had in common, especially in times of crisis, was doctrinal allegiance. That Calvinists and High Anglicans or Methodists and Scottish Presbyterians consorted at times did not negate the signs by which one believer espied evil in the beliefs of another. Methodists were especially talented at expressing Christian love as doctrinal disgust, above all, with those Unitarian intellectuals – they were also called Arians – who admired Christ as a sublimely moral but completely *human* being. Charles Wesley, prolific writer of hymns, called upon the Holy Trinity to show no mercy to Unitarians:

> O might the blood of sprinkling cry
> For those who spurn the sprinkled blood
> Assert Thy glorious Deity,
> Stretch out Thine arm, Thou Triune God!
> The Unitarian fiend expel,
> And chase his doctrine back to hell.
> (Manning 1942: 17)

If the hymn has worked its spell, those like the pioneering scientist and rational dissenter Joseph Priestley, the essayists William Hazlitt and Charles Lamb, and one of England's greatest poets, Coleridge, may be conversing today with Satan, for all were connected to Unitarianism. Priestley probably escaped hell, as he did riotous mobs, by fleeing to America. Coleridge found salvation, so we must assume, by converting to Trinitarian Anglicanism. We can only wonder about the fate of Hazlitt, who vaulted over Unitarianism into permanent philosophical radicalism, or Lamb, who clung stubbornly to the Arian heresy.

Religious hatred, or at least its invective, would gradually yield to liberal religious reform. Statutory acceptance of Catholics, Jews, and Dissenters into civic life would not be complete until the 1880s, but it had begun in the 1790s and was increasingly codified in the Reform Acts of 1832 and 1867. Laws of toleration calmed religious antagonisms during expanding capitalist industrialism, which, like all productive systems, was impossible without social order. Such laws eventually shortened the reach of religion. By the 1890s it was no longer necessary to test beliefs in order to assure social usefulness. This gradually accepted toleration was far from spiritual indifference. The invisible hand of the market still traced the mysterious ways of God. Capitalism incorporated, as it does today, many spiritual strains, one example of which is defined by Max Weber in *The Protestant Ethic and the Spirit of Capitalism*. But such spirituality was not defined with machine-like precision. If faceless supernatural authority was vital to prosperity, individuals of all religious stripes bowed even to its dim shadow. Catholicism, Judaism, and Dissenting Protestantism were all eventually drawn into the apparatus of state, economy, and culture. To be sure, religion would long continue to lay vulgar shibboleths even on the tongues of great poets – T. S. Eliot, another Unitarian convert to Anglicanism, comes to mind. But the British embrace of spiritual variety slowly effaced both established and Nonconformist Christianity as, at best, the Empire's high moral force and, at worst, its shabby moral alibi.

Some religious shifts occurred almost imperceptibly amidst Christian spiritual exercises that had hardly changed in two hundred years. That most important of Christian preparations – for early death – obviously did not need much revision. Many people, above all laborers, lived arduous, brief lives, dying between the ages of 30 and 40. True, there were Methuselan wonders like Wordsworth who died at 80, and the indefatigable Hannah More, who published her moral tracts until the age of 90. More typically, Keats died at 26, Shelley at 29, Byron at 36, Austen at 42, Wollstonecraft at 38. Someone like Keats, who disdained religious superstition, prepared for early death by writing sonnets, while nearly everyone else read printed sermons or listened to them in Anglican cathedrals or Dissenting chapels. Prayers were offered up at morning, noon, and night. Life at birth, marriage, and death was marked by the solemn words of the Anglican *Book of Common Prayer* or of Dissenting hymns. When the devout were not praying or singing, they were reading their sermons, the Bible, poetic renderings of the Psalms, polemical religious pamphlets, and among their favorite books, John Bunyan's *The Pilgrim's Progress* (1678, 1684) whose hero, Christian, they cheered on to Paradise.

The souls of Dissenters were attended to mostly in solitude or in the modest chapel's choral singing. The souls of middle-class and aristocratic sinners were succored by an Anglican rector, vicar, or curate – in short, the high and the low of the established clergy. Whether a wealthy dilettante who lived in London far from his parish or a poor, zealous shepherd of his flock, the parson was important in social and economic life. And he could wear many hats. He could be a natural scientist, a progressive agricultural reformer, a cranky justice of the peace. He could be Thomas Malthus, frightening all of Britain with nightmares of engulfing population, an itinerant preacher trotting on horseback from village to village, or an urbane essayist like Sydney Smith. These motley Christian soldiers gained luxurious or pitiful livings from their parishes, but most earned enough with which to court, for instance, the likes of Jane Austen's women. Her clergymen, always awkward lovers, can be duplicitous boors like Mr Collins in *Pride and Prejudice* (1813) or kind men like Edward Ferrars in *Sense and Sensibility* (1811). Austen pushes spirituality into the margins when describing husband hunting, for her women have less need of God to find conjugal happiness than they do of good taste and common sense. But nowhere in her irony is the value of even a superficial layer of religion called into question, no more than it was by the most radical critics of society. William Cobbett, for instance, that belligerent radical Tory, in his *Rural Rides* (1822–6), lashed out at most Anglican parsons, together with Quakers and Jews, as hypocritical blood-suckers of the nation's wealth. But he also defended religion as a guarantee of a free-born Englishmen's liberty. Tom Paine was often shunned, even by radical friends, not only because, as it was rumored, he was a disagreeable drunk, but also because some whiffed the smell of atheism about him.

Atheism was not, at least before Shelley, a common Romantic revolutionary principle – it was reason for shame. And, indeed, when the young Shelley published *The Necessity of Atheism* (1811), he committed an act of social disorder which led to his being expelled from Oxford. Seven years later he would begin his lifelong exile on the Continent. In Great Britain, as in America and Europe, deep or superficial religious belief was an ordinary part of a morally ordered life. Within the swaying moral order, however, writers held, not only to strikingly various Christian doctrines, but radically different conceptions of the nature of religion itself. At one extreme were the guardians of orthodox religion and morality. The moralizing tribes were legion. Cobbett despised them as those who earnestly wished to convince the poor of the blessedness of their condition. The Gospels declared that the wretched poor had a better chance of getting to heaven than the rich. At the other extreme are Blake's wildly radical "Christian" notions of the mind which countered the moralizing of writers like Hannah More and of those of the Society for the Propagation of Christian Knowledge. "Pity would be no more / If we did not make somebody poor," was Blake's response to the jejune simplicities of Christian moralizing. Many other contraries and confluences could be traced through Austen's High Church civility, Wordsworth's and Coleridge's early radical rationalism and their later Tory Anglicanism, Keats's rejection of Christian superstitions, Byron's contempt for Christian hypocrisy and guilt, or Shelley's atheistic – or as his Victorian admirers preferred – his *agnostic* politics and poetics. In order to suggest how such various opinions and even religious styles bristle together or clash with one another, we must glance back to just before the French Revolution, when religion and reason were sometimes strongly, sometimes only delicately, connected.

The Fragility of Enlightenment

In the last half of the eighteenth century, the middling classes, the aristocracy, the high and the low Anglican clergy, the angry Dissenting preachers, the country gentry, the artisans, the poor working classes were all born with expectations of a direct relation to God. This immediacy was important even among Anglicans, who come as close to Catholic mediation as is possible for a Protestant, but it was also politically indispensable to Protestant Dissenters – Quakers, Baptists, Anabaptists, Methodists, Unitarians, Presbyterians, and the like. That direct relation to God with the Inner Voice and the Inner Light implied also a direct inspiration from even the most cryptic words of the Bible. One need only think back to *The Adventures of Robinson Crusoe* (1719), which, like *The Pilgrim's Progress*, was very widely read, to remember how, alone on his island, Robinson interprets the ups and downs of his day with often ambiguous passages of the Scriptures. This heritage of Protestant faith in the immediacy of God's word echoing in the individual mind informs British Romanticism, no less than

Catholic ritual informs quite differently French and some German Romanticism.

Some of those with the Inner Light and whom both the Church and the chapel trained to be submissively devout were inevitably seduced by the great English Deists or French Jansenists, by skeptics from Montaigne to David Hume or at least by the rational dissent of Arians like Joseph Priestley. And once tempted to adopt the ideas of outlandish French philosophical deists like Voltaire and Rousseau, our perhaps once devout believer was, in the eyes of orthodox Christians, lost to the true God. Our convert to reason would, of course, grant that, even in doubting an orthodox God, some form of God, indeed some form of divine something at the center of things, was a good idea. Voltaire wryly insisted that, indeed, his wife, his tailor, and his accountant should remain devout believers, but that the living, thinking, feeling, and dying of enlightened thinkers should be done with reason, by which the mind sees itself and things as they are, without supernatural mystery or fear of transcendent punishment. Many dissenting, deist, similar "theist," and rationalist ideas were congenial to pious believers who cherished mental independence and political liberty. But not all rationalist and religious tendencies in the 1790s sat well together. The rationalism which led to materialism, historical necessity, and an absent deity produced the intellect one sees in Thomas Paine's *The Age of Reason* (1793–4). But others – well-read, articulate artisans, for instance, and admirers of technological progress – could also be, if they did not enjoy the vagueness of Deism, God-fearing Bible-thumpers, with fever in their eyes and promises of fire and brimstone on their tongues. Influential books like John Locke's *Essay on Toleration* (1667), of course, helped to establish common political assumptions among such varieties of religious and rationalist thinkers. And even those who sought supernatural revelation grounded the mind in the physical world with Locke's *An Essay Concerning Human Understanding* (1690).

No Romantic writer, in fact, however drawn to Platonism or Neo-Platonism, visions, fantasies, allegorical dreams, or folkloric superstitions, ever leaves this Lockean empiricist tradition behind. Everything begins in the senses, after which the senses can be played with, jumbled together in kinesthesia, set against or with each other in visionary correspondences, associated with a godly voice, as they later were by the orthodox Coleridge, or made into intimations of transcendence as they were by Keats and Shelley. The Protestant Inner Light that survives in British Romanticism may have a distant origin in God but it often shines immediately upon and as if within the stuff of the world. It may be that no human impulses to transcendence ever escape the metaphors drawn from the phenomenal world. But Romantic transcendence rarely seems to want to fly beyond the matrix of sensual metaphor. This was as true of Locke as it was of Coleridge, who never disengaged his mind from the excitement of sensual impressions. He actually drove those sensual impressions into the center of supernatural apprehension. The primordial Romantic spiritual event is actually a spiritualized empiricist moment, a heuristic moment, or an epistemological model of beginnings, in which the new Romantic Adam is born, one who must feel the electric connections of body and mind before he can understand the origins of God. William Blake anathematized Voltaire and Rousseau and mocked the empiricist who could not see – as Blake could – an entire world in a grain of sand. But even he insisted on precise sensual perception of that very grain of sand. As he makes clear in *Milton* (1809–10), the world begins anew with the birth of William Blake, a new Adam of poetic consciousness, into whom Milton's soul had entered through the left big toe, now inhabiting a body burning with joyful perceptions of the defining lines of all individualized life, all sharply perceived material things.

Many ideas separated revealed religion and its frightening mysteries from rationalist belief in metaphysical transparency and universal benevolence. But passionate believers and lukewarm Deists are to be found on the same side in struggles for tolerance and individual liberty. English Calvinist rage, for instance, that of the revolutionary seventeenth century, can be glimpsed still in late eighteenth and early nineteenth-century party politics. Severe Calvinists could actively struggle for political liberty even as they accepted their catastrophic inheritance of sin and possible eternal damnation. On the other hand, readers of Rousseau's writings on humankind's original goodness, though wary of Rousseau himself, saw the reasonableness of his political ideas based on an assumption of human goodness. A cheerful deist like Benjamin Franklin, too pragmatic to be either a Calvinist or a Rousseauist, contemplated in the 1780s the prospect of human progress in his American ambassadorial office in Paris, certain that God was kind, that people were good, and that the world was not all that bad. But what in the 1790s was to happen in those Parisian streets where the good-humored Franklin once strolled disrupted social accord between, on the one hand, Cathedral and chapel, and, on the other, religion and reason. The hope for progress and for more personal liberty and for what the American Declaration of Independence called a *right* to happiness – all such good will for many Europeans stopped suddenly short.

The fall of the Bastille in 1789 incited in Britain, besides newspaper headlines and the government's fear, common congratulations for the Revolution from dissenting groups and radicals of less devout persuasion. Although decried by Edmund Burke in *Reflections on the Revolution in France* (1790), writers like Blake, Wordsworth, Southey, Coleridge, as well as journalists and even moderate Church of English ministers who envisioned a French constitutional monarchy, looked hopefully upon events. Sanguinity, however, especially from 1793 on, turned pale as pamphlets, newspapers, books, and fleeing French émigrés told of how guns, pikes, and the guillotine were bringing forth rivers of blood. This was blood of a new kind. In his *The French Revolution: A History* (1837), upon which Dickens drew to write *A Tale of Two Cities* (1859), Thomas Carlyle claimed that what happened in 1793, that is, seemingly indiscriminate massacre, was something for which language had not yet found a name. What seemed beyond a name was neither mass violence nor the sheer volume of blood – far from it. Killing many thousands at a time was new to no one. History, long before the Shoah and the specter of nuclear apocalypse, had been filled with those proud to have been the agents of human extermination. Religious and political memory bristled with images, to name just a few, of Joshua's founding of Israel, the Roman flattening of Carthage, the Catholic erasure of the Albigensians, and the Black Legend, with which Protestants adorned the facts to make sixteenth-century Catholic *conquistadores* even more exterminatory than they were. Explanations for all such horrors and their fantastical exaggerations abounded in the works of those who honored and those who denigrated religious and imperial violence. But the French Revolution placed upon a stage – it was indeed a very theatrical revolution – a people acting, not for God, Satan, or only for nation and empire; but in their own name in search of liberty, social justice, nature, and reason. When Parisian revolutionaries worshiped with grand pomp at spectacular altars of Nature and Reason, they were worshiping themselves. The original theoretical rupture is there in Rousseau's *Social Contract* (1762), which extended Locke's theories to reinforce the idea that government was no longer established by a spiritual covenant but by contractual agreement with the people. Robespierre, the most demonized of French Revolutionaries, revered Rousseau. This well-known reverence invited observers to link intellectually ruptured religious covenants and the exterminating angel of revolutionary self-righteousness. The revolutionaries had, indeed, reached back to the Old Testament, proudly calling their political policy the *Terreur* and themselves *terroristes*. That rhetoric struck pious observers as sacrilegious effrontery. A primordially frightening, wrathful God had been given a purely human face. The new humanly determined contract began as arrogant iconoclasm and ended in revolutionary cannibalism. The *terroristes* had first devoured God, then each other.

Those with an unshakeable religious belief in traditional concepts of good and evil easily accounted for and condemned the French Terror. This was not so easy for philosophical radicals and rationalist dissenters. For some observers, the events of the 1790s transformed reason and religion into *one* beast with two heads. The center of European civilization that formerly was God was shown by rationalism to inspire debilitating primitive fear, but where did modern Terror come from if God and his Satan were now erased? An immensely popular book like Godwin's *Enquiry Concerning Political Justice* (1793) argued that rationality, free of God and left to itself, would produce a benevolent, just society. In the very same year in which Godwin published his popular book, the Terror undermined those arguments. It could now be imagined that the human mind left to its own devices could become as fanatic as any that Christianity had produced. Not everyone, of course, was bewildered by the Revolution. Philosophers like Immanuel Kant, essayists like Arthur Young and William Hazlitt, radicals like William Blake and William Cobbett all kept faith with the notion that the Revolution was, for all its violence, a step forward for humanity. Blake's system of psychic contraries protected him from historical shock because his system, by definition, depended upon such extremes – of love and anger, peace and violence. But for many, especially for poets like Wordsworth and Coleridge, who had cut loose from traditional religion, the Revolution, if it did not destroy the rational foundations of social hope, certainly fractured them.

This is not to say that everything instantly changed. Literary historians have shown how writers in Britain after the French Revolution continued all through the first decades of the nineteenth century to link their politics, reactionary or "liberal," to the confrontations of Dissent and the Church (Woodring 1970, Ryan 1997). But simultaneously, and over many more decades, the question of an unfathomable origin of violence, subject neither to religious nor rationalist understanding, began to take shape in all European culture, thrusting Wordsworth, Coleridge, and Southey (along with others in Germany and France) into intellectual limbo. Wordsworth and Coleridge would slowly climb out of that limbo and return to the Church. But the newly revealed beast of the 1790s does not simply slouch towards Bethlehem to be transfigured by a new, adjusted coupling of eighteenth-century reason and religion. Nor does it simply come to rest in the day-to-day politics of the Romantics. Wordsworth, Coleridge, and Southey returned to conventional worship and to conservative Tory politics. But this return to orthodoxy was a psychic retreat, for they continued to be haunted by the social hope that had crashed amidst the violence of the 1790s.

Coleridge, for example, would never stop thinking about his poem *The Rime of the Ancient Mariner* (1798, 1800, 1816), which clearly confronts the origin of violence. And though it is a poem one can tie to Unitarian ideas, Coleridge, even later as an orthodox Anglican, would never disown it, one of the most complex religious poems in the English language. The significance of his story can only be pondered by the Mariner's mesmerized listener and by us, his readers. In this working out of meaning, even Coleridge, the Anglican Tory, believed that neither religion nor reason by itself could produce civilized order or allow escape from what had exploded in the French Revolution as a kind of primordial human violence. Coleridge cultivated, along with every other Romantic writer, his version of a new mental faculty that had to precede any hope in purely rational political or sacramental religious order, and he, like all other Romantic writers, called this mental faculty by an old name – the imagination.

Imagination, or Spiritual Reinvention

Of all British cultural concepts, the most complex is that of the Romantic imagination. It cannot be defined with only a few principles, for it is a complex sense – and no more than a sense – of a new de-Christianized or re-Christianized world. Imagination is not only creativity, invention, genius, or mental fecundity. It involves more than inventing a story or painting a compelling picture, although Romantic imagination includes all such creativity. Romantic imagination is a meta-faculty, like that in Descartes' thinking thing, that can only be conceived of by itself. It is the mind observing sensations and impressions – and above all the mind observing itself while it observes its sensations, impressions, the world, and beliefs. A sign of this shifting self-consciousness is the Romantic obsession with trying and trying again to define what imagination was, is, or can be. Understanding this self-conscious complexity is not made easy by the fact that now, long past the moment of its Romantic emergence, the aura of the imagination still haunts sophisticated intellectual as well as popular platitudes. No matter that grand, metaphysical concepts of imagination have been deflated in modern culture. It still flourishes in both sclerotic but dominant ideals and in counter-cultural spasms of liberation.

Imagination in its contemporary forms – in its extreme apprehension, for instance, of what André Gide in his *Journals* of 1893 called the *mise en abyme*, the infinite regression into mental mirrors of mental mirrors – has imposed itself on those trying to understand it, to the point that it has become an unquestioned mental given. And even in its more mundane and less disconcerting versions, as when politicians invoke new political and social "visions," echoing Shelley's transformation of poets into the ultimate legislators, the Romantic imagination remains a hovering presence. The presence sheds its aura also upon the narrated or archetypal *unconscious*, which also is like the sea or the sky in that it is just there – a part of the mind that, despite psychology or neural surgery, remains unexplainable by any other part of the mind. Not everyone attains this imagination, as conceived by the Romantics. And it is not enough simply to have it; *it must also leave its mark in time and space*. It must shape human memory. Without both its emotional effect and its historical presence, we assume that even the most brilliant imagination is, as Thomas Gray proclaims in *Elegy in a Country Churchyard* (1751), simply "wasted." Indeed, those in whom the imagination is at work are touched by a form of saving intellectual grace, which saves the self not in eternity but in social time. Pascal, the seventeenth-century Jansenist mathematical genius and religious epistemologist, claimed that the imagination always lost its way in contemplating the hidden God. This claim is reversed by the British Romantics. For them God would not simply remain hidden, he would completely disappear without the grace, not of Christ, but of the human imagination. In this sense, Romantic imagination, like its modern derivatives, is a rich reflection or, if we prefer more sober words, a simulacrum of a once purely religious idea.

Romantic writers did not, of course, invent the idea of imagination. They put it together out of old and not-so-old ideas, parts here and there of elaborate systems like Plato's or the eighteenth-century *je ne sais quoi* of aesthetic mystery, pieces of old theories of memory as decaying yet recaptured thought, or eighteenth-century psychologies drawn from all that is the opposite of Platonism – empirical associationism, replete with physiological vibratiuncles, cellular somethings shimmering in reticulated neurological webs. All such mental bric-a-brac was at times excluded from, at others tied to, grander memories of epic and adventurous Protestant vision, allegorical dreams, and the vestiges of the Stoic *recta ratio*, or accumulated wisdom and reason. Out of all these and other elements – too many to mention here – the Romantics made of the imagination something it had never been. And they put it to uses previously unknown.

Reimagining God

For eighteen centuries in Christian Europe, the ultimate object of reverence was, as it still is for most people, nothing less than God. In the poem that remained the most important for all English readers, *Paradise Lost* (1667), a Protestant poem of classical restraint, the epic poet can only justify the ways of God to humankind if God helps him in every utterance. Romantic imagination, however, changes the doctrine by which divine presence is revered. In a world where, for intellectuals, God became opaque, a concretized human imagination became as necessary to God as God was to all previous history. Even if Coleridge traced poetic imagination back to Yahweh's declaration "I am that I am," it is in the poetic imagination that the ancient God would be sensually and ideally recovered. In society and culture at large God's presence was, of course, still felt to be clearly there. Many writers then, as today, wrote as sincere Protestants, Catholics, or mystics. Romantic imagination, however, allowed those without a truly immediate God – and with anguish at that absence – to write with the same power, if not with the same confidence, as the orthodox or mystical believer.

Because thought itself seemed unthinkable outside a Christian context, it is not surprising that Romantic poets wrote in Christianity's verbal shadow. The religious words or phrases of the day in Romantic writing now linger in whispering footnotes. But they once jumped from the page with a life now mostly lost to us. Arthur Young, for instance, in his *Travels in France during the Years 1787, 1788, and 1789* (1792), points to the word "regeneration," one of the common revised theological words of revolutionary *terroristes*. The new French political resonance of this old word, combining Christian hope and revolutionary liberation, would not be lost on Young's British Protestant audience. The connected word, "unregenerate," in Coleridge's "The Eolian Harp" (1795), codifies a Protestant notion concerning salvation that identifies the speaker as a potential spiritual friend or enemy, depending on whether one is Methodist or Calvinist, and on what one means exactly by unregenerate. And all this in a poem where erotic pantheism, once expressed, is then suppressed with a bow to orthodox Christianity. Assuming that Coleridge's readers were attuned to the new, revolutionary connotations of regeneration evoked by Arthur Young, the word "unregenerate" might have had a strange new resonance. Most readers probably heard only the theological connotations of the word, which were, however, enough to electrify it with conflicting religious sensibilities. Many Protestant believers today still commonly use the word "unregenerate." Many other readers have not the slightest idea of what it means. Unfortunately the word dies within the poem unless it is *felt* in its religious entwinement. When Coleridge used the word "unregenerate," he called up powerful apocalyptic fear and trembling, set in severe counterpoint to the equally powerful and joyful pantheist eroticism of the poem.

Many crucial words in Romantic literature are packed in this way with theological meanings Romantically recontextualized. Perhaps because the Christian word "grace" had a long history of bloody violence attached to it, Romantics tended to avoid it. On the other hand, "joy" could resonate with memories of apocalyptic splendor even in the lyrics of the atheist Shelley, singing only of flowers or the breeze. Many writers of the day may use, in one place or another, all the old religious words but often substitute, for instance, "dejection" for "despair," "power" for "God," "peace" for "grace," "symbols" for "signs," "voice" for "Word," "intensity" for "passion," or, quite famously, "Beauty" for "Truth." These semantic substitutions position the writers less as expressing spiritualized emotion or religious memory than as self-consciously interpreting their perceptions of the emotion. Despair, for instance, as a theological device, brilliantly kept even the unbeliever within the fold. Because it is a sin, *despair*, however painful, defines the spirit of the unbeliever in God's universe. But *dejection* is concretized in the individual mind, free to define its particular loss, its particular void, its particular pain.

Blake's are the most elaborate of poetic variations upon Christianity of any poet of the age. But his transformations of God and Satan into mental faculties are, after all, a recalling of human projections back down to the mind from the heavens. And there in the marvelous mind of Blake, God and Satan occupy a new stage, from which Blake hisses at priestly mystery and Christian mumbo-jumbo in, for instance, *The Marriage of Heaven and Hell* (1794) or *The Book of Urizen* (1795). It would be wrong to think that Blake was not a Christian, but he was a Christian of an antinomian tradition in which God's grace became nearly synonymous with the simple joy of being alive. That joy is incomplete unless liberated from the obsessive, timorous death-consciousness of traditional Christianity. Death in Blake is, indeed, a secondary matter, and hence his modest interest in everything that touches on what might happen after death. His Christianity was so radical as to pass out of Christianity into something else. He transforms straight Christian paths to heaven and hell into painful mental cycles. The mind in such poems as "The Mental Traveller" (1803) traces a circle, in which the end meets its beginning, eternally dismantling, reshaping, and dismantling all over again the God hovering within the thought that produced him.

Redesigning cycles of life and death, however, raised the danger of entrapment in cycles apparently new but theologically ancient. And if the new poet and the old priest try, as Blake believed, to make poetry simply in different ways, are not the old priest and the new poet, even in their differences, somehow the same? Hence the many Romantic attempts to define what a poet is – marking differences from the religious prophet, yet granting to the poet ancient prophetic gifts. Even in the most radical challenges to a Judeo-Christian God, the poet must avoid sophistications of the trap that catches Satan in *Paradise Lost*. When Satan cries out rebelliously "Evil be thou my good!" he trumpets a false cry of liberation. God has set the defining term "good" of which "evil" can only be its reversed reflection. The false dialectic in Satan's claim allows God his eternal primacy. God will always have the last word, if he is always granted the first. The problem was to write one's way out of this suffocating Alpha and Omega of Judeo-Christian discourse, using many of its words and concepts, without sliding back into it or finding new words for religious emotions translated into psychic states. Sometimes the poets twist that discourse into new psychic forms, by borrowing its expression, or, more rarely, throwing it over, as Byron's anguished hero of *Manfred: A Dramatic Poem* (1817) tries to do. Manfred moves beyond Milton's Satan in claiming that the mind is "its own place" and the maker of its own "heaven and hell," but there is no more compelling Protestant reminiscence in the liberated mind than facing heaven and hell caught between good and evil inwardly. St Paul, in his letter to the Romans, defines a not dissimilar new psychic slavery in the sinner liberated from the old slavery of the Mosaic law. The nineteenth century would have to await Nietzsche for a glimpse of how one might think completely beyond a

Christian system of good and evil or slavery and freedom. Still, Romantic writers did confront a wide audience's religious sensibilities, and showed how and why those sensibilities needed to be changed, striking examples of which appear in the works of Byron and Scott.

Byron's fame was instantaneous with the publication of the First Canto of *Childe Harold* (1812). His immense celebrity, his world-weariness, his cavalier sexuality, and his image as a mad, bad child, diseased by the Spirit of the Age, cannot be underestimated. Thomas Carlyle, in *Sartor Resartus* (1831), thought Byron's discontent dangerous enough to advise the public to stop reading him: "Close thy Byron; open thy Goethe" (Carlyle 1831: 143). Bertrand Russell reserves an entire chapter for the "Byronic" in his *History of Western Philosophy* (1945: 746–52), for there are few historical contradictions more revealing than trying to cast off the religious ghost, while sickening unto death in its grip. Scott's own fame as a popular poet was eclipsed by the scurrilous Byron until he recaptured it as the author of the Waverly novels, between 1815 and 1825. The effect of Scott's astounding influence upon the novel in Europe and America was to produce, for a new social world, historical narrations of old ideas and patterns in a "Romanticized" past. This fictionally ordered past would often spill out later in nineteenth-century Britain and America as cultural nostalgia, nationalizing myths, sentimental ethnic and even racist longing. But dogs are not responsible for their fleas, and chanting nationalist claptrap was not part of Scott's serious intentions. He is a complex narrator of religious sensibility. He can, for instance, in *The Heart of Midlothian* (1818), present a theologically pure and moving Presbyterian heroine like Jeanie Deans and, at the same time, her father, Douce Davie Deans, whose theological purity belongs to a savage past. Scott's novels display both Protestant and Catholic political causes, whose doctrines, sects, manipulators, or maddened fanatics, fictional or historical, drive toward historical dead-ends. Although Scott is often considered the reactionary and Byron the liberal, when it comes to their portrayal of religion, rigid categories obscure the related effects of their writing. With the same effectiveness as Byron, who ridiculed religious hypocrisy and moral "cant," Scott relegates much religious fervor to absurd fanaticism or folkloric antiquarianism. Although they are in so many obvious ways dissimilar, both Byron and Scott measure social good against religious doctrines that are dangerous, whether expressed in posturing or in sincerity.

But whether the Romantic writer was instantly famous, like Byron or Scott, or slowly taken up, like Wordsworth, Coleridge, Keats,

Shelley, and last of all Blake, Romantic reshaping of religious sensibilities was a long, adaptive process. If it is true, as T. E. Hulme once wrote, that Romanticism is "spilt religion" (1936: 118), it did not spill in one splash but as a constant flood of contradictory sensibilities, in poems that both troubled and consoled readers. Such poems only gradually led to secularization of the spiritual. The most read of nineteenth-century poets did not include the Romantics but, as Stephen Prickett points out, writers like the Anglican priest and theologian John Keble whose *Christian Year*, first published in 1827, "sold an average of 10,000 copies a year for fifty years" (Prickett 1976: 104). *Christian Year* appeared a few years before Macaulay's appreciation of Shelley, whose genius, he says, had turned "atheism itself into a mythology" (1831/1907: 403). But most readers were having none of that, and continued to take their religious mythology from the pulpit, in their hymns, and in Keble's Christian sentiment.

From the 1790s to the 1830s, many readers, even those reading Byron and Scott, were still reading James Thomson's *The Seasons* (1730), enjoying the mild religious satire of Robert Burns's "A Cotter's Saturday Night" (1785), or were plunged in the Calvinism of William Cowper's *Olney Hymns* (1779). Writing by women from the 1750s translated Christian ideas into domestic sentiments of novels or moral dialectics of the theater, as in Joanna Baillie's *Plays upon the Passions* (1798–1812), which were for a time much more popular than the works of Blake, Wordsworth, or Coleridge. The spiritual preoccupations of the major Romantic poets do not intensely affect intellectuals until decades after the publications of the texts in which they occur. Blake, today a popular English poet, was virtually unread before the end of the nineteenth century. To read Shelley's *Prometheus Unbound* in the 1820s was a different experience from reading it in the 1880s, after readers had also read George Eliot's translation of Strauss's *The Life of Jesus* (1846) in which the spiritual becomes primarily the historical Jesus, or Charles Darwin's *On the Origin of Species* (1859) in which God is reduced to overseeing a universe of biological accidents.

And yet the transfigurations of God and the gradual displacement of religious sentiment are also constant throughout nineteenth-century literature. Two examples will have to stand for many that would show how writers continued, decade after decade, to reshape religious and aesthetic sensibilities. Our first example comes from Thomas Macaulay's review of Thomas Moore's *Life of Byron* (1830) – a defense of Byron against hypocritical readers and narrow-minded critics. Macaulay easily dismisses the reading public, scandalized by rumors of Byron's supposed degeneracy, as "ridiculous" in "its periodical fits of morality":

> Once in six or seven years our virtue becomes outrageous. We cannot suffer the laws of religion and decency to be violated. We must make a stand against vice. We must teach libertines that the English people appreciate the importance of domestic ties. Accordingly some unfortunate man, in no respect more depraved than hundreds whose offences have been treated with lenity, is singled out as an expiatory sacrifice. At length our anger is satiated. Our victim is ruined and heart-broken. And our virtue goes quietly to sleep for seven years more. (Macaulay 1830/1907: 616)

Although Macaulay defended Byron against this English hypocrisy, he nevertheless agreed that his poetry was marked by "incorrectness," that is to say, by overblown sentiments and a lack of decorum. He writes here in eighteenth-century aesthetic terms and appeals to the neo-classical concept of "imitation." Nothing could be further from what was gradually being established as the new Romantic sensibility, the replacement (as M. H. Abrams points out) of the "lamp" for the "mirror" and new claims for the moral substance of the imagination. But Macaulay, though still wielding the aesthetic terms of "imitation," then slides toward another test for good poetry and it is not that of the eighteenth century, but a test that measures "the creative power" and "the vision and the faculty divine" (1830/1907: 630). He is quoting from Wordsworth's *The Excursion* (1814), as it was quoted by Coleridge in his *Biographia Literaria* (1817). Macaulay thought that Byron had not risen to these mental ideals, but clearly they were now the ideals to be achieved, located far to the side of traditional religion and far above the maddened, hypocritical crowd. The quoted words are all "romantically" religious, even theological. And by this time they have become consecrated words in the secular Romantic discourse of imagination.

Finally, Romantic imagination coming to the aid, not of failed, false religion, but of failed reason, appears dramatically in a text published over 30 years after Macaulay's, in John Stuart Mill's *Autobiography* (1873). In the famous Chapter V, "A Crisis in My Mental History," the brilliant political thinker recounts a period of severe dejection. His great predecessor was Jeremy Bentham, a thinker of logical rigidity who wielded the criteria of pleasure and pain and "the greatest happiness of the greatness number" to define ideal social goals. Mill knew the limitations in Bentham's utilitarian philosophy, as we see in his essays on Bentham and Coleridge (1838–40), but Mill himself had been educated and worked with those ideals by which social happiness might someday be achieved. That is, until the day when something came upon him, something he compares to what a Methodist might have felt as "the first 'conviction of sin'" (Mill 1873/1989: 112).

The analogy is a self-conscious one, for Mill takes pains to describe his dejection, or what we would call "depression," as one not related to religious despair. His sense of emptiness in life did not occur because he had discovered that there was no God. Mill had understood that long before. He had died, not to God, but to the world. To be born again he needed a new power, one to which he was oblivious as a rational atheist. It was the power by which the poetic imagination reconnected one's self to the outer world of nature, things, and humanity. This new redemptive power was transmitted to him by Wordsworth's poems:

> They seemed to be the very culture of the feelings, which I was in quest of. In them I seemed to draw from a source of inward joy, of sympathetic and imaginative pleasure, which could be shared in by all human beings . . . made richer by every improvement in the physical or social condition of mankind. . . . There have certainly been, even in our own age, greater poets than Wordsworth; but poetry of deeper and loftier feeling could not have done for me at that time what his did. I needed to be made to feel that there was real, permanent happiness in tranquil contemplation. Wordsworth taught me this, not only without turning away from, but with a greatly increased interest in, the common feelings and common destiny of human beings. (1873/1989: 121)

Mill, like Macaulay before him, certifies Romantic imagination, which did not replace God or return readers to God. It musically captured the natural world, the human energy within it, and the mind observing itself observing this world. This connecting power in imagination brought the mind back to itself. Mill did not suffer his depression after any violent historical event, as Romantic writers did after the French Revolution. But the imagination they constructed was suitable for such a mental crisis as Mill's when, without religious belief, the mind lost faith in itself. What Wordsworth brought to Mill, the social utilitarian, was not a replacement for God, but an anchoring in feelings connected with the world that had been lost along with social optimism in the 1790s, and which made Romantic imagination a matter of mental survival. It is just this mental survival that Mill sought.

Mill provides a link between our contemporary sensibility and that of the Romantics. After all, during the twentieth century, the most brutish in all history, losing faith in reason is not all that different from losing faith in God. And that loss is displayed throughout twentieth-century literature to be often as catastrophic as the loss of religious faith had been in the literature of the nineteenth.

The Gods in Twilight

Many cultural blurs – many more than have been discussed here – arose in Romantic transfigurations of religion. The eighteenth-century sublime, for instance, and its traditional godly qualities of distant power, and even terror, perceived in art and nature, dissolved into the self-conscious Romantic sublime. Memory, even of the gods, was drawn into what Thomas De Quincey, the English Opium-Eater, called in *Suspiria de Profundis* (1845) the "palimpsest" of the human brain. And that suspicion was absorbed into modern forms of the clinically mapped unconscious, where, although now it seems itself a mythical place, Freud first began to trace the illusions of religion. Hope, without which there is no Christianity, was driven by poets like Shelley or philosophers like Schopenhauer into the force of human will, and found a home also in secular, even Marxist, politics. Such transformations are part of the constant modern secularization of religion. Romantic self-consciousness, indeed, prepares for the modern attempt to deconstruct secularized religious discourse and to locate what Kenneth Burke in *Rhetoric and Religion* (1961) called the "god-term" in aesthetic and social semantics. And yet it is Romantic self-consciousness that fashions many new god-terms. One must study, then, both what is taken apart and what has been ideologically put back together.

Religious ruptures and recuperations of religion extend from the Romantics all through twentieth-century literature. And in the social sciences also there has been an osmosis, over the last two centuries of Romanticism and Christianity in the study of religion itself. From Jakob and Wilhelm Grimm to Emile Durkheim's sociology of religion or Georges Dumezil's analyses of Indo-European myth or Mircea Eliade's descriptions of the sacred and profane, Romantic conceptions peek from behind notions of an undying religious imagination. In this sense, if Romanticism, at least amongst intellectuals, displaced Christianity, it also gave it an enduring ideological power in complex transfigurations and erasures that are far from complete. We sense these when we agree with Nietzsche that God is dead and when we look about and see that he obviously is not, or when we realize that Western society is no longer Christian and that it still very much is. T. S. Eliot, in *Christianity and Culture*, captured this blur with a useful banality: "a society has not ceased to be Christian until it has become something else" (1939/1988: 10). Eliot's resigned expectation of continual transfiguration with no sense of what it was to be had been anticipated decades before by the sociologist Durkheim: "the ancient gods grow old or die, and others are not yet born. Hence the futility of . . . old historic memories artificially reawakened: it is from life itself, and not from a dead past, that a living cult can emerge" (Durkheim 1912/2001: 322–3). Modern transfigurations of God, which began in the seventeenth century, are for us still most immediately grounded in post-French revolutionary Romanticism. Romantic poems and stories still speak to contemporary cultural anguish. Many contemporary writers know, as Romantic writers did, how to wait, not for the return of the old gods, but for the arrival of the new. Those writers seem also to know, like the Romantics, that, if indeed the new gods turn out to be false and ugly, we must live simply in and for the world, as intelligently as we can, with no gods at all.

References and Further Reading

Abrams, M. H. (1953/1958) *The Mirror and the Lamp: Romantic Theory and the Critical Tradition*. New York: Norton.

Abrams, M. H. (1971) *Natural Supernaturalism: Tradition and Revolution in Romantic Literature*. New York: Norton.

Balfour, Ian. (2002) *The Rhetoric of Romantic Prophecy*. Stanford, CA: Stanford University Press.

Barth, J. Robert, S. J. (2003) *Romanticism and Transcendence: Wordsworth, Coleridge, and the Religious Imagination*. Columbia: University of Missouri Press.

Brantley, R. E. (1994) *Locke, Wesley, and the Method of English Romanticism*. Gainesville: University of Florida Press.

Burke, Kenneth. (1961) *The Rhetoric of Religion: Studies in Logology*. Berkeley: University of California Press.

Canuel, Mark. (2002) *Religion, Toleration, and British Writing, 1790–1830*. Cambridge, UK: Cambridge University Press.

Carlyle, Thomas. (1831/2001) *Sartor Resartus: The Life and Opinions of Herr Teufelsdrockh in Three Books*. Berkeley and Los Angeles: University of California Press.

Davie, Donald. (1978) *The Gathered Church: The Literature of the English Dissenting Interest, 1700–1930*. New York: Oxford University Press.

Durkheim, Émile. (1912/2001) *The Elementary Forms of Religious Life*. Oxford: Oxford University Press.

Eliot, T. S. (1939/1988) *Christianity and Culture: The Idea of a Christian Society and Notes Towards the Definition of Culture*. San Diego, CA: Harcourt Brace Jovanovich.

Engell, James. (1981) *The Creative Imagination: Enlightenment to Romanticism*. Cambridge, MA: Harvard University Press.

Fairchild, H. N. (1957) *Religious Trends in English Poetry, Vol. IV, 1830–1880*. New York: Columbia University Press.

Frei, H. W. (1974) *The Eclipse of Biblical Narrative: A Study in Eighteenth and Nineteenth Century Hermeneutics*. New Haven, CT: Yale University Press.

Frye, Northrop. (1982) *The Great Code: The Bible and Literature*. New York: Harcourt Brace Jovanovich.

Gill, F. C. (1937) *The Romantic Movement and Methodism: A Study of English Romanticism and the Evangelical Revival*. London: The Epworth Press.

Hulme, T. E. (1936) "Romanticism and Classicism," in *Speculations*, ed. Herbert Read (pp. 113–40). London: Routledge.

Jager, Colin. (2007) *The Book of God: Secularization and Design in the Romantic Era*. New Brunswick, NJ: Rutgers University Press.

Kirschner, S. R. (1996) *The Religious and Romantic Origins of Psychoanalysis*. Cambridge, UK: Cambridge University Press.

Macaulay, Thomas Babington (1830, 1831/1907) "Moore's Life of Lord Byron" and "John Bunyan" in *Critical and Historical Essays*, vol. II. (pp. 399–410, 613–42), ed. Ernest Rhys. J. M. Dent & Co. London.

Maniquis, Robert M. (2002) "Filling Up and Emptying out the Sublime," in Robert M. Maniquis (ed.), *British Radical Culture of the 1790s* (pp. 369–405). San Marino, CA: Huntington Library Press.

Manning, B. L. (1942) *The Hymns of Wesley and Watts: Five Informal Papers*. London: Epworth Press.

Mellor, Anne K. (2000) *Mothers of the Nation: Women's Political Writing in England, 1780–1830*. Bloomington: Indiana University Press.

Mill, John Stuart. (1873/1989) "A Crisis in My Mental History. One Step Onward," in *Autobiography*, John M. Robson (pp. 111–144). London: Penguin Books.

Olsen, G. W. (ed.). (1990) *Religion and Revolution in Early Industrial England: The Halévy Thesis and its Critics*. Lanham, MD: University Press of America

Prickett, Stephen. (1976) *Romanticism and Religion: The Tradition of Coleridge and Wordsworth in the Victorian Church*. Cambridge, UK: Cambridge University Press.

Prickett, Stephen. (1996) *Origins of Narrative: The Romantic Appropriation of the Bible*. Cambridge, UK: Cambridge University Press.

Priestman, Martin. (2000) *Romantic Atheism: Poetry and Freethought, 1780–1830*. Cambridge, UK: Cambridge University Press.

Reardon, B. M. G. (1985) *Religion in the Age of Romanticism: Studies in Early Nineteenth Century Thought*. Cambridge, UK: Cambridge University Press.
Rupp, George. (1986) *Religion in England 1688–1791*. Oxford: Clarendon Press.
Russell, Bertrand. (1945) *A History of Western Philosophy*. New York: Simon and Schuster.
Ryan, Robert. (1997) *The Romantic Reformation: Religious Politics in English Literature, 1789–1824*. Cambridge, UK: Cambridge University Press.
Thompson, E. P. (1993) *Witness Against the Beast: William Blake and the Moral Law*. Cambridge, UK: Cambridge University Press.
Weber, Max. (1905/2001) *The Protestant Ethic and the Spirit of Capitalism*. London: Routledge.
White, Daniel. (2007) *British Romanticism and Early Religious Dissent*. Cambridge, UK: Cambridge University Press.
Woodring, Carl. (1970) *Politics in English Romantic Poetry*. Cambridge, MA: Harvard University Press.

Chapter 2

Romanticism and Empire

Saree Makdisi

The Romantic Age came to a sudden end on February 2, 1835. It ended, as it had begun, with a shift in British attitudes towards empire. For just as the inauguration of the era of British Romanticism had been announced by Sir William Jones's 1772 "Essay on the Poetry of the Eastern Nations," its demise was signaled by Thomas Macaulay's "Minute on Indian Education," which was presented in the context of a debate over the East India Company's education policy in February 1835. Jones's essay had helped make available to British writers a whole new cultural and literary world, on which – their appetites having already been whetted earlier in the century by translations (genuine and otherwise) of the *Arabian Nights* – they would steadily feast for the following five decades, transforming themselves and British literary culture in the process. Macaulay's 1835 essay, however, scorned Jones and anyone who took seriously his advice to seek inspiration and gather raw material for poetry from what he regarded as the backward and thoroughly degenerate East, and hence it marked the termination of the cultural and literary project that had been inaugurated by Jones. In between Jones and Macaulay, British Romanticism emerged, grew, flourished – and died.

The empire was not Romanticism's only area of interest, of course, and not everything about the Romantic period can be reduced to the question of imperialism. But what Raymond Schwab has identified as the Oriental Renaissance of the late eighteenth century made available far more than explicitly imperial matters to European writers and audiences. According to Schwab (and other more recent scholars: see the further reading list below), the Romantic interest in difference and otherness – surely one of the period's dominant concerns, if not *the* overriding concern – was largely enabled by the enormous vistas of cultural difference made available by the empire and, in particular, by the steady flow of knowledge and textual innovations coming back to Europe from the East: translations from Arabic, Persian, and Sanskrit; new forms of poetry and of drama; whole new fields for literary inspiration, innovation, exploitation. "Both geographically and historically, what had been lacking through the centuries and what would come to dominate everything was cultural dissonance, a sense of *the dissident*," Schwab argues. "The known world had been wholly classical before 1800. Or, in a sense, it had been a classified world. Homer was simultaneously the essential beginning and the culmination" (Schwab 1984: 23). The forms of knowledge and of discourse made available by the empire changed all that forever, and prompted Europeans to think beyond – and to revolt against – the classical and neo-classical paradigms that they had inherited from the eighteenth century; in other words, they led directly to Romanticism.

Even if the empire was not the only area of concern, it was certainly something of an obsession throughout the Romantic period. With the notable exception of William Blake, every single major writer in the period (and most of the minor ones as well) had at least a passing flirtation with imperialism or its major cultural manifestation, Orientalism. Many authors (e.g., Lord Byron, Robert Southey, Jane Austen, Walter Scott, Charlotte Dacre, Percy Shelley, Elizabeth Hamilton, Tom Moore, Walter Savage Landor) had significant imperialist or Orientalist works, if not long-standing, career-long engagements with the East. Moreover, the interest in imperialism invested virtually all areas of cultural production, including those that, at first glance, ought to have had nothing to do with the empire (such as arguments for and against the rights of man and of woman, or country-house novels, or even the most seemingly withdrawn and other-worldly forms of nature poetry).

Of course, the interest in empire was not limited to the Romantic period, but, rather, spanned British literature from at least the time of Shakespeare's *The Tempest* (1611) through at least the first third of the twentieth century. Romantic imperialism, however, had a flavor of its own, quite distinct from what came before and what would follow afterwards. Much of that distinctiveness had to do with the period's transitional nature, and, in particular, with its location at the cusp of very different attitudes toward progress and modernity – hence its interest in the forms of otherness (the archaic, the residual, the remainders of a mythic past) generated both by the empire and by the concomitant tendency toward the standardization and ultimately the homogenization of everyday life in Britain itself, which was the other by-product of increasing modernization.

Romanticism has long been seen as a cultural counterweight – even as a form of resistance – to a materially and economically progressive age, an age of scientific discoveries, technological inventions, and the resulting acceleration in economic productivity (and hence material wealth, but also exploitation and brutalization) that came from both. That acceleration was identified by William Wordsworth in the Preface to *Lyrical Ballads* (1800) with the "multitude of causes, unknown to former times," that were, he says, "acting with a combined force to blunt the discriminating powers of the mind, and, unfitting it for all voluntary exertion, to reduce it to a state of almost savage torpor. The most effective of these causes," Wordsworth adds, "are the great national events which are daily taking place, and the increasing accumulation of men in cities, where the uniformity of their occupations produces a craving for extraordinary incident, which the rapid communication of intelligence hourly gratifies" (Wordsworth 1800/1994: 436).

Anticipating Wordsworth's critique of commercial (or rather capitalist) culture, one of the forerunners of Romantic poetry, Oliver Goldsmith, had warned in *The Deserted Village* (1770) that "where wealth accumulates . . . men decay" (Goldsmith 1770/1876: 12). Adapting Goldsmith's line to their own age, and to the increasing progress underlying Britain's rapid industrialization, many of the period's greatest writers warned that economic progress and what was called "improvement" came with a very heavy social, cultural, and even psychospiritual price. This concern features prominently in Romanticism, and ranges from William Blake's proverb, in *The Marriage of Heaven and Hell* (1790–3), that improvement may make straight roads, but "crooked roads without improvement are roads of Genius," to Percy Shelley's assertion, in *Queen Mab* (1813), that "the venal interchange / Of all that human art or nature yield; / Which wealth should purchase not, but want demand," had "For ever stifled, drained, and tainted" the "full fountain" of "boundless love." And it remains there toward the very end of the Romantic age – albeit at the opposite end of the political spectrum from Blake and Shelley – in Robert Southey's contention in the *Colloquies on the Progress and Prospects of Society* (1829), that, for all its material wealth, the age of steam engines and cotton mills was increasingly peopled by a race of people who were intellectually and spiritually impoverished, if not bankrupt altogether.

That Romanticism was critical (or at least suspicious) of the forms of material progress that both enabled and were subservient to the aggressive, domineering, all-conquering spirit of capital, is hardly an original observation. This is, indeed, practically the only theme that ties together lifelong radicals such as Blake and Shelley to conservatives, and indeed anticapitalist reactionaries, like the later Southey and Wordsworth (or, for that matter, twentieth century neo-Romanticists like J. R. R. Tolkien).

That attitudes toward the empire provided the surest and most obvious indication of the extent of that spirit and its grip on cultural production, is, however, perhaps a somewhat less obvious claim. But in assessing its relationship to its cultural others, late eighteenth-century Britain (the Britain of Sir William Jones and Edmund Burke) was not yet convinced that technological or socioeconomic development automatically implied cultural "improvement" as well – much less that Britain's technological prowess and economic power necessarily translated into claims of cultural supremacy over other civilizations, particularly in the East (which was, and would remain, the major site of imperial activity after the loss of the American colonies). Britain might command the technological means that gave it the ability to conquer other countries, but that did not, as Burke repeatedly warned, imply that the British were in a position to assume any kind of cultural superiority over peoples "who framed their laws and institutions prior to our insect origins of yesterday." Moreover, according to Burke, the colonial administration of India should not be undertaken on the basis of attempting to transform India, to make it British by trying to impose a supposedly superior British culture on it. "If we undertake to govern the inhabitants of such a country, we must govern them upon their own principles and maxims, and not upon ours," Burke insists. "We must not think to force them into the narrow circle of our ideas; we must extend ours to take in their system of opinion and rites, and the necessities which result from both" (Burke 1788/ 1860, vol. 3: 301–2).

For Macaulay, however, writing at the other end of the surge of imperial activity and interest from 1772 to 1830 (a period in which over 150 million people were brought under British imperial control), Britain's technological superiority, as manifested in its imperial power, was *precisely* what allowed Britons to proclaim the inherent superiority of their own culture – and to dismiss other cultures with utter disdain. Henceforth, the colonial mission would be as much a project of cultural transformation as of material exploitation (with the former supposedly compensating for the latter):

> To have found a great people sunk in the lowest depths of slavery and superstition, to have so ruled them as to have made them desirous and capable of all the privileges of citizens, would indeed be a title to glory all our own. The scepter may pass away from us. Unforeseen accidents may derange our most profound schemes of policy. Victory may be inconstant to our arms. But there are triumphs which are followed by no reverse. There is an empire exempt from all natural causes of decay. Those triumphs are the pacific triumphs of reason over barbarism; that empire is the imperishable empire of our arts and our morals, our literature and our arts. (Macaulay 1833, quoted in Stokes 1989: 45)

For Macaulay, then, progress and imperial power underlay the imperative to understand that material "improvement" separated Britain from its colonial others.

As far as Macaulay was concerned, however, "improvement" not only separated Britain from its colonial others, but from its own backward past. Thus, for Macaulay, nostalgia for a lost past in Britain was little better than interest in quaint forms of exoticism from faraway lands – both were dangerous forms of delusion. Both, however, proved to be essential to Romanticism, which is exactly why Macaulay's condemnation of the interest in imperial otherness (and indeed cultural difference in general) is ultimately inseparable from his more general repudiation of Romanticism, in the figure of the Poet Laureate, Robert Southey. I will shortly return to Macaulay's criticism of Southey, but first I want to clarify what was at stake in the relationship between imperial activity and cultural difference during the Romantic period, particularly as expressed in Orientalism.

The late eighteenth-century Orientalism that helped to inspire Romanticism was markedly different from the forms of Orientalism that had preceded it. It was increasingly concerned with knowledge of the Oriental other for the purposes of imperial administration: it was instrumental, purposeful, expedient. "Every accumulation of knowledge, and especially such as is obtained by social communication over whom we exercise a dominion founded on the right of conquest," wrote Warren Hastings, the Governor-General of Bengal, in the preface to the first English translation (1785) of the *Bhagavad-Gita*, "is useful to the state." Early eighteenth-century Orientalism seemed, by contrast, much more innocent, even innocuous: it was concerned with moral instruction (of Britons, not Orientals), or, quite simply, with mere novelty and entertainment value. The early eighteenth-century split between entertainment and instrumental knowledge (or even knowledge as such) is illustrated by the fact that the publication of Antoine Galland's *Les mille et une nuits* in 1704 was swiftly followed by the first of many English translations of the *Arabian Nights Entertainments*, and inspired a wave of other "translations," amendments, variations, "discoveries" of new tales or fragments, and even something of a cottage industry in quasi-Oriental storytelling and essay writing; whereas Barthélemy d'Herbelot's 1697 *Bibliothèque orientale*, a compendium of Oriental knowledge, was never translated into English, presumably because there was no market for it, even though Galland himself had edited d'Herbelot's manuscript and had had it posthumously published for him in French.

Knowledge of Eastern cultures and literatures would assume an entirely different status by the end of the eighteenth century. Romantic-era Orientalism differed from earlier eighteenth-century Orientalism partly because of the fact that (thanks to the work of Jones and others) it was based on a far greater knowledge of the East than had been available previously (which was essentially the *Arabian Nights* and its derivatives); and partly because it was – necessarily – much more heavily invested in Britain's imperial project than had been the case with earlier forms of Orientalism. For this form of Orientalism emerged as an almost accidental by-product of the policy instituted by Warren Hastings to govern the East India Company's possessions in their own languages (or at least those of their learned elites). As late as the 1750s, knowledge of Indian languages in the ranks of the East India Company was still very limited. But with the change in policy as ordered by Hastings, in the 1770s the Company started systematically using local languages in its government of India, which obviously entailed British officials acquiring knowledge of those languages, in order, as Hastings put it, to "adapt our Regulations to the Manners and Understanding of the People, and Exigencies of the Country" (quoted in Cohn 1996: 26). Hastings ordered the extraction and circulation of Oriental knowledge for the purposes of command, not mere entertainment. He encouraged the translation of classic texts into English as well as a process of acculturation that would enable Englishmen to study Indian languages and literatures in order to master Indian culture from within. As Javed Majeed points out, the urge "to draw 'orient knowledge from its fountains pure'" was applied both to the process of legal codification and to the process of generating imaginative works and works of fiction (Majeed 1992: 52). "Entertainment" itself, in this context, assumed an expressly political and administrative function, so that the cultural and the political were quite inseparable.

This was the period when the British began to produce an apparatus of knowledge: grammars, treatises, dictionaries (e.g., Sir William Jones's *Grammar of the Persian Language*, 1771) – and translations of more and more Oriental works, both legal (e.g., Halhed's *Gentoo Laws*, 1776) and literary or cultural (e.g., Charles Wilkins' translation of the *Bhagavad-Gita*, 1785). As Bernard Cohn points out:

> Seen as a corpus, these texts signal the invasion of an epistemological space occupied by a great number of Indian scholars, intellectuals, teachers, scribes, priests, lawyers, officials, merchants, and bankers, whose knowledge as well as they themselves were to be converted into instruments of colonial rule. They were now to become part of the army of babus, clerks, interpreters, sub-inspectors, munshis, pandits, qazis, vakils, schoolmasters, amins, sharistadars, tahsildars, deshmukhs, darogahs, and mamlatdars who, under the scrutiny and supervision of the white sahibs, ran the everyday affairs of the Raj. (Cohn 1996: 21)

Thus, Cohn concludes, "the conquest of India was the conquest of knowledge" (1996: 16).

However, the translations from Arabic, Persian, and Sanskrit, as well as the whole epistemological project of which they represented a crucial component, not only provided the textual materials for imperial rule – they would also inspire a whole generation of British writers. It was in this context that the work of Sir William Jones became so prominent. But while Jones (who worked as a judge in the East India Company) argued for the practical application of the knowledge obtained from this Oriental renaissance, he also insisted that the process of extracting all this knowledge served far more than a merely instrumental function. Europeans, he argued, would gain from this immense Oriental learning a cultural resource that they could go on to use for their own aesthetic purposes. Asia, according to Jones, is "the nurse of sciences, the inventress of delightful and useful arts, the scene of glorious actions, fertile in the productions of human genius, abounding in natural wonders, and infinitely diversified in the forms of religion and government, in the laws, manners, customs, and languages, as well as in the features and complexions of men" (Jones 1784/1977: 2); it also offers a source of literary inspiration to Europeans. "I must request," Jones writes in the conclusion to one of his essays on the poetry of the eastern nations, that

> in bestowing these praises on the writings of Asia, I may not be thought to derogate from the merit of the Greek and Latin poems, which have been justly admired in every age; yet I cannot but think that our European poetry has subsisted too long on the perpetual repetition of the same images, and incessant allusions to the same fables: and it has been my endeavour for several years to inculcate this truth, that, if the principal writings of the Asiaticks, which are reposited in our public libraries, were printed with the usual advantage of notes and illustrations, and if the languages of the Eastern nations were studied in our great seminaries of learning, where every other branch of useful knowledge is taught to perfection, a new and ample field would be opened for speculation; we should have a more extensive insight into the history of the human mind; and we should be furnished with a new set of images and similitudes; and a number of excellent compositions would be brought to light, which future scholars might explain and future poets might imitate. (Jones 1772/1777: 189–90)

What Jones proposed, then, was to establish the cultural and literary parallel to the extraction of material wealth from the East, and to transfer both sets of treasures safely back to Britain. Following Jones, the British interest in Orientalism (and hence the empire) quickly matured from being merely a passing fad to an essential component of the much broader process of cultural and political self-definition that was taking place at the end of the eighteenth and beginning of the nineteenth centuries.

The irony here is that that process of self-definition, though it was inspired by contact with other cultures, ultimately came to be more about the *self* being defined than about the cultural *others*, the fascination with which had inspired self-awareness in the first place. For the process of gaining power over the other fundamentally required knowing not only what made the other "different," but also, in effect, what made the self the "same" (or in other words, collectively speaking, what made "us" who "we" are). The world of cultural difference that Jones proposed to explore thus both enabled and required a firmer sense of the identity from which it marked a departure. In other words, Britain's imperial relationships compelled British writers to articulate what it was that made Britain different from its others. In defining the Orient as a field of study, they had also to define an Occident against which the Orient's cultural difference could be measured and assessed. This entailed the emergence of an altogether new, modern sense of

British imperial and national subjectivity, a sense of self that could be defined against the Asiatic others who were subjected to the empire.

Self-definition quickly came to take over from the process of other-definition that had originally inspired it. And in the process, the Orient gradually started being thought of as a site that grounded the deeply ambivalent thoughts, worries, fears, and desires of the British self who had gained – or at least claimed – epistemological and narrative as well as political and administrative power over it. If the Orient became an obsession in the Romantic period, in other words, it was in ways that, paradoxically, had increasingly little to do with the Orient itself (even with the Orient as a cultural and political construction rather than an actual place, as Edward Said argued), and more and more to do with Britain's sense of itself. Even with the work of Jones coming out in fresh editions through the 1780s and into the 1790s, the Orient was increasingly seen not merely as a source of entertaining stories, innovative literary forms, and fascinating themes and images, but rather as an exciting site of danger, sensuality, and eroticism: a place that threatened even the most knowledgeable of outside rulers with corruption. Nowhere was this theme played out more distinctly than in the 1788–95 trial of Warren Hastings, nominally for high crimes and misdemeanors, but really for having in effect "gone native" and become monstrously Orientalized himself.

Because articulations of the sense of self (collective, social, national, imperial, and individual) were among the overriding concerns of the Romantic period, and because the sense of self that emerged during this period was so inextricably bound up with the circumstances of imperial rule, the Orient was inevitably one of the period's focal points. This explains why an interest in Orientalism recurs throughout the corpus of Romanticism, including in areas that at first glance ought to have nothing to do with the Orient at all – because the Orient had become essential to virtually every attempt to articulate a sense of selfhood or subjectivity. For the sense of self that was articulated through the 1790s and on into the nineteenth century was predicated on a sense of Western identity, a feeling of superiority over a supine and unmanly Eastern other. The contrast between the manly, honest, sober, virtuous Western self and the effeminate, luxurious, lazy, indulgent Eastern other permeates all forms of discourse in the Romantic period. Apart from everything else, for example, Wordsworth's project in the *Lyrical Ballads* was also to rescue poetry from being merely a matter of those by then notoriously Oriental traits of "amusement and idle pleasure," "idleness and unmanly despair," and to affirm instead an explicitly "manly" style, one available to the "sound and vigorous mind" of the Western self. This involved creating a new kind of reader as well as a new kind of author. For if the genius of the Poet represents "an advance, or a conquest," Wordsworth asks, "is it to be supposed that the reader can make progress of this kind, like an Indian prince or general – stretched on his palanquin, and borne by his slaves? No; he is invigorated and inspirited by his leader, in order that he may exert himself; for he cannot proceed in quiescence, he cannot be carried like a dead weight" (Wordsworth 1815/1988: 82). Only an explicitly Western reader, obviously, is capable of the kind of self-discipline that Wordsworth insists his poetry requires.

By the early nineteenth century, then, the distinction between West and East, as well as the attendant distinction between the Western self (controlled, regulated, rational, efficient, productive) and the Eastern self (undisciplined, irrational, emotional, wasteful, unproductive), had developed into a general principle that more and more Britons could take for granted. For most, it was important to validate the Western sense of self, which became, for example, one of the vital discourses of the radical culture that emerged in the 1790s and would be consolidated into respectability by the 1830s. For some, there would always be something dangerous or worrying about the Western sense of self and the supposedly rational self-control that had taken it to the point of nearly total homogenization. (When Blake complained, toward the end of his life, that "Englishmen are all Intermeasurable One by Another," he was referring in part to his sense that the rational, limited subjectivity essential to Orientalist discourse was inherently suffocating and entrapping, not just mind-numbingly homogenizing; he was also registering again his refusal to participate in that form of discourse or the imperialist political project from which it was inseparable. See Makdisi 2003: 204–59.) For others, there would always be something appealing about the Eastern self and its lack of standardization and self-control (it is this sense of attraction to the East that would, for example, draw Byron to it for most of his career and almost all of his best, and best-known, writing).

Nevertheless, the distinction between West and East, Occident and Orient, would become general, even institutionalized, by the end of the Romantic period, the time when Macaulay was preparing to write his "Minute on Indian Education," which would sound the death-knell of Romanticism. The arguments that would be worked out most fully in the Minute were, however, already anticipated in Macaulay's devastating 1830 review of Southey's *Colloquies* in the *Edinburgh Review*.

Southey brings to a task demanding the highest intellectual and moral qualities of the philosophical statesman, writes Macaulay, "two faculties which were never, we believe, vouchsafed in measure so copious to any human being, the faculty of believing without reason, and the faculty of hating without a provocation." It is, Macaulay adds, "most extraordinary, that a mind like Mr Southey's, a mind richly endowed in many respects by nature, and highly cultivated by study, a mind which has exercised considerable influence on the most enlightened generation of the most enlightened people that ever existed, should be utterly destitute of the power of discerning truth from falsehood" (Macaulay 1830/1965: 25).

Macaulay's Southey is not only incapable of distinguishing truth from falsehood while hating without provocation and believing without reason; he exceeds even Burke's "fierce and ungovernable sensibility," with which, according to Macaulay, Southey shares strong affinities. For while Burke "chose his side like a fanatic, and defended it like a philosopher," and while he could "defend the wildest course by arguments more plausible than those by which common men support opinions which they have adopted after the fullest deliberation," in the mind of Southey:

> reason has no place at all, as either leader or follower, as either sovereign or slave. He does not seem to know what an argument is. He never uses arguments himself. He never troubles himself to answer the arguments of his opponents. It has never occurred to him, that a man ought to be able to give some better account of the way in which he has arrived at his opinions than merely that it is his will and pleasure to hold them. It has never occurred to him that there is a difference between assertion and demonstration, that a rumour does not always prove a fact, that a single fact when proved, is hardly foundation enough for a theory, that two contradictory propositions cannot be undeniable truths, that to beg the question is not the way to settle it, or that when an objection is raised, it ought to be met with something more convincing than 'scoundrel' and 'blockhead.'" (Macaulay 1830/1965: 27)

In case all this has not already helped us to identify Southey as essentially a bilious old nabob – which, not coincidentally, is how Macaulay mocks the apparition of Thomas More in the *Colloquies* – there remains one more moment in this thoroughgoing Orientalization of the Poet Laureate (for Orientalization is precisely what this is), by the end of which Southey seems of a piece with the Orient, "its vast cities, its gorgeous pagodas, its infinite swarms of dusky population, its long-descended dynasties [and] its stately etiquette." For, Macaulay concludes, drawing on what was by the 1830s the full spectrum of Orientalist thought,

> it would be absurd to read the works of such a writer for political instruction. The utmost that can be expected from any political system promulgated by him is that it may be splendid and affecting, that it may suggest sublime and pleasing images. His scheme of philosophy is a mere day-dream, a poetical creation, like the Domdaniel cavern, the Swerga, or Padalon [references to Southey's Oriental epics], and indeed it bears no inconsiderable resemblance to those gorgeous visions. Like them, it has something of invention, grandeur, and brilliancy. But, like them, it is grotesque and extravagant, and perpetually violates even that conventional probability which is essential to the effect of works of art. (Macaulay 1830/1965: 27)

It should come as no surprise, then, that – having Orientalized it – Macaulay should find Southey's work intellectually and aesthetically barren, since that was also his assessment of Oriental culture in the "Minute on Indian Education," which he turned to shortly after his review of Southey. He argues in that document that India's vernacular languages "contain neither literary nor scientific information," and that the sum total of historical information contained in even the learned languages of India (Arabic, Persian, Sanskrit) "is less valuable than what may be found in the most paltry abridgments used at preparatory schools in England." This too should hardly come as a surprise, since, according to the "Minute," those learned languages express "medical doctrines, which would disgrace an English farrier, – Astronomy, which would move laughter in girls at an English boarding school, – History, abounding with kings thirty feet high, and reigns thirty thousand years long, – and Geography, made up of seas of treacle and seas of butter" (Macaulay 1835/1999: 58).

Perhaps in part because Macaulay launched his attack on Southey at exactly the same time as he was deepening his interest in Oriental and imperial affairs, Southey thus emerges from this critique a thoroughly Orientalized figure, privileging belief over reason, mixing truth and falsehood, expressing hatred without provocation, and conveying a philosophical system which, precisely like those of the Orient, might perhaps offer glimpses of pleasure, grandeur, affect, sublimity – though at the expense of being finally negated or overcome by a dreamlike extravagance, excessive irrationality, and of course intellectual barrenness. Southey's Orientalization is not merely inseparable from what Macaulay claims are his intellectual and philosophical faults: it expresses those faults exactly. Southey is Orientalized to the extent that he is wrong, misguided, deluded, irrational, inaccurate, and extravagant; and he is wrong, misguided, deluded, irrational, inaccurate, and extravagant precisely to the extent that he is Orientalized.

In thus Orientalizing Southey, Macaulay is signaling the abrupt end of one version of Orientalism – the one that had emerged in inextricable association with Romanticism in the 1780s and 1790s – and the emergence of another. What we can locate in Macaulay, in other words, is the triumphant expression of a new attitude toward the East, which in effect announced the termination not only of what we might think of as the spectacular Orientalism of the Romantic period, but of the aesthetic politics of Romanticism itself. Not only did Macaulay's argument register a whole new attitude toward the cultural politics of empire: it did so in a way that necessarily condemned the infatuation with otherness that was so essential to Romanticism.

While it drew on Oriental languages and cultures, however, Southey's Orientalism was never intended to be merely derivative, but rather to adapt quasi-authentic cultural materials for European aesthetic and political projects: in other words, to produce imaginative works that would tap into the considerable accumulation of Oriental knowledge flowing into Europe at the time, even while betraying and ultimately undermining the very cultures on which they were modeled. This simultaneous foundation on and departure from the new field of knowledge being developed in the East is what enabled Southey to claim that his Oriental epics – *Thalaba the Destroyer* and *The Curse of Kehama* – differed from the actual Oriental texts and traditions in which they were, however, rooted.

Although works like *Thalaba* devote considerable energy to the construction and elaboration of their complex Oriental settings, the Orient here serves merely as one setting for what Southey conceived of as a universal history, in which different cultures might be read alongside one another, rather than according to a rigid hierarchy with European cultures lording it over supposedly inferior non-European cultures. Thus he would often cut from one culture to another as a way of asserting not merely their interrelationship but their interdependence – and in so doing, he would substantially head off any European claims to superiority based on cultural difference. In a note to the lines in *Thalaba*, "Praise to the Lord our God, / He gave, he takes away," for example, Southey acknowledges what might be considered by some to be the strangeness of placing "a Scripture phrase in the mouth of a Mahommedan; but," he explains, "it is a saying of Job, and there can be no impropriety in making a modern Arab speak like an ancient one." Moreover, he adds in the notes to *Thalaba*, that rather than using a line from the Koran, "I thought it better to express a feeling of religion in that language with which our religious ideas are connected" (Southey 1801/1845: 36). Here, quite explicitly, Southey is articulating a view of cultures surprisingly similar to Blake's: for it is only if the same concepts (like Blake's Poetic Genius) are manifested and articulated differently in different cultures that it could make sense to suggest that a line from the Bible could stand in for one from the Koran – that we could, paradoxically, best approximate the spirit of Islam by invoking the Bible. In another passage of *Thalaba*, Southey borrows a line from what he says is a traditional English ballad – which he cites in full in the notes – and transposes it to an Arab context. Again, this suggests a certain degree of commonality among cultures.

This repeated cultural cross-fertilization undoubtedly boosted the cosmopolitan energies of Southey's works; it also helped him to deploy the Orient as a spectacular setting for moral instruction. Using the Orient this way was of course, in itself, nothing new by the early nineteenth century (Addison and Steele had deployed the tactic a hundred years earlier), but in the context of expanded knowledge and greater imperial commitments such a gesture had altogether different significance in the early nineteenth century, as the more charitable views of people like William Jones started to fade away, to be gradually replaced by the outright cultural hostility of people like James Mill, Charles Grant, and, ultimately, Macaulay himself. Many of the concerns that Southey elaborates in the spectacular setting of *Thalaba* are identical to the concerns he would elaborate in his explicitly English works, notably the *Colloquies*, and such essays as "On the Rise and Progress of Popular Disaffection" or "On the Means of Improving the People."

Not only, for example, does *Thalaba* evoke the same concern for the instruction of "the multitude" that would prove one of the dominant concerns of Southey's essays on England, it also offers a warning of what happens to societies that allow material concerns to eclipse their moral and religious commitments. The warning issued by Aswad in one of the early passages of *Thalaba* is precisely the kind of lesson that one finds reiterated throughout Southey's work, especially the work devoted to England:

> Boy, who hast reached my solitude,
> Fear the Lord in the days of thy youth!
> My knee was never taught
> To bend before my God;
> My voice was never taught
> To shape one holy prayer.
> We worshipped Idols, wood and stone;
> The work of our own foolish hands
> We worshipped in our foolishness.
> Vainly the Prophet's voice
> In frequent warning raised, –
> "REPENT, AND BE FORGIVEN!"
> We mocked the messenger of God;
> We mocked the Lord, long-suffering, slow to wrath.
> (Southey 1801/1845: 216)

Here once again a distinctly Christian line – "repent, and be forgiven" – is spoken by a Muslim, and the well-known Muslim hostility to idolatry and the worship of material things is seen to bear an uncanny resemblance to the warning echoing through England in the late eighteenth and early nineteenth centuries, of the moral dangers associated with commercial growth. Certainly, this is one of the recurring themes of Southey's *Colloquies*, whose main concerns are the moral consequences of "the uncontrolled dominion of that worldly spirit which it is the tendency of the commercial system to produce and foster," and hence the "undisputed and acknowledged supremacy" which Mammon – a false god like the false idols of *Thalaba* – "seems to have obtained in commercial countries, and in no country more decidedly than in this [England]." The ghost of Thomas More goes on to point out that "The spirit which built and endowed monasteries is gone," and asks Montesinos, "Are you one of those persons who think it has been superseded for the better by that which erects steam-engines and cotton-mills?" (Southey 1829/1831: 154, 158). Clearly, for Southey, not only do steam and steel represent the modern-day equivalent of the primitive wood and stone idols denounced by Aswad, but the need to assert the moral rehabilitation of societies in which the spirit of materialism has gone out of control applies no more to the Orient than it does to England itself, where Southey advocates a system of national education (including moral and religious instruction) that might extend the benefits of civilization to "those classes who are brutalized by the institutions of society" (p. 132).

Clearly, too, the brutalized workers of England – victims of a system that, according to the ghost of More, is founded on "slavery direct or indirect, abroad or at home," and that "employs men unremittingly in pursuits unwholesome for the body, and unprofitable for the mind" – are no better off, no more intellectually and culturally developed, than the Arab workers in *Thalaba*, where we see that only "the labour and the pain of multitudes" made possible the creation of the short-lived material wealth of Ad, whose people discover far too late that the Lord does not hear the prayers abroad of those "who made no prayers at home" (Southey 1801/1845: 218). The threat of moral decay brought about by the unchecked pursuit and accumulation of material wealth links the fate of the English to that of Indians and Arabs, cultures tied together in the face of a common enemy. Southey's cosmopolitan surveys of cultures threatened by the worldly spirit of vulgar materialism refuses to privilege one society over another, much less one over all the others.

Southey's commitments rested, however, on an extremely unstable set of assumptions, which were themselves built on the shifting terrain of arguments concerning imperial policy running through Southey's entire career, from the 1780s to the 1830s. It is not surprising, then, that his position should be shot through with contradictions. Ironically, for example, it was Southey's universalist and cosmopolitan interests (which were derived from one stage of imperial policy, in the 1780s and 1790s) that led to his advocacy of the evangelical attitude toward Britain's imperial possessions in Asia (which would take hold in a radically – indeed deliberately – contradictory set of imperial policies in the early nineteenth century). The kind of Orientalism elaborated by Southey, as well as by other writers, from Walter Savage Landor to Tom Moore and Lord Byron, was not the only form of Orientalism in the Romantic period – it existed in sharp contrast with, for example, the distinctly more hostile Orientalism of writers such as the Comte de Volney, Shelley, and De Quincey – but it emerged in the gap arising between these different stages of imperial rule. When that gap closed, with the consolidation of a new set of attitudes, embodied in new policies (of which Macaulay was one of the prime advocates), these contradictions would themselves be resolved, and it would become more difficult, if not impossible, to engage in the kinds of spectacular Orientalist projects that so interested Southey (or Byron, or Moore).

We can locate this gap in the transition from the approach to imperial policy advocated by Warren Hastings in the 1770s to the new policies that would be first announced in the Cornwallis reforms of 1793 but would only really come to be put into practice after 1813, and would not actually be consolidated until after the debates in the

1830s in which Macaulay's "Minute on Indian Education" would prove such a significant intervention. The irony here is that, although Southey was profoundly interested in and influenced by the work emerging from the Oriental Renaissance of the 1780s and 1790s, he was also a champion of the very same evangelical approach to India called for by men like Charles Grant and William Wilberforce, whose hostility to Eastern cultures was unflinching.

Macaulay, on the other hand, did not suffer from such contradictions or their attendant anxieties, which is why he could be so sweeping in his condemnation both of Southey and of the Oriental literatures in which the Poet Laureate was actually (for all his retrospective attempts at denial and distancing) very interested. Macaulay saw nothing of value in Oriental civilization, let alone any possible source of inspiration for anyone writing for what he claimed was the most enlightened generation of the most enlightened people that ever existed.

Eric Stokes argues that little of the cultural hostility revealed by Macaulay in such texts was new, that "everywhere his speech rings with ideas which the elder Charles Grant and Wilberforce had uttered nearly forty years before" (Stokes 1989: 45). But it is important to note that despite the similarities, there were also some profound differences between Macaulay's position and the older evangelical position which he would draw on. For one thing, Macaulay sought to a certain extent to secularize what had been a frankly religious discourse.

More significantly, however, even when he echoed older voices, Macaulay's position suffered from none of the contradictions that hobbled theirs: for while their approach might have been considered conservative in an English context (i.e., upholding what it conceived of as the traditional culture), it was radically destabilizing in the imperial context – seeking to uproot and destroy local institutions and traditions and to replace them with new imports. Macaulay, on the other hand, was all for radical transformation in England as well as in India – even if he thought that government, in the form of the East India Company, was ideal for the task in India, and hopeless at it in England – and was an eager advocate of what Marx would later identify as the mission to "put an end to all feudal, patriarchal, idyllic relations," to "tear asunder the motley feudal ties that bound man to his 'natural superiors,'" to batter down Chinese walls and "force the barbarians' intensely obstinate hatred of foreigners to capitulate," and to compel them to "introduce what it calls civilization into their midst" (Marx and Engels 1848/2002: 222–4).

As much as the various imperial and Oriental questions, in fact, this is what manifestly distinguishes Macaulay's position from Southey's; or, to be more precise, this is what fuses Macaulay's attack on Southey's Oriental tendencies to his critique of Southey's domestic politics. For Macaulay, progress unfolds across all cultures and all times. Thus, if it falls to England to bring enlightenment to India in the nineteenth century, and if the English are now the most enlightened people that ever existed, that is only because England and the English received enlightenment from others in their turn. "What the Greek and Latin were to the [English] contemporaries of More and Ascham, our tongue is to the people of India," Macaulay argues in the "Minute on Indian Education." "Had our ancestors . . . neglected the language of Cicero and Tacitus; had they confined their attention to the old dialects of our own island; had they printed nothing and taught nothing at the universities but Chronicles in Anglo-Saxon, and Romances in Norman-French, would England have been what she now is?" (Macaulay 1835/1999: 58). Clearly not, for Macaulay – which explains both his unremitting hostility toward Eastern cultures and his profound disagreement with Southey.

For on Macaulay's reading of Southey's *Colloquies*, the Poet Laureate is as much an advocate of obstinate traditions and worn-out customs – if not quite Chinese walls – stubbornly trying to keep the spirit of innovation and progress at bay as the sages and *ulema* of the East. Southey, according to Macaulay,

> abhors the spirit of the present generation, the severity of its studies, the boldness of its inquiries, and the disdain with which it regards some old prejudices by which his own mind is held in bondage. He dislikes an utterly unenlightened age; he dislikes an investigating and reforming age. The first twenty years of the sixteenth century would have suited him perfectly. (Macaulay 1830/1965: 59)

Macaulay's point here is twofold. For while he obviously wishes to contest Southey's assessment of the reality of England's material progress, and to argue that the common people are far better off in the nineteenth century than they were in some idyllic and mythical preindustrial age of the Romantic imagination, he also wants to argue against the use of images as political devices in the first place, which is what he accuses Southey of doing – and not only with regard to the Orient, but with regard to England itself. Southey's investment in spectacular Orientalism is here revealed to be inextricable from his investment in a more general economy of images. For Macaulay, on the other hand, in exactly the same way that it is essential to show that the splendid and affecting – "sublime and pleasing" – images of the Orient amount to little more than day-dreams and fantasies, it is also essential to show that it is folly to elaborate would-be political or philosophical arguments on the basis of images alone. Hence the absurdity of trying to assess the comparative value of manufactures and agriculture according to the prettiness of the landscapes associated with them is exactly indicative of the absurdity of substituting prettified aesthetics for serious political economy, or in other words abandoning hard-nosed reason in the name of image and spectacle.

This is precisely what Macaulay accuses Southey of doing. Not only is the Poet Laureate utterly destitute of the power of discerning truth from falsehood, and guilty of that peculiarly Oriental sin of believing without reason and hating without provocation; he is also guilty of substituting images for realities – another Oriental trait:

> Government is to Mr. Southey one of the fine arts. He judges of a theory, of a public measure, of a religion or a political party, of a peace or a war, as men judge of a picture or a statue, by the effect produced on his imagination. A chain of associations is to him what a chain of reasoning is to other men; and what he calls his opinions are in fact merely his tastes.... Mr. Southey's political system is just what we might expect from a man who regards politics, not as a matter of science, but as a matter of taste and feeling. (Macaulay 1830/1965: 25–6)

For Macaulay, of course, progress is made possible precisely by allowing science and discipline to override not only taste and feeling, but also long-established customs, stubborn prejudices, and outmoded practices – in England as much as in India.

The Orient – and Orientalist investments such as Southey's – represent for Macaulay the embodiment of the pursuit of the spectacular rather than the material, and of the foolhardy substitution of an image economy for genuine political economy. As far as Macaulay is concerned, they are both to be brought under control and disciplined; a process that would involve the eradication of forms of thought incompatible with the disciplinary logic of a new age – an age which spectacular Romanticism itself would not survive. For the new imperial policies advocated by Macaulay, image and spectacle would henceforth be entirely secondary in their importance when compared to genuine material realities. Since it is impossible to educate the mass of the population of India, Macaulay argues, "we must at present do our best to form a class who may be interpreters between us and the millions whom we govern; a class of persons, Indian in blood and colour, but English in taste, in opinions, in morals, and in intellect" (Macaulay 1835/1999: 61). For such an imperial project, clearly, the Romantic investment in the spectacle of difference would be turned on its head, outward difference would serve only to mask internal, and hence genuine, sameness – and it is the sameness, rather than the difference, that would count. And the exhilarating, threatening, sublime spectacle of Oriental alterity would be defused at last.

References and Further Reading

Burke, Edmund. (1788/1860) "Speech Opening the Impeachment of Warren Hastings, Day One," in *The Works of Edmund Burke*, 3 vols (pp. 285–387). New York: Harper and Brothers.

Cohn, Bernard. (1996) *Colonialism and its Forms of Knowledge: The British in India*. Princeton, NJ: Princeton University Press.

Fulford, Tim, and Peter Kitson (eds). (1998) *Romanticism and Colonialism: Writing and Empire, 1780–1830*. Cambridge, UK: Cambridge University Press.

Goldsmith, Oliver. (1769/1876) *The Deserted Village*, ed. E. T. Stevens. London: Longmans.

Jones, Sir William. (1772/1777) "Essay on the Poetry of the Eastern Nations" in *Poems Consisting Chiefly of Translations From the Asiatick Languages*, 2nd edn (pp. 163–90). London: W. Bowyer and J. Nichol.

Jones, Sir William. (1784/1977) "A Discourse on the Institution of a Society, for Enquiring into the History, Civil and Natural, the Antiquities, Arts, Sciences, Literature, of Asia, By the President." In *The Works of Sir William Jones in Thirteen Volumes* (vol. 2, p. 3). Delhi: Agam Prakashan.

Leask, Nigel. (1992) *British Romantic Writers and the East: Anxieties of Empire*. Cambridge, UK: Cambridge University Press.

Macaulay, Thomas. (1830/1965) "Southey's Colloquies on Society," in *Macaulay: Critical and Historical Essays*, ed. Hugh Trevor-Roper (pp. 25–69). New York: McGraw-Hill.

Macaulay, Thomas. (1835/1999) "Minute on Indian Education." In Barbara Harlow and Mia Carter (eds), *Imperialism and Orientalism: A Documentary Sourcebook* (pp. 56–61). Oxford: Blackwell.

Majeed, Javed. (1992) *Ungoverned Imaginings*. Oxford: Clarendon Press.

Makdisi, Saree. (1998) *Romantic Imperialism*. Cambridge, UK: Cambridge University Press.

Makdisi, Saree. (2003) *William Blake and the Impossible History of the 1790s*. Chicago: University of Chicago Press.

Marx, Karl, and Friedrich Engels. (1848/2002) *The Communist Manifesto*, ed. Gareth Stedman Jones. Baltimore: Penguin.

Said, Edward. (1978) *Orientalism*. New York: Pantheon.

Said, Edward. (1993) *Culture and Imperialism*. New York: Knopf.
Schwab, Raymond. (1984) *The Oriental Renaissance: Europe's Rediscovery of India and the East, 1680–1880*, trans. G. Patterson-Black and V. Reinking. New York: Columbia University Press.
Southey, Robert. (1829/1831) *Sir Thomas More; Or, Colloquies on the Progress and Prospects of Society*. London: Murray.
Southey, Robert. (1801/1845) *Thalaba the Destroyer*, in *Poetical Works* (pp. 213–312). London: Longman.
Stokes, Eric. (1989) *The English Utilitarians and India*. Delhi: Oxford University Press.
Wordsworth, William. (1988) *Selected Prose*, ed. John Hayden. Harmondsworth, UK: Penguin.
Wordsworth, William. (1994) *Selected Poems*, ed. John Hayden. Harmondsworth, UK: Penguin.

Chapter 3

"Associations Respect[ing] the Past": Enlightenment and Romantic Historicism

Anthony Jarrells

From the moment that "Romanticism" emerged as a critical concept – in the second half of the nineteenth century – it described a period that not only succeeded a previous age of Enlightenment but also opposed it. In his *History of English Literature*, published in 1864, Hippolyte Taine argued that poets like Robert Southey, Samuel Taylor Coleridge, and William Wordsworth had "violently broken" with eighteenth-century canons of taste and knowledge and had looked past the Enlightenment to the Middle Ages and the Renaissance for their models (Taine 1864/1873, vol. 3: 423). Indeed, even before there was such a thing as "Romanticism," Francis Jeffrey characterized the same three poets as "dissenters" from "established systems of poetry and criticism," and as "perpetually brooding over the disorders by which [civilization's] progress has been attended" (Jeffrey 1802: 63, 71). To be sure, Romantic writers themselves had a hand in constructing what Mark Salber Phillips calls the "myth" of a "wholly abstract and detached" Enlightenment (Phillips 2003: 446). When friends advised Wordsworth to "prefix" his poems with a "systematic defence" of his poetic theory, he rejected the suggestion because, as he explained in his Preface to *Lyrical Ballads* (1800), he did not want to be suspected "of reasoning [the reader] into approbation" of his poetry. Poetry is not systematic or reasonable; it is, as Wordsworth famously claimed, the "spontaneous overflow of powerful feelings" (Wordsworth and Coleridge 1800/1991: 242).

Twentieth-century critics and editors of anthologies in large part continued to stress a decisive break between an Enlightenment characterized by reason and abstraction and a Romanticism that privileged imagination and feeling. M. H. Abrams' influential book of 1953, *The Mirror and the Lamp*, for instance, uses the metaphor of a mirror to describe the literature of the eighteenth century, which aimed to reflect the world and the underlying laws of nature. Romantic writers, however, strove not so much to reflect the world as to project themselves onto it and to create it in their own image. Like a lamp – a "radiant projector" – Romantic writing "makes a contribution to the objects it perceives" (Abrams 1953: viii). For Abrams, Wordsworth's Preface is a paradigmatic example of the "displacement" of a mimetic theory of art by one that was "expressive" (p. 22).

A significant effect of the historicist turn in the 1980s was that it challenged the long-held notion of a Romantic/Enlightenment break. By historicizing the texts, writers, and ideologies of the period – that is, as Jerome McGann explains, "by placing [Romantic characterizations] in a critical context which attempts to understand them in terms other than their own self-definitions" – "new" historicist critics complicated many of the ideas and oppositions taken for granted in earlier accounts (McGann 1983: ix). Marilyn Butler, for instance, argued that the social pressures exerted on and by literary movements persist across periods in ways that suggest coexistence rather than succession (Butler 1981: 180). And in his book-length study of Romantic historicism, *England in 1819* (1998), James Chandler situates the emergence of the new historicism itself as a repetition of a constitutive Romantic practice: that of dating texts and of regarding them as products of a specific age or period. Chandler's focus is Romanticism. But the distinctive form that emerges in the period is a product of Enlightenment-era theories of "uneven development" – particularly as they featured in the work of William Robertson and John Millar (Chandler 1998: 127–8).

The heightened attention to the Enlightenment occasioned by the historicist turn in Romantic studies has highlighted the important place of Scotland for understanding how Romanticism engages, extends, and reorients Enlightenment. Chandler's book is one influential example of this. Katie Trumpener's *Bardic Nationalism* (1997) is another. Trumpener shows how the materials and perspectives that comprise two of the Romantic period's most distinctive genres – the national tale and the historical novel – originated in "the investigative journeys of the Enlightenment" and the "controversies" surrounding the authenticity of James Macpherson's "Ossian" poems (1760–3), which were thought to be translations of a third-century Scottish epic (1997: 101). And more recently, in *Scott's Shadow* (2007), Ian Duncan examines Romantic-period Edinburgh as a major site of literary production in the period, one where periodical genres like the magazine and fictional genres like the novel assumed their modern forms. Duncan's account of this "cultural" capital of the nineteenth century uncovers the "fiction-making" processes that underpin "modern sovereignty." Central to this account is the figure of Walter Scott, the writer most responsible for making the novel "the ascendant genre of national life" (Duncan 2007: 28). The "philosophical authority" for the novel's ascendancy, however, derives, says Duncan, from the Scottish Enlightenment empiricism of David Hume (2007: xii).

What is it, we might ask, about Scotland's situation in the period that enables us to grasp connections across what otherwise are thought to be distinct periods? And if Scotland is such an important site for understanding these connections, why has it not featured similarly in earlier historicist work on the period? In his landmark study of *The Historical Novel* (1937), for instance, Georg Lukács marks Scott as the progenitor of the genre but barely registers the specifically Scottish context and subject matter of his work. Lukács does link the representation of history in Scott's novels to the "realist literary traditions of the Enlightenment"; but the Enlightenment he has in mind is largely a Continental one (Lukács 1937/1983: 33). It is above all the philosophy of G. W. F. Hegel that provides the "philosophic basis" for the new, progressive conception of history that features in Scott's novels (p. 28). As Chandler explains, though, to associates Romantic historicism in Britain with Hegel is to miss what is truly distinctive about the period. Thus Chandler himself not only emphasizes a British – and specifically a Scottish – framework for understanding both Scott and Romantic historicism; he argues that the theory of historical stages that underpins the historicism of the period comes from the comparative model of history developed by the philosophical historians of the Scottish Enlightenment.

This move from a Continental to a specifically Scottish context for Romantic historicism may seem parochial in its emphasis – a move toward the merely regional or provincial. But I would suggest that it is in fact the opposite. The philosophical historians of the Scottish Enlightenment were uniquely situated to grasp the unevenness of historical development: eighteenth-century Scotland's geographical and linguistic divisions (between Highland and Lowland; east and west;

Gaelic, English, and Scots), and its "anomalous position" with regards to colonialism – as both colonizer and colonized – made it ideal for exploring the fissures, the uneven character, of modernity itself (Davis, Duncan, and Sorensen 2004: 2). The theories and explanations put forward by the philosophical historians of the mid-eighteenth century comprised attempts to account for as well as to smooth over these divisions. The resulting approaches – conjectural history, political economy, rhetoric and belles-lettres – not only provided the newly unified kingdom with a necessary narrative of Britishness; they became part of a global trade in books and ideas that stretched from Edinburgh and Glasgow to London, Dublin, Paris, Philadelphia, and beyond (Sher 2006: 23–4).

Romantic-period writers continued to engage with and revise these Scottish Enlightenment ideas. But the terrain of engagement, as Duncan suggests, shifted from history to fiction as the novel became the form *par excellence* for representing national life. To illustrate this shift of terrain and this engagement, I will turn first to assessments of Enlightenment philosophical history in two of the most influential periodicals of the Romantic period: the *Edinburgh Review* and *Blackwood's Edinburgh Magazine*. My particular focus here will be the place Scott's fiction occupied in the war of ideas waged in the period. Next, I will turn to a genre which Scott helped to make popular but which came to challenge the historicism implicit in his novels: the tale. In the regional tales such as those published in *Blackwood's*, we find one of those minor or secondary genres in which, as Phillips suggests, the pressures and strains of the period – and for us, of Romantic historicism itself – are made especially visible (Phillips 2000: 15).

National Intellect and National Feeling

In 1819, Walter Scott's future son-in-law and biographer, John Gibson Lockhart, published *Peter's Letters to his Kinsfolk*, a semifictional account of literary life in Romantic Edinburgh. Although Lockhart adopts the persona of an outsider – of a Welsh "odontist" visiting Scotland – as a writer and de facto editor at *Blackwood's Magazine*, he was in fact very much on the inside of the political and cultural disputes raging in the city. Throughout his account, for instance, Lockhart's eponymous narrator laments the continued cultural influence of what he terms "the philosophers of the last age":

> The generation of Hume, Smith, &c. left matters of feeling very much unexplored, and probably considered Poetry merely as an elegant and tasteful appendage to the other branches of literature, with which they themselves were more conversant. Their disquisitions on morals were meant to be the vehicles of ingenious theories – not of convictions of sentiment. They employed, therefore, even in them, only the national intellect, and not the national modes of feeling. (Lockhart 1819, vol. 2: 360)

The oppositions implied in this passage are the very ones which have long served to separate Enlightenment and Romanticism. Theory and intellect are made to stand against feeling and sentiment; and among the "branches of literature," philosophical – or what Lockhart would call "sceptical" – history, is pitted against "Poetry," a genre that allowed for a deeper representation of national life.

The occasion of Peter's ruminations on Scottish Enlightenment philosophy is what Lockhart describes as the "long undisputed tyrannical sway" of Francis Jeffrey and the *Edinburgh Review* – the premier vehicle of Scottish Enlightenment thought in the period (vol. 2: 204). Founded in 1802 by four Whig lawyers frustrated with the Tory administration of Henry Dundas, the *Edinburgh Review* remained, in 1819, the most influential periodical in Britain. *Blackwood's*, in fact, was founded in 1817 in large part to oppose the dominance of the *Edinburgh Review*'s Whiggism with strong Tory principles. But as the lengthy treatment given to Enlightenment philosophers in *Peter's Letters* suggests, this Whiggism characterized not just an opposing political affiliation but also a particular view of history, one that was "sociological" in its approach, and which regarded modern, commercial society as the inevitable highest stage of history (Kidd 1993: 7). Jeffrey had been a student of Dugald Stewart and of John Millar, both Enlightenment Whigs and disciples of Adam Smith. Under his editorship, the *Edinburgh Review* developed a model of professionalized authorship to compete with Tory patronage networks, and a broad, political-economic outlook that stressed a gradualist approach to reform.

Lockhart found a "splendid" exception to the Whig rule of Jeffrey and friends in the work of Walter Scott. "While all the rest were contenting themselves with exercising and displaying their speculative acuteness," writes Lockhart, "he had the wisdom . . . to grapple boldly with the feelings of his countrymen" (Lockhart 1819, vol. 2: 360–1). In a climactic scene that appears in volume two of *Peter's Letters*, Lockhart's narrator travels to Abbotsford to meet Scott, "the patriarch of the National Poetry of Scotland" (p. 351). The scene is important in its implications as it represents both a physical move away from Jeffrey's Edinburgh/*Edinburgh* and an ideological move back to a sentimental strain attributed earlier in the text to Wordsworth and Robert Burns (both of whom Jeffrey fails fully to appreciate). "By enquiring into and representing the modes of life in earlier times," writes Lockhart, Scott

> employs the imagination of his countrymen, as a means of making them go through the personal experience of their ancestry, and of making them acquainted with the various courses of thought and emotion, by which their forefathers had their genius and characters drawn out – things to which, by the mechanical arrangements of modern life and society, we have been rendered too much strangers. (Lockhart 1819, vol. 2: 350)

In his account of the Abbotsford visit, Lockhart makes clear a certain ideological connection between Wordsworth, "the great Poet of the Lakes," and Scott, "the great Poet of Scotland." Where Wordsworth had claimed in his Preface that his poetry might "counteract" the sapping of national sentiment and degrading of national taste resulting from "a multitude of causes, unknown to former times": war, revolution, capitalism (Wordsworth and Coleridge 1800/1991: 249), Scott, it was hoped, would do the same by reclaiming Scottish traditions and associations equally obscured by "modern life."

Although Scott had no official connection to *Blackwood's*, his figure and authority were crucial for the image the magazine constructed of itself in the early years of its existence. If "modern life" was the concern of the *Edinburgh Review*, *Blackwood's* would counter that periodical's professionalized, political-economic ethos by promoting a sense of "national culture" – that is, by foregrounding those traditional settings and associations lost in the general sweep of commercial progress (Duncan 2007: 48–9). In part, this meant preserving a sense of Scotland's own distinct history, much of which had been "subverted" in the philosophical histories of the Enlightenment (Kidd 1993: 7). The magazine's Edinburgh base was part of this; but so was the decision to include original works of fiction – especially Scottish regional tales. It is not that the writers at *Blackwood's* were nationalist in the sense of being anti-English. Rather, they thought that the best way to participate in the political and economic union with England was by maintaining a sense of Scottish national identity. As Lockhart explains, "An union of national interests *quoad* [i.e., regarding] external power, relates chiefly to the future." But "associations," he insists, "respect the past" (Lockhart 1819, vol. 2: 355).

The importance of the word "associations" in Lockhart's writing derives not from the Lockean philosophy that was so influential on eighteenth-century thought, but rather from the idea that ones values and identity are shaped by shared notions of place and tradition. Associations are thus social: they are bonds that hold a people together. Like the fields and hills that "had laid / Strong hold" on the "affections" of Wordsworth's Michael, they evoke "A pleasurable feeling of blind love" (Wordsworth, 1800, "Michael," ll. 74–8). Such blind love of place and tradition is precisely what the ingenious theories and skeptical histories of the Enlightenment had undermined – in part by constructing a more broadly British identity for Scots, and in part by challenging, often inadvertently, the religious foundations of tradition. As Scott's work demonstrated (for Lockhart, at least), fiction could represent, even embody, the deep attachments to local and traditional associations which *Blackwood's* opposed to the Enlightenment Whiggism of the *Edinburgh Review*.

Of course, not all readers of the period agreed with Lockhart's assessment of Scott. William Hazlitt, for instance, praised the "candour and comprehensiveness" of Scott's view of history even as he labeled Scott's genius "degraded" by his affiliation with "the lowest panders of a venal press" – a reference to Lockhart and *Blackwood's* (Hazlitt 1825/1932: 68). And in an *Edinburgh Review* piece on the collected "Waverley Novels," published in 1832, the reviewer concluded that "We have seen nothing in the writings of Walter Scott . . . which indicates that he regards with an evil eye the increasing spirit of modern improvement" (quoted in Kidd 1993: 266).

While twentieth-century scholars of the period have in large part accepted Lockhart's separation of Enlightenment intellect and Romantic feeling, they have mostly followed Hazlitt and the anonymous reviewer of the Waverley novels in seeing Scott as a figure whose connections to Enlightenment philosophical history were at least as pronounced as any to *Blackwood's* brand of Romantic nationalism. Like Jeffrey, Scott too attended Stewart's Edinburgh University lectures on political economy. He was also an important early reviewer for the *Edinburgh Review* and a member of the Edinburgh Speculative Society. Even more than Scott's explicit links to Enlightenment thinkers and institutions, however, critics from Lukács to Chandler, Kidd, Trumpener, Duncan, and Saree Makdisi have pointed to the Whiggish approach to history that underpins the novels themselves. The following oft-quoted passage from the "postscript, which should have been a preface," in *Waverley* (1814), highlights a perfect literary instance of the Enlightenment-era theory of uneven development:

> There is no European nation which, within the course of half a century, or little more, has undergone so complete a change as this kingdom of Scotland. The effects of the insurrection of 1745 – the destruction of the patriarchal power of the Highland chiefs – the abolition of the heritable jurisdictions of the Lowland nobility and barons – the total eradication of the Jacobite party, which, averse to intermingle with the English, or adopt their customs, long continued to pride themselves upon maintaining the ancient Scottish traditions and manners – commenced this innovation. The gradual influx of wealth, and extension of commerce, have since united to render the present people of Scotland a class of beings as different from their grandfathers as the existing English are from those of Queen Elizabeth's time. (Scott 1814/1986: 340; cf. Chandler 1998: 135, Makdisi 1998: 73)

Scottish Enlightenment historians like Robertson, Smith, and Millar argued that all societies pass through different temporal "stages" of development, which include hunting, shepherding, agriculture, and commerce (Smith 1762/1978: 14). But while all societies presumably pass through each stage, they do not do so at the same rate. One society can thus be compared with another by understanding the stage occupied by each at the moment of analysis. In his *History of the Reign of Charles V* (1769), for instance, Robertson compares the "rude" manners of the ancient Germans with those of present-day Native Americans, a "race" of men "still ... nearly in the same political situation" (Robertson 1769/1792, vol. 1: 250).

Likewise, in the Scott passage quoted above, the passing of two generations in Scotland is compared to the passing of over two centuries in England. One would have to go back to sixteenth-century England, in other words – to the time of Queen Elizabeth – to find a state of society equivalent to that of mid-eighteenth-century Scotland. Though such changes must appear dramatic in hindsight, it is only from the more advanced position that they appear at all. "The change," writes Scott, "though steadily and rapidly progressive, has, nevertheless, been gradual; and like those who drift down the stream of a deep and smooth river, we are not aware of the progress we have made, until we fix our eye on the now distant point from which we have drifted" (Scott 1814/1986: 340). As in Robertson's *History of Scotland* (1759), Scott implicitly gives credit to the progressive changes that have occurred in Scotland to the union with England. Indeed, the simile Scott uses to render time in spatial terms – as a river – would continue to be a useful one for comparing the progress of colonized nations with the more advanced state of England. "Going up that river was like travelling back to the earliest beginnings of the world," says Marlow, the narrator of Joseph Conrad's *Heart of Darkness* (1899), a novel that begins by comparing the Congo at the end of the nineteenth century and the Thames at the time of the Roman conquest (Conrad 1899/1988: 35).

That Lockhart positions Scott on the "feeling" side of the Enlightenment/Romantic opposition and thus misses or conveniently ignores the Enlightenment features in his work can be accounted for by the political battles raging in the period. But this does not mean that the national feeling Lockhart attributes to Scott's poetry and to the Waverley novels is itself a complete fiction. Looking beyond the figure of Scott, it is clear that many writers from the period challenged the generalizations of Enlightenment history with an intensified focus on feeling and place. I would suggest that the "stadial" or progressive view of history identified by Chandler and Makdisi – where societies advance through successive stages of history – represents one of two different but related historicisms in the period. A second approach, derived from Germany, offered Lockhart (and many other British Romantic writers) a philosophical basis from which to critique the progressive and universalizing assumptions implicit in the first. This second approach did not come from Hegel, however, but rather, for Lockhart, from Friedrich Schlegel.

In 1818, Lockhart translated Schlegel's 1812 *Lectures on the History of Literature* for William Blackwood. It was in this work that he found the "feeling" he missed in the generation of "Hume, Smith, &c." Schlegel refers, for instance, to "two common principles" on which "every work of imagination must more or less proceed": "First, on the expression of those feelings which are common to all men of elevated thinking; and secondly, on those patriotic feelings and associations peculiar to the people in whose language it is composed, and on whom it is to exert its nearest and most powerful influence" (Schlegel 1812/1818, vol. 1: 6–7). Where for Lockhart the skeptical reasoning of Enlightenment intellect had done nothing but "vitiate the pedigree of national sentiment and associations," in Schlegel's work he saw the possibility of a different approach, one where sentiment and poetry might restore a sense of the nation (Lockhart 1818: 510). As Schlegel explains, "National consciousness, expressing itself in works of narrative and illustration, is HISTORY" (Schlegel 1812/1818, vol. 1: 16).

This second form of historicism – the German *historismus* – is the more commonly understood referent of "historicism" (Hamilton 1996: 2–3). But the word has also been used – sometimes confusingly – to describe the progressive-Enlightenment history that German writers like Johann Gottfried Herder and Schlegel challenged. "Historicism rightly culminates in universal history," writes Walter Benjamin, for whom the term refers first and foremost to the idea of "homogenous, empty time" – a kind of grammar or template through which societies or nations progress (Benjamin 1939/1968: 261–2). More relativistic in its approach to different societies (or cultures), *historismus* not only asserts the importance of religious and patriotic feeling, it also critiques the implicit position of universality from which Enlightenment historical comparisons are made (Dietze 2008: 74). This latter approach would come to characterize Romantic ideology, in which the general (politics and society) is subsumed by the particular (culture and individual consciousness) and in which different cultures are understood to develop their own distinct national forms. As the work of Chandler, Makdisi, and Dipesh Chakrabarty reminds us, however, the progressive historicism of the Enlightenment remained powerfully influential well into the Romantic period. My point here is not to suggest that Romantic historicism is in fact one or the other of these two – the Scottish or the German, the progressive or the relativist. Nor is it constituted by the displacement of one by the other. Instead, this second, German-oriented model of historicism constitutes a significant strain on the model of history that British Romantic writers inherited from the Scottish Enlightenment. Romantic historicism, in other words, is not a unified ideology or movement – either this or that. It is a tension that pervades ideologies and texts across the period. To grasp this tension and to better understand what it might mean for both Romanticism and historicism, it is necessary to look beyond the single example of Scott, important as his example is, and toward what Phillips calls the "broader system of genres" in which the newly historical genre of the novel participated (Phillips 2000: 10).

Secondary Scottish Novels

In an *Edinburgh Review* piece on "Secondary Scottish Novels," published in 1823, Jeffrey compares 12 books by Lockhart, John Galt, and John

Wilson – all *Blackwood's* writers – to any one novel by Scott. "In the arduous task of imitating the great novelist," Jeffrey writes, "they have apparently found it necessary to resort to the great principle of the division of labour; and yet they have not come near to equal the work of his single hand" (Jeffrey 1823: 159). Jeffrey finds material to praise in works like Lockhart's *Adam Blair* (1822) and Galt's *Annals of the Parish* (1821). Compared with the richness and coherence of Scott's fiction, though, the individual achievements of Lockhart, Galt, and Wilson amount only to very good imitations of the various parts of Scott's whole; their work is "secondary," that is, in that it is both an incomplete version of the Scottian novel and also, curiously, a subspecies of the type. Jeffrey is of course not alone in characterizing Lockhart, Galt, and Wilson as so many minor figures in an age of Scott. But to leave the slippery terrain of literary merit and to turn instead to genre is to open up a different set of relations between these texts and writers – relations that can be characterized as spatial rather than hierarchical. Galt, for instance, did not regard his books as novels. He characterized them as "theoretical histories," or, more generally, as "tales" (Galt 1833, vol. 2: 219). To see them similarly is to see what Jeffrey misses – a generic form in which the materials of history that Scott so skillfully synthesized are differently configured. Indeed, what I have described as the tension of Romantic historicism can be usefully explored by better understanding what a tale was in and to the Romantic period. For if the tale is in fact a minor or secondary genre (and this remains open for debate), it is nevertheless one whose features clearly register the pressures and strains of "history" in the period when fiction emerged as the representative form of national life.

As publishing statistics provided by Peter Garside suggest, Galt was not the only writer in the period to call his work a "tale." By 1820, the word "tale" surpassed both "romance" and "novel" as the most popular generic designation for a work of fiction. It would account for over 34 percent of all titles published in the decade that followed (Garside 2000: 50–1). But tales are difficult to define because the word was used in a variety of ways in the period and for a variety of reasons. Sometimes, like "romance," "tale" was used synonymously with "novel." In 1816, for instance, Walter Scott published the first of his "Tales of my Landlord" series, which included *The Black Dwarf* and *Old Mortality* (the series would later include *The Bride of Lammermoor*, *The Heart of Midlothian*, and *A Legend of Montrose*). Scott's own review of his "Tales" for the *Quarterly* opens with the following sentence: "These *Tales* belong obviously to a class of novels which we have already had occasion repeatedly to notice" (Scott 1817/1968: 238). For Scott, that is, "tales" belong to the same class as the first three of his Waverley "novels" (*Waverley, Guy Mannering,* and *The Antiquary*). But the word "tale" could also be used to signal something that was *not* a novel. "The following work is offered to the public as a Moral Tale – the author not wishing to acknowledge a Novel" (Edgeworth 1801/1994: 3). So writes Maria Edgeworth in the advertisement to her 1801 novel, *Belinda*. By 1801, Edgeworth had already published two collections of "Moral Tales" and "Moral Tales for Young People," and *Castle Rackrent; an Hibernian Tale*. After *Belinda*, she would go on to publish several more novels under the title "Tales of Fashionable Life," a series that in turn greatly influenced Scott.

But when writers like Galt, James Hogg, Mary Russell Mitford, or Washington Irving attached the word "tale" to their works, they seem to have meant something different by it. For one, they seem to have meant something shorter than *Old Mortality*: something less, that is, than three volumes. Scott himself eventually subscribed to this logic. After the market crash of 1826 which left him nearly ruined, Scott was required to use the future profits of three already commissioned works to pay off creditors. The profits from two of these works – *Woodstock* and the *Life of Napoleon* – were given over to Scott's creditors. The third was supposed to have been an unnamed novel. To satisfy his own financial needs at the time Scott thus set out to write something that was not a novel – something that might be allowed to remain in his hands (and which was originally commissioned by Robert Cadell as a small Eastern tale). As Claire Lamont explains, *Chronicles of the Canongate* (1827) was published in two rather than three volumes because any new "novel" by Scott would "be claimed . . . for the creditors" (Scott 1827/2000: 293). Even so, the two volumes of Scott's *Chronicles* contain only three tales and a lengthy, tale-like introduction. Hogg's *Winter Evening Tales*, by contrast, which was published in 1820 and which was his most successful work of prose fiction, included 22 tales in two volumes. Many of these tales had been published previously in periodical form – whether in Hogg's own short-lived literary magazine, *The Spy*, from 1810–11, or in the early numbers of William Blackwood's *Edinburgh Monthly Magazine*, as "Tales and Anecdotes of the Pastoral Life."

The tale as a genre went hand-in-hand with the periodical – and with the magazine, in particular. Size, or portability, was an obvious factor; but so was the flexible character of the tale, its mix of the mundane and the marvelous, the oral and the written, and the fictional and nonfictional. Tales could both offset and blend with the more general political and review pieces that surrounded them. What truly distinguishes the tale, however, is the unique way the genre intermixes what I've described as the two different historicisms of the period. In Scott's *Waverley*, for example, the peculiarities of the local are introduced, highlighted, and even to a certain extent fetishized. But ultimately these peculiarities are assimilated into a larger narrative of national progress. It is this narrative, in fact, that allows Scott to aestheticize the violence of Scotland's Jacobite past and to occlude the force of the Hanoverian response. In Hogg's tales, by contrast, the important national-historical moments of the Waverley novels – 1715, 1745 – are described as "but secondary mementos" to the catalogue of terrible storms by which Hogg chronicles rural life. These "red lines in the shepherd's manual," writes Hogg, "stand in bloody capitals in the annals of the pastoral life" (Hogg 1820/2002: 372). The conditions of local life highlighted by these storms often resist assimilation into a larger, progressive account. Values and modes of living thought to have passed away are shown to continue in the present moment, existing alongside national progress and continuously calling it into question. But not negating it.

As I suggested above, the local features and associations given prominence in the tales of the period embodied, to an extent, a sense of national feeling found lacking in Enlightenment history. Hogg's *Winter Evening Tales* may highlight rural concerns, traditional hierarchies and kinship networks, and local history. But they betray an equally strong engagement with those ingenious theories of the Enlightenment that served to eclipse local history: with the "progress of improvement," that is, with political economy, and with what Lockhart called "the mechanical arrangements of modern life" (Lockhart 1819, vol. 2: 350). Although their west-of-Scotland settings make for a very different scene from the parish of Ettrick that features in Hogg's fiction, Galt's tales also reveal this tension between larger narratives of progress and the local histories that do not always fit comfortably within them.

When he started writing for *Blackwood's*, in 1819, Galt had some experience writing fiction of the kind that the magazine was already publishing. Among other things, in 1813 he had written a book he called "The Pastor," about rural life in the west of Scotland. When he brought the manuscript to Archibald Constable (publisher of the *Edinburgh Review* and the Waverley novels), Constable rejected it on the grounds that the public was not interested in Scottish stories. Galt's "philosophical sketches" of small town Scottish life began appearing in *Blackwood's* in 1820 under the title "The Ayrshire Legatees." Blackwood was so pleased that he agreed to publish Galt's earlier, rejected piece – now renamed the *Annals of the Parish* (1821) – and a second series, "The Steam-Boat." Both "The Ayrshire Legatees" and "The Steam-Boat" were also published separately in single volumes. All three were among the books reviewed by Jeffrey in his piece on "Secondary Scottish novels."

Galt proposed a general title for the combined pieces, "Tales of the West"; but Blackwood rejected the title as unnecessary. Whether Galt's use of the word "tale" signified something different from a novel (as I suggested for Scott it did not) can be seen from the account Galt provided of his work from this period in his *Autobiography* (1833):

> It may be necessary to explain that I do not think the character of my own productions has been altogether rightly regarded. Merely because the incidents are supposed to be fictitious, they have been all considered as novels, and yet, as such, the best of them are certainly deficient in the peculiarity of the novel. They would be more properly characterized, in several instances, as theoretical histories, than either as novels or romances. A consistent fable is as essential to a novel as a plot is to a drama, and yet these, which are deemed my best productions, are deficient in this essential ingredient. (Galt 1833, vol. 2: 219)

The phrase "theoretical history" comes from Dugald Stewart, who used it to describe the characteristic Scottish Enlightenment procedure of deducing what *may* have been from what *is* – or, as Stewart says, of showing "from the known principles of human nature" how the various parts of something like a language or a society or religion "might gradually have arisen" (Stewart 1793/1811–12: 449–50). This species of philosophical investigation is labeled "theoretical or conjectural history."

Galt had read some of the conjectural histories of the Scottish Enlightenment while writing his *Life of Cardinal Wolsey* (1812). In his *Literary Life* (1834), published just a year after the *Autobiography*, he says he found little of use in the work of William Robertson but praises Hume for drawing "the most sagacious inferences" concerning circumstances and events which he could not have known about through documented sources (Galt 1834, vol. 1: 72–3). The genre's dependence upon fiction – upon conjecturing about the prehistory of a given object of investigation – obviously appealed to Galt. His *Annals of the Parish*, for instance, began, he says, as an attempt "to observe and to conjecture in what respects the minister of a rural parish differed from the general inhabitants of the country" (1834, vol. 1: 152). But conjectural history's ultimate status as *history* was clearly also important to Galt. Works like *Annals of the Parish* detail the enormous changes that occurred in eighteenth-century Scotland – the industrialization of the weavers, the new and vast networks of trade that connected Glasgow to London, the West Indies, and North America, and the changing face of town and country. But they do so in ways that balance sentiment and objectivity.

Thus, in the passage above, when Galt claims that his works are "deficient" in "consistent fable," which is for him the defining feature of the novel, we can grasp his point in a couple of different ways. In the eighteenth century, the word "fable" referred primarily to fiction – a "story not founded on fact" (*OED*). But it could also refer to the plot of a play or poem. Galt's use of the word seems to refer to both senses. Like Scott's historical novels, his tales recount real historical events and include real historical personages. Unlike Scott's novels, they are deficient in a plot that develops these events and personages in ways that make them fully cohere or that unify them in a single perspective.

But if Galt's tales are not novels of the kind Scott wrote, they are also not conjectural histories of the kind written by Robertson or Hume. This fundamental doubleness of the genre – for Jeffrey, it equates with lack of coherence – can be accounted for by the increased strain put upon conjectural history by the more relativistic historicism that featured so explicitly in *Blackwood's* and which cast a skeptical eye upon the universalizing principles of conjectural history itself. This doubleness becomes clear on another occasion when Galt describes his work as "theoretical history." While recounting the origins of *Annals of the Parish* in his *Literary Life*, Galt again emphasizes the book's overall lack of plot – "the most material feature of the novel" (Galt 1834, vol. 1: 155). His own "notion," he says, was "to exhibit a kind of local theoretical history, by examples, the truth of which would at once be acknowledged" (p. 226). The addition of the word "local" to "theoretical history" highlights a small but important difference between Galt's tale and the progressive historicism of the Scottish Enlightenment. A "local" theoretical history is in a sense a contradiction in terms. The conjectural historians of the Enlightenment were indeed interested in the deviations of climate or terrain that might affect the progress of a given society or shape its peculiar character. But these remained deviations – exceptions that proved the rule of nature. Galt, like Herder before him, is more interested in the deviations themselves – not necessarily at the expense of human nature or progress, but not as something to be subsumed by it, either. The narrator of *Annals* says, "What happened in my parish was but a type and index to the rest of the world" (Galt 1821/2001: 142). He follows this statement with a curious addition: "We had, however, one memorable that must stand by itself" (p. 142), a reference to a 70-year-old transplanted American industrialist marching "crously" with "lean, shaking hands" following a false report of a French man-of-war on a nearby Highland loch.

Unlike "The Ayrshire Legatees" and "The Steam-Boat," *Annals of the Parish* was not written and published serially – although Hogg thought it should have been and Galt himself claimed to have reworked the whole based on the structure of "The Ayrshire Legatees." The book is divided into 51 brief "chapters," each arranged chronologically by year. Characters reappear across years, of course; and the same narrator's voice links the separate chapters. But there is little consistency of plot. The chapters read like 51 separate tales as the account of each year is simply divided into a description of memorable events or characters. Chronology is the only real unity in the narrative; like the steam ship in Galt's *Blackwood's* series, it serves as a device for bringing together tales related by time and place, but little else. Written as a sort of parish diary, *Annals of the Parish* recounts the Reverend Micah Balwhidder's years as minister of Dalmailing. These years – 1760–1810 – overlap nearly exactly with the reign of George III. As Balwhidder explains,

> it was thought a wonderful thing, and everybody spoke of me and the new king as united in our trusts and temporalities, marvelling at how the same should come to pass, and thinking the hand of providence was in it, and that surely we were preordained to fade and flourish together.... (Galt 1821/2001: 3)

Despite the humor of the comparison, the issues and considerations that might occupy a monarch in the second half of the eighteenth century do indeed overlap with the "temporality" of Balwhidder's parish. There are references to and descriptions of the American rebellion, the Gordon Riots, the Irish Uprising, and the French Revolution; changes in textile manufacturing following the advent of steam technology; and the building of new toll roads to facilitate advances in trade and agriculture. But these events are mixed, for any given year, with various omens, portents, and superstitions, petty rifts and thefts, religious schisms, and – in 1772 – a "Caesarian operation" performed upon a

Muscovy duck that had stuffed its "crap" with "as many beans as filled a mutchkin stoup" (p. 53). "My task, says Balwhidder, "is to describe what happened within the narrow bound of my pasturage" (p. 63).

The subtle irony implicit in Galt's narration suggests that we are not supposed to take the Reverend fully at his word. Balwhidder's own sources are experience and local history, neither of which necessarily translates into "the rest of the world." Our knowledge of this as readers, though, does not make Balwhidder untrustworthy or ridiculous (though the book is funny). His limitations of perspective in fact serve to make his account more historical. Like the first *Statistical Account of Scotland*, published in 21 volumes between 1791 and 1799, Galt's *Annals* offers a detailed view of parish life. Unlike the *Statistical Account*, Galt resists the overarching aim of creating a complete picture of Scotland. When Sir John Sinclair conceived of his ambitious project, he asked hundreds of parish ministers to answer questions about topography, population, agriculture, industry, and local custom in their parishes. His aim, he said, was "to lay the foundation of a great, methodological, and complete survey of Scotland," and in doing so, to ascertain the "progress of national improvement" (Sinclair 1791–9, vol. 3: xi). Galt's narrator, however, has mixed feelings about the progress of national improvement: "it's hard to tell wherein the benefit of improvement in a country parish consists," he exclaims about a change in parish fashions following the introduction of a new schoolmistress (Galt 1821/2001: 41). Throughout Balwhidder's account, improvement is associated with providence. But the local effects of war, uprising, colonial expansion, and industrialization have left Galt's narrator somewhat skeptical regarding any overall benevolence in God's – not to mention Adam Smith's – plan.

Romantic Historicism and Postcolonial Critiques of Modernity

At the heart of Romantic historicism as I've discussed it here is a tension between progressive, Enlightenment history and an approach that challenges the Enlightenment emphasis on universals. The first originated in the philosophical histories of the Scottish Enlightenment; the second found its way from Germany to Britain through periodicals like *Blackwood's*. Works such as Galt's *Annals of the Parish* exhibit this tension more openly than do the historical novels of Scott, which have so often featured in accounts of Romantic historicism. In Galt's tales – indeed, in the genre itself – we see both a serious engagement with the progressive historicism of writers like Hume, Smith, and Stewart and a strongly inflected relativism suggestive of the historicism of Herder and Schlegel. As such, Galt's tales do not so much exchange the universal of Enlightenment history for the provincial of Romantic nationalism; they "provincialize" Enlightenment itself in the Romantic period. In his study of "postcolonial thought and historical difference," *Provincializing Europe* (2000), Dipesh Chakrabarty introduces the idea of a provincialized Europe – a "Europe," that is, which is no longer the inevitable and implied subject of all history, and which is no longer given the pride of place in accounts of modernity (first Europe, then elsewhere). His important rethinking of postcolonial criticism stresses the importance of Enlightenment categories for understanding historical difference even as it works "to see the modern as inevitably contested" and "to write over the given and privileged narratives of citizenship with other narratives of human connections" (Chakrabarty 2000: 46).

This, I have argued, is what Romantic-period tales do: they offer narratives of human connections that resist the logic of progress and inevitability without rejecting it. In doing so, they not only suggest the relevance of Romantic historicism for postcolonial debates about history, modernity, and difference; they provide a model for the kind of history writing Chakrabarty himself calls for, one which is both analytical and affective. While Jeffrey characterized the tales of Galt as incomplete parts of a bigger whole, we might, by way of rebuke, give the final word to his nemesis, Lockhart: in Romantic-period tales we see not only the national intellect, but also the national modes of feeling.

Note

An early version of this essay was delivered as a talk at Edinburgh University's Institute for Advanced Studies in the Humanities. I would like to thank the Institute for the Visiting Research Fellowship that brought me to Edinburgh. Very special thanks go to the director of the Institute, Susan Manning, and to Ruth Perry, John Docker, and Alex Thomson for helpful comment and critique.

References and Further Reading

Abrams, M. H. (1953) *The Mirror and the Lamp: Romantic Theory and the Critical Tradition*. New York: Oxford University Press.

Benjamin, Walter. (1939/1968) "Theses on the Philosophy of History," in *Illuminations*, ed. Hannah Arendt, trans. Harry Zohn (pp. 253–64). New York: Schocken.

Butler, Marilyn. (1981) *Romantics, Rebels and Reactionaries: English Literature and its Background, 1760–1830*. Oxford: Oxford University Press.

Chakrabarty, Dipesh. (2000) *Provincializing Europe: Postcolonial Thought and Historical Difference*. Princeton, NJ: Princeton University Press.

Chakrabarty, Dipesh. (2008) "In Defense of *Provincializing Europe*: A Response to Carola Dietze," *History and Theory* 47: 85–96.

Chandler, James. (1998) *England in 1819: The Politics of Literary Culture and the Case of Romantic Historicism*. Chicago: University of Chicago Press.

Conrad, Joseph. (1899/1988) *Heart of Darkness*, ed. R. Kimbrough, 3rd edn. New York: Norton.

Davis, Leith, Ian Duncan, and Janet Sorensen (eds). (2004) *Scotland and the Borders of Romanticism*. Cambridge, UK: Cambridge University Press.

Dietze, Carola. (2008) "Toward a History on Equal Terms: A Discussion of *Provincializing Europe*," *History and Theory*: 69–84.

Duncan, Ian. (2007) *Scott's Shadow: The Novel in Romantic Edinburgh*. Princeton, NJ: Princeton University Press.

Edgeworth, Maria. (1801/1994) *Belinda*, ed. K. Kirkpatrick. Oxford: Oxford University Press.

Galt, John. (1821/2001) *Annals of the Parish*, ed. Ian Campbell. Edinburgh: The Saltire Society.

Galt, John. (1833) *The Autobiography of John Galt*, 2 vols. London: Cochrane and M'Crone.

Galt, John. (1834) *The Literary Life, and Miscellanies, of John Galt*, 3 vols. Edinburgh: William Blackwood.

Garside, Peter. (2000) "The English Novel in the Romantic Period," in P. Garside and R. Shöwerling (eds.), *The English Novel, 1770–1829: A Bibliographical Survey of Prose Fiction Published in the British Isles* (vol. 2, pp. 15–103). Oxford: Oxford University Press.

Hamilton, Paul. (1996) *Historicism*. London: Routledge.

Hazlitt, William. (1825/1932) *The Spirit of the Age*. In *The Complete Works of William Hazlitt*, ed. P. P. Howe, vol. 11. London: J. M. Dent.

Hogg, James. (1820/2002) *Winter Evening Tales*, ed. Ian Duncan. Edinburgh: Edinburgh University Press.

Hogg, James. (1829/1995) *The Shepherd's Calendar*, ed. Douglas S. Mack. Edinburgh: Edinburgh University Press.

Jeffrey, Francis. (1802) "Southey's Thalaba: A Metrical Romance," *Edinburgh Review* 1: 63–83.

Jeffrey, Francis. (1823) "Secondary Scottish novels," *Edinburgh Review* 39: 158–95.

Kidd, Colin. (1993) *Subverting Scotland's Past: Scottish Whig Historians and the Creation of an Anglo-British Identity, 1689–c. 1830*. Cambridge, UK: Cambridge University Press.

Lockhart, John Gibson. (1818) "Remarks on Schlegel's History of Literature," *Blackwood's Edinburgh Magazine* 3: 497–511.

Lockhart, John Gibson. (1819) *Peter's Letters to his Kinsfolk*, 3 vols. Edinburgh: William Blackwood.

Lukács, Georg. (1937/1983) *The Historical Novel*, trans. H. and S. Mitchell. Lincoln: University of Nebraska Press.

Makdisi, Saree. (1998) *Romantic Imperialism: Universal Empire and the Culture of Modernity*. Cambridge, UK: Cambridge University Press.

McGann, Jerome. (1983) *The Romantic Ideology: A Critical Investigation*. Chicago: University of Chicago Press.

Phillips, Mark Salber. (2000) *Society and Sentiment: Genres of Historical Writing in Britain, 1740–1820*. Princeton, NJ: Princeton University Press.

Phillips, Mark Salber. (2003) "Relocating Inwardness: Historical Distance and the Transition from Enlightenment to Romantic Historiography," *PMLA* 118: 436–49.

Robertson, William. (1769/1792) *The History of the Reign of the Emperor Charles V*, 4 vols. London: T. Cadell.

Schlegel, Friedrich. (1812/1818) *Lectures on the History of Literature, Ancient and Modern*, trans. J. G. Lockhart, 2 vols. Edinburgh: William Blackwood.

Scott, Walter. (1814/1986) *Waverley: or, 'Tis Sixty Years Since*, ed. Claire Lamont. Oxford: Oxford University Press.

Scott, Walter. (1817/1968) "Tales of my Landlord," in *Sir Walter Scott on Novelists and Fiction*, ed. Ioan Williams (pp. 238–59). London: Routledge and Kegan Paul.

Scott, Walter. (1827/2000) *Chronicles of the Canongate*, ed. Claire Lamont. Edinburgh: Edinburgh University Press.

Sher, Richard. (2006) *The Enlightenment and the Book: Scottish Authors and their Publishers in Eighteenth-Century Britain, Ireland, and America*. Chicago: University of Chicago Press.

Sinclair, John (ed.). (1791–9) *The Statistical Account of Scotland. Drawn from the Communications of the Ministers of the Different Parishes*, 21 vols. Edinburgh: William Creech.

Smith, Adam. (1762/1978) *Lectures on Jurisprudence*, ed. R. L. Meek, D. D. Raphael, and P. G. Stein. Oxford: Clarendon Press.

Stewart, Dugald. (1793/1811–12) "Account of the Life and Writings of Dr. Smith," in *The Works of Adam Smith*, LL.D., 5 vols. London: T. Cadell.

Taine, Hippolyte. (1864/1873) *A History of English Literature*, trans H. Van Laun, 4 vols. Edinburgh: Edmonston and Douglas.

Trumpener, Katie. (1997) *Bardic Nationalism: The Romantic Novel and the British Empire*. Princeton, NJ: Princeton University Press.

Wordsworth, William and Samuel Taylor Coleridge. (1800/1991) *Lyrical Ballads*, ed. R. L. Brett and A. R. Jones, 2nd edn. London: Routledge.

Chapter 4

Nationalisms in Romantic Britain and Ireland: Culture, Politics, and the Global

Miranda Burgess

From W. B. Yeats's lament for "Romantic Ireland" in "September 1913" to Hugh Trevor-Roper's screed against what he saw as Walter Scott's "romantic Celtic fantasies" in *The Invention of Tradition*, the association between nationalism and British Romanticism is of long and broad standing in the literature on both (Hobsbawm and Ranger 1983: 30). While it has often been the subject of dismissiveness (whether unthinking or programmatic) or untheorized biographical speculation, the connection is as much the outcome of historical confluence and intellectual influence as it is the creation of a retrospective rhetorical linkage. Yet the reflexive linkage of Romanticism and nationalism is an imperfect shield against the underlying challenges of definition and analysis that dog each area of inquiry, most insistently at the points where the two areas converge.

In his field-defining 1983 study of the literary and political history of nationalism, *Imagined Communities*, Benedict Anderson highlighted what he called the "philosophical poverty and even incoherence" of the phenomenon he was discussing (1983/1991: 5). The same year saw the publication of Jerome McGann's *The Romantic Ideology*, which called for a "new, critical view of Romanticism and its literary products" by urging its readers to historicize writings too long regarded as above the fray of the material world (1983: 1). While McGann insisted on the coherence of the ideology he identified, his approach sparked a parallel challenge to the logic of British Romanticism as a movement and, inevitably, as a period. For Anderson, scholars run up against the incoherence of nationalism: "Nation, nationality, nationalism – all have proved notoriously difficult to define, let alone to analyse" (Anderson 1983/1991: 3). With respect to Romanticism in Britain, Marilyn Butler's formulation is similar, and similarly influential: "English Romanticism is impossible to define with historical precision because the term itself is historically unsound" (Butler 1988: 37).

One response is to turn from description to etiology – from the thing itself, in other words, to the processes that have made it. For the study of Romantic nationalism, a way in opens at the convergence of what Anderson called "print-capitalism" and the emphasis in the best recent intellectual histories of Romanticism on the history of English as a discipline (e.g., Siskin 1998, Chandler 1998). In the British context, the critical role played by print culture in the history of Romantic nationalism has complicated, and been complicated by, the historical distinctions – equally legible as international and infranational – between Scotland, Ireland, England, and Wales. Britain's unique situation in the early nineteenth century, as what might in retrospect be called the origins of the modern multiethnic nation state, in turn resulted in a competition between political and cultural nationalisms both in the print cultures of the period itself and in subsequent cultural and intellectual history as well as a (perhaps unique) attunement to the increasingly global scene in which nation states had to operate.

Culture, Revolution, and Nationalisms in Britain

In his *Reflections on the Revolution in France* (1790), Edmund Burke declared his affection for what he had come to call "our national character": that blend of "natural entrails" and "inbred sentiments," all of which "bear the stamp of our forefathers" in the double sense of inheritance supported by education, that govern men's conduct "in England" (Burke 1790/1989: 137). It may seem ironic that the Irish philosopher and parliamentarian Edmund Burke became, perhaps, the most influential exponent of British nationalism in the Romantic period. I want to suggest that there is nothing ironic about it.

Certainly Burke's declaration in *Reflections* was in marked contrast to his earlier repeated assertions that national characters were purely situational, the product of education and governance alone. In his unfinished *Tracts Relating to the Popery Laws* (1765), for example, Burke had insisted that any weaknesses generally visible among Irishmen were not registers of any intrinsic disposition but rather had resulted from "the most unparalleled oppression" (Burke 1765/1991: 479). It is also the case that the *Reflections* make a greater investment in Englishness than Burke had often been willing to make in his writings on Ireland, or than contemporary caricaturists such as James Gillray (who often portrayed him as a skinny Jesuit) wanted to give him credit for. Burke's conception of Englishness is, in short, more relational than essential.

The changing and relational perspective on national character evident in contrasting the *Reflections* with Burke's earlier writings on Ireland and India was typical of a fluidity, or perhaps an ambivalence, that is generally apparent in the writing about nations that was published in Britain in the period. A similar movement between perspectives on nations is apparent not only across the span of Burke's career but also, in a briefer space, across the careers of more progressive political philosophers such as William Godwin, whose rewrite of *Political Justice* in 1796 reconsidered and significantly tempered his insistence, three years earlier, that "The operations of law and political institution" on national character are "important and interesting," while physical causes are "trifling and unworthy of notice" (Godwin 1793, vol. 1: 57, 64). It is possible to see Burke's own shifting national identifications as symptomatic of such an ambivalence toward national identity – and, at the same time, of the continued fluidity of the category.

In a frequently cited essay on the relationships between the categories of "race" and "nation" in European thought, Nicholas Hudson tracks the "gradual separation" of one from the other across the eighteenth and into the early nineteenth century (Hudson 1996: 248). Whereas the word "nation" had once encompassed a notion of blood ties that worked in close proximity to aristocratic ideologies of family, these meanings came to cling to "race" instead, at least until the reunion of the two terms in the later nineteenth century. In the intervening period, "nation" came to signify something linguistic and participatory, institutional and governmental. Hudson's conclusions substantially concur with Eric Hobsbawm's widely influential general history of European nationalism, *Nations and Nationalism since 1780* (1990). Hobsbawm argues that it was not until after 1830 that the tension between ideas of the nation-state based on territorial boundaries and collective participation (what we might call politics) and those based on birth and on language or inherited tradition (what we might call culture) created an irreconcilable division between the earliest advocates of nation-states – "revolutionary-democratic" reformers – and later nationalist understandings of the state as an ethnocultural entity (Hobsbawm 1990: 20).

Hobsbawm's insistence that nation in this period "means no more than a territorial state" echoes arguments throughout Enlightenment philosophy and history, from John Locke's *Two Treatises of Government* (1690) to Jean-Jacques Rousseau's *Social Contract* (1762), that dominated British nationalist thinking in the period. It helps to explain why Ernest Gellner's rival account of *Nations and Nationalism* (1983) has had a comparatively limited impact on the scholarship on British Romantic nationalism. For Gellner, nationalism is the manufacture of a fictitious national culture by "nationalist intellectuals," who respond to the shift from agrarian to industrial modes of production, and to the resulting popular experience of economic, geographical, and cultural displacement, with "warm and generous ardour on behalf of . . . peasants and workers" (Gellner 1983: 61).

Some nationalist writers in Romantic Britain and Ireland – Scott, for example, or Sydney Owenson – did on occasion, in Gellner's terms, "don . . . folk costume and trek . . . over the hills, composing poems in the forest clearings," or very nearly so (Gellner 1983: 61). But they simultaneously tended to display extreme self-consciousness about their own fiction-making process and its role in the politics of the nation state. In *The Antiquary* (1816), Scott's protagonist declares that a poet is free to narrate any national history he chooses, "free of the corporation, and as little bound down to truth or probability" (Scott 1816/1829, vol. 5: 195). For Scott, as Ian Duncan has recently illustrated in detail in *Scott's Shadow* (2007), nations are outcomes and vehicles of cultural production; they are not fictions disguised as tradition. Personal and national profits accrued to Owenson from her social appearances as a "Wild Irish Girl," but her accounts of being "denied the civilized privileges of sofa and chair" and displayed like "'the beautiful hyena that was never tamed' of Exeter Change" demonstrate a sophisticated awareness of the fictions involved and their ambiguous political effects (Owenson 1829, vol. 1: 76). In Owenson's *Florence Macarthy* (1818), the protagonist, a returning expatriate Irishman with a romantic love of country, is also a "brave Guerilla chief whose life and fortune have been devoted to South American independence" under the *nom de guerre* "the Librador" (Owenson 1818, vol. 3: 49). Owenson's sometimes sentimental portrait of what another of her heroes calls "purely natural, national character" coexists alongside an explicitly revolutionary-democratic politics (Owenson 1806/1999: 65).

Activities like Owenson's and Scott's place another spin on arguments that nationalism is incoherent. They demonstrate the extent to which the divorce between ethnocultural thinking and nationalism and national identity became final only quite late in the game, and to which it allowed, in the meantime, for the continued cooperation of the partners, not least for the ends of statist – even explicitly democratic and reformist – thought and action.

Nation, State, and Public Sphere

In examining the approach to national identity that characterizes Burke's paradigmatic Romantic nationalism, it is essential to take note of the noises in the background. The swing between political historical and ethnocultural accounts of the nation that is so striking in comparing the *Reflections* to the *Tracts on the Popery Laws* takes place to the buzzing of reformist "grasshoppers." "I have often been astonished," Burke writes to his correspondent in France,

> considering that . . . the mutual intercourse between the two countries has lately been very great, to find how little you seem to know of us. I suspect that this is owing to your forming a judgment of this nation from certain publications, which do, very erroneously, if they do at all, represent the opinions and dispositions generally prevalent in England. The vanity, restlessness, petulance, and spirit of intrigue of several petty cabals, who attempt to hide their total want of consequence in bustle and noise, . . . makes you imagine that our contemptuous neglect of their abilities is a mark of general acquiescence in their opinions. (Burke 1790/1989: 136)

Several elements in this passage help explicate the character of Romantic nationalism by highlighting aspects of nationalist thought that are implicit in most of the recent histories I have cited so far. First, as Hobsbawm, Gellner, and Anderson have established, nationalisms tend to emerge at times of social, economic, and political change, often accompanied, as in Burke's case, with a sense of ideological and/or political embattlement. Second, even in the Romantic period, nationalism remained as much rhetoric as disposition or movement. Thus the Dublin-born and Irish-educated Burke could level accusations of outlandishness – the condition of being an intruder in "this nation" and a stranger to what is "general" to the British people (*gens*) or indeed to the human species (*genus*) – at English writers such as the Dissenting clergyman Richard Price, the chief grasshopper of his pamphlet and, subsequently, could extend his accusations indiscriminately to the radical London woman of letters Mary Wollstonecraft and the expatriate Thomas Paine, along with others in their circles. Third and most crucially, the ethnocultural register of Burke's nationalism intensifies in its encounters with those he represents as apostates from an inherited and innate British identity. Apostasy and encounters alike take place in and between printed texts, suggesting that Romantic nationalism is, most fundamentally, a phenomenon of print culture.

In responding to the *Reflections* in their own printed works, Wollstonecraft and Paine turn Burke's nationalist rhetoric back on itself. Each uses a double technique of accusation and irony, at once mocking Burke's nationalism and reclaiming the national terrain. In her *Vindication of the Rights of Men* (1790), for example, Wollstonecraft attacks what she takes to be Burke's corrupt misunderstanding of inherently progressive British values: "Security of property! Behold, in a few words, the definition of English liberty" (Wollstonecraft 1790/1989: 14–15). However, in her novel *The Wrongs of Woman* (1798), in a moment of bitter parody, she places a speech about "French principles" in the mouth of a judge who declares that he is performing the duty of an "Englishman" in denying divorce to a grievously suffering wife (Wollstonecraft 1798/1996: 199).

Similarly, in the first part of his *Rights of Man* (1791), Paine reminds the reader that the British monarchy, whose heritability grounds the inherited national character of Britain in Burke's *Reflections*, began with invasion from France by a "plunderer of the English nation" and "son of a prostitute" – a man whose foreign and illegitimate birth endangered the very succession it founded (Paine 1791/1989: 120). At the same time, however, he argues that Burke's pamphlet administers a "poison . . . to the English nation" by upholding a royal succession whose establishment and continuance alike betray what Paine characterizes as Britain's "fundamental" and "common principle": the existence of a natural "right resident in the nation" (pp. 54–6). As for Burke himself, Paine insists, "He writes neither in the character of a Frenchman nor an Englishman, but in the fawning character of that creature, known in all countries as a friend to none, a *Courtier*" (p. 136). In this reading of Burke, it is Burke who is the alien. The cosmopolite is unmasked as a faithless betrayer of the British nation – even as Paine objects to Burke's nationalist rhetoric.

Paine and Wollstonecraft figure prominently in Gerald Newman's *Rise of English Nationalism* (1987), a social and cultural history. Newman views Romantic nationalism as a deeply held ideological position that begins as a rhetorical tactic: the weapon of a rising bourgeoisie against a hereditary socioeconomic elite, wielded as often by novelists such as Frances Burney as by political writers like Paine. For Newman it is trade rather than politics that sets the scene for this process. In an England defining itself through a modernizing economy that has resulted in increased trade relations with Europe and America, and in a newly capitalist economy dominated by erstwhile aristocrats, it is useful to propagandize against domestic elites for being corrupt in their cosmopolitanism, and against cosmopolitanism itself as a consequence and expression of unpatriotic, corrupt, or faithless Francophilia. In this analysis, nationalisms emerge from the vertical tension between a self-identified group and those that group designates as outsiders and opponents, eventually becoming spatialized as a division between the nation and its others.

Newman's argument helps to account for the persistence of ethnocultural distinctions in Romantic nationalist thought despite its primarily political economic aims and origins, and even in those variants that take a progressive stance. It opens a useful perspective on the rhetorical similarities between Burke and his English Jacobin opponents, though its explanatory power is somewhat weakened by an inattention to the distinction, and the complicated relationship, between English and British nationalisms. Above all, such a class-based analysis complicates any simple opposition between conservative and radical reforming politics in the period. A critic of Romantic nationalism such as David Simpson might highlight what he takes to be the tendency of British Romantic writers, such as William Wordsworth, to fixate on the defining eccentricities of individual or national character, posing the apparently methodless thought of uneducated subjects against the sweeping and universalizing claims of progressive political theory (Simpson 1993: 40–63). For Newman, in contrast, Wordsworth may be understood, for example, as a more progressive writer than Byron, for Byron was part of the cosmopolitan elite that was challenged by Wordsworth's detailed attention to uneven development at home.

As Craig Calhoun argues in *Nationalism* (1997), ethnic bonds are part of the rhetoric of state-making from the beginning and persist, as rhetorical outcomes and ends, in the modern liberal nation-state as well. It is this continuing relation that has lent modern nation-states their ability to seem convincingly primordial and to be subjectively felt by their nationals, despite coming into existence in response to modern political needs and despite their essentially institutional character. As a result, Calhoun understands cultural, if not specifically "ethnic," nationalism as, in many cases, complementary with "a liberal, cosmopolitan discourse emphasizing the freedom of all peoples" (Calhoun 1997: 86). At its best, as Calhoun has recently reiterated in *Nations Matter* (2007), nationalism has been, and can be, a critical force in ensuring the justice of cosmopolitanism (in the Romantic period) and globalization (from 1989 to the present): "democracy," he reminds his readers, "depends on solidarity" (Calhoun 2007: 166). Implicitly, both continue to depend, as they have since the beginning, on the condition of the field of letters.

When conservative writers like Burke turn nationalist rhetoric against radical practitioners such as Wollstonecraft, Paine, Joseph Priestley, William Cobbett, and William Godwin, to name a few of their targets, they are doing so as part of a battle over the character of the true England that is construed as an inheritance but nevertheless remains dependent on political change. Who can best restore an embattled ancient nation, whether metaphorized as a landed estate or defined by a heritage of parliamentary independence, and rescue its values of sincerity and collective sacrifice from thralldom to a Francophile faction, whether that faction is viewed as an aristocratic or revolutionary force? More to the point, what form will restoration take? In offering a plurality of written answers to these questions, the intellectuals and poets of the 1790s and early nineteenth century make a "national aesthetic" of Romanticism, but they also approximate the ideal nation state to the debates taking place within it (Newman 1987: 111). In this sometimes explicitly cultural analysis, the most salient location of culture lies in the work of writing and rhetoric: in the field of cultural production itself.

What is especially salutary about Calhoun's and Newman's analyses is the insistence that nationalist cultural production cannot be reduced, as Trevor-Roper and others would have it, to disingenuous myth-making aimed at a credulous consumer, any more than it can be linked solely to political quietism or reaction. Rather, they remind historians of letters of what Jürgen Habermas argued in *Structural Transformation of the Public Sphere* (1962, English translation 1989): that the field of cultural production – also called, in this period, the republic of letters – is widely perceived in the Romantic period as both a vehicle and a model for political action and change (Habermas 1989: 60–2). Contemporary responses to this perspective on writing vary widely, from William Hazlitt's assertion that "the French Revolution might be described as a remote but inevitable result of the invention of the art of printing" (Hazlitt 1830/1931, vol. 13: 38) to Burke's elegy for the

French, who have, in his view, "been drawn and trussed . . . like stuffed birds in a museum" and "filled . . . with chaff and rags, and paltry blurred shreds of paper about the rights of man" (Burke 1790/1989: 137). To these opposing perspectives must be added the more skeptical viewpoint typified by Isaac Disraeli's remark that "the politics of this state [i.e. the republic of letters] consist rather in words . . . than in actions, or their effects" (D'Israeli 1791: 31).

It is in this context that Jane Austen's Henry Tilney, in *Northanger Abbey* (1818), characterizes "the country and the age in which we live" as one in which "social and literary intercourse is on such a footing; where every man is surrounded by a neighbourhood of voluntary spies, and where roads and newspapers lay every thing open" (Austen 1818/2003: 145). To read Austen's account of a Britain in which not only writers but also, and more significantly, reading audiences contribute to the national character is to recognize what is, for the scholarship on Romantic nationalism, the most significant flaw of culturally attentive histories such as Newman's and Calhoun's, as well as related work on the role of culture in the political projects of Britain, Britishness, and empire. There has been a relative inattention to the demand side, to the desires and activities of readers.

The gaps have been supplemented to some degree by analyses such as Linda Colley's discussion of the consumption of jingoistic cheap print by working-class Protestants in her book *Britons: Forging the Nation* (Colley 1992/2005: 20–9). But histories of nationalism in Britain should benefit still more from the "systems approach" to the history of print culture advocated by William St Clair in *The Reading Nation in the Romantic Period* (2004), whereby tracking data such as sales figures and print runs while tracing distribution networks and the printed record of reviewer and (where available) reader response allows these intersecting histories to compensate for one another's blind spots. St Clair's notion of British national culture as that of a "reading nation" is a useful supplement to Anderson's account of the origins of nationalism. For Anderson, "print-capitalism" emerged, alongside capitalism generally, in the wake of a modernization process that saw the breaking up of once vast religions into smaller faiths, the recession of ties between monarchy and religion, and the need for administrative vernaculars to combat the decline of Latin as a *lingua franca*. Its chief donation to nationalism was a sense of cultural and linguistic community across vast spaces, by inculcating the sense of a uniform transnational temporality and within it, through the imagination of compatriots simultaneously engaged in identical reading in a standardized printed vernacular, the sense of a community existing in national space and time. Anderson has charted the ways in which print capitalism made use of Romantic-period infrastructure and technological developments, such as the improved post roads and canal system Austen points to. Analyses following St Clair's model would add an attention to "reading constituencies, with cohorts joining and leaving," and with diverse expectations and modes of response, official and otherwise (St Clair 2004: 267).

Such work could make particular common cause with recent scholarship on the history of the institution and discipline of "English literature," and especially with the emphasis placed there on the role of anthologies – that pedagogical book form, the printed counterpart of the commonplace book. The Romantic anthology's purposes included the inculcation of a standardized vernacular language that, once refined into a catalogue of audibly familiar and "literary" references and devices, became the ground for a common national culture (Guillory 1993: 93, Siskin 1998: 94). When Jane Austen mocked the genre by making it the preferred reading of Mrs Elton in *Emma* (1816), she gave contemporary voice to precisely that question of reading cohorts that would come to preoccupy St Clair. In preferring to encourage "exchange of opinion" about books after careful reading and rereading by diverse individuals and groups, Austen questioned both the worth and the efficacy of inculcating a uniform literary culture (Austen 1818/2003: 23). Not least, to read the scholarship on the history of print culture in conjunction with the history of the discipline of English is to suspect that the competition and overlap between political and cultural nationalisms in Romantic-period Britain might result from some such jostling between the overlapping publics that, as Austen insisted, must make up the republic of letters.

Scotland and the Britishness of Romantic Cultural Production

Implicit in the anthologies whose rise marks the origins of "English literature" as a heritage and a discipline is something like a displacement of English by British culture after the mid-eighteenth century. The inclusion of Scottish and Irish writers amid the canon of English literature is a case in point, and one with Romantic origins (Wright 1997: 352–4). Some sense of the potential felt by at least some contemporaries in this emerging sense of a relatively capacious Britishness is apparent in the enthusiastic buy-in of Scottish writers in the latter part of the eighteenth century and the beginning of the nineteenth. Most paradigmatically, James Thomson, who wrote "Rule Britannia" (1740), the triumphal anthem of a British nationalism based on naval superiority and an associated ethos of commercial range and freedom, was a Scottish poet. In an 1819 pamphlet that was to become a standard in the Edinburgh tourist trade, Scott, too, celebrated the mingling of "two nations, who, speaking the same language, professing the same religion, and united in the same interests, seem formed by GOD and Nature to compose one people" (Scott 1819: 34). His rhetoric of cultural commonality and shared commercial interests demonstrates a familiar mix of the political, historical, and ethnocultural strands of Romantic nationalism, here dedicated to the progress of Britain. It is also worth noting Scott's prominence, as part-owner of the printing shop that produced his novels and of one of the leading periodicals that reviewed them, among the "print-capitalists" who played a leading role in nineteenth-century British nationalism.

More recently, scholarship has alternately highlighted and problematized Britain's inclusiveness in ways that turn on the distinction between anticolonial (or, in Scotland's case, peripheral) nationalisms and the demands of imperial states whose origins were themselves forged in nationalist claim. As Calhoun notes, the "discourse of nationalism can be employed equally in the service of unification or secession" (Calhoun 1997: 103); in turn, unification can be understood by contemporaries as a progressive move toward inclusion or as an exercise in unwanted political and cultural dominance from the center. Moreover, as we have already seen, the making of the British nation required politics and culture to work especially closely together. As a result, as Robert Crawford has shown in *Devolving English Literature* (2000), "English literature" had, from the beginnings of its institutionalization, an unusual heterogeneity and geographical range. But Crawford's book also includes the provocatively titled chapter "The Scottish Invention of English Literature," which adds a specifically literary, and specifically critical, dimension to the work of historians, such as Colley, who trace the origins of British nationalism, and British national character, to the professional, economic, and imperial ambitions of Scottish writers in particular (Crawford 2000: 16–44).

In attempting to ascertain the character and degree of resistance to Britain and British nationalism during the Romantic period, therefore, it is necessary to turn to the closely related history of Scotland, and of Scottish nationalism, at the turn of the nineteenth century, more particularly to print culture and the institutions of literary and linguistic instruction. Until recently, it had been the scholarly consensus that the dominant nationalisms in Romantic Scotland were wholly British in their political orientation and cultural aims or indeed, as Nairn asserts, that there was no Scottish nationalism in Romantic Scotland (Nairn 2003: 94). More recently, however, such analyses of Romantic nationalism in Scotland have given way to at least two rival schools of thought, best summarized by reference to Duncan's *Scott's Shadow* (2007) and Katie Trumpener's *Bardic Nationalism* (1997) on the one hand and to Crawford and Colley on the other.

In his analysis of the period of cultural and political consolidation that followed the visit of George IV to Scotland in 1822, Duncan has argued that Scotland's "national identity" became "split between a political and economic dimension (imperial Union) and a supplemental cultural one (national distinctiveness)" (Duncan 2007: 17). In this analysis, Scotland confirms and brings to market its cultural distinction even as it participates in Britain. Trumpener concurs, though she understands the process rather differently: for Trumpener, nineteenth-century Scottish culture becomes self-consciously "British" only once it is exported to the colonies, especially in printed form. There it aids, for example, in defining a Canadian identity that distinguishes itself from the national character of America by means of its "transimperial" association with metropolitan Britain (Trumpener 1997: 244–7).

Crawford's and Colley's thinking, however, originates with an earlier period. A wholesale substitution of Britain for England, Crawford argues, was bequeathed to English and Scottish schools by eighteenth-century Lowland intellectuals. Books such as Hugh Blair's *Lectures on Rhetoric and Belles Lettres* (1783) typically announced themselves as designed "for the initiation of Youth" as they seek to "form their Style, or to prepare themselves for Public Speaking or Composition" (Blair 1783, vol. 1: iv–v). They operated on the assumption that language is an index of "national character" and thus offer the implicit promise of enabling successful language users to assist in shaping the nation, not least through participation in public life (Blair 1783, vol. 1: 206). Once the Parliament of Scotland had acceded to Union with England and Wales in 1707, access to real political and economic power was at stake in the standardization and pedagogical portability of English as a language and English literature as a common culture. As a result, Scots intellectuals took a prominent part in producing the rhetorics, grammars, and anthologies that defined and purveyed a common British culture.

The cost of access to power in Britain was an extraordinary level of linguistic and literary achievement by individual upper- and middle-class Scots under the tutelage of Blair and the numerous other rhetoricians and elocutionists who urged the Scots to lose what they described as a dialect, accent, or brogue. Crawford argues that this achievement itself came at a price: what he characterizes as the suppression of Scotland's original culture. Janet Sorensen has considerably complicated this analysis in *The Grammar of Empire in Eighteenth-Century British Writing* (2000) by demonstrating that rhetorical instruction leveled the differences between multiple, often polyglot languages *within* Scotland, a process that established protocols for the later export of English literary and language instruction to the colonies, not least by Scottish functionaries.

The effects of this leveling process remain clearly audible, and clearly incomplete, in Scott's *The Antiquary*. In this novel, working-class Scots and elderly Scotswomen of any class speak Scots; all English people, well-born Scotsmen, and young educated women speak English. Arguments are had about the worth or worthlessness of Gaelic (here represented as a dead rather than a living language), and the learned title character Jonathan Oldbuck engages in the audible code-switching of the imperfectly bilingual (or, in this case, multilingual) speaker: "And what possessed you, *dumosa pendere procul de rupe?* – though *dumosa* is not the appropriate epithet – What the deil, man, tempted ye to the verge of the craig?" (Scott 1816/1829, vol. 5: 116). This speech, which follows the rescue of Oldbuck's dearest friends from a cliff face, shows Oldbuck speaking Scots when he is extremely excited (a rare occurrence) and a pedantic, deliberate, often archaic English mixed with Latin or Greek at other times. The implication of speeches like this one is that Oldbuck has learned his English as he has his classical languages, polishing it with the aid of rhetorics and grammars. In *The Antiquary*, more than any other of his novels, Scott draws attention to the emergence, the stakes, and the uneven development of English as a British vernacular.

Notwithstanding the preoccupation of even so enthusiastic a Briton as Scott with such questions of uneven development, Colley describes the relation of Scots to Britain and its nationalism as essentially one of opportunity, chiefly opposed by an insular and retrograde English nationalism. Hers is a viewpoint that has recently been seconded by T. M. Devine in *Scotland's Empire* (2003), with its compelling description of Scots having "colonized" the imperial process (Devine 2003: xxvi). As a result, the main residual nationalism of the late eighteenth century, Colley proposes, was a Scotophobic phenomenon. Its bugbears were the figures of Charles Edward Stuart, the Young Pretender, in his afterlife as a French courtier, and the third Earl of Bute, Prime Minister of Britain from 1762 to 1763. This recourse to Englishness reached a climax in John Wilkes's journal *The North Briton* in the early 1760s.

Yet Wilkes's nationalism could be politically progressive as well as xenophobic, mingling as it did fears about the economic consequences of union with concerns about increasing royal prerogative and the decreasing power of voters to determine the character of Parliament (Colley 1993/2005: 106). Treating Bute and Stuart as twin emblems of the Scots permitted Wilkes and his followers to associate Scotland with France and thereby to underscore the urgency of confronting a dangerously proximate enemy eager to impose its absolutist sympathies and imperial ambitions on England. Additionally, Bute was a convenient scapegoat as Wilkes unsuccessfully attempted to draw off the threat of prosecution for seditious libel by emphasizing Bute's influence on the king rather than the misdeeds of the monarch himself, even as Wilkes drew considerable attention to the latter.

Moreover, though by the time of the American Revolution an inclusive British nationalism – built on a triple alliance of Protestant religion, commerce, and imperial participation – was superseding Wilkite and other forms of English reaction, the consequences for Scotland and its nationalisms were neither simple nor uniform. War in America, followed by continental war and imperial expansion, allowed numerous Scotsmen the opportunity and scope to distinguish themselves by their contributions to Britain, thereby confirming the worth of Scotland and Scots in metropolitan eyes (Colley 1993/2005: 127–30). By this means the Scots consolidated their status as "North Britons," participants in a common culture as well as a common enterprise in Britain and overseas. Yet by highlighting the continuing evidence for uneven development, Scottish Romantic writers remind readers of the need to maintain the balance sheet of nationalism's gains and losses: at home, in peripheries and metropole, and abroad, in Britain's empire.

Irish Nationalisms, Debate, and Transnational Exchange

The years following the 1603 union of the English and Scottish crowns had seen an economic, political, and linguistic union so complete that for many Scots "there were no barricades" on the road to success in

London (Anderson 1983/1991: 90). These conditions were already in place before the signing of the Act of Union of 1707, which was to bring about the "incorporating union" of Scotland with England. They would continue to hold irrespective of any price paid by Scots at home or the fulminations of Wilkes and his followers. The linguistic availability of English made the benefits of a prenational and as yet unnamed condition of Britishness available to arrivals from Scotland well before the voting into being of "one Kingdom by the Name of Great-Britain," as the Articles of Union had it.

Though they lacked such ease of access to England's literary capital, Irish writers and intellectuals made their way to London in significant numbers throughout the eighteenth and early nineteenth centuries. Some became major figures in the emerging "British" literature. In Charles Robert Maturin's 1808 novel *The Wild Irish Boy*, Lady Montrevor, a sophisticated *salonnière* and member of the ruling Protestant Ascendancy, laments what she calls the "mental absenteeism" prevalent in Ireland (Maturin 1808, vol. 2: 311). The phrase describes the situation in which Romantic-period Irish artists and intellectuals must with few exceptions leave Ireland for London if they are to be able to distinguish, or indeed to support, themselves, precisely because of the vexed relations then existing between Ireland, the predominantly Anglo-Irish Ascendancy, and Britain. The implied comparison to the absenteeism of eighteenth- and nineteenth-century Irish landlords is apt, for the Irish brain drain Montrevor points to is represented as a capital flight comparable to the landlords' lack of financial investment in their property. The causes are more than merely analogous. Montrevor's words suggest that Ireland's culture, and cultural production, are damaged by the same conditions of Ascendancy governance that united the most radical nationalists with the most moderate reformers in criticism of its economic and social effects. It is worth noting that Montrevor, herself a returned absentee, views Ireland as the "Siberia of the British dominions" (Maturin 1808, vol. 2: 299).

Taken together, these features of Romantic-period Ireland highlight the unusual character of early nineteenth-century Irish international involvements, which resulted less from the call of opportunity abroad, or in London, than from a generally shared sense of a lack of it at home. Whereas uneven development in other jurisdictions may have produced a defensive, resistant brand of nationalism, Ireland's situation seems to have made its residents look outward. In their case, this geographical breadth of gaze was a measure not of the absence of nationalism but of its pragmatic coexistence with a cosmopolitan impulse, a relationship that has continued to be debated into the twenty-first century, and which has been the subject of renewed interest in the context of Ireland's emergence as a so-called Celtic Tiger.

It is relevant here that Montrevor's remarks highlight Ireland's continuing situation as an object requiring exegesis, Joep Leerssen's *"explicandum,"* that is, at the same time, a focus of argument, conversation, and above all of *writing*, in Ireland, Britain, and beyond (Leerssen 1997: 38). If we were to characterize Ireland (then as now) as a *disputandum*, therefore, we would also be highlighting its status as perhaps the aptest index of the close but complicated relationship between Romantic nationalism and the public sphere, both globally and locally. The relationship between the cultural and political nationalisms of Romantic Ireland, in particular, has been the subject of considerable unresolved debate. In the Ireland of the period there existed well-developed separate threads of cultural and political nationalism among some writers and thinkers even as others continued to insist on the inseparable union of politics with culture. The result is a complex matrix of incrementally different nationalisms, leading to some dispute over where a given figure ought to be placed on the grid, or whether such a figure was nationalist at all.

The popularity of antiquarian nationalisms in Romantic-period Ireland is a case in point. More than in England or Scotland, these nationalisms delighted in the discovery and cataloguing of artifacts, material or linguistic, which adherents presented as surviving evidence of an ancient nation, and which spurred practitioners to reconstruct the national traditions they declared themselves to have lost. In engaging in these acts of reconstruction, antiquarian nationalists collapsed space and time into the small room they called a nation, scanning landscapes as historical evidence and reading history as a set of enforced disjunctions made visible, even allegorical, by impact on the land. Scholarship on the antiquarian nationalisms of Romantic Ireland has often understood them as a reactionary longing for a heroic, historically undifferentiated, and purely fictive past (Leerssen 1997: 10–11, 68). Until recently, the cultural nationalist texts of the period have rarely been taken seriously by historically minded scholars, who have seen them as exercises in genteel nostalgia, deceptive or self-deceiving.

Owenson's novel *The Wild Irish Girl* (1806) frequently sets its plot aside in order to present antiquarian histories of things – "the ancient costume of the Irish nobles" (now made of coarser cloth); "the original ancient Irish harp" (now played only among ruins) – supported by extensive footnotes (Owenson 1806/1999: 47, 71). Meanwhile,

Owenson's *Lay of an Irish Harp; or Metrical Fragments* (1807) made mournful parallels between fragmented poetic form and what it presents as a fractured nation:

> 'Tis said *oppression* taught the lay
> To him – (of all the "sons of song"
> That bask'd in Erin's brighter day)
> The *last* of the inspir'd throng;
> That not in sumptuous hall, or bow'r,
> To victor chiefs, on tented plain,
> To festive souls, in festal hour,
> Did he (sad bard!) pour forth the strain.
> (Owenson 1807: 3–4)

This characteristic tone of melancholy in the face of cultural loss, as well as the vogue such works helped excite in Britain for picturesque tours to Ireland, have led to their dismissal as trite consolations for Union or as embarrassing examples of everything that was wrong with Romantic nationalism: a wholesale evacuation of political engagement. Some recent scholarship, however, notably Trumpener's *Bardic Nationalism*, has viewed such works as the bearers of an anticolonial nationalist impulse, a critical stance that enumerates a political history of violent conquests. It is also possible to understand these antiquarian nationalist works squarely within a transnational context, as exercises in the marketing of Ireland and Irish nationalism, bringing home the profits (all but one of Owenson's books were published first in London) even as they address readers who have the power to bring about political and economic change, whether directly or through international suasion – an instance of the role of print culture in Romantic political nationalism, as Ina Ferris's *The Romantic National Tale and the Question of Ireland* (2002) has pointed out in depth.

Trumpener proposes that cultural nationalism, not least in its antiquarian form, emerges from Irish writing in response to British nationalism in the Romantic period. It emerges from a collision between the genres of British enterprise in the peripheries – the land survey, often conducted by government, and the picturesque tour, its civilian counterpart, each of which engages in a kind of discursive land clearance readying the scene for repopulation and development – and an assertive local experience insistent on its own presence in the scene (Trumpener 1997: 37–127). Chief among Irish cultural nationalist genres was the national tale, a fluid, transnational, politically variable form. All these genres, transformed from within by their encounters with one another, are as mutually dependent as the nations they help form and whose relations they help to mediate. Ferris argues that the Ireland of the Romantic period is the scene of multiple and unresolvable rhetorical competitions, each sparked by "encounter with forms of in-betweenness" (Ferris 2002: 14). The national tale, as it was pioneered by Owenson and developed by Maturin and by John and Michael Banim between 1806 and the late 1820s, is a profoundly "civic" form, its encounters between genres and rhetorics a model for the global public sphere these writers wish at once to shape and to turn to Ireland's benefit (Ferris 2002: 46). This is an explicitly civic, or political, nationalism that is energetically transnational and culturally focused from the start.

Similar debates surround the phenomenon usually viewed as the leading exemplar of political nationalism in Romantic-period Ireland: the United Irishmen movement. Scholars have reached no lasting consensus on the exact positioning of the United Irishmen – architects of the major failed rebellion of 1798 – with respect to the range of Irish nationalisms. Avowed opponents of "rule . . . by Englishmen, and the Servants of Englishmen" and advocates for "a *cordial Union* among ALL THE PEOPLE OF IRELAND" leading to "AN EQUAL REPRESENTATION OF ALL THE PEOPLE IN PARLIAMENT," they saw themselves as activists in the spirit of "the great Æra of Reform" characterized by "unjust Governments . . . falling in every quarter of Europe" (*Declaration, Resolutions, and Constitution, of the Societies of United Irishmen*).[1]

Some of the difficulty in assessing the quality of United Irish nationalism stems from the distribution and fate of the divisions and alliances within contemporary reaction to the Union of Ireland with Britain in 1801. In the beginning, the Protestant Ascendancy opposed the Union as a measure likely to undermine their economic supremacy over the land and give undue rights to the largely Catholic peasantry who worked it. Progressive thinkers in Ireland and Britain tended to be for it, often for economic reasons based on an analogy with Scotland, but sometimes also because they considered it a species of state reform. When the Union did not result in Catholic emancipation, as the two Parliaments that agreed to it had promised, progressives as different as Owenson and Byron rapidly turned against it. Still others sought to reform it, often because the historical concord of progressive politics with Dissenting religion created sympathy for those experiencing conflict with a state church (Ferris 2002: 4–6).

The United Irishmen themselves mingled cultural and political agitation, domestic and international activity in ways that have proved equally difficult to parse. How important is their involvement in cultural nationalist activities such as the Belfast harpers' festival of 1792, at which the harp was born as a national and nationalist symbol, or the Romantic nationalist verse writing of the intellectual William Drennan and the revolutionary and diplomat Theobald Wolfe Tone, which often resembled the work of the sentimental Owenson (Thuente 1994)? Was this a republican movement betrayed by alliance with the ethnocultural nationalism of the rural, Catholic Defender movement from early on, resulting in sectarian bloodshed during the 1798 rebellion? Or did the United Irish politics of radical reform continue to resemble the spirit and demands of their contemporaries the United Scotsmen or the London Corresponding Society, though inflected by a different political context (see Whelan 1996: 129–30)? Is it useful to think of the United Irishmen as a cosmopolitan or global association, emphasizing their documented ties with French and American revolutionary figures, or does the sectarian violence of 1798 trump any such account? Can the civic and cultural nationalism of the United Irishmen be characterized as their own transnational take on what Margaret Jacob (2002) has called an "international republican conversation"? The rich variety of argument about these questions is a legacy of the productive tensions between culture and politics, home and away, in the nationalisms of Romantic Ireland, as well as the sheer volume of writing about Ireland in the period.

Romantic Nationalisms and Global Modernity

The national tale was exported during the Romantic period to the English-speaking British colonies, where it furnished tools for the new kinds of nationalism to be developed by former British settlers as they became Australian and Canadian. It is in tracking such matters as the mobility of genres and its global effect on print culture and on nations that the scholarship on Romantic Ireland – and, indeed, on British and Irish Romanticism generally – makes its most forward-looking contributions to the broader study of nationalisms and nations. Such a Romanticist literary history refuses any separation between nationalism and global thinking, yet it makes a continuing claim for the relevance of nationalism, and national identity – in its cultural as well as its civic form, as a body of Irish, or of British, common knowledge.

The Romantic-period narrative of Ireland's constant transnational exchanges suggests that nationalism may no more than any other tradition be simply bequeathed and inherited. Rather, it is dynamically fractured, pulled against itself by its origins in the debates on transnational politics and uneven development *within* the British Isles. While the nation offers a seductive and apparently primordial model of social cohesion, it can never fully achieve internal stability. These relations between uneven development, nationalism, and transnational exchange explain why the study of Irish and Scottish Romanticisms remains at the forefront of scholarship both in Romanticism generally and Romantic nationalism in particular. In turn, the study of Romantic nationalisms in general provides an occasion for the analytic meeting of metropolitan, peripheral, and colonial nationalisms, civic and cultural, in a long historical context. If "nationalist discourse" is, as Calhoun has put it, an offshoot of "global cultural flow," there is no more useful perspective than Romantic studies to bring to bear on the origins, contexts, and continuing potential of the global itself (Calhoun 1997: 10).

Note

1 The pamphlet *Declaration, Resolutions, and Constitution, of the Societies of United Irishmen* (1791?) is available at Eighteenth Century Collections Online.

References and Further Reading

Anderson, Benedict. (1983/1991) *Imagined Communities: Reflections on the Origin and Spread of Nationalism*, 2nd edn. London: Verso.

Austen, Jane. (1818/2003) *Northanger Abbey*, ed. James Kinsley and John Davie. Oxford: Oxford University Press.

Blair, Hugh. (1783) *Lectures on Rhetoric and Belles Lettres*, 3 vols. Dublin: Whitestone.

Burke, Edmund. (1765/1991) *Tracts Relating to the Popery Laws*. In *Writings and Speeches*, ed. R. B. McDowell (vol. 9, pp. 434–82). Oxford: Clarendon.

Burke, Edmund. (1790/1989) *Reflections on the Revolution in France*. In *Writings and Speeches*, ed. L. G. Mitchell (vol. 8, pp. 53–293). Oxford: Clarendon.

Butler, Marilyn. (1988) "Romanticism in England." In Roy Porter and Mikulas Teich (eds) *Romanticism in National Context* (pp. 37–67). Cambridge, UK: Cambridge University Press.

Calhoun, Craig. (1997) *Nationalism*. Buckingham, UK: Open University Press.
Calhoun, Craig. (2007) *Nations Matter: Culture, History, and the Cosmopolitan Dream*. New York: Routledge.
Chandler, James. (1998) *England in 1819: The Politics of Literary Culture and the Case of Romantic Historicism*. Chicago: University of Chicago Press.
Colley, Linda. (1992/2005) *Britons: Forging the Nation, 1707–1837*, 2nd edn. New Haven, CT: Yale University Press.
Crawford, Robert. (2000) *Devolving English Literature*, 2nd edn. Edinburgh: University of Edinburgh Press.
D'Israeli, Isaac. (1791) *Curiosities of Literature*. London: Murray.
Devine, T. M. (2003) *Scotland's Empire, 1600–1815*. London: Lane.
Duncan, Ian. (2007) *Scott's Shadow: The Novel in Romantic Edinburgh*. Princeton, NJ: Princeton University Press.
Ferris, Ina. (2002) *The Romantic National Tale and the Question of Ireland*. Cambridge, UK: Cambridge University Press.
Gellner, Ernst. (1983) *Nations and Nationalism*. Ithaca, NY: Cornell University Press.
Godwin, William. (1793) *Enquiry Concerning Political Justice*, 2 vols. Dublin: White.
Guillory, John. (1993) *Cultural Capital: The Problem of Literary Canon Formation*. Chicago: University of Chicago Press.
Habermas, Jürgen. (1989) *The Structural Transformation of the Public Sphere: An Inquiry into a Category of Bourgeois Society*, trans. Thomas Burger with Frederick Lawrence. Cambridge, MA: MIT Press.
Hazlitt, William. (1830/1931) *Life of Napoleon Buonaparte*. In *Complete Works*, ed. P. P. Howe, vols. 13–14. London: Dent.
Hobsbawm, Eric. (1990) *Nations and Nationalism since 1780: Programme, Myth, Reality*. Cambridge, UK: Cambridge University Press.
Hobsbawm, Eric and Terence Ranger (eds). (1983) *The Invention of Tradition*. Cambridge, UK: Cambridge University Press.
Hudson, Nicholas. (1996) "From 'Nation' to 'Race': The Origin of Racial Classification in Eighteenth-Century Thought," *Eighteenth-Century Studies* 29: 247–64.
Jacob, Margaret. (2002) "Sociability and the International Republican Conversation." In Gillian Russell and Clara Tuite (eds), *Romantic Sociability: Social Networks and Literary Culture in Britain, 1770–1840* (pp. 24–42). Cambridge, UK: Cambridge University Press.
Leerssen, Joep. (1997) *Remembrance and Imagination: Patterns in the Historical and Literary Representation of Ireland in the Nineteenth Century*. Cork: Cork University Press.
Maturin, Charles Robert. (1808) *The Wild Irish Boy*, 3 vols. London: Longman.
McGann, Jerome. (1983) *The Romantic Ideology: A Critical Investigation*. Chicago: University of Chicago Press.
Nairn, Tom. (2003) *The Break-Up of Britain: Crisis and Neo-Nationalism*. Urbana, IL: Common Ground.

Newman, Gerald. (1987) *The Rise of English Nationalism: A Cultural History, 1740–1830*. New York: St. Martin's.

Owenson, Sydney. (1806/1999) *The Wild Irish Girl: A National Tale*, ed. Kathryn Kirkpatrick. Oxford: Oxford University Press.

Owenson, Sydney. (1807) *Lay of an Irish Harp; or Metrical Fragments*. London: Phillips.

Owenson, Sydney. (1818) *Florence Macarthy: An Irish Tale*, 4 vols. London: Colburn.

Owenson, Sydney. (1829) *The Book of the Boudoir*, 2 vols. New York: Harper.

Paine, Thomas. (1791/1989) *The Rights of Man, Part I*. In *Political Writings*, ed. Bruce Kuklick (pp. 49–144). Cambridge, UK: Cambridge University Press.

Scott, Walter. (1816/1829) *The Antiquary*. In *The Waverley Novels*, vols. 5 and 6. London: Cadell.

Scott, Walter. (1819) *Description of the Regalia of Scotland*. Edinburgh: Ballantyne.

Simpson, David. (1993) *Romanticism, Nationalism, and the Revolt Against Theory*. Chicago: University of Chicago Press.

Siskin, Clifford. (1998) *The Work of Writing: Literature and Social Change in Britain, 1700–1830*. Baltimore, MD: Johns Hopkins University Press.

Sorensen, Janet. (2000) *The Grammar of Empire in Eighteenth-Century British Writing*. Cambridge, UK: Cambridge University Press.

St Clair, William. (2004) *The Reading Nation in the Romantic Period*. Cambridge, UK: Cambridge University Press.

Thuente, Mary Helen. (1994) *The Harp Re-strung: The United Irishmen and the Rise of Irish Literary Nationalism*. Syracuse, NY: Syracuse University Press.

Trumpener, Katie. (1997) *Bardic Nationalism: The Romantic Novel and the British Empire*. Princeton, NJ: Princeton University Press.

Whelan, Kevin. (1996) *The Tree of Liberty: Radicalism, Catholicism and the Construction of Irish Identity, 1760–1830*. Cork: Cork University Press.

Wollstonecraft, Mary. (1790/1989) *Vindication of the Rights of Men*. In *Works*, ed. Janet Todd and Marilyn Butler (vol. 5, pp. 1–60). New York: New York University Press.

Wollstonecraft, Mary. (1798/1996) *The Wrongs of Woman: or, Maria. A Fragment*, ed. Gary Kelly. Oxford: Oxford University Press, 1996.

Wright, Julia M. (1997) "'The Order of Time': Nationalism and Literary Anthologies, 1774–1831," *Papers in Language and Literature* 33: 339–65.

Chapter 5

"With an Industry Incredible": Politics, Writing, and the Public Sphere

Paul Keen

In its review of Mary Wollstonecraft's *A Vindication of the Rights of Woman* (1792), the *Monthly Review* announced that:

> Philosophy, which, for so many ages, has amused the indolent recluse with subtle and fruitless speculations, has, at length, stepped forth into the public walks of men, and offers them her friendly aid in correcting those errors which have hitherto retarded their progress toward perfection, and in establishing those principles and rules of action, by which they may be gradually conducted to the summit of human felicity. (*Monthly Review* 1792: 198).

The image of Philosophy stepping outside of its inherited boundaries in order to circulate in more "public" contexts echoed Joseph Addison's memorable comment in *The Spectator* No. 10: "It was said of *Socrates*, that he brought Philosophy down from Heaven, to inhabit among men; and I shall be ambitious to have it said of me, that I brought Philosophy out of Closets and Libraries, Schools and Colleges, to dwell in Clubs and Assemblies, at Tea-Tables and in Coffee-Houses" (Addison and Steele 1711/1907: 38–9).

The readers of the *Monthly Review; or Literary Journal* (founded in 1749) would have appreciated the significance of Addison's broader emphasis on the complex internal relations within the literary field. His article, which was simultaneously an announcement of literary success and an articulation of the terms in which he wished that success to be understood, inscribed a pedagogical ambition (to enable his readers "to be let into the Knowledge of ones self") within a jubilant recognition of commercial relations that included both his audience ("this great City" which was "inquiring Day by Day after these my Papers") and his "Publisher [who] tells me that there are already Three Thousand of them distributed every Day" with "Twenty Readers to every Paper." It was a frankly (if partially ironically) reformist agenda driven less by a leveling impulse than by a search for a new code of social distinction appropriate to a commercial society: an attempt to "recover" his readers "out of that desperate State of Vice and Folly into which the Age is fallen" by instilling in them a degree of polite sociability which would "distinguish [them] from the thoughtless Herd of their ignorant and inattentive Brethren" (Addison and Steele 1711/1907: 38).

All of these issues would return with a vengeance in the Romantic period: questions of who was writing and publishing what, how it circulated, who and how extensive its audience was, and what the effect of reading should be on individual readers and on society in general. If, as Henry Cockburn remarked about the French Revolution, "Everything, not this or that thing, but literally everything, was soaked in this one event," few cultural phenomena were more vehemently implicated and obsessively scrutinized than the world of print (Cockburn 1856/1974: 73). In an age in which politics soaked into every corner of society, the magnitude of the implications of questions about the nature and role of modern literature as an unprecedented communicative force were exposed as they had never been. It became virtually impossible to discuss either – politics or print – in ways that were not, at some level, bound up with one another. I will focus my examination of these issues on three particular years: 1792 and 1818, years of fierce political unrest in which all of these questions were the subject of intense debate, and 1802, a period of relative calm marked by significant developments within the literary field itself. And I will ground each of these discussions in an account of a particular text. In the case of the two later years I have chosen a journal, one well remembered (the *Edinburgh Review*) and one largely forgotten (the *Yellow Dwarf*) though both were influential and innovative literary experiments that helped to reconfigure existing ideas about cultural authority. But for 1792 I have chosen a very different type of text, the controversy over Thomas Paine's publication of *Rights of Man*, Part Two. This controversy found its focus in Paine's subsequent trial (*in absentia*) for seditious libel, but it also encompassed several individual texts, from *Rights of Man*, Parts One and Two, to Paine's response to the trial in his "Letter Addressed to the Addressers," all of which circulated widely within radical print culture in the period. Treating these as elements of a single broader text (the Paine controversy) highlights the multiple ways that discourse traveled across a range of highly mediated literary and cultural sites, and, related to this, the fluency of political participants as readers of a wide variety of different kinds of written and social texts. The period was typified by what James Chandler, borrowing from Claude Lévi-Strauss, describes as "a hot chronology" – a time when writers and readers were forced by the pressures of the day to wrestle in overt and highly self-conscious ways with questions about the conditions within which their own literary efforts were inscribed (Chandler 1998: 3). The answers they developed were both particular to their historical moment and significant in much broader ways as analyses of the changing nature of the literary field.

For many reformers, the most powerful means of establishing the authority of reason, liberty, and justice, was literature, understood not as an aesthetic category but as a communicative domain enabling a wide-ranging debate on issues of public importance. In November 1788, on the eve of the French Revolution, the *Analytical Review or History of Literature, Domestic and Foreign, on an Enlarged Plan* (published by Joseph Johnson) declared that "Literature, by enlightening the understanding, and uniting the sentiments and views of men and nations, forms a concert of wills, and a concurrence of action too powerful for armies of tyrants" (*Analytical Review* 1788, 2: 324). Literature may not have been the only phenomenon capable of ensuring the success of this process, but for many reformist thinkers it was "the most important by far." Nor were these interventions limited to individual publications. The periodical press rarely failed to emphasize its own important role in these discussions. The *Monthly Review* insisted that, "Among all the modes which have been devised for the purpose of diffusing knowledge among mankind, none is so effectual as that of periodical publications." Aligning itself with the politicized nature of these debates, it added that "no subject is more proper for such publication, than the general science of politics, so interesting, and, we will add, so intelligible to the community at large" (*Monthly Review* 1792, 9: 230).

Anxieties generated by the revolutionary potential of this reformist vision centered on a tension inherent in the *Monthly Review*'s reference to the "public" in their Wollstonecraft review. The ultimate issue for many loyalists was not the strategic one of whether public opinion could be successfully mobilized on the side of Church-and-King but, more fundamentally, whether the very idea of public opinion had any useful social role whatsoever. The fact that the idea of public opinion has become such a commonplace today can make it difficult to remember that the idea had its own particular history, but critics in the Romantic period already recognized both the modernity of the concept and the extent to which its relatively recent emergence was itself bound up with the transformative power of print. As Isaac D'Israeli put it in *Curiosities of Literature* (1791), "the taste for books, so rare before the fifteenth century, has gradually become general only within these four hundred years: in that small space of time the public mind of Europe has been created" (D'Israeli 1791: 1). For reformers, this idea of "the public mind" – the *Analytical Review*'s "concert of wills" which would be "too powerful for armies of tyrants" – was the cornerstone of hopes for social progress, but for many conservatives, the danger was not that this or that opinion could be misguided (though this was also a problem) but rather that the idea of public opinion itself was fundamentally irreconcilable with social harmony. Edmund Burke's *Reflections on the Revolution in France* (1790) offered a compelling vision of social order that was based on the blessings of mystification or a deeply shared willing suspension of disbelief rather than on what Burke portrayed as the corrosive effects of extended public debate inflamed by a spirit of critical inquiry. None of the problems which now plagued France and which threatened to manifest themselves in England had existed, Burke suggested, in the days before the advent of this "public mind." "But now," he warned, thanks in large part to the inflammatory power of print,

> all is to be changed. All the pleasing illusions, which made power gentle, and obedience liberal, which harmonized the different shades of life, and which, by a bland assimilation, incorporated into politics the sentiments which beautify and soften private society, are to be dissolved by this new conquering empire of light and reason. All the decent drapery of life is to be rudely torn off. All the superadded ideas, furnished from the wardrobe of a moral imagination, which the heart owns, and the understanding ratifies, as necessary to cover the defects of our naked shivering nature, and to raise it to dignity in our own estimation, are to be exploded as a ridiculous, absurd, and antiquated fashion. (Burke 1790/1986: 171)

For those who believed, with Burke, that this "wardrobe of a moral imagination" was crucial to social harmony, print's ability to facilitate wide public debate on seemingly endless issues was inherently alienating rather than liberating. It was not that people might collectively decide on the wrong thing, but, far more seriously, that indulging people in the idea that they were better off by debating every aspect of their society was itself the wrong thing. Nor, conservatives frequently stressed, would these would-be reformers be content with mere debate once they had ventured onto the slippery slope of political activism. A correspondent to the *Gentleman's Magazine and Historical Chronicle* (a London publication founded in 1731) wrote to convey his revulsion with "this scribbling age, when every man who can write composes a pamphlet, and every journeyman bookseller erects himself into a publisher... when the press and the sword are alike familiarly appealed to" (*Gentleman's Magazine* 1792, 62: 934).

As Jon Klancher has argued, these tensions were exacerbated by a nervous awareness of the erosion of traditional boundaries between different reading audiences. In the politically turbulent atmosphere that developed after 1789, these boundaries fragmented into a "scene of a cultural struggle demanding a new mental map of the complex public and its textual desires, a new way to organize audiences according to their ideological dispositions, their social distances, and the paradoxically intense pressure of their proximity as audiences" (Klancher 1987: 15).

The Trials of Literature in 1792

In an essay which has become a kind of a manifesto for our own age's interest in print culture, Robert Darnton argued that rejecting "the great-man, great-book view of literary history" in favor of an approach which could accommodate the important role of "literary middlemen" would "open up the possibility of rereading literary history. And if studied in connection with the system for producing and diffusing the printed word, they could force us to rethink our notion of literature itself" (Darnton 1990: 152–3). Nearly two centuries earlier, a number of people were already insisting on a similar approach, including no less a figure than King George III. On May 21, 1792, the King issued a proclamation warning that "divers wicked and seditious writings have been printed, published, and industriously dispersed, tending to excite tumult and disorder." The Proclamation announced that the government was determined "to repress [these] wicked and seditious practices... and to deter all persons from following so pernicious an example." But it went a great deal further in commanding "all our Magistrates in and throughout our Kingdom of Great Britain" to "make diligent enquiry, in order to discover the Authors and Printers of such wicked and seditious writings ... and all others who shall disperse the same" (Royal Proclamation 1792/1995: 121–2). The focus was not merely on the legality of particular texts or on the broader issue of freedom of speech but, as Addison had suggested in a very different spirit, on sociological questions of how texts circulated, who was printing and publishing them, and how far the question of audience helped to establish the criminality of a text.

These issues were debated in a range of contexts but the forum in which they received their most dramatic and explicit consideration was a series of trials for seditious libel, the most famous of which was Thomas Paine's 1792 trial for *Rights of Man*, Part Two. Paine's lawyer, Thomas Erskine, insisted that it was a trial, not only about the freedom of the press, but about the relevance of these broader questions raised by the Proclamation. "You cannot be justified in finding it criminal," Erskine told the jury, "because published at *this* time, unless it would have been a criminal publication under any circumstances, or at *any other* time" (Erskine 1810, vol. 2: 94), or because of Paine's attempt to encourage his book's "circulation amongst classes of men unequal to political researches" (p. 93). Far from sidestepping the question of audience, Attorney General Sir Archibald Macdonald emphasized the determining influence of the social context of the book's publication and distribution. It would not suffice, he warned the jury, to proceed "by simply reading to you the passages which I have selected, and leaving it entirely to your judgement" (vol. 2: 46). A close reading, no matter how judicious, could not produce an adequate interpretation; this task depended on a correct appreciation of wider mediating factors that had more to do with circulation than content. Macdonald had not charged Paine for *Rights of Man*, Part One (1791), he told the jury, because "Reprehensible as that book was, extremely so, in my opinion, yet it was ushered into the world under circumstances that led me to conceive that it would be confined to the judicious reader, and when confined to the judicious reader, it appeared to me that such a man would refute as he went along" (Erskine 1810, vol. 2: 47–8).

What Macdonald meant by this was that Part One had sold for the relatively expensive price of three shillings – the same price as Edmund Burke's *Reflections on the Revolution in France* (1790). But Paine had released Part Two as a sixpenny pamphlet, a decision that undermined the security of this "judicious" reading community:

when I found that another publication was ushered into the world still more reprehensible than the former; that in all shapes, in all sizes, with an industry incredible, it was either totally or partially thrust into the hands of all persons in this country, of subjects of every description. . . . I thought it behoved me upon the earliest occasion, which was the first day of the term succeeding this publication, to put a charge upon record against its author. (Erskine 1810, vol. 2: 48)

The Attorney General's correlation between criminality and class hierarchy was a firmly established point. Authors were to be treated differently depending on whether they were interested in promoting the exchange of ideas – "with an industry incredible" – or inciting people to violence. And the determining factors in this distinction, which was fundamental to ideas about the transformative power of literature, had as much to do with the book trade as with the ideas that were being traded. The point was frequently repeated that the use of an accessible style at a cheap enough price was more of a crime than were the seditious ideas that were being offered.

In his "Letter Addressed to the Addressers," written in the summer of 1792 in response to the seditious libel charge, Paine warned that

> It is a dangerous attempt in any government to say to a nation, *"thou shalt not read."* This is now done in Spain, and was formerly done under the old government of France; but it served to procure the downfall of the latter, and is subverting that of the former; and it will have the same tendency in all countries; because *thought* by some means or other, is got abroad in the world, and cannot be restrained, though reading may. (Paine 1792/1987: 368)

The government's coercive legal maneuvers could never achieve their intended effect, Paine argued, because they only highlighted its moral weakness, and in doing so, placed the law itself (rather than the reformers) in a position of guilt. "The *Rights of Man* is a book calmly and rationally written," he challenged his prosecutors, "why then are you so disturbed?" (1792/1987: 367). Reversing the government's sense of the incriminating nature of his plebeian audience, Paine insisted that creating as wide an audience as possible was the best means of establishing a correct judgment about his book's moral worth: "Let every man read and judge for himself, not only of the merits and demerits of the work, but of the matters therein contained, which relate to his own interest and happiness" (p. 374).

Paine's was the first of a series of arrests aimed at reining in popular debate but, as Kevin Gilmartin has reminded us, it is a mistake to reproduce radicals' accounts of conservatives as frightened and selfish reactionaries lashing out at democratic changes which they simply could not understand or which seemed to threaten their inherited privileges (Gilmartin 2006). All of this was certainly true, to varying degrees, of many conservatives in the period, but, as Gilmartin demonstrates, others also recognized the need to make the case for loyalism directly to working-class readers in ways that were every bit as innovative as the wretched Jacobin innovators they decried. In some ways they needed to be inventive. Appealing to public opinion on behalf of a politics that was itself deeply suspicious of the very idea of public opinion necessarily created tensions that could only be accommodated through considerable stylistic dexterity. Taking his cue from Mark Philp's account of "vulgar conservatism" – which rejected Burke's insistence that "the vulgar were the object of conservative thinking, not intended participants in it" in favor of an approach which directly engaged the lower orders – Gilmartin explores the means by which writers across a range of genres forged "a mode of public argument and political organization" that appealed to popular readers in ways that neutralized the tensions within this endeavor (Gilmartin 2006: 21–2). Nor was this simply a matter of strategic necessity. As Gilmartin also demonstrates, many loyalist writers fused a comforting rhetoric of tradition with genuine programs of extensive social reform. The most ambitious of these writers may well have been Hannah More, whose *Cheap Repository Tracts* insistently rejected the stabilizing force of custom in favor of "an aggressive national movement to reform the social order" that was "as thoroughgoing and closely reasoned as anything in Jeremy Bentham or Robert Owen" (Gilmartin 2006: 59, 71). For evangelicals like More, reform may have amounted to rooting out the sorts of loutish vices that they associated with the aberrant masculine world of tavern life rather than democratic enfranchisement, but that did not make their reformist aspirations any less ambitious. More's real genius may have been her ability to present such an extensive vision of change in ways that seemed on the surface to offer a comforting deference to inherited traditions. In doing so she and other "vulgar conservatives" helped to rejuvenate the idea of loyalism in ways that would make it attractive to a newly politicized general public.

Nor, as Wollstonecraft and More insisted in strikingly similar terms, were these debates about the connections between literature and the social order waged in terms of class alone. Wollstonecraft's explicitly gendered insistence in *Rights of Woman* that "it is a farce to call any being virtuous whose virtues do not result from the exercise of its own reason," situated women's aspirations in terms of this broader spirit of enlightened progress (Wollstonecraft 1792/1989: 90). Lamenting women's superficial and irrational state, she blamed "a variety of concurring causes" including "a false system of education gathered from the books written on this subject by men who, considering females rather as women than human creatures, have been more anxious to make them alluring mistresses than affectionate wives and rational mothers" (p. 73). However deeply opposed More may have been to Wollstonecraft's brand of radical reform, her comment that "it is a singular injustice which is often exercised towards women, first to give them a most defective Education, and then to expect from them the most undeviating purity of conduct" reflected a similar resistance to the double standards of an unreformed patriarchal order (More 1799, vol. 1: ix).

However intense their other differences, conservative and reformist critics could find some common ground in their disdain for the miserable quality of many new publications. Descriptions of these literary problems were often as alarmist as conservatives' apocalyptic accounts of the French Revolution. A letter in the April *Gentleman's Magazine* derided "the miserable *gleanings* of mercenary, incompetent, vain, and idle scribblers" which were filling "our schools and circulating libraries." "Every writer should draw from his own proper fund of knowledge whatever he presents to the public," it warned, "otherwise the number of mean and fraudulent publications will be perpetually encreasing ... and there will be an end to all ingenuity, dignity, character, honour, and propriety in the Republick of Letters" (*Gentleman's Magazine* 1792, 62: 322). These judgments reflected an underlying anxiety about the instability of the book trade as it was transformed by "the efforts of many booksellers, based on new promotional techniques, advertising, and more adventurous retail and distribution," all of which helped to undermine the oligarchy of London publishing houses which had controlled and regulated the business (Raven 2001: 17). "In the final decades before the introduction of steam-driven mechanized printing in 1814, English booksellers brought out an immense diversity of books, pamphlets, newspapers, general and specialist magazines, periodicals, and part-issues that could reach every town in the three kingdoms" (Raven 2001: 1). Fears about literary decline and revolutionary upheaval converged in what Jon Mee characterizes as the age's more diffuse anxieties about print culture as an anarchic terrain in which "words were circulated in print... distanced from a controlling authorial identity, open to misappropriation, and likely to merge with and further infect the uncertain and oceanic passions of the anonymous crowd" (Mee 2002: 2).

The "Promise of their Labours": Literary Professionalism in 1802

A decade later, the public mood was very different. Disenchantment with the French Revolution whose violent excesses seemed to confirm Burke's dire predictions, the government's determined campaign of political repression, the backlash against radical advocates of the rights of women after Mary Wollstonecraft's death in 1797, and the intellectually numbing effects of a protracted war which placed a premium on uncritical patriotism, all combined to destroy the reform movement's momentum. The decline of popular radicalism took the edge off debates about who was writing, publishing, and reading what, at what price, and how it was being circulated. But at the same time, the diminished threat of revolution at home and the Peace of Amiens with France, signed in March 1802, provided breathing space to reflect on the literary implications of the previous decade's struggles. In its account of the conservative John Bowles's *Reflections on the Conclusion of the War*, the first edition of the *Edinburgh Review or Critical Journal* (launched in October 1802) insisted that the peace would be a death warrant, not "of the liberty and power of Great Britain" as Bowles predicted, but of the success of intemperate authors, and therefore, of "Mr. Bowles [sic] literary reputation." "The truth is," the *Edinburgh Review* explained, "if Mr. Bowles had begun his literary career at a period when superior discrimination, and profound thought, not vulgar violence, and the eternal reputation of rabble-rousing words, were necessary to literary reputation, he would never have emerged from that obscurity to which he will soon return." The subordination of "intemperate passions" to a more thoughtful public mood made way for a literary atmosphere capable of moving beyond antagonistic polemics (*Edinburgh Review*, 1: 94–5). In doing so it may have prepared the way for a cultural revolution led by the *Edinburgh Review* itself.

As Ian Duncan has argued, the *Edinburgh Review*'s style and format represented a groundbreaking intervention which radically altered the relations of cultural authority that structured the Romantic literary field in ways that acknowledged a new relation to the worlds of commerce and politics (Duncan 2005). On the one hand, the continuity between the *Edinburgh Review*'s expansive vision and eighteenth-century literary journals' broad focus reflects the *Review*'s philosophical alignment with the cosmopolitan ideal of a republic of letters that had fragmented under the weight of the political pressures of the previous decade. But it also reflects an ideological continuity between the *Edinburgh Review*'s overtly Whig politics and the legacy of Scottish Enlightenment thinkers such as Adam Smith, David Hume, Adam Ferguson, and Francis Hutchison, whose work had helped to articulate a progressivist vision of a modern commercial society stabilized by an ethos of polite sociability and animated by an intellectual community whose ideas would become diffused throughout an increasingly enlightened public. Francis Jeffrey's antagonistic reviews of Wordsworth's poetry are well known, but however interested the *Edinburgh Review* was in poetry (and in novels and drama), the first number reviewed sermons, travel writing, poetry, scientific and medical treatises, and discussions of the utility of country banks and of Britain's paper credit system.

While the *Edinburgh Review* may have been traditional in the breadth and heterogeneity of its literary commitments, its style and format marked a revolution in the periodical press. Rejecting the tendency of existing periodicals such as the *Monthly Review* and the *Critical Review* to publish monthly in order to offer an account of every new publication, the Advertisement in the first *Edinburgh Review* proudly noted that "it forms no part of [its] object, to take notice of every production that issues from the press." On the contrary, it was their intention "to be distinguished, rather for the selection, than for the number, of its articles." Nor, they suggested, was this a sacrifice. "Of the books that are daily presented to the world, a very large proportion is evidently destined to obscurity.... The very lowest order of publications are rejected, accordingly, by most of the literary journals of which the Public is already in possession." Rather than replicating these existing journals, the *Edinburgh Review* made a virtue of its difference by publishing quarterly rather than monthly, and extending its articles "to a greater length, than is usual in works of this nature" (n.p.). In doing so it established a new model of critical authority which it figured as capable of redressing the anarchic state of modern literature.

As Duncan has emphasized, this amounted to far more than a matter of changing stylistic priorities. Confronted with the fragmentation of the older ideal of the republic of letters, the *Edinburgh Review*'s disavowal of political neutrality and often dramatic expression of critical authority, coupled with the insistence of Archibald Constable (the

Review's publisher) that all authors be paid for their work, amounted to a bold reinterpretation of inherited codes of literary professionalism in terms suited to nineteenth-century social and political realities. The *Edinburgh Review* gained its prominence, not by trying to undo the fragmentation of the republic of letters or deny the intrusion of politics into every aspect of civil life – "not [into] this or that thing, but literally everything" – but by insisting on a heightened judicial posture capable of bringing some sort of coherence to a cultural field where a myth of unity was no longer possible. Acknowledging the radical interfusion of culture and commerce, as well as the impossibility of political neutrality or critical objectivity in a postrevolutionary age, the *Edinburgh Review* simultaneously reflected the extensive cultural influence of the Scottish legal community and formulated a new model of literary professionalism capable of responding to the pressures of Britain's industrial strength in a politically saturated age.

In doing so, however, it was forced to address the politically compromised nature of any model of professionalism indebted to the ideas of the Enlightenment. Burke's damning correlation of the corrosive effects of Enlightenment thought with the barbarities of the French Revolution steadily gained ground in the early nineteenth century, most dramatically in Coleridge's later writings. In order to formulate a convincing model of literary professionalism, the *Edinburgh Review* would need to confront these insinuations about the diabolical connections between a politics of authorial distinction and revolutionary national politics head-on. That it did so by way of a review of Jean Joseph Mounier's *De L'Influence attribuée aux Philosophes, aux Francs-Maçons, et aux Illuminés, sur la Revolution de France* in the lead article of its first number suggests the extent to which Jeffrey recognized both the high stakes and the discursive complexities of this revisionary project. In his *Reflections on the Revolution in France*, Burke had blamed the "political Men of Letters" who "contrived to possess themselves, with great method and perseverance, of all the avenues of literary fame" in order to foster resentment towards the *ancien régime* (Burke 1790/1986: 211–12). Rejecting both Burke's conspiracy theory and Mounier's wholesale exoneration of France's "philosophers," the *Edinburgh Review* allowed that, however innocent they may have been of the dark conspiracies suggested by Burke, "the writings of those popular philosophers who have contended for political freedom, had some share in bringing about the revolution in France." It immediately qualified this charge, however, by insisting on a related distinction between influence and intention. The "designs" of the *philosophes* "were pure and honourable; and the natural tendency and promise of their labours, was exalted and fair. They failed, by a fatality which they were not bound to foresee; and a concurrence of events, against which it was impossible for them to provide" (*Edinburgh Review* 1802, 1: 9–11). The *Edinburgh Review*'s argument was important because the debate was about far more than a correct understanding of the origins of the Revolution; what was ultimately at stake in these discussions was the Enlightenment ideal of literature as the basis of a public sphere which, as the *Analytical Review* had put it, "forms a concert of wills, and a concurrence of action too powerful for armies of tyrants" (*Analytical Review* 1788, 2: 324).

The *Edinburgh Review*'s enormous success and its explicit Whig affinities paved the way for similar quarterlies such as the *Quarterly Review* (1809) and *Blackwood's Magazine* (1817), both of which held equally strong Tory loyalties. Duncan has rightly suggested that however vigorous their differences, the stature of all three journals reflected Edinburgh's importance as a city whose influence marked "a new kind of national capital – not a political or commercial metropolis, but a cultural and aesthetic one" (Duncan 2005: 48). But it was a weekly periodical launched the same year as the *Edinburgh* by a theatrically self-conscious Englishman which would have the greatest impact in the turbulent years after Napoleon's defeat. William Cobbett launched his weekly *Political Register* while still an ardent loyalist, but by 1804 he had grown disenchanted and had adopted the radical sympathies which would help to revolutionize periodical literature when he started producing a cheap twopenny edition in November 1816. Cobbett would need to wait, however, until a new political crisis generated the conditions within which his influence could fully establish itself. The Pitt government's draconian campaign in the 1790s, combined with the numbing effects of a war that spanned more than a decade, against the increasingly threatening specter of Napoleon's imperialist ambitions would all but extinguish the reform movement in Britain. In his 1812 *Reflector* essay "The English Considered as a Thinking People, in Relation to Late Years," Leigh Hunt bemoaned the decline of genuine critical debate which, he argued, had once been England's most compelling distinction. But the eventual conclusion of the war three years later simultaneously removed the need for solidarity against an ambitious foreign enemy and released a vast number of discharged soldiers back into a social order in which they could not always find a place. Along with a severe economic depression, the war's end thus encouraged an atmosphere of political restlessness that would culminate in a new era of revolutionary upheaval. Cobbett may have been the most influential of this period's new wave of radical journalists, but few magazines bridged the gap between politics and culture, and between middle-class and popular radicalism, than the *Yellow Dwarf*, published by Leigh Hunt's brother, John.

Print Politics in 1818

If the French Wars had curbed any resurgence of the reform movement, the years after Napoleon's defeat were, according to E. P. Thompson, the "heroic age of popular Radicalism" (Thompson 1963/1980: 691). The year 1818 saw relative calm and therefore an opportunity to reflect on the implications of the previous year when tensions created by the economic hardships of 1816, crippling levels of taxation, and the specter of a bloated patronage system had flamed into talk of revolution after a minority of protestors had broken away from a meeting at Spa Fields and rioted on December 2, 1816, and then again after an alleged assassination attempt on the Prince Regent on his departure from Parliament on January 28, 1817. Skeptics insisted that the "assassination attempt" was nothing more than a stone thrown through the window of the royal carriage. The government was unable to produce any corroborating evidence, but still used the incident as a pretext to suspend Habeas Corpus, introduce new prohibitive legislation known as the "Gagging Acts," and embark upon a new series of political arrests.

The extremity of the government's response generated an important discussion, not only about who should be reading what, but also about the government's role in policing the limits of public debate and regulating the circulation of texts. As the January 7 edition of T. J. Wooler's *The Black Dwarf* put it, looking back on the political struggles of the year, "the Press was armed in favour of Reform to a degree unprecedented" (*Black Dwarf* 1818: 3). The first several editions of John Hunt's *Yellow Dwarf*, launched on the first Saturday of 1818, focused on the legal implications of one of the most important cases of the previous year: William Hone's trials for blasphemous libel for publishing politically inflected parodies of the Catechism, the Litany, and the Athanasian Creed. Defending himself successfully on all three charges, Hone had turned the trials, held on successive days in December 1817, into political texts in themselves. But the *Yellow Dwarf*'s analysis of Hone's trials subordinated an interest in the trials to an investigation of the dubious legality of the government's use of *ex-officio* information which, it explained by way of a quotation from Blackstone's *Commentaries*, were reserved for cases "so high and dangerous" that "a moment's delay would be fatal" (Keen 2003, vol. 2: 221). The March 7 edition protested against the subsequent arrest of two vendors for selling Hone's pamphlets. Not only had the pamphlets' innocence already been established in court, vendors were traditionally immune from the requirement of bail. Taking the case to its logical extreme, the *Yellow Dwarf* posed the question of what would happen if "the publisher of the *Morning Post* or the *Times*" were charged with a libel. The government would have to "demand bail from all the vendors who had sold a copy of the Paper, and fill Newgate with newsmen and with the boys who hawk the Papers about the streets" (p. 293).

The *Yellow Dwarf* warned that the government's position reflected the same double standard about freedom of expression that Paine's trial had exposed in 1792. "It is the circulation of a work amongst the lower orders, not the nature of the work itself, which . . . determines the guilt; and what is strangest of all, 'its *systematic* circulation in cheap magazines.'" It would have been a pleasant change, the *Dwarf* continued, for the government to have spelled the hypocrisy of this position out in clearer terms itself.

> We should have seen, that a paper which would pass unpunished if sold for a shilling, would be "reprehensible" at sixpence-halfpenny, and "literally poison" if sold for a penny; – that any thing which the people choose to read must be libellous, but that Ministerial parodies, which were stupid and did not circulate, should not be punished . . . that blasphemy could not exist on hot-pressed paper, or even in Treasury Journals; – that nothing which was read by the rich alone could be mischievous. (Keen 2003, vol. 2: 294)

At his own trial for blasphemous libel two years later, the radical preacher Robert Wedderburn would protest against the same "conspiracy of the poor, to keep them in ignorance and superstition." He would not have been charged, Wedderburn insisted, if he "had asserted the same things a thousand times, in a different phraseology . . . but because my audience were humble people who would not have understood fine-spun discourses, and delicate allusions, I am condemned for addressing them in the vulgar tongue" (Wedderburn 1820: 17).

If these questions were familiar from the 1790s, there were also crucial changes. The most important of these was the appearance of an array of "cheap weekly magazines," as they routinely described themselves. William Cobbett had led the way on November 16, 1816, when he produced a twopenny version of his *Political Register* in order "to make it move *swifter*" by avoiding the stamp tax (Cobbett 1816, 31: 610). Other radical weekly magazines quickly followed. Their most remarkable quality may have been the clarity with which they identified themselves as part of an important new phenomenon. Whatever difficulties social historians may have had with Thompson's argument that the working class "was present at its own making" (1963/1980: 8) the weekly magazines worked hard to emphasize that this was precisely the case with them. The first edition of the *Gorgon*, launched in May 1818, warned that

> CORRUPTION has not yet encountered a more formidable and dangerous enemy, than in the circulation of cheap, weekly publications. . . . Before the commencement of these weekly papers, the labouring classes were, in a great measure, precluded from political information. . . . But how wonderfully is the scene changed in the last eighteen months. (Keen 2003, vol. 3: 7)

Comparing the "*old* Press," which "was exclusively devoted to either of the two aristocratical Factions," with "the establishment of cheap publications," which had transformed the Press into "a mighty engine in the cause of truth, and the rights of man" early the next year, it declared that "the people ought to part with their lives, rather than give up this valuable auxiliary to their claims" (p. 280). The radical magazines gave voice to an often spontaneous overflow of powerful feelings on a weekly basis without the luxury of tranquil recollection. As Gilmartin emphasized in *Print Politics* (1996), their greatest achievement may have been the relentlessness and sophistication with which they hammered home a shared insistence on radical print culture as a diffuse and overlapping set of practices that extended well beyond their own acts of authorship.

Some of the most important literary events of 1818 were oral rather than printed. S. T. Coleridge built on his growing literary reputation by embarking on two concurrent lecture series, on the history of philosophy on Monday nights, and on Shakespeare on Thursday nights, in competition with William Hazlitt's lectures at the Surrey Institution (some of which were attended by John Keats). One of Coleridge's favorite themes during these years was the demise of the "evil days" of Enlightenment rationalism. "I am happy to see and feel that men are craving for a better diet than the wretched trash they have been fed with for the last century," he announced (Coleridge 1818/2000:

239–40). But this was more a case of wishful thinking than accurate judgment. As political tensions intensified, Enlightenment rhetoric, with its emphasis on the power of critical debate amongst a broad and increasingly educated populace, was gaining a renewed authority within the radical press. "It is to promote the great work of enlightening the minds of the people, and preparing them for those changes which must infallibly come, that we have commenced the present publication," announced the lead article of the first *Gorgon* (Keen 2003, vol. 3: 8). William Hazlitt's powerful essay "What is the People," published in the March 7 and 14 editions of the *Yellow Dwarf*, insisted that "the full and free development of the public opinion must lead to truth, to the gradual discovery and diffusion of knowledge" (Keen 2003, vol. 2: 304). The key to this, the January 17 edition of the *Yellow Dwarf* explained, was the press:

> As every man for himself cannot undertake to collect the evidence on political questions, there must necessarily be a class of persons who undertake to collect the facts and arrange the arguments in such a shape, that others may speedily decide on them. . . . The conflicting testimony and reasoning is conveyed through the kingdom by means of the press. (Keen 2003, vol. 2: 239)

Hazlitt's prominence within the pages of the *Yellow Dwarf* reflected the rich fusion of poetry and politics that animated the circle that had gathered around the Hunt brothers, and that found expression in the appearance of some of the age's most exciting poetry within the journals, including Percy Shelley's "Ozymandias," published in the "Original Poetry" section of the January 11 edition of the Hunts' *Examiner*, which three weeks later began a glowing three-part review of Shelley's major publication that year, *The Revolt of Islam*. In the end, reformers' faith in the transformative power of "*the wrongs of the People proclaimed by an omnipotent* PRESS" proved to be as overoptimistic as Coleridge had been in his obituary for this Enlightenment commitment to the radical potential of critical exchange (Keen 2003, vol. 3: 63). As the economy improved and the repressive effects of the Gagging Acts took their toll, the revolutionary moment passed. But even if it had not been able to exploit the revolutionary impulse of the postwar years, the radical weekly press provided a valuable account of some of the most important aspects of the literary field as it was crystallizing into the disciplinary form that is today the subject of renewed inquiry. The *Yellow Dwarf*'s response to the effects of the

Suspension of Habeas Corpus Act the previous year focused on a shift in the division of knowledge that would ultimately constitute the modern categories of literature and philosophy. The tendency of eighteenth-century thinkers to use these words interchangeably, or in ways which considerably overlapped, reflected the Enlightenment's belief in the reformist power of print as a medium of critical exchange encouraging the pursuit of knowledge. The term "philosophy" had been central to Addison's sense of his literary efforts and to the *Monthly Review*'s account of Wollstonecraft's *Vindication*. But it was precisely this sense of fusion that was under pressure from repressive government interventions.

The *Yellow Dwarf* offered a perceptive and telling obituary for an older and more historically engaged sense of both of these forms of intellectual endeavor – literature and philosophy – in its discussion of the Suspension Act:

> just so much philosophy is permitted to be taught as will not interfere with the selfish views of a ruling faction, just so much truth as will tend to support their cause, just so much literature as can exist without the aid of manly knowledge. . . . Philosophy is thus disjoined from that political science of which it should be the ground-work; partial, garbled, and mangled truth is made to serve the purposes of falsehood; and literature, is made a meagre barren substitute for it. (Keen 2003, vol. 2: 254)

Raymond Williams was surely right to suggest that this "dissociation" of what had been seen as "interlocking interests" was "in part a product" of the Romantic period (Williams 1958: 48). But the *Dwarf*'s argument is proof that this transition was not uncontested, nor did its implications go unnoticed. The Romantic period is better remembered for the vigor and sophistication with which fundamental questions about literature were debated – a discursive struggle of which we today are increasingly aware.

References and Further Reading

Addison, Joseph, and Richard Steele. (1711–12/1907) *The Spectator*, ed. G. Gregory Smith. London: J. M. Dent.

Behrendt, Stephen (ed.). (1997) *Romanticism, Radicalism, and the Press*. Detroit: Wayne State University Press.

Burke, Edmund. (1790/1986) *Reflections on the Revolution in France*, ed. C. C. O'Brien. London: Penguin.

Chandler, James. (1998) *England in 1819: The Politics of Literary Culture and the Case of Romantic Historicism*. Chicago: University of Chicago Press.

Chandler, James and Kevin Gilmartin (eds). (2005) *Romantic Metropolis: The Urban Scene of British Culture, 1780–1840*. Cambridge, UK: Cambridge University Press.

Cobbett, William. (1802–35) *Cobbett's Weekly Political Register*. London: William Cobbett.

Cockburn, Henry. (1856/1974) *Memorials of His Time*, ed. K. Miller. Chicago: University of Chicago Press.

Coleridge, Samuel Taylor. (1818/2000) "Lectures on the History of Philosophy," in *The Collected Works of Samuel Taylor Coleridge*, ed. Kathleen Coburn, vol. 8. Princeton, NJ: Princeton University Press.

Darnton, Robert. (1990) *The Kiss of Lamourette: Reflections in Cultural History*. New York: Norton.

D'Israeli, Isaac. (1791) *Curiosities of Literature, Consisting of Anecdotes, Characters, Sketches and Observations, Literary, Critical, and Historical*. London: John Murray.

Duncan, Ian. (2005) "Edinburgh, Capital of the Nineteenth Century," in James Chandler and Kevin Gilmartin (eds), *Romantic Metropolis: The Urban Scene of British Culture, 1780–1840* (pp. 3–45). Cambridge, UK: Cambridge University Press.

Duncan, Ian. (2007) *Scott's Shadow: The Novel in Romantic Edinburgh*. Princeton, NJ: Princeton University Press.

Erskine, Thomas. (1810) *The Speeches of Thomas Erskine*, comp. James Ridgway, 2nd edn, vols. 2 and 3. London: J. Ridgway.

Fontana, Biancamaria. (1985) *Rethinking the Politics of Commercial Society: The Edinburgh Review, 1802–1832*. Cambridge, UK: Cambridge University Press.

Gilmartin, Kevin. (1996) *Print Politics: The Press and Radical Opposition in Early Nineteenth-Century England*. Cambridge, UK: Cambridge University Press.

Gilmartin, Kevin. (2006) *Writing Against Revolution: Literary Conservatism in Britain, 1790–1832*. Cambridge, UK: Cambridge University Press.

Habermas, Jürgen. (1962/1989) *The Structural Transformation of the Public Sphere*, trans. Thomas Burger. Cambridge, MA: MIT Press.

Hunt, Leigh. (1812) "The English Considered as a Thinking People, in Relation to Late Years," *The Reflector* I: 1–16.

Keen, Paul. (1999) *The Crisis of Literature in the 1790s: Print Culture and the Public Sphere*. Cambridge, UK: Cambridge University Press.

Keen, Paul (ed). (2003) *The Popular Radical Press in Britain, 1817–182*, vols 2 and 3. London: Pickering & Chatto.

Klancher, Jon P. (1987) *The Making of English Reading Audiences, 1790–1832*. Madison: University of Wisconsin Press.

Lackington, James. (1792) *Memoirs of the First Forty-Five Years of the Life of James Lackington*. London: James Lackington.

Maniquis, Robert M. (ed.). (2002) *British Radical Culture in the 1790s*. San Marino: Huntington Library Press.

Mathias, T. J. (1797) *The Pursuits of Literature, or What You Will: A Satirical Poem in Four Dialogues*, 3rd edn. London: T. Becket.

Mee, Jon. (2002) "Mopping Up Spilt Religion: The Problem of Enthusiasm," available online at *Romanticism on The Net* 25: 1–11. <http://www.erudit.org/revue/ron/2002/v/n25/006009ar.html>.

More, Hannah. (1799) *Strictures on the Modern System of Female Education*, 2 vols. London: T. Cadell and W. Davies.

Paine, Thomas. (1791–2/1987) *The Rights of Man*. In *The Thomas Paine Reader*, ed. Michael Foot and Isaac Kramnick (pp. 200–364). London: Penguin.

Paine, Thomas. (1792/1987) "Letter Addressed to the Addressers," in *The Thomas Paine Reader* (pp. 365–86).

Pig's Meat; or Lessons for the Swinish Multitude. (1793) Ed. Thomas Spence, vol. 1. London: printed for T. Spence.

Raven, James. (2001) "The Book Trades," in Isabel Rivers (ed.), *Books and Their Readers in Eighteenth-Century England: New Essays* (pp. 1–34). London and New York: Leicester University Press.

Royal Proclamation. (1792/1995) In *Political Writings of the 1790s*, ed. Gregory Claeys (vol. 7, pp. 121–2). London: William Pickering.

Thompson, E. P. (1963/1980) *The Making of the English Working Class*. London: Penguin.

Wedderburn, Robert. (1820) *Trial of the Rev. Robert Wedderburn*, ed. Erasmus Perkins. London: printed for the editor.

Williams, Raymond. (1958) *Culture and Society, 1780–1950*. New York: Harper.

Wollstonecraft, Mary. (1792/1989) *A Vindication of the Rights of Woman*. In *The Works of Mary Wollstonecraft*, ed. Janet Todd and Marilyn Butler (vol. 5, 61–266). London: William Pickering.

Chapter 6

Romantic Justice: Law, Literature, and Individuality

Mark Schoenfield

From the earliest Greek drama to the latest season of television, the law has been an object of veneration and satire, respect and disdain. Yet what defines law, as either a concept or institution, varies historically. Issues of rights, property, individuality, and national sovereignty both transform legal thought and receive expression within it. Romantic literature uses the law for novelistic purposes; lost wills and illegal marriages drive romance plots, while crimes and their adjudication structure Jacobin novels. But such works also subject law to a critical analysis by challenging the coordination of "the law" as a conceptual ideal coextensive with, or subordinate to, justice, and the legal institutions – trials, writs, assizes – as the practical enablers (or disrupters) of that ideal. Romantic-age parodist William Combe stated the conflict in his 1815 verse "The Catchpole":

> LAW is, or should the offspring be
> Of Justice and Humanity...
> But, 'tis the Practice that confounds it,
> Winding its mystic Nonsense round it;
> ... drugg'd with Pleadings, Justice slept.
> (Combe 1815/1903: ll. 1–2, 12–13, 18)

The struggle between ideals and institutions touched on the expression of individual liberty, the tensions between natural and legal rights, and the modern understanding of the individual as both subject to the law but sovereign within his or her own person, as both an economic agent and a private person.

Economic Transformation, Law, Print Culture

Karl Polanyi identifies the century encompassing literary Romanticism as the "Great Transformation" in European economics. From around 1750, he argues, commodification begins to supply "a vital organizing principle in regard to the whole of society" (Polanyi 1944/1957: 71–2).

Land, once the stabilizing mark of status, entered the marketplace when primogeniture, entailments, and other legal devices limiting the sales of property were weakened or stripped away and enclosures multiplied, sweeping public lands into private profits. Labor, subject to the wage-earning regimes of factories and other industrial organizations, reshaped individuals' understanding of the social potential of their own bodies, and consequently of familial obligations and marital potentials. As Mary Robinson's Mr Bradford – the gouty, acquisitive tradesman in her novel *The Natural Daughter* (1799) – gloats, status itself was manipulated as a saleable product, as merchants purchased, married, and pleased their way into the aristocracy (Robinson 1799/2003: 93–7). Writing from the late Romantic vantage point of 1831, Thomas Love Peacock conveys the extent of commodification within polite society when his Lady Clarinda delights in her own market value: "Mr. Mac Quedy, the Modern Athenian, who lays down the law about every thing, [and] ... turns all the affairs of this world into questions of buying and selling ... has satisfied me that I am a commodity in the market, and that I ought to set myself at a high price" (Peacock 1831/1981: 162). Such economic shifts depended on and solidified two key components of modernity: the *great nation states* with their imperial ambitions and bureaucratic governance; and *the modern individual*, who functioned as producer, consumer, capitalist, spouse, professional, and – implicated in all the prior categories – subject before the law. In this same period, from about 1750 to 1835, the modern author emerges, through copyright and other legal interpellations, as a paradigmatic subject before the law, at once producer and proprietor. Mark Rose notes that "the emergence of the mass market for books, the valorization of original genius, and the development of the Lockean discourse of possessive individualism" all coincide with "the long legal and commercial struggle over copyright" that blended "Lockean discourse and the aesthetic discourse of originality"; under these conditions, "the modern conception of the author as proprietor was formed" (Rose 1988: 159).

Reforms engaged all institutional systems in late eighteenth-century Britain and brought others, including new judicial formations, into existence. A new legal conception of divorce evolved from individualist principles; the nation state's investment in trade and military authority sparked a consolidation and expansion of the Admiralty court, the institution that resolved disputes over seized property and enemy combatants. These changes depended upon a professionalized legal system and an ideology circulated through the "social text," Jon Klancher's term for the cultural frames by which individuals read their relations to both institutions and their own individuality (Klancher 1987). Without extensive cultural representation – provided by new genres of the novel, occasional poems published in periodicals, and histories that located the seeds of innovations within past rituals – the courts could not have enacted their many transformations.

Because the interests of authors and the law only sometimes coincided, biographies reveal mutual dependencies and antagonisms. For example, Charlotte Smith reshapes her anguish over legal disputes into her elegiac stanzas. Sarah Zimmerman summarizes the economic and legal conditions under which Smith began writing professionally. She notes that Smith looked to publication when her husband was imprisoned for debt, in order to "maintain the family's social standing" until the estate of her father-in-law could be settled and provide her children with the education she wanted. Her father-in-law's will, however, "generated legal entanglements that remained unresolved throughout that career" with the Chancery suit reaching resolution only after her death. "As a result, Smith's temporary venture into the literary marketplace lasted twenty-two years" (Zimmerman 1999: 40). In *The Old Manor House* (1793), rich and greedy Mr Whitly explains the workings of chancery, with which Smith was all too acquainted:

> "Your brother Phill, d'ye see, says he's heir at law, and so there's a Chancery law-suit about it – But we knows that a will's a will, and the longest purse will carry the day. – Well! the upshot of all is, that, heir at law, or not heir at law, your brother, if he can carry on the suit, which folks be pretty dubious about, will never get no part of it." (Smith 1793/2002: 408)

In poetry like her *Elegiac Sonnets*, such blunt expression was transmuted into an abstract and sentimental vein; comparing herself to a lunatic, she writes:

> *He* has no *nice felicities* that shrink
> From giant horrors; wildly wandering here
> He seems (uncursed with reason) not to know
> The depth or the duration of his woe.
> (Smith 1797/1993: LXX: ll. 11–14, p. 61)

The lunatic is spared the self-consciousness that Smith's legal tribulations – rendered as sublime "giant horrors" – has forced upon her, a curse of "reason." Despite the abstraction, the poem relies on the biographical context implicit in the prefaces of the accretive *Elegiac Sonnets* and reinforced by reviewers such as the *Gentleman's Magazine* writer who hopes "that the misfortunes she so often hints at, are all imaginary," since all readers "must have perused her very tender and exquisite effusions with diminished pleasure, could we have supposed her sorrows to be real" (quoted in Zimmerman 1999: 48–9). Having it both ways like the sonnets themselves, the reviewer invokes and denies a specific context, one in which his magazine, a public cultural statement intended to reinforce masculine privilege as a natural and legal value, would be implicated.

Many Romantic-age writers, like Smith, had legal entanglements: Byron's alleged duels, as well as his marital and copyright struggles, contribute to the tactical polemics of *Don Juan*; the Wordsworths' protracted difficulties about their father's estate influenced William's career and self-awareness; Francis Jeffrey and other reviewers were lawyers, and legal training infuses their critical practice. Simultaneously, propriety, manners, and other social aesthetic norms depended on the ability of legal society to reinforce and promulgate such norms; consequently, judges not only ruled in court, but were substantial public figures. Lord Eldon evinced an awareness of his stature as a public exemplar, recalling that James Boswell, lawyer and by then famous author, "called upon me at my chambers in Lincoln's Inn, desiring to know what would be my definition of *Taste*." Eldon refused to answer because Boswell "would publish it, and I did not choose to subject my notion of it to public criticism" (Eldon 1960: 99).

If the law depended upon cultural representations to circulate the fame and honor of its practitioners and the justice of its judgments, lawyers were also wary of them as tools easily appropriated by reformists and revolutionaries. In the 1770s, Lord Mansfield expressed skepticism about the press; Northumberland was opining on the "comfort" of the newspaper at breakfast, and Mansfield answered: "Your Grace likes the *comfort* of reading the newspapers – the *comfort* of reading the newspapers! Mark my words . . . those newspapers, if they go on as they now do, will most assuredly write the Dukes of Northumberland out of their titles and possessions, and the country out of its King" (quoted in Twiss 1844, vol. 1: 112). The future Lord Eldon, standing by, did mark these words, and, as Attorney General, headed up prosecutions against the press and, in 1794, against the London Corresponding Society, which used print to assemble a network of reformists. In 1798, he introduced a bill to prevent the publication of newspapers "by persons not known" (Twiss 1844, vol. I: 304). This statute extended a common-law notion that an anonymous publication, incapable of maintaining a copyright, was unprotected against piracy. Because anonymity acted as an extrajudicial license that helped evade sedition laws, the court promoted declared authorship as a check on such power. Authors and publishers like Cobbett, however, garnered their popularity by courting prosecution, publishing from prison, and using trials as the occasion for ideological declarations. The battle of the law and the press was waged over an aesthetics of justice, as Mansfield's alarmed repetition of "comfort" intimates.

Poetic Justice: Aesthetics for the Law

For both Charlotte Smith, whose justice in Chancery was delayed until after her death, and for Lord Eldon, who presided over Chancery for much of Smith's litigation, justice was a social norm intimately tied to, but not fully correspondent with, legal practice. While such justice had antecedents in religious authority and local traditions that continued to influence Romantic understanding of the term, "justice" denotes a dependence between those social practices like art and marketing that structure beliefs about fairness, and those legal institutions that intervene within a wide range of social relations by implementing regulations and consequently inculcating abstract ideals of fairness. Late eighteenth-century Britons warily eyed (and influenced) the dramatic legal reforms of revolutionary France and simultaneously absorbed the reverberating discourse of Natural Rights set in motion by the American Revolution. Because "justice" was contested in ways that shaped an emerging national identity, economy, and literature, legal developments infused and depended upon a broadly cultural, often specifically literary context. That law could stray from justice was a theme rampant in literature; Thomas Love Peacock initiates the plot of *Nightmare Abbey* (1818) through this distinction: "Mr. Glowry returned from London with the loss of his law-suit. Justice was with him, but the law was against him" (Peacock 1818/1981: 49). More often, literature revealed an ultimate alignment between the law and justice, even if it required a panoply of unlikely events such as the desperate discovery of lost documents, as in Maria Edgeworth's *Patronage* (1814), or the criminal's own mind disclosing and punishing his guilt, as in Walter Scott's *Ivanhoe* (1819) and *The Iron Chest*, George Colman's (1796) stage adaptation of Godwin's *Caleb Williams*. Even Peacock's Glowry, contemplating his failed lawsuit, understands it as a symptom of "the depravity of this degenerate age," suggesting an earlier time in which law and justice coincided.

Thomas De Quincey, in his legally inflected assessment of Alexander Pope's poetry, insists on both a continuity and tension between judicial and "poetic justice." The latter, he writes, does not mean a justice that differs by its object from the ordinary justice of human jurisprudence:

> it means a justice that differs from common forensic justice by the degree in which it *attains* its object, a justice that is more omnipotent over its own ends, as dealing – not with the refractory elements of earthly life, but with the elements of its own creation, and with materials flexible to its own purest preconceptions. It is certain that, were it not for the Literature of Power, these ideals would often remain amongst us as mere arid notional forms; whereas, by the creative forces of man put forth in literature, they gain a vernal life of restoration, and germinate into vital activities. (De Quincey 1848/1890: 57)

De Quincey argues that a "Literature of Power," embodied most consistently in Homer and Milton, activates the idealism on which justice depends and, by its currency in culture, makes it available to ordinary tribunals, whether courts adjudicating criminal and civil matters, periodical reviews assessing contemporary literature, or daily manners arbitrated in aristocratic drawing rooms. The confluence De Quincey articulates between literature and law, although influenced by contingent factors such as the dynamic presence of legal reformers like Samuel Romilly (who captured the social imagination in ways that paralleled Lord Byron's more spectacular fame), and the various legal crises generated by King George III's putative madness and George IV's marital strife, registered more systematically as a consequence of the emerging modern legal state. Its professionalizing procedures, its development of evidence and trial proceedings, its escalating representations within the public press, and most dramatically, the law's commitment to – and fear of – the economic autonomous subject, necessitated what Terry Eagleton denominates a "legal aesthetics." He observes that this aesthetics helps produce a "human subject" that, "like the work of art itself, discovers the law in the depths of its own free identity, rather than in some oppressive power" (Eagleton 1990: 19). It follows, Eagleton suggests, that "the law becomes the form which shapes into harmonious unity the turbulent content of the subject's appetites and inclinations" (p. 23).

Amid this transformation, law intensifies as a topical object of consumer desire. Trials were watched by capacity crowds and recounted in newspapers and on stages; Gary Dyer has described *Ashford v. Thornton* (1817) in which the defendant, a brutish man accused of murder and rape, declared his right to trial by battle by throwing down a glove; this bizarre trial prompted several plays and pamphlets and influenced *Ivanhoe* (Dyer 1997). The Wordsworths and Coleridge, after attending the trial of John Hatfield, the Keswick Impostor who seduced Mary Robinson, contributed to what Coleridge termed the "counterfeit Hatfields and Marys in abundance – in farces, melodramas, and novels" and other texts (quoted in Gatrell 1994: 335); Mary Robinson thus appears in Wordsworth's *Prelude* as the Maid of Buttermere (Christensen 2000).

Legal machinations also become key plot points for innumerable novels across the political spectrum. In *Caleb Williams*, William Godwin presents analogies between legal institutions and other purveyors of justice. Fleeing his master, the accused Caleb feels compelled to return by Mr Forster's letter: "if your conscience tells you, 'You are innocent,' you will, out of all doubt, come back." Doing so is "of the utmost consequence to your future honour and character" (Godwin 1794/2000: 242). Caleb's private conscience and his public reputation depend on his willingness to enter the machinery of the law, a system that extends across the novel's geographies – from the country estates where landowners serve as Justices of the Peace, to the city prisons that Godwin models on John Howard's sociological *State of the Prisons* (1777), to the mock trial the outlaws perform in the forest, emblem of natural law. Such Jacobin novels not only describe engagements with the law, but acknowledge the legal scrutiny that summons them into political discourse; Godwin – explaining the initial suppression of his "Preface" because of the treason trials of the London Corresponding Society – notes that "Terror was the order of the day; and it was feared that even the humble novelist might be shown to be constructively a traitor" (1794/2000: 56). As Nancy Johnson observes, "This overtly political fiction, published in the volatile 1790s, provides a comprehensive inquiry into the development of a theory of rights which has long been at the core of the relationship between the individual and the law" (Johnson 1994: 99).

The law, through such public representation, acts as a reservoir for metonymies and analogies of general conduct; for example, in Jane Austen's *Mansfield Park* (1814), Edmund characteristically admonishes his elder sister, "In all points of decorum, *your* conduct must be law to the rest of the party" (Austen 1814/2001: 161). In a more satirical mode, Christopher Anstey's son published his dialogue in 1808 between a bookseller and an exasperated author who declares:

> Sure the law would not hang me for taking the pains
> To knock out an ill-judging bookseller's brains! (Anstey 1808: 144–5)

The "author" asserts that the law would look to *poetic* justice on such "pressing occasions" rather than operate by its own inflexible regulations. This couplet both parodies the law's increasing monopoly on justice, in which disputes previously settled by duels, private contracts, or local rituals had become the province of the courts, and signals the law's increasing interest in regulating texts through sedition, libel, copyright, and other common-law practices.

Not only did imaginative literature postulate a relation of law to justice; the legal system itself developed an aesthetics of justice. As the law sought an increasing scope of jurisdiction – incorporating local customs into Common Law, formalizing an array of marriage and contract practices and invalidating others, shifting the spectacle of criminal justice from the execution to the trial – its monopolistic claims articulated "poetic justice" as a supplement of its formalist procedures. For example, in order to aid the developing economy, Chief Justice Mansfield worked to reduce "the doctrine of consideration," in which a contract was validated by an actual physical, bodily event, to "a shadowy and harmless fiction," so that signatures on the contract were sufficient to validate it (Holden 1955: 133). Yet, reduced to a "shadowy and harmless fiction," the doctrine retained an aesthetic force, allowing Mansfield and other judges to continue to claim the authority of precedence. This understanding of contract arises as part of the courts' shift from the body to the text as locus of truth. To achieve such legerdemain, in its displays, procedures, and self-representations, the law integrated a poetics of justice as a strategy of legitimization. Desmond Manderson has argued that "a writ, like a sacrament, is 'iconic'

– what matters is the constant ritual reenactment of the form and not its content or purpose" (Manderson 2000: 38). In this sense, although the specifics of a case – the particular witnesses, the accusation, the jurors – belong to the domain De Quincey characterizes as "forensic justice," its formal elements ritualistically invoke a communal poetic justice grounded in the reiterative structures of language, in the materiality – clothing, architecture, acoustics – of the court, and even in the arcane absurdities of anachronistic legal procedures.

William Blackstone explains in his monumental *Commentaries on the Laws of England* (1765–9) that contemporary judges seek to remodel commercial law, yet must avoid "soliciting any great legislative revolution in the old established forms" (Blackstone 1769/1979, vol. 3: 268). Blackstone has in mind his friend Lord Mansfield who insisted that "the daily negotiations and property of merchants ought not to depend on [legal] subtleties and niceties, but on rules easily learned and easily retained" (quoted in Heward 1979: 101). Blackstone solved this conundrum through a metaphor that enveloped practical forms within poetic justice:

> We inherit an old Gothic castle, erected in the days of chivalry, but fitted up for a modern inhabitant. The moated ramparts, the embattled towers, and the trophied halls, are magnificent and venerable, but useless. The inferior apartments, now converted into rooms of convenience, are chearful and commodious, though their approaches are winding and difficult. (Blackstone 1769/1979, vol. 3: 268)

This metaphor substitutes an image of harmony for a historical antagonism, a rhetorical device that anticipates a displacement that Jerome McGann identifies as characteristic of conservative Romantic ideology. Blackstone's emphasis on aesthetic response delineating a sublime outline – "magnificent and venerable" – and a beautiful interior – "chearful and commodious" – is characteristic of other legal theorists such as David Hume and Edmund Burke, but also recurs in the ritualized language of indictments and other judicial documents. It was, for example, typical of indictments for violent crimes to refer to the devil. Thus, at the start of James Hadfield's trial for treason, he was accused first of "being moved and seduced by the instigation of the devil as a false traitor" against the king; only after this mystical, ritualized language do the "overt acts" – namely purchasing gunpowder and then shooting at the king in a theater – get mentioned (*Trial of James Hadfield* 1800/1820: 1283).

The public perception of trial by jury balanced an aesthetic that intimated idealized consistency and the tactical contingencies by which particular juries were comprised and reached acceptable, unfathomable, or counterfactual verdicts. The jury was of particular significance in the transformation from the body as the site of knowledge to a rational system (constituted through language) in which truth was a professional product applicable equally to the body or other forms of property. For the chivalric practices invoked by Blackstone's gothic metaphor, the truth, whether of guilt, debt, or social status, emerged through rituals of the body such as trial by ordeal and performances of oaths and was confirmed by bodily punishments such as hanging, evisceration, and branding. Despite Blackstone's claim that the jury was an Anglo-Saxon institution that grounded Norman law, the modern jury took shape in the sixteenth and seventeenth century. At the time, the refusal to plead before a jury resulted in a defendant being "put to the *peine forte et dure*: pressed by weights until he either agrees or expires"; in 1772, this invocation of the body was abolished and the "refusal to plead or consent to jury trial" was considered the equivalent of a "plea of guilty" (Bentley 1998: xiii). This movement deemphasizes the body in comparison to the word. The modern legal system, although still insistent on its right to summon both the body of the accused and – by impaneling jurors – the body politic itself, increasingly emphasized verbal evidence, rudimentary expert testimony, and expanded responsibility for lawyers in conducting trials.

In public debate, the reliability of the jury merged with arguments about the consolidation of state power, freedom of the press, and reform movements. Although the genre of the legal novel reached fruition in the Victorian era, in Mary Shelley's *Frankenstein* (1818), Walter Scott's *Heart of Midlothian* (1818), James Hogg's *Confession of a Justified Sinner* (1824), to select novels from an array of genres and political perspectives, jury trials appear in modes that stage the juries as the bearers (or misguided proponents) of common sense. The pseudonymous "R," a letter-writer to the *Gentleman's Magazine* proclaimed in 1792 that the "slender capacities" of juries "scarcely enable them to discriminate plaintiff from defendant" and proposed to limit the role to "gentlemen" who possessed "education, rank, and property" ("R" 1792). The *Gentleman's* conservative argument correlates the standards of reasonableness and representation to sufficient class status. In his *Anecdote Book*, however, Lord Eldon reported a case from that same year that turned on the legal definition of a "gentleman." The judge began his summation to the jury thus:

Mark Schoenfield

> Gentlemen of the jury, when I see you in that box, I call you *gentlemen*, for I know you are such: custom has authorized me: and from your office there, you are entitled to be called *gentlemen*. But out of that box, I do not know what may be deemed the requisites that constitute a *gentleman*: therefore I can give you no direction. (Twiss 1844, vol. 1: 131)

Although here presented whimsically, the right of a jury, *by virtue of being a jury*, to represent and determine the meaning of "gentleman" gestures toward the cultural authority that juries had garnered. Bringing the category of "gentleman" under the law represents a considerable shift from the understanding that gentlemen – in their guises of land-owners, justices of the peace, legislators – made the law.

The tension between classes mitigated in this narrative could also erupt in the disagreements between juries and the conservative judges who dominated the judiciary from the 1790s through the Regency. Edward Law, Lord Ellenborough, presided on three successive days over three separate trials of the radical publisher William Hone for libel. Marcus Wood has demonstrated that the publisher's success – defending himself, Hone achieved three acquittals, despite Ellenborough's insistence on his guilt – stemmed from a rhetoric aligning the jury's class sentiments with his own. "The Verdicts of Three Honest Juries," an 1817 broadside, exults:

> How majestic is Law! How it swells and looks big;
> How tremendous its brow! And how awful its wig!
> But the frowns of a Judge was not valued a fig –
> By the Verdicts of Three Honest Juries, huzza!
> (quoted in Wood 1994: 96)

Punning on "Law" as both the law and Edward Law and on "Honest" as fair yet favoring Hone (hone-est), these lines depict a contest between jury and judge in which the unintimidated jury emerges as the superior reader of Hone's texts and of the social text of justice. In trials actually concerned with texts, such as copyright and libels, cultural norms of representation were vital as a standard and also subject to revision by agents within the trial – defendant, prosecutor, judge, jurors – but representation was at issue in other jury trials as well, including those regarding wills, contracts, and criminal statutes (by which Parliament altered common law).

Public encomia over trial by jury confirmed a self-image of the British citizenry and an aesthetic that valued impartiality, coherence, and rationality. A key legal fiction needed to position juries at the core of English justice was the invention of the "reasonable man" as a standard for interpretation: he was the ideal reader of a contract; the ideal subject who made political representation possible through his collective similarity; the ideal husband into whom a wife, surrendering both rights and property, could be safely gathered; in short, the ideal citizen. The jury provided the means to insert the reasonable man as a unifying figure into a common law that was disparate, contradictory, and uneasy about the distinction between public wrongs (crimes) and private wrongs (torts). As a juror, this figure would act – under the discipline of court procedure, the scrutiny of the press, and the pressure of 11 comrades – without reference to his own allegiances while lawyers, bolstered by the politeness rituals of the court, modeled reasonableness in their rhetoric.

The Lawyer: Public Figure, Parodic Subject

Newspapers in the Romantic period regularly presented trials as stories, complete with descriptions of the scenes, audience reactions, and the characters of the lawyers. Laura Korobkin notes that the narrative structure of trials, especially in opening and closing statements, "utilize preexisting components familiar to their constructors from stories they have read, heard, watched, or told" (Korobkin 1998: 13); in the print culture of Romanticism, these narratives functioned in the dissemination of the court's and the individual lawyer's reputation. Thomas Erskine, regarded as the greatest criminal defense lawyer of the age, repeatedly invoked romance, heroic epic, even journalistic tales. Typically, by inserting himself into his client's story, he would construct a defense lawyer's *Bildungsroman* that finds its completion in the jury's acquittal. In part, the seepage between courtroom and press allowed this strategy. In his unsuccessful defense of Thomas Paine, for example, Erskine refers to the "calumnious clamour, that, by every art, has been raised and kept up against me: In every place, where business or pleasure collect the public together, day after day my name and character have been the topics of injurious reflection." Erskine announces that, despite these attacks, "I have no complaint to make, either against the printers of these libels, nor even against their authors" whether motivated by "honest prejudices" or "personal malice" (Erskine 1813, vol. 1: 276). Such calumny could not influence his decision to defend Paine, because doing so is a matter of his character, a constitutional obligation, and – through the intersection of these

– a defense of the British constitution. Erskine thus shifts the argument from the content of Paine's book to the duty, shared by jurors, judge, and advocates alike, toward the constitution.

In his own narratives, Erskine's defendants appear in a variety of guises. Sometimes he drew on the Jacobin plot of the commoner facing the encroaching monstrosity of a state apparatus – one always carefully distinguished from the present court; other times, the defendant appeared within the domestic comedy of manners, or as the hero defending the shores of a country. Another strategy Erskine used successfully was transmuting a particular case into an example of a general principle. In the trial of James Hadfield (1800), Erskine mounted an insanity defense for Hadfield, who had shot at the king in a theater; apparently, Hadfield thought that God had demanded his own death, and as he would not commit the sin of suicide, he decided that shooting at the king guaranteed his own execution. Thus, as Erskine positions his defense, Hadfield attempts to implicate the court in his madness, by making it the agent of his desire to die; Erskine, himself, however, represents the very moment in which he is speaking as antithetical to such manipulation: "The scene in which we are engaged, and the duty which I am not merely *privileged*, but *appointed* by the authority of the Court to perform, exhibits to the whole civilized world a perpetual monument of our national justice" (Erskine 1813, vol. 1: 497). Erskine's theatrical language – "scene," "perform," "exhibits" – situates the trial as an ideological event that rehearses not only "national justice" but a nation bound together *by* justice. Erskine's defense accumulated pity for the accused. First, his insanity came, according to the expert testimony of a anatomist, from wounds sustained while fighting on behalf of the nation in the service of the King's brother. Second, shortly before going to the theater, he had attacked his child, despite being a dutiful and loving father. These events delicately invoked the King, the defender and beloved patriarchic of the nation, whose own madness haunted the trial. Erskine stars in and stage-manages the trial by telling a variety of stories – comic views of madness run harmlessly astray, solemn recountings of tragic violence from delusions – and thereby mingles public sympathy for the king with his client's pitiable condition.

Between 1770 and 1830, the professionalization of the court occurred unevenly across the geography of Great Britain and its courts of Law, Equity, Consistory, and other administrative ones. But many of the basic dynamics of the shift – and especially the rise of the lawyer – are allegorized in Maria Edgeworth's *Castle Rackrent*

(1800). The overt story, told by "Old Thady," is the decline of the Rackrent family through four successive generations, but the corresponding subplot is the rise of Thady's son Jason, from servant to agent to attorney who, as the novel ends, is poised to consolidate the estate under his ownership. This rise acknowledges the changing dependency of the aristocracy. Servants who, like Thady, regard themselves as part of the family and protect the family's reputation as a desideratum, yielded to professional fee-taking professionals, as the estate's wealth required increasingly sophisticated management. If, under the earlier owner, Sir Patrick, tenant–landlord relations were a matter of custom and handshakes, by Sir Condy's time, these relations are governed by contracts and leases. Early on, the first Sir Rackrent dies and in the midst of his funeral, his "body was seized for debt" by "villains [who] acted under the disguise of the law" (Edgeworth 1800/1999: 11); the body serves as the site at which the truth of the debt is contested, and the heir, Murtagh, "on account of this affront to the body, refused to pay a shilling of the debts, in which he was countenanced by all the best gentlemen of property . . . the moment the law was taken of him, there was an end of honor to be sure" (p. 12).

The authority of "gentlemen of property" adjudicates the domain of honor, and, as the bizarre duel that kills Sir Kit attests, such authority peculiarly combines manners and power. Writing for the *Westminster Review* (July 1825), Charles Hay Cameron found that the justification for dueling, the "reciprocal right of challenge and liability to be challenged," possessed "sufficient reason of all the polish and decorum to be found in our manners" (Cameron 1825: 21). Manners depend on a horizon of violence in which "the honour of a gentleman is in his own keeping and can only be vindicated by his own right hand." The *Westminster* acknowledges the cultural aesthetics that must balance "the wisdom of civilized men" and the threatening horizon of "a recourse to a savage state" (p. 22). Dueling, highly legalistic in its procedures yet in itself illegal, proves a solidifying supplement to a legal system never fully complete. But the duel within *Castle Rackrent* is not merely a quasi-legal procedure, but a metonym for the disciplinary procedures by which class operates on and through the body – including heavy drinking (as a sign of virility), Sir Kit's wife's imprisonment, and the continual deprivations and binges of the peasantry.

The end of the novel, however, discounts the body as a locus of truth, and replaces it with a legal debate, which comes, in place of the ceremonial funeral, "immediately" after Sir Condy's death: "my lady Rackrent . . . and Jason, immediately after my poor master's death, set about going to law about that jointure; the memorandum not being on stamped paper, some say it is worth nothing, others again it may do; others say, Jason won't have the lands at any rate" (Edgeworth 1800/1999: 96). This dispute about the authority of textuality raises questions of both law and equity. The legal issue is whether Condy's "memorandum" is a valid document transferring property to his wife. Rather than "gentlemen" articulating a standard, the debate is between "some" who say yes, and "some" who say no. This indeterminate group constitutes a kind of jury pool. Others, however, argue that regardless of the legal issue, equity – the notion of justice – would prevent Jason's acquiring the land. Debate has replaced the duel; the "memorandum" has displaced the body, the court has carved out a segment of the public discourse for itself, and Edgeworth's parodic mode opens the question of how to value these changes.

Manners, Novels, and Property

Edmund Burke insisted on the necessary connection between justice, national affection, and manners. In *Reflections on the Revolution in France* (1790), he makes this argument by demonstrating not the lawlessness of the new French state, but the disconnection between its proliferating laws – "laws are to be supported only by their own terrors . . . In the groves of *their* academy, at the end of every vista, you see nothing but the gallows" – and its aesthetics, metonymized in the beautiful Marie Antoinette (Burke 1790/2001: 240). Her rude treatment verified that "the age of chivalry is gone." Burke, echoing Blackstone, invokes "chivalry" as the aesthetic horizon for power experienced not as coercion but through a sentimental grasp of justice:

> [The] public affections, combined with manners, are required sometimes as supplements, sometimes as correctives, always as aids to law. The precept given by a wise man, as well as a great critic, for the construction of poems, is equally true as to states: – *Non satis est pulchra esse poemata, dulcia sunto.* There ought to be a system of manners in every nation, which a well-formed mind would be disposed to relish. To make us love our country, our country ought to be lovely. (Burke 1790/2001: 241)

Burke quotes Horace's *Ars poetica* to insist that the aesthetics of the state mirror that of poetry. The formal arrangements, the ornamentation, the balance of the sublime and the beautiful contribute not only to the manners of a nation, but to the metonymic chain that renders laws consistent with desire and affection. Decrying the fate of the French monarchy and focusing on the disordered crowd that seizes the queen of France, Burke plies the connections between the aesthetic and the judicial: "Justice is grave and decorous, and in its punishments rather seems to submit to a necessity, than to make a choice" (Burke 1790/2001: 83).

Building on David Hume's analogy between justice and manners, the former operating in the public domain and the latter functioning among friendships, Burke, in his "First Letter on a Regicide Peace," asserted continuity between manners and laws rooted in bodily aesthetic response:

> Manners are of more importance than laws. Upon them, in great measure, the laws depend. The law touches us but here and there, and now and then. Manners are what vex or soothe, corrupt or purify, exalt or debase, barbarize or refine us, by a constant, steady, uniform insensible operation, like that of the air we breathe in. They give their whole form and colour to our lives. (Burke 1796: 242)

As David Kaufmann notes of Austen's *Sense and Sensibility*, this widely accepted analogy validated a novelistic recourse to metaphors of the law to explain judgments within smaller spheres. Thus Austen's heroines Elinor Dashwood, Emma Woodhouse, Fanny Price, and Elizabeth Bennett all use terms of "acquittal" and guilt in considering the manners and behavior of potential suitors. From Austen's perspective, an appropriate individualism represented a coherent engagement with the prescribed world of manners, and a continual recognition that laws, both civil and criminal, impinged upon that world. In *Pride and Prejudice* (1813), after Darcy's rejected marriage proposal, he writes Elizabeth an exculpatory letter explaining his behavior toward Wickham; he begins by asking that she "pardon the freedom with which I demand your attention; your feelings, I know, will bestow it unwillingly, but I demand it of your justice" (Austen 1813/2002: 219). Justice here is predicated on a social responsibility that, like that of the juror, is indifferent to individual sentiment; Darcy asserts a right – replicating *habeas corpus* – to be heard before a competent tribunal (Elizabeth's competency is emphasized in references to her sense, judgment, and reason). Darcy's defense registers legal conundrums of the day. He asserts, "Of what he has particularly accused me, I am ignorant; but of the truth of what I shall relate, I can summon more than one witness of undoubted veracity"; Darcy invokes the ancient right to know the charges against him, a right that received current attention as criminal jurisdiction began providing defendants with copies of indictments prior to the trial. As Elizabeth considers Darcy's testimony and contrasts it with Wickham's assertions, she is positioned as a juror determining the credibility of evidence; struck by Wickham's "impropriety," "indelicacy," and "inconsistency," terms that modulate between legal and aesthetic registers, Elizabeth acquits Darcy and finally acknowledges her feelings for him.

"Individualism" persisted in the Romantic period simultaneously as "a social mechanism," as P. S. Atiyah has observed, and as "a value-based ideal, an aspiration" (Atiyah 1979: 256). Among the specific legal interventions that helped construct individual autonomy as a social practice were the development of an array of contractual options and the court's increasing suspicion of entails – wills or deeds that restricted the sale of property and directed its inheritance in perpetuity. Because they bound property to the desires of its prior owners, entails deprived current owners of flexibility in the use or sale of the property. Although intended to provide social stability, they were clumsy mechanisms for an increasingly mobile economy. In *Pride and Prejudice*, the feudal arrangement of the "entail," by which Mr Bennett's daughters will find themselves dispossessed, represents an ancient patriarchy that impinges on the present. When Mrs Bennett complains, "There is no knowing how estates will go when once they come to be entailed," she indicates that the anachronistic legal instrument produces the uncertainty that, within feudal arrangements, it is meant to forestall – the uncertainty of inheritance (Austen 1813/2002: 100). If, for feudalism, the stability of property was the central tenet of the law, under the regime of emerging capital, the fluidity of property – dependent upon widened contractual rights – represents a new legal landscape.

Among the most dramatic alterations in the law was the expansion of contract law. "Shortly after 1800 the very concept of contract in English law and theory changed its character, and the executory contract became the paradigm of contract theory" (Atiyah 1979: 420). An executory contract was enforceable once the contract had been executed based on the declared intent of competent parties, without additional consideration, action, or ritual. The replacement of the marriage or family entailment as the paradigm for contract with the executory contract meant a further emphasis on individual choice that aligned marriage law with individualism. The judge William Scott, considering a husband's claim for an annulment based on his insanity when the marriage was contracted, argued that in contract law, a party can certainly use a "defect of incapacity" to "invalidate a contract of marriage, [just] as well as any other contract." He acknowledges, and rebukes, contrary and "obscure dicta, in earlier commentaries" that "prevailed in the dark ages, of the mysterious nature of the contract of marriage, in which its spiritual nature almost entirely obliterated its civil character" (*English Reports* 1900: 601).

The familial space marked by the ideology of executory contract reorganized, and in some ways intensified, patriarchal hegemony. The increased freedom of women to choose their spouses became part of the mechanism of gender control. Within the household, measured speech and enforced silence became an analogue to the freely chosen status as civil *femme covert* (literally, "covered woman," and referring to a married woman's status of having her rights bound into her husband's), a choice which constrained public speech – the making of contracts, wills, and even libels. In *Evans v. Evans*, William Scott explained that the court's insistence on the rigid enforcement of marital contracts served "the greater and more general good": Spouses "become good husbands and good wives, from the necessity of remaining husbands and wives; for necessity is a powerful master in teaching the duties which it imposes" (*English Reports* 1900: 467). The law here coerces manners, or at least the appearance of manners, based on the initial freedom of electing the contract (despite the social pressures that impinged on this choice). Scott repeatedly remonstrated about domestic civility, and although rhetorically, he directs this towards both husband and wives, the material effects of his rulings consistently regulated women more strictly than men. In *Soilleux v. Soilleux* (1802), the wife sues for divorce primarily on the grounds of adultery (although cruelty is also alleged). She runs a girls' boarding school and has five daughters; in such a household, Scott insists, "the purest manners ought to be observed by every person in it; particularly by him [the husband], whose example was likely to have so much influence" (*English Reports* 1900: 586). Although Scott rebukes the husband, the case's villain turns out to be Mary Wiltshire, whom Soilleux seduced (had he simply continued repeated unsuccessful efforts to seduce women, there would have been neither adultery nor grounds for divorce). Scott's train of reasoning turns on the compliance of Wiltshire to the norms of feminine speech on behalf of ideals of virtue:

> Before this period her master had persecuted her with the same odious addresses, and she had complained of them; but after this discovery she makes no complaint, nor expresses any uneasiness whatsoever. Is that

the conduct of a person who is averse to the gross importunities of such a man? . . . [Complaint] is the natural and necessary conduct of an innocent woman in such a situation. (*English Reports* 1900: 587)

The boarding school is a metonym of the new economy, in which women have economic and social potential that must be constrained by concomitant obligations. What is "natural" for a woman is consequently and equally "necessary." Justice, as both a concept and a cultural invocation of national affection, allowed for an abstract discourse in which the "natural" and "necessary" could be continually realigned, in keeping with new economic imperatives, even in the midst of public disagreement about what counted as either natural or necessary. If Austen's novels explore, in the realm of manners, the rhetoric of the natural and the necessary, then Austen – and indeed the entire genre of the novel of manners – draws on and contests legal paradigms as much as the more overt Jacobin novel. To be a woman, as to be an author, was to have an identity constructed under the regime of the law.

For the modern individual, the law both enabled and restricted modes of being. It permeated social and private spaces, and shaped the rhetoric of nationhood. While many writers challenged the practice of law or the operation of specific laws, literature as a whole represented an ideal of justice that both individuals and institutions could strive to occupy. Without the literary representation of justice, legal institutions would not have developed as they did, underpinning the individual as a bearer of rights and property and securing the modern author. At the same time, such literary representations foreclosed more radical transformations and possibilities by grounding their realism, and even romance, on norms of "the rational man."

References and Further Reading

Anstey, Christopher. (1808) "Appendix: Containing the Author's Conversation with His Bookseller," in *The Poetical Works of the Late Christopher Anstey*, ed. John Anstey (pp. 167–86). London: Cadell and Davies.

Atiyah, P. S. (1979) *The Rise and Fall of Freedom of Contract*. New York: Oxford University Press.

Austen, Jane. (1813/2002) *Pride and Prejudice*, ed. Robert Irvine. New York: Broadview Press.

Austen, Jane. (1814/2001) *Mansfield Park*, ed. June Sturrock. New York: Broadview Press.

Barr, Mark. (2005) "The Lyric Dispensation: Coleridge, Mosaic Law, and Equivocal Authority in 'The Eolian Harp'," *Studies in Romanticism* 44: 293–316.

Barrell, John. (2000) *Imagining the King's Death: Figurative Treason, Fantasies of Regicide 1793–96.* New York: Oxford University Press.

Bentley, David. (1998) *English Criminal Justice in the Nineteenth Century.* London: Hambledon Press.

Blackstone, William. (1765–9/1979) *Commentaries on the Laws of England: A Facsimile of the First Edition*, 4 vols. Chicago: Chicago University Press.

Burke, Edmund. (1790/2001) *Reflections on the Revolution in France*, ed. J. C. D. Clark. Stanford, CA: Stanford University Press.

Burke, Edmund. (1796/1991) "First Letter on a Regicide Peace," in *The Writings and Speeches of Edmund Burke*, ed. R. B. McDowell and William Todd, 9 vols (vol. 9, pp. 187–264). Oxford: Clarendon Press.

Cameron, Charles Hay. (1825) "British Code of Duel; A Reference to the Laws of Honour and the Character of Gentleman," *Westminster Review* 4: 20–32.

Christensen, Jerome. (2000) "Romantic Hope: The Maid of Buttermere, the Right to Write, and the Future of Liberalism," in *Romanticism at the End of History* (pp. 129–52). Baltimore: Johns Hopkins University Press.

Combe, William. (1815/1903) "The Catchpole," in *The English Dance of Death* (pp. 127–35). London: Methuen.

De Quincey, Thomas. (1848/1890) "The Poetry of Pope," in *The Collected Writings of Thomas De Quincey*, ed. David Masson (vol. 11, pp. 51–95). Edinburgh: Black.

Dyer, Gary. (1997) "*Ivanhoe*, Chivalry and the Murder of Mary Ashford," *Criticism* 39: 388–408.

Eagleton, Terry. (1990) *The Ideology of the Aesthetic.* Oxford: Blackwell.

Edgeworth, Maria. (1800/1999) *Castle Rackrent, An Hibernian Tale*, ed. G. Watson. New York: Oxford University Press.

Eldon, Lord, John Scott. (1960) *Lord Eldon's Anecdote Book*, ed. A. L. J. Lincoln and R. McEwen. London: Stevens & Sons.

English Reports. (1900) [Reprint of English court reports from 1220 to 1866] Ed. A. Wood Renton et al., 176 vols., vol. 161. London: Stevens.

Ennis, Daniel. (2002) *Enter the Press-Gang: Naval Impressments in Eighteenth-Century British Literature.* Newark: University of Delaware Press.

Erskine, Thomas. (1813) *The Speeches of the Hon. T. Erskine*, ed. Thomas Ridgway, 5 vols. New York: Eastburn, Kirk, and Co.

Fluck, Winfried. (2003) "Fiction and Justice," *New Literary History* 34: 19–42.

Gatrell, V. A. C. (1994) *The Hanging Tree: Execution and the English People, 1770–1868.* New York: Oxford University Press.

Godwin, William. (1794/2000) *Caleb Williams*, ed. G. Handwork and A. A. Markley. New York: Broadview Press.

Hankinson, Knut. (1981) *The Science of a Legislator: The Natural Jurisprudence of David Hume and Adam Smith.* New York: Cambridge University Press.

Hessen, Carla. (1991) "Enlightenment Epistemology and the Laws of Authorship in Revolutionary France, 1777–1793," in Robert Post (ed.), *Law and the Order of Culture* (pp. 109–37). Los Angeles: University of California Press.

Heward, Edmund. (1979) *Lord Mansfield*. London: Barry Rose.

Holden, J. M. (1955) *The History of Negotiable Instruments in English Law*. London: University of London Press.

Holdsworth, William. (1956–82) *A History of English Law*, ed. A. L. Goodhart and H. G. Hanbury, 7th edn, 17 vols. London: Methuen.

Johnson, Nancy. (1994) "Rights, Property and the Law in the English Jacobin Novel," *Mosaic* 27: 99–120.

Kaufmann, David. (1992) "Law and Propriety, *Sense and Sensibility*: Austen on the Cusp of Modernity," *ELH* 59: 385–404.

Klancher, Jon. (1987) *The Making of English Reading Audiences, 1790–1832*. Madison: University of Wisconsin Press.

Korobkin, Laura. (1998) *Criminal Conversations: Sentimentality and Nineteenth-Century Legal Stories of Adultery*. New York: Columbia University Press.

Manderson, Desmond. (2000) *Songs without Music: Aesthetic Dimensions of Law and Justice*. Berkeley, CA: University of California Press.

O'Reilly-Fleming, Thomas. (2001) "From Beasts to Bedlam: Hadfield, the Regency Crisis, McNaughton and the 'Mad' Business in Britain, 1788–1843," in Jane Moriarty (ed.), *The Role of Mental Illness in Criminal Trials* (pp. 103–26). New York: Routledge.

Peacock, Thomas Love. (1818, 1831/1981) *Nightmare Abbey and Crotchet Castle*, ed. R. Wright. New York: Penguin.

Pocock, J. G. A. (1985) *Virtue, Commerce, and History*. New York: Cambridge University Press.

Polanyi, Karl. (1944/1957) *The Great Transformation: The Political and Economic Origins of Our Time*. Boston: Beacon.

"R." [pseudonym]. (1792) "Imperfections of Juries," *Gentleman's Magazine* 72: 1194.

Robinson, Mary. (1799/2003) *The Natural Daughter; With Portraits of the Leadenhead Family*. In *A Letter to the Women of England and The Natural Daughter*, ed. Sharon Setzer. New York: Broadview Press.

Rose, Mark. (1993) *Authors and Owners: The Invention of Copyright*. Cambridge, MA: Harvard University Press.

Rose, Mark. (1998) "The Author as Proprietor: *Donaldson v. Becket* and the Genealogy of Modern Authorship," *Representations* 23: 51–85.

Schoenfield, Mark. (1996) *The Professional Wordsworth: Law, Labor, and the Poet's Contract*. Athens: University of Georgia Press.

Smith, Charlotte. (1793/2002) *The Old Manor House*, ed. Jacqueline Labbe. New York: Broadview Press.

Smith, Charlotte. (1797/1993) *Elegiac Sonnets*, 8th edn. In *The Poems of Charlotte Smith*, ed. Stuart Curran. New York: Oxford University Press.

Trial of James Hadfield. (1800/1820) In *A Complete Collection of State Trials*, compiled by T. B. Howell et al. (vol. 27, pp. 1281–1356). London: T. C. Hansard.

Twiss, Horace. (1844) *The Public and Private Life of Lord Chancellor Eldon, with Selections from his Correspondence*, 3 vols. London: J. Murray.

Wood, Marcus. (1994) "Radicals and the Law: Blasphemous Libels and the Three Trials of William Hone," in *Radical Satire and Print Culture* (pp. 96–154). Oxford: Clarendon Press.

Woodmansee, Martha. (1984) "The Genius and the Copyright: Economic and Legal Conditions for the Emergence of the 'Author,'" *Eighteenth-Century Studies* 17: 425–48.

Zimmerman, Sarah. (1999) *Romanticism, Lyricism, and History*. Albany: State University of New York Press.

Chapter 7

Natural History in the Romantic Period

Noah Heringman

By the 1760s, men and women in Great Britain, and throughout Europe, were practicing various life and earth sciences in a wide range of social settings. The umbrella term "natural history" defined this large body of practices, understood not as "science" but as a descriptive approach to the study of nature that included collecting (and/or selling) specimens, classifying them, and writing and reading natural history texts. Natural philosophy, in its prestigious Newtonian form, provided the explanatory counterpart to natural history; for some contemporaries natural history was only a supplement to the laws of nature posited by Newtonian physics. Before 1800, natural history was not evolutionary and even today can still be understood "without reference to time" (*OED*), in a sense that survives from the Latin root *historia*. But as its popularity grew, the status and temporal scope of natural history expanded dramatically. By the mid-eighteenth century natural history already had a celebrity to rival Newton, in the Swedish professor Carolus Linnaeus. The vast influence of Linnaeus's *System of Nature* (1735) eventually led to new applications of natural knowledge in domains ranging from mining to colonial plant transfer – both especially crucial to Britain's global influence in the late eighteenth century. By the early nineteenth century new institutions were in place for the study of life and earth sciences, and a protoevolutionary concept of deep time had emerged from the natural history of fossils. I hope to show in this essay that natural history in its persistent popular forms also provided a forum for critical engagement with institutionalized science, a critical engagement far more sophisticated than the unreflective hostility often (wrongly) attributed to Wordsworth and other Romantic poets.

"The Favourite Science"

Followers of Linnaeus in England included many humble fieldworkers and collectors as well as wealthy amateurs who became celebrities in their own right, including the Duchess of Portland (Margaret Bentinck), Thomas Pennant, and Sir Joseph Banks. The Scottish naturalist Robert Ramsay praised Pennant's work in glowing terms in 1772, concluding that "Natural History is, at present, the favourite science over all Europe, and the progress which has been made in it will distinguish and characterise the 18th century in the annals of literature" (Ramsay 1772: 174). A later assessment confirms that the years around 1770 were seminal for the careers of Pennant and Banks and for natural history in general: "Natural history was [then] succeeding ... to much of that transcendent popularity among the learned which natural philosophy had, for the last hundred years, almost exclusively possessed" ("Sir Joseph Banks" 1807: 377). This 1801 essay credits two important patrons with the triumph of natural history during the last quarter of the eighteenth century: Linnaeus (1707–78), who among other achievements developed the binomial nomenclature still used in the life sciences today; and George III, the "farmer King" who ascended the throne in 1760 with the promise that "science, learning, and, in particular, natural history, and distant discovery, would long be in honour at court" (p. 378). Sir James Edward Smith, who founded the Linnaean Society in London in 1788, declared in his inaugural *Discourse on the Rise and Progress of Natural History* that he was "induced to consider the present age as one of the most propitious to the study of Nature" (Smith 1798: 152). William Smellie's 1100-page *Philosophy of Natural History* (1790–99) also includes a narrative of progress in which living British naturalists have taken the lead in "enriching the science of Natural History" with new methods and new discoveries (Smellie 1799: 74).

Smellie, unlike the three other naturalists, did not belong to a social elite. But despite the difference in social class, Smellie concurred with Pennant, Banks, and Smith that natural history was the "favourite" or characteristic science and literature of their time. Many people who lacked a classical education, social status, or money to amass equipment and specimen collections also practiced natural history during George's reign (1760–1820). Traditional and economically necessary practices of rural working men and women – such as gathering medicinal plants, showing caves and other "natural wonders" to urban tourists, or collecting fossils for sale – were increasingly recognized and incorporated as natural history. As the achievement of an outsider who earned his place in the scientific and literary establishment, Smellie's career exemplifies another vital aspect of Romantic natural history: it was accessible. Smellie's *Philosophy* sets out to "save . . . time and study" (1799: 77) for readers who are not equipped to amass and read all the primary literature – readers perhaps not unlike the youthful Smellie himself, who studied natural history on the side as a printer's apprentice and then made himself an expert when his newly founded printing firm produced the first edition of the *Encyclopaedia Britannica* (1768–71).

Today natural history no longer has a stable disciplinary identity like the five bodies of scientific knowledge described by Frederick Burwick elsewhere in this volume. These and other specialized disciplines have become dominant, but the protean inclusiveness of natural history lingers on, and provides one argument for thinking about natural history as the quintessential Romantic science. Major public collections, especially in France, introduced forms of display that still endure in a more typically Victorian institution, the natural history museum (cf. Spary 2000: 221). Now science is understood to operate behind the scenes at these museums, producing nature for the public: this culture of expertise, too, took shape in the Romantic period. The period abounded with popularizing works of natural history, ranging from didactic and encyclopedic works in prose, such as Smellie's, to Romantic poems, including Erasmus Darwin's *The Botanic Garden*, Charlotte Smith's *Beachy Head* (discussed at length in this essay) and William Blake's *The Book of Thel* (a parody of such works). The range of popular and learned periodicals on scientific subjects broadened significantly in the 1790s. Smith justified the creation of the Linnaean Society and its publications by arguing that the *Philosophical Transactions of the Royal Society of London* could no longer hold all the new discoveries in natural history (Smith 1798: 156). Banks, as president of the Royal Society from 1778, promoted natural history as a focus of that body, but nevertheless the growth of natural history prompted the separate creation not only of the Linnaean Society – which covered two of the traditional "branches" of natural history, botany and zoology – but also of the Geological Society (1807), which covered the third branch, mineralogy, and consolidated it with other currents in earth science. A proliferation of smaller natural history societies around the country helped to maintain inclusiveness and variety (Knell 2000, cf. Roche 1996).

This tremendous diffusion of natural history was driven by another crucial factor: exploration. The voyage of Captain Cook on the *Endeavour* (1768–71) was one of the first explicitly scientific voyages of discovery and remains unique for its privately funded research operations in natural history. Banks brought a staff of eight on the voyage and took full advantage of the collecting opportunities presented by Polynesia, New Zealand, and Australia, whose fauna, flora, and minerals were virtually unknown to Europeans at that time. Although the *Endeavour* voyage was soon followed by many other distinguished voyages of discovery, Smith still refers to it in 1788 as "that celebrated voyage round the world" (p. 151), expecting his listeners to know which one he means. Smith's reference becomes more clear as he goes on to claim (patriotically) that Britain's public collections in natural history – the "natural history cabinet" of the British Museum and the Royal Botanical Gardens at Kew – are the best in the world: these collections both drew heavily on the collection that Banks amassed on this voyage and continued to augment by mobilizing collectors around the globe. The professional life science research that operates behind the scenes today at natural history museums still bears the imprint of wealthy amateurs such as Banks and Smith who transformed the learned societies into scientific institutions. Today's amateur naturalists also carry on the tradition of self-educated researchers such as Smellie and occasionally they still make their mark in a highly professionalized scientific community: one recent example is the discovery of the tyrannosaur "Sue" by commercial fossil dealers Susan Hendrickson and Peter L. Larson in 1990.

The flowering of natural history is an essential aspect of Romanticism because natural history was, among other things, a major literary genre: it was both a literary and a scientific practice based on fieldwork. A great many authors in the Romantic period, including the Romantic poets, wrote on natural history in one form or another. The rural clergyman Gilbert White, like most naturalists at the time, wrote innumerable letters containing queries and observations. By collecting and editing his own letters to Thomas Pennant and another prominent naturalist, he created the classic of the natural history genre: *The Natural History and Antiquities of Selborne* (1789). White's brother and publisher, the London bookseller Benjamin White, specialized in natural history and also published works by Pennant and others. Smith's *Discourse* refers to the Linnaean and Royal Societies repeatedly as "literary societies," and Smellie, in his *Philosophy*, analyzes natural history as a species of "composition" (II.2). Smellie was also a major popularizer: he produced the first English translation (1780–5) of the most important and widely read work of natural history in eighteenth-century Europe, the Comte de Buffon's *Histoire naturelle*. The most popular natural history in England, also inspired by Buffon, was Oliver Goldsmith's *History of the Earth and Animated Nature* (1774 and many later editions), a colorful synthesis of modern and premodern sources. One group of scholars has even proposed a new way of dating Romanticism based on events in the history of science, 1768–1833 (Fulford, Lee, and Kitson 2004: 4–5). Major cultural events (such as the *Endeavour* voyage) provide one important avenue for explaining the close historical relationship between Romanticism and natural history; so too do analytic categories such as colonialism (Bewell 2004) and print culture (Yeo 2001, O'Connor 2007). The proliferation of new learned societies is also critical because these institutions – with their lectures, collections, and numerous publications – inaugurated the specialized disciplines associated with modern science, and because they were clearly understood at the time as redrawing the literary landscape.

The next section takes up this redrawing of boundaries primarily in terms of the conflict between natural history and natural philosophy, but one of its consequences – the increasing demand for writing based closely on fieldwork – is also clearly linked to the practice of such writers as William and Dorothy Wordsworth and John Clare. After turning to print culture and colonialism in the following sections, the essay concludes with a brief study of one poem, Charlotte Smith's *Beachy Head*, that touches on all three of these domains and suggests some reasons why natural history has not, until recently, influenced the "annals of literature" as Robert Ramsay expected.

Natural History and Natural Philosophy

Well into the nineteenth century, the English reading public and even most "scientists" (as they began to call themselves in 1833) still thought primarily in terms of two larger domains of natural knowledge: natural history and natural philosophy (comprising physics, astronomy, and aspects of chemistry and medicine). Our story begins with the conflict between these two domains. According to one postmodern historian, "disciplines are political structures that mediate crucially between the political economy and the production of knowledge" (Lenoir 1997: 47). On this view, the rise of natural history in Britain – its ramification into disciplines – would be tied to the growth of the British Empire, which came to dominate political economy in the later eighteenth century. Natural history was vital for the classification, redistribution, and economic exploitation of "new" plants, animals, and minerals from colonial territories. At the same time, consensus on the scope of natural philosophy began to weaken; according to Richard Yeo, the term was "already under stress by 1765" (Yeo 1999: 321). Some thinkers continued to see natural history as "the poor relative of natural philosophy" (p. 325), partly because they saw it as merely descriptive, whereas Newtonian natural philosophy actually explained the forces of nature. Nonetheless, natural philosophy eventually yielded to more specialized physical science disciplines at least partly because of the increasing influence of natural history.

Romantic-era specialization also ensured the survival of more popular forms of natural history, though arguably at the cost of their perceived rigor. Natural history today – from bird-watching to museum-going to nature writing to the more expert narratives of Stephen Jay Gould – owes something both to the early nineteenth-century division of labor that gradually marginalized popular practice and to Romanticism as traditionally understood, as a form of nonspecialist nature writing. Samuel Taylor Coleridge was one of a number of systematic idealist thinkers who supported the unified ideal of natural philosophy and opposed scientific specialization. But the same slow, seemingly inevitable process that fragmented natural philosophy also gradually produced various earth, plant, and animal sciences in place of the three traditional branches of natural history, while the name "natural history" stuck to a set of ostensibly unrigorous cultural practices. Arguably, natural history is the older science: both its empirical and its literary components can be traced to the *Naturalis Historia* of Pliny the Elder (23–79 CE) and to the Renaissance revival of classical learning. But as natural history was revived, natural philosophy as handed down from Aristotle was completely transformed by Copernicus and his followers, especially by Isaac Newton, and became a competing disciplinary structure based on a formal, mathematical language for physical and astronomical knowledge. Life sciences and physical sciences have continued to compete for dominance even as more and more specialized and hybrid forms have surfaced: these transformations help to explain why "natural history ... seems to have come to an end so often," as James Secord has put it (J. Secord 1996: 449).

Noah Heringman

In 1778 Sir Joseph Banks became president of the Royal Society, assuming the office held by Newton from 1703–27: to all interested contemporaries, this change powerfully signified that natural history was gaining ground on the prestige of natural philosophy. The same contemporary biographer who described the once "transcendent" but now threatened popularity of natural philosophy summed up Banks's accomplishments in the first half of his career:

> That the culture of the breadfruit tree has been successfully introduced into our West India isles; that the colony in New South Wales has been reared to its present prosperity; that the natural history of the great territory of New Holland is continually more and more explored; and that even amidst the wars which now desolate the earth, the general commerce of men of learning and science is not entirely interrupted; are so many benefits, for which the warmest gratitude of philanthropy and science is due to Sir Joseph Banks. ("Sir Joseph Banks" 1807: 405)

Other eighteenth-century presidents, such as Sir Hans Sloane, were interested in natural history, but Banks promoted it as a piece of the society's agenda. Thomas Pennant was one Fellow of the Royal Society who lobbied for a greater emphasis on natural history, and the science benefited greatly from Banks's private activities as a collector and networker, alluded to in the quotation above. But Banks evidently had little interest or ability in mathematical sciences and published very little of his own research. Many members of the society therefore resented Banks deeply: they published pamphlets against him and circulated reports that he was nothing more than a wealthy amateur using the position to promote his class interests. Banks had been eagerly lampooned in cartoons and in verse when he returned on the *Endeavour* in 1771, and a new crop of satirists were happy to publicize the conflicts in the Royal Society, which became known as the Dissensions of 1783–4.

Banks's social status and influence within the controversial government of George III help to explain the broad public interest in scientific politics suggested by the more than two dozen satires against him that were published by 1790. Banks's promotion of natural history formally linked the pursuit of natural knowledge with the expansion of the British Empire, and hence politicized not only the Royal Society but also the public discourse about science, which became more closely tied to the interests of the social elite who stood to benefit the most from imperial expansion. This link to colonialism provides one item in the formidable catalogue of objections to natural history brought to light

Figure 1 "The Natural___ist." Anonymous engraving from "Simon Snip," *The Philosophical Puppet Show* (London, 1785). Courtesy of Special Collections, Lehigh University Libraries, Bethlehem, Pennsylvania, USA.

by the controversy of 1783–4, which showed that natural history could be both popular and tremendously unsettling at the same time.

The frontispiece to one of the satires, *The Philosophical Puppet Show* (Figure 1), dramatizes many of these objections. Banks is seated on a throne, signifying his abuse of the presidency in the service of a social elite; in fact, one of his policies was to admit some fellows on the basis of their wealth, with the idea that they would patronize research – a reasonable position in an academy that did not enjoy state funding, as those in Paris and other European capitals did. But the legend on the dais declares that ignorance, arrogance, and pride form the basis of Banks's power. The dunce's cap signifies that he is more a "natural" – in the colloquial sense of "half-witted person" (*OED*) – than a naturalist. The magnifying glasses suggest a narrowly empirical interest in minutiae. Banks's specimen, the suspiciously phallic marine shell, reminds the cartoon's audience of his South Sea voyage on the *Endeavour*, which had involved much-publicized sexual adventures with native women on Tahiti. On Banks's left, King George approaches with a letter to the Tahitian queen, suggesting that the government is allowing Banks too much authority over colonial policy. Critics of Linnaean "sexual botany" – the system promoted by Banks, Erasmus Darwin, and many others – routinely conflated human sexual excesses with Linnaeus's hugely successful method of classifying plants by the number of "male" stamens and "female" pistils in their flowers (Bewell 1996). Apart from their erotic aspects, the various specimens depicted in this scene further suggest that Banks's natural history is a mere connoisseurial interest in curiosities, while their presentation by the two figures on the left evokes Banks's network as a system of collecting tribute from the colonies. Limitations of space prohibit full discussion of this image, but most of its details are clarified by the accompanying 37-page text, a puppet play preceded by a lengthy preface by the supposed author, "Simon Snip, FRS," a tailor and puppeteer (see also Fara 1997).

Ironically, the accessibility that made natural history so popular in print and in practice during the Romantic period proved a tremendous liability to Banks, who was charged more or less unjustly with intellectual unfitness for more rigorous science: "Preach not to me of theoretic art; / I – like a whore – profess the practic part," declares the Banks puppet in the play (Snip 1663: 17). The twentieth-century distinction between pure and applied science might also help to explain this charge: although applied physics certainly had its imperial uses, in navigation especially, some natural philosophers placed an absolute

Natural History in the Romantic Period

priority on "pure" mathematical forms of inquiry and condemned the seemingly vulgar life sciences. The pamphlets and satires on Banks count as natural history publications only in a secondary sense. But the controversy underscores the richly paradoxical situation of Romantic natural history: Banks was chastised at the same time both for being elitist and for corrupting polite learning with a "low" cultural practice accessible to all.

Natural History and Print Culture

The crucial distinction between natural history and natural philosophy was that the former called for fieldwork, the component that kept natural knowledge accessible to a generalist public, both in the field and on the printed page (Yeo 2001: 64–5, 136, Jardine 1991: ch. 1). Relatively little life-science research during the heyday of natural history was conducted in the laboratory. Identification and description in the field were essential, if in somewhat different ways, for both the laborer spending his Sunday in the fields outside Manchester and the ambitious young naturalist sent overseas by a learned society to contribute to the Linnaean classification of global nature. While "artisan botanists," as Anne Secord calls them, had much more limited access to publication, both kinds of fieldwork gained publicity from the burgeoning domestic tour genre, which often featured natural history (A. Secord 1996). In *Beachy Head* (1807), Charlotte Smith pointedly took a geological description from Gilbert White's local narrative rather than drawing on philosophical theories of the earth, and she developed a profitable sideline in didactic works on natural history. Wordsworth and Coleridge, themselves promoters of domestic tourism, were also (with Byron) among the enthusiastic readers of Alexander von Humboldt's celebrated narratives describing his exploration of South American natural and cultural history (1799–1804).

The map of learning for general readers ramified into more and more branches and various print publications competed to give them an overview. The encyclopedia and the middlebrow journal represent two of the available schemes for conceptualizing the system of knowledge as a whole. Both of these differed from the increasingly professional and compartmentalized view of natural knowledge that gave rise to the British Association for the Advancement of Science in 1833; and they differed as well from the encyclopedic philosophy of German Idealism promoted by Coleridge. The *Encyclopaedia Britannica* was first published in 1771 and was in its third edition by 1797. William Smellie gave a significant emphasis to natural history in compiling the first edition and the number of related entries continued to grow. A prospectus declared that in the second edition, "Natural History . . . will be found more fully, more accurately, and more scientifically detailed, than in any other Dictionary whatever" (*A New Edition* 1788: 5). Richard Yeo has shown that the third edition relied much less on compilers and capitalized instead on the desire of expert contributors to give their particular specializations an official presence (Yeo 2001: 184–5). But cost increased with length, and the *Britannica*'s Enlightenment premise also became subject to critique: philosophers including F. W. J. von Schelling, Coleridge, and G. W. F. Hegel (in his own *Encyclopedia* of 1816–32) questioned the encyclopedia's exhaustive analysis of knowledge, privileging instead a unified view of knowledge as process (Rajan 2004: 6). The new periodicals took specialization for granted, but created what might be termed a mosaic of knowledge in process by including monthly items from as many as possible of the proliferating subfields of both natural history and natural philosophy.

Two natural history-related journals from the Romantic period have been published continuously ever since: William Curtis's *Botanical Magazine* (founded 1787) and *The Philosophical Magazine* (founded 1798), now strictly a physics journal. The early specialization of Curtis's magazine attests to the popularity of botany in particular, while *The Philosophical Magazine* contributed to the popularization not only of astronomy, chemistry, and physics, but also of natural history in all its branches, as well as industrial technology. This journal merits a brief case study in part because it absorbed two competitors (in 1814 and 1828) that had long and successful runs of their own. The editor, Alexander Tilloch, included many new discoveries of plants and animals around the globe, often excerpting or translating the highly literary descriptions of the naturalists and travelers who made them. But *The Philosophical Magazine* was not an amateur publication in the pejorative sense. The majority of contributions – many by distinguished naturalists such as J. F. Blumenbach, H. B. de Saussure, and Humphry Davy – were reprinted from a stunning variety of British, Continental, and American learned journals. More important, Tilloch kept his readers abreast of developments on the Continent during the long years of war with France, when French periodicals themselves were extremely difficult to obtain and other English sources were scarce. For example, Tilloch was the first journalist to report substantially on the research of Georges Cuvier, who was to become the most influential figure for English geology and paleontology after the Napoleonic Wars. In 1798 the *Philosophical Magazine* carried a summary of "Citizen Cuvier's" latest research on fossil bones and continued to report on his work almost annually through the end of the war. In 1806 Tilloch printed a complete translation of Cuvier's "Memoir upon Fossil and Living Elephants" in three installments running to 30 densely printed pages. The Royal Society's *Philosophical Transactions*, by contrast, first alludes to Cuvier in 1801 and includes only a few brief mentions prior to 1816 (though he was made FRS in 1806). The *Philosophical Magazine* thus preserved the international dimension of the public sphere for readers during the years of war with France. I am referring here specifically to what Thomas Broman has termed the "authentic public sphere" created in Germany in the 1790s by scientific periodicals for general readers, which subjected all new domains of knowledge to broad-based public scrutiny or "criticism" (Broman 1998: 140).

Tilloch helped to expand the "thinking public" not only by providing international coverage but also by making it affordable. The Royal Society was privately supplied with the publications of French savants during the war years, and readers of the society's *Philosophical Transactions* had access to some European contributions in both natural history and natural philosophy, but the costs of membership, and even a single volume of the journal, were prohibitive. The *Philosophical Magazine* was a bargain, comparatively, at one shilling and sixpence per monthly number – about 100 densely printed octavo pages – though readers had to put up with smaller print, smaller margins, and fewer illustrations. The densely packed pages of *A Natural History of Fishes, and of Reptiles, Insects, Waters, Earths, Fossils, Minerals, and Vegetables, Compiled from the Best Authorities* (1795), a very small duodecimo volume, further help to conjure up a readership of more modest means. The *Philosophical Transactions*, by contrast, resembles in quality the large-format illustrated "plate books" in natural history and antiquities that were intended as much for elegant display as for study. Robert Thornton's *The Temple of Flora* (1798–1807), an outrageously lavish series of botanical color plates in the largest or "atlas folio" format, cost nearly £40,000 to produce; and Banks spent an estimated £7,000 and employed close to two dozen artists over many years to prepare illustrations for a multivolume plate book on the natural history of the *Endeavour* voyage that was never actually published. The amply illustrated fourth edition of Pennant's *British Zoology* (1776–7, including a new preface that provides a good short introduction to natural history) aimed at usefulness as well as elegance, but even the octavo printing (two pounds eight shillings for four volumes) would not have been affordable to most readers of *The Philosophical Magazine*.

The proliferation of new genres, new readers, and new paths to authorship in Romantic natural history also gave a new prominence to women. Didactic works on botany, such as Priscilla Wakefield's *An Introduction to Botany* (1796) and Lady Charlotte Murray's *The British Garden* (1799), became common during the 1790s. Charlotte Smith's poem *Beachy Head*, as I hope to show, foregrounds the tension between a feminized, morally instructive botany and a problematic geology that produces anxieties related to gender and nation. Erasmus Darwin's *Plan for the Conduct of Female Education* (1797) lists numerous sources in botany but notes that there is "no proper introductory book" in mineralogy, thereby confirming a gendered division of natural history in place since the 1760s (Darwin 1797: 42, 125, Shteir 1996: 19). Darwin described his own earlier Linnaean poem *The Loves of the Plants* (1789) as a set of "diverse little pictures, suspended over the chimney of a Lady's dressing-room" (Darwin 1791/1824: vii). The scandalized reaction to Darwin's poetry in the 1790s, however, unsettled the association between botany and femininity and pointed to these intimate allusions as confirming the link between botany and illicit sexuality suggested by Banks's experience on Tahiti. The clergyman Richard Polwhele, for example, condemned Linnaean botany and included several character sketches of botanically interested women in his satire *The Unsex'd Females* (1798).

The controversy over botany, sex, and gender has been much studied by scholars (see also Schiebinger 2004). It is important here because it illustrates the powerful political implications that attached to the expanded franchise on natural history – and to "nature's progressive history" itself (J. Secord 2000: 498) – in the wake of the French Revolution: natural history provided one important stage for the defining Romantic-era contests over gender and representation detailed elsewhere in this volume.

Colonial Knowledge Work

The voluminous traffic in colonial natural history has led one Romanticist to call it the fundamental "European nature-making activity" of the period (Bewell 2004: 18). Colonial natural history also incorporated the study of cultures – of native peoples in their physical environments – and has therefore been crucial for historians of colonialism, anthropologists, postcolonial theorists, and historians of science, as well as students of Romanticism. The concept of "informal imperialism" helps to explain its importance: in many areas not directly subject to European military or political control, natural history and other cultural practices helped indirectly to establish European hegemony. Recent work by Romanticists reinforces the consensus that the precedent of the *Endeavour* voyage cemented the connections between ethnography, natural history, and colonialism (Bewell 2004: 7, Fulford et al. 2004: 4–5). In addition to thousands of plant and animal specimens so far unknown to Europeans, the *Endeavour* also transported a Polynesian man and boy, Tupaia and Taiyota, who died en route to England after contributing invaluable service as interpreters and navigators. Cook's second voyage succeeded in returning with another Tahitian, Omai, who became a London celebrity in the mid-1770s.

Not only did native people become specimens, but the scientific work of the *Endeavour* depended on extensive contact with native peoples, especially on Tahiti (or "Otaheite"), where the ship remained anchored for three months to observe the transit of Venus across the sun – this was Cook's official mission. As we have seen, popular understanding of this work routinely conflated social and sexual contact between British and Polynesians with botanical collecting and taxonomy. The crew relied to some degree on trade and more so on native generosity for food and knowledge of the territory. Banks, Daniel Solander, Sydney Parkinson, and others on board also made extensive ethnographic observations and collections and relied on native botanical knowledge. Natural history and ethnography thus became more firmly linked, and the link was reinforced by scores of subsequent British, French, Russian, and other voyages and the attendant "explosion in natural history print culture" (Bewell 2004: 21). If natural history is "*the* colonial science *par excellence*" (p. 11), this is partly because a biogeographical worldview was in place from the beginning of European colonization. Biogeography sought and found causal connections between living beings, including humans, and the climate and terrain in which they lived. European thinkers from Michel de Montaigne to Adam Ferguson drew upon travelers' reports of Native Americans living in harmony with Nature for their theories of human development. Buffon's *Histoire naturelle* (1749–89) included over 400 pages on "The Natural History of Man" (in Smellie's translation); much of this addressed environmental factors and used colonial data. The dioramic displays of "early man" in the Natural History Museum in

New York, among many others, reflect this continuing association between natural history and ethnography.

Antiquarianism, however, in the guise of "popular antiquities," remained the disciplinary umbrella for much local ethnographic work. Domestic travel narratives, local history, and topographical poetry typically surveyed both natural history and antiquities, a connection preserved in White's *The Natural History and Antiquities of Selborne*. In fact, Banks's active affiliation with the Society of Antiquaries is an important reason for the ethnographic emphasis given to colonial natural history by the *Endeavour* voyage. Sydney Parkinson, the primary artist-naturalist on this voyage, developed a parallel interest in ethnography, presumably inspired both by the example of Banks and by a course of antiquarian and historical reading that he brought on board (Joppien and Smith 1985: 51–52). Parkinson formed a large collection of the tools, weapons, textiles, and other artifacts of South Pacific peoples, and compiled vocabularies of their languages that remained standard for decades. Although employed officially as a botanical draftsman, his own writing emphasizes ethnobotany much more than Linnaean classification (which was the main goal of Banks and Solander). Parkinson amassed his ethnographic knowledge and collections in his own time: a shipmate noted that he "frequently sat up all night" to work on these projects after completing his drawings for Banks (Parkinson 1772/1972: xi). The distinction between his paid and unpaid work became an issue when Parkinson died at sea and Banks appropriated his manuscripts and collections. The late artist's brother managed to obtain manuscript materials and publish a version of Parkinson's journal in spite of Banks's attempts to suppress it, as the brother, Stanfield, bitterly recounts in his preface.

As one of the earliest critical accounts of Banks's methods, this preface remains a vital document. Stanfield bases his claim to Sydney's effects not only on his legal status as executor but on an argument concerning the proper domain of a natural history professional. Stanfield praises "the accuracy he aimed at, not only in the particular walk of his profession of natural history, but also in describing the persons, languages, customs, and manners of the natives of the several islands and continents they visited" (Parkinson 1772/1972: vii). This distinction between ethnography in this extended sense and the professional domain of natural history led him to challenge publicly (if unsuccessfully) Banks's "title" to artifacts, manuscripts, and "anything but the drawings in natural history, which only my brother was employed to execute" (p. xii). Sydney Parkinson's 1,300 drawings of plants and animals from the voyage remain the most important part of his legacy; the disputed collection was surely dispersed, but examples were engraved for Parkinson's *Journal*, and similar artifacts became strongly associated with the visual record of Banks himself – including the canoe paddle and round basket, depicted on the front of the dais (see Figure 1 above), and the cloak, which echoes the Maori cloak worn by Banks in the famous portrait by Benjamin West (1773). If Parkinson had survived, he probably would have continued his rise from relatively humble origins to something like professional status. Many colonial artists and naturalists attained a significant degree of gentility (cf. Spary 2000: 76). One noteworthy case is that of Maria Sibylla Merian, remembered by Sir James Edward Smith in 1788 as "a monument of female perseverance" for her early fieldwork in South America (Smith 1798: 101–2).

The fieldwork of colonial naturalists circulated in a wide range of printed and visual forms. The most expensive publications, like Merian's *Insects of Surinam*, included gorgeous hand-colored engravings from sketches made in the field. But visual images and displays were also available to a wider public for as little as one shilling (roughly £2 or $4 today). One shilling was the initial price of admission to the Panorama in London's Leicester Square, a 90-foot rotunda created by Robert Barker in 1794 for the display of his massive 360-degree paintings (described in detail by Gillen D'Arcy Wood elsewhere in this volume). Several recent scholars have explored the panorama's role in popularizing colonial natural history and antiquities (Aguirre 2005, Ziter 2003), and natural history featured prominently in other exhibitions and displays as well (O'Connor 2007, Pascoe 2006).

The ample recent scholarship in this field has also emphasized the uses of natural history for colonial exploitation, its connections with racism and slavery, particularly in West Africa and the Caribbean (Coleman 2005, Tobin 2005). Others have noted that these darker aspects of colonial natural history were offset, for Romantic poets including Coleridge and Robert Southey, by other colonial projects that seemed to promise social and cultural "improvement" (Fulford et al. 2004: 120–1), a sense echoed in the glowing catalogue of Banks's accomplishments quoted earlier from his biography in *Public Characters*. Saree Makdisi's essay in this volume further explores the many contradictions of colonialism. In this context it is worth noting that recent scholarship has shown the relationship between colonialism and Romantic natural history to be politically complex, reciprocal, and central to the public sphere.

Fossils and History in *Beachy Head*

The intense scholarly focus on colonial natural history makes it almost disorienting for the student of British Romanticism to return to the assertively local and national representations of Nature in many of the Romantic poets. If, as Alan Bewell argues, "Nature first appeared primarily as a colonial import" (Bewell 2004: 14), this would help to explain why domestic nature, too, "appears . . . as if seen for the first time" by Romantic poets (p. 5). Several of the colonial studies describe Britain, quoting Bruno Latour, as an imperial "center of calculation," the London that housed the colonial administration and the learned societies described in the first part of this essay. Even the quintessential English landscape of Gilbert White's Selborne, connected to London and empire only by a line of correspondence, shows surprising traces of globalization, as Tobias Menely has recently argued (Menely 2004). At the same time, however, White remains an important touchstone for what might be called a nativist Romanticism. Although one-third of White's *Selborne* is addressed to Thomas Pennant, who was active in colonial natural history, his most frequently cited authorities are two locally oriented English natural theologians of the early eighteenth century, John Ray and William Derham. The tradition of *local* natural history can be traced via Ray and Robert Plot to William Camden's *Britannia* (1586), a compendium of county histories. Theresa Kelley has shown that John Clare and Charlotte Smith, two of White's avid readers among the Romantic poets, insisted on vernacular English names for local plants and actively resisted the colonizing imperatives of Linnaean taxonomy (Kelley 2003: 234).

Smith's last poem, *Beachy Head* (1807), reflects on natural history in the context of a local narrative that owes as much to the tradition of Camden and White as to the Miltonic tradition from which she draws her blank verse idiom. Smith made a spectacular entry on the literary scene with her *Elegiac Sonnets* (eight editions, 1784–97), a few of which are set on coastal cliffs, and a number of closely observed coastal scenes (among others) in her novels suggest more than a casual interest in natural processes. As several critics have shown, Smith gained considerable expertise in natural history by writing her *Rural Walks* (1795) and other didactic works in verse and prose, especially on botany (Pascoe 1994: 194–5). *Beachy Head* unfolds a long descriptive meditation on the geological feature after which it is named – a 530-foot chalk cliff overlooking the English Channel – and the surrounding acres of Sussex coast in southeast England. The poem delves deeply into the natural and cultural history of a landscape rich with personal and political associations. The chalk formation is largely identical to the chalk on the French side of the channel, and Smith registers an anxiety over this proximity that was typical for English observers after so many years of war with France. A spectator on Beachy Head could have witnessed the landing of William the Conqueror in 1066, as Smith notes, and could also have witnessed a rare naval defeat by the French in 1690 (l. 158n.). The chalk itself makes for a thin, unforgiving soil, which Smith highlights in her portrait of rural poverty, but as a consequence fossil shells often appear on the surface. These shells provide the occasion for Smith's engagement with the transformation of mineralogy into geology in the first half of *Beachy Head*.

While Smith engages consistently with botany throughout, especially in the second half, her encounter with geological questions in the poem is more localized and strongly marked by anxiety. Precisely this geological anxiety makes *Beachy Head* worthy of close examination as a contribution to Romantic natural history. Fossil shells (and other "organic remains") always played a prominent role in the mineralogical branch of natural history because they resembled the living things that formed the other branches. As Smith was writing her poem fossils were just beginning to be appropriated by a new geohistorical science, which fused the old domains of mineralogy, geognosy (earth structure), and geogony (theories of its origin). In the year that *Beachy Head* was published, a new learned society in London adopted a controversial French name for this science: geology (Rudwick 2005: 448). Smith (who died while she was finishing the poem in 1806) could not have known of the new Geological Society, but her poem displays a deeply ambivalent awareness of newly ambitious earth science. *Beachy Head* makes geology a paradigm case for the tendency toward "vague theories" and "vain dispute" in current science, advocating instead the traditional and more inclusive practices of natural history. The Geological Society's founders drew on the same national traditions of skepticism and empiricism to portray theorizing, conversely, as an error committed by amateurs who distorted their scanty local observations to support hypotheses derived from Continental thinkers. Thus a national institution was justified as an empirical research network that would check theoretical excesses. But critics of the Geological Society and other elite institutions objected that they tended to marginalize "practical men" and (implicitly) women by appropriating their knowledge and controlling publication. In this respect, *Beachy Head* should be seen as part of a broad concurrent endeavor to keep the earth legible for nonspecialists. Yet in some ways, Smith's half-repressed fascination with French theory in a time of war links her just as closely to the Geological Society as to the nature poets, women travel writers, and self-taught geological fieldworkers who remained outside it.

From the beginning of her poem Smith resists the pressure to narrate the origins of Beachy Head from her observations. In so doing, she acknowledges a growing divide between natural history and the new geology. Theresa Kelley has pointed out Smith's ambivalence concerning the kind of history that might be appropriate to what she herself termed a "local poem" (Kelley 2004). Smith sets forth a traditional, static natural history – in which fossils are or ought to be considered on the same temporal plane with living plants – partly to foreground the dynamic and troubled *human* history of this landscape. Thus she rejects natural theology at the beginning of the poem, which imagines "the Omnipotent / Stretch[ing] forth his arm" to divide England from the continental land mass (ll. 5–6), by appending a contradictory footnote. The theological vision, according to this note, is both scientifically and politically inadequate, and God is not mentioned elsewhere in the poem. But if the geological evidence cannot be used to argue a divine origin, neither can it justify the newer kind of naturalistic explanation. Smith professed to know nothing about the new chronology being developed since the late 1790s by Cuvier and Blumenbach in Europe, according to which fossils documented a vast history entirely prior to and separate from human beings. But she nonetheless explicitly denies that the fossil evidence alone can account for the origin of Beachy Head in a later, more sustained geological meditation (ll. 368–419). Charlotte Smith's pointed interest in fossils is all the more remarkable at a time when fossils were still "peripheral" for most English geologists, as Martin Rudwick has put it, and as James Parkinson – the only member of the new Geological Society who was active in this field – himself complained in 1811 (Rudwick 2005: 466, Parkinson 1811: 324).

Remembering the fossils she found on the Sussex Downs in younger years, Smith's narrator entertains three possible explanations for her youthful observation that these shells seemed to be made of the same chalk that surrounded them (ll. 372–89). She dismisses in one line the possibility that the ocean once reached the top of the cliffs now towering above it, leaving the possibility that fossils are sports of nature – a traditional explanation dating back to classical antiquity – and the possibility that the chalk is a seabed uplifted from its original position, closer to the more recent, historical kind of explanation. Smith gives the most serious attention to this last hypothesis, underscoring its imaginative and explanatory power by attributing it to Gilbert White in her footnote. A comparison with White's *Selborne* shows that Smith has modified the theory while retaining White's diction, betraying her intellectual investment (Smith 1807/1993: 382n, White 1789/1853: 120–1 [Dec 9, 1773]). Yet the preceding long note, with its labored ambiguity, seems to consign all geological explanation to a realm of vain presumption – not for religious reasons, but because it is conjectural and perhaps also inimical to the curiosity and wonder celebrated in the verse. "I have never read any of the late theories of the earth," Smith assures us, "nor was I ever satisfied with the attempts to explain many of the phenomena which call forth conjecture in those books I happened to have had access to on this subject" (p. 375n.). In the verse, she takes this insufficiency as evidence for the vanity of science in general:

> Ah! very vain is Science' proudest boast,
> And but a little light its flame yet lends
> To its most ardent votaries, since from whence
> These fossil forms are seen, is but conjecture,
> Food for vague theories, or vain dispute,
> While to his daily task the peasant goes,
> Unheeding such inquiry. (ll. 390–6)

Given the timing of this poem, it seems likely that Smith is challenging the new geology's claims of expertise and professionalism. On the one hand, she seems to accept the geologists' claim to be on the cutting edge of science, its "most ardent votaries," anticipating the substitution by which "science" later came to mean natural science exclusively. But this metonymy proves less flattering than it seems, as she goes on to charge geology with harboring science's vaguest theories and most vain disputes. Smith's note identifies geology with "theories of the earth," a concept already in disrepute with those ambitious for geology, including Humphry Davy and Jean-André Deluc. Smith drives home this pejorative sense by comparing this sort of theorizing about fossils with antiquarianism: she mocks the antiquaries who "fancy [they] can trace" the remains of Roman fortifications on this coast (ll. 404–10), and goes on to observe in another equivocal note that the elephant bones found near Beachy Head have been claimed both as historical evidence of Roman colonization and as prehistoric specimens or relics of the "universal deluge" (1807/1993: 412n.).

Smith suggests that she saw the fossil bones of such an animal in Paris in 1791, and she may also be remembering the so-called mammoth exhibited by Rembrandt Peale in London in 1802. At this point the poem decisively abandons geology and history in favor of botany (l. 441). But Smith's detailed references, including the bones, the Parisian natural history museum, and even the resistance to theory itself, all betray a curiosity about the emerging discipline of geology that contradicts her stated hostility to science. This ambivalence registers, in part, her unwillingness to be excluded from serious science writing on the grounds of gender, but also participates in a long skeptical-empirical tradition.

There are surprising parallels to *Beachy Head* in the first English scientific study of the chalk formation, published in the Geological Society's *Transactions* in 1814 by the self-educated geologist Thomas Webster. Although Webster, unlike Smith, acknowledges the extensive correlation of the French and English chalk, he does echo her indecision concerning the relative positions of land and sea (Webster 1814: 251) and declares that "the origin of . . . the chalk formation . . . remains one of those hidden mysteries on which all the speculations of geologists have not thrown any certain light" (p. 245). Webster also includes a sublime anecdote of a local vicar's near-fatal adventures "near the brink of the precipice" of Beachy Head (1807/1993: 191–2n.).

Smith concludes her poem with a legend of the vicar's early eighteenth-century predecessor, Parson Darby, who did not escape with his life. Pursuing his vocation of saving drowning mariners, Smith's parson resides in a cave under the cliff where he himself finally drowns in a storm scene that underscores the instability of the chalk: "the bellowing cliffs were shook / Even to their stony base, and fragments fell / Flashing and thundering on the angry flood" (ll. 718–20). As the bones of Parson Darby mingle with the bones of sailors and the shells of animals from long-gone epochs, it becomes difficult to disentangle Beachy Head's natural hostility to human cultivation (and indeed that of the whole extensive chalk formation) from the long history of human hostilities encouraged by its geographic setting. The impossibility of drawing clear distinctions between social and natural history (and likewise between theory and observation) fuels the anxiety so palpable in what Anne Wallace has termed the "fossil scene" of *Beachy Head*, in the poem's forceful shifts from natural to historical topics and back again, and in its very choice of this locale (Wallace 2002: 81). Inasmuch as these marine fossil species seem both to demand and to elude ecological explanation, Smith's anxiety could be related to the "Romantic anxiety about species" that Ashton Nichols describes as leading to the view of nature as "an ecological system" (Nichols 1997: 136).

Conclusion

Like some of the best geology of her time, Smith's *Beachy Head* shows a keen awareness both of the intense theoretical interest of geological questions and the limitations of geological theorizing. In so doing, the poem provides an index of the resistance early geology encountered in asserting disciplinary control over these questions. I have emphasized the production of new institutions and new disciplines as one of the defining developments in the period's natural history. Although Wordsworth's lament, "we murder to dissect," does not accurately summarize the Romantic attitude toward science, the discourse of natural history did provide a forum for criticism of new developments in natural knowledge, such as increasing institutional control. The traditional cultural elements of natural history served diverse constituencies equally well: if its accessibility was a rallying point or even a subject of nostalgia for Smith in 1806, it provided an angle of attack for the Royal Society Dissenters in 1783, and helped to pave the way for a new form of professionalism for Thomas Webster, Sydney Parkinson, and many others. I have also emphasized the circulation of natural history in many forms of print to many classes of readers: for Smith and her publishers, the expensive quarto volume containing *Beachy Head and Other Poems* was the high end of a repertoire that extended down to the tiny duodecimo printings of Smith's *Rural Walks* and other didactic works. Smith's innovative use of footnotes as a counterdiscourse (Labbe 2003: 59) also illustrates new possibilities created by natural history in print. Colonialism hovers on the periphery of the poem, especially at the beginning, as Theresa Kelley has suggested (Kelley 2004: 311). Kelley's main thesis concerning *Beachy Head* – that it wrestles with the contradictions between local history and universal history – points to a still more fundamental reason for the importance of the poem in any consideration of Romantic natural history.

Georges Cuvier's work on fossils has been credited by intellectual historians as a revolutionary step toward the "epistemic shift" (Foucault) in modern understandings of nature. Most of Romantic natural history – the new institutions, the forms of print, and the colonial projects detailed here – operated under the aegis of Linnaean classification, seeking to integrate all natural phenomena into one system. But after Cuvier, the Linnaean organization had to be broken up into chronological phases. Many organisms, Cuvier insisted, had become extinct; living species could not be found to match fossil species supposedly transported by a flood; and naturalists were suddenly confronted with a totally different order of time and history. Smith probably knew little of Cuvier's work, but she recognized that the traditional view of fossils, as represented by Gilbert White, was threatened – and she seems uncannily to anticipate the English fossil craze that followed Robert Jameson's 1813 translation of Cuvier. Natural history, as a descriptive science, did not traditionally imply a chronological dimension. Naturalists had viewed fossils as "documents" of former times since the seventeenth century, but until now that history had always been viewed as coterminous with human history, a history that could be traced in the human record. The concept of "deep time" as a history vastly greater than, and at best analogous to, human history, was acknowledged very gradually in England because of the persistence of natural theology. But Smith's sharp questioning of "antiquarian" theories of fossils suggests other grounds for resistance to deep time. If fossils and their beds can now be read as documents of "nature's own history" (Rudwick 2005: 348), any reading of a landscape runs the risk of naturalizing the social history of that landscape. *Beachy Head's* insistent antipastoral attention to social inequality and war struggles against such a naturalization of social conditions.

Smith's poem registers the disjunction between human and natural history that was one ironic result of the Romantic flowering of the natural history disciplines. This survey of Romantic natural history has itself focused much more – perhaps to a fault – on the human history of print, institutions, and colonialism than on the natural objects or, as Banks called them, "the subjects of natural history." The Romantic cultivation of nature has had other ironic results as well. The knowledge of nature went hand in hand with the mastery of natural resources, one long-term consequence of which has been environmental degradation that could hardly be envisioned in Romantic writings (with the possible exception of Byron's "Darkness"). But along with exploitation of nature on a global scale and intensified specialization, the Romantic period also generated a common language for engaging respectfully with the natural world. The language used by scientists and nonscientists alike for cultivating environmental awareness and preservation owes something both to Romantic poetry and to popular natural history of the period. So too does any global effort toward the restoration or preservation of indigenous plant, animal, and human communities. Finally, as suggested by *Beachy Head*, the preface to Sydney Parkinson's *Journal*, and perhaps even *The Philosophical Puppet Show*, one of the most vital legacies of Romantic natural history may be the capacity for critical engagement with science and its institutions.

Note

For their kind help in the preparation of this essay I should like to thank Jay Gupta, Elizabeth Hornbeck, Jon Klancher, Ted Koditschek, and the incomparable Crystal Lake.

References and Further Reading

Aguirre, Robert D. (2005) *Informal Empire: Mexico and Central America in Victorian Culture*. Minneapolis: University of Minnesota Press.

Bewell, Alan. (1996) "'On the Banks of the South Sea': Botany and Sexual Controversy in the Late Eighteenth Century" in David Philip Miller and Peter Hanns Reill (eds), *Visions of Empire: Voyages, Botany, and Representations of Nature* (pp. 173–93). Cambridge, UK: Cambridge University Press.

Bewell, Alan. (2004) "Romanticism and Colonial Natural History," *Studies in Romanticism* 43: 5–34.

Broman, Thomas. (1998) "The Habermasian Public Sphere and 'Science *in* the Enlightenment'," *History of Science* 36: 123–49.

Buffon, Georges Louis Leclerc, Comte de. (1780–5) *Natural History, General and Particular*, trans. William Smellie, 9 vols. Edinburgh: Printed for William Creech.

Cantor, Geoffrey, Gowan Dawson, Graeme Gooday, Richard Noakes, Sally Shuttleworth, and Jonathan R. Topham. (2004) *Science in the Nineteenth-Century Periodical: Reading the Magazine of Nature*. Cambridge, UK: Cambridge University Press.

Coleman, Deirdre. (2005) *Romantic Colonization and British Anti-Slavery*. Cambridge, UK: Cambridge University Press.

Darwin, Erasmus. (1791/1824) *The Botanic Garden. A Poem, in Two Parts . . . with Philosophical Notes*. London: Jones & Co.

Darwin, Erasmus. (1797) *A Plan for the Conduct of Female Education in Boarding Schools*. Derby, UK: J. Johnson.

Fara, Patricia. (1997) "The Royal Society's Portrait of Joseph Banks," *Notes and Records of the Royal Society of London* 51, 2: 199–210.

Foucault, Michel. (1966/1970) *The Order of Things. An Archaeology of the Human Sciences*. New York: Random House.

Fulford, Tim, Debbie Lee, and Peter J. Kitson. (2004) *Literature, Science, and Exploration in the Romantic Era: Bodies of Knowledge*. Cambridge, UK: Cambridge University Press.

Goldsmith, Oliver. (1774) *An History of the Earth, and Animated Nature*, 8 vols. London: Printed for J. Nourse.

Hawley, Judith (gen. ed.). (2003–4) *Literature and Science, 1660–1834*, vols. 3–5. London: Pickering & Chatto.

Heringman, Noah (ed.). (2003) *Romantic Science: The Literary Forms of Natural History*. Albany: SUNY Press.

Heringman, Noah. (2009) "'Very Vain is Science' Proudest Boast': The Resistance to Geological Theory in Early Nineteenth-Century England," in Gary D. Rosenberg (ed.), *Emergence of Modern Geology and Evolutionary Thought from the Scientific Revolution to the Enlightenment*. Boulder, CO: Geological Society of America.

Jardine, Nicholas. (1991) *The Scenes of Inquiry: On the Reality of Questions in the Sciences*. Oxford: Clarendon.

Jardine, Nicholas, J. A. Secord, and E. C. Spary (eds). (1996) *Cultures of Natural History*. Cambridge, UK: Cambridge University Press.

Joppien, Rüdiger, and Bernard Smith. (1985) *The Art of Captain Cook's Voyages*, vol. 1: *The Voyage of the* Endeavour, *1768–1771*. New Haven, CT: Yale University Press.

Kelley, Theresa M. (2003) "Romantic Exemplarity: Botany and 'Material' Culture," in Noah Heringman (ed.), *Romantic Science: The Literary Forms of Natural History* (pp. 223–54). Albany: SUNY Press.

Kelley, Theresa M. (2004) "Romantic Histories: Charlotte Smith and *Beachy Head*," *Nineteenth-Century Literature* 59, 3: 281–314.

Knell, Simon J. (2000) *The Culture of English Geology, 1815–51: A Science Revealed Through Its Collecting*. Aldershot, UK: Ashgate.

Labbe, Jacqueline M. (2003) *Charlotte Smith: Romanticism, Poetry, and the Culture of Gender*. Manchester: Manchester University Press.

Lenoir, Timothy. (1997) *Instituting Science: The Cultural Production of Scientific Disciplines*. Stanford, CA: Stanford University Press.

Menely, Tobias. (2004) "Traveling in Place: Gilbert White's Cosmopolitan Parochialism," *Eighteenth-Century Life* 28: 46–65.

Miller, David Philip and Peter Hanns Reill (eds). (1996) *Visions of Empire: Voyages, Botany, and Representations of Nature*. Cambridge, UK: Cambridge University Press.

A New Edition in Quarto, Corrected, Improved, and Greatly Enlarged. (1788). Edinburgh: Elliot and Kay.

Nichols, Ashton. (1997) "The Anxiety of Species: Toward a Romantic Natural History," *The Wordsworth Circle* 28, 3: 130–6.

Nichols, Ashton (ed.) (2004) *Romantic Natural Histories: Selected Texts with Introduction*. Boston: Houghton Mifflin.

O'Connor, Ralph J. (2007) *The Earth on Show: Fossils and the Poetics of Popular Science, 1802–1856.* Chicago: University of Chicago Press.

Parkinson, James. (1811) "Observations on Some of the Strata in the Neighborhood of London, and on the Fossil Remains Contained in Them," *Transactions of the Geological Society* 1: 324–54.

Parkinson, Sydney. (1772/1972) *A Journal of a Voyage to the South Seas, in his Majesty's Ship, The Endeavour.* Adelaide: Libraries Board of South Australia.

Pascoe, Judith. (1994) "Female Botanists and the Poetry of Charlotte Smith," in Carol Shiner Wilson and Joel Haefner (eds), *Re-Visioning Romanticism: British Women Writers, 1776–1837* (pp. 193–209). Philadelphia: University of Pennsylvania Press.

Pascoe, Judith. (2006) *The Hummingbird Cabinet: A Rare and Curious History of Romantic Collectors.* Ithaca, NY: Cornell University Press.

Peterfreund, Stuart. (2003) "'Great Frosts and . . . Some Very Hot Summers': Strange Weather, the Last Letters, and the Last Days in Gilbert White's *The Natural History of Selborne*," in Noah Heringman (ed.), *Romantic Science: The Literary Forms of Natural History* (pp. 85–110). Albany: SUNY Press.

Rajan, Tilottama. (2004) "Philosophy as Encyclopedia: Hegel, Schelling, and the Organization of Knowledge," *The Wordsworth Circle* 35: 6–11.

Ramsay, Robert. (1772) "To the Lovers of Natural History," *Scots Magazine* 34: 174–5.

Roche, Daniel. (1996) "Natural History in the Academies," in Nicholas Jardine, J. A. Secord, and E. C. Spary (eds), *Cultures of Natural History* (pp. 127–44). Cambridge, UK: Cambridge University Press.

Rudwick, Martin J. S. (2005) *Bursting the Limits of Time: The Reconstruction of Geohistory in the Age of Revolution.* Chicago: University of Chicago Press.

Schiebinger, Londa. (2004) *Plants and Empire: Colonial Bioprospecting in the Atlantic World.* Cambridge, MA: Harvard University Press.

Secord, Anne. (1996) "Artisan Botany," in Nicholas Jardine, J. A. Secord, and E. C. Spary (eds), *Cultures of Natural History* (pp. 378–93). Cambridge, UK: Cambridge University Press.

Secord, James. (1996) "The Crisis of Nature," in Nicholas Jardine, J. A. Secord, and E. C. Spary (eds), *Cultures of Natural History* (pp. 447–59). Cambridge, UK: Cambridge University Press.

Secord, James. (2000) *Victorian Sensation: The Extraordinary Publication, Reception, and Secret Authorship of Vestiges of the Natural History of Creation.* Chicago: University of Chicago Press.

Shteir, Ann B. (1996) *Cultivating Women, Cultivating Science: Flora's Daughters and Botany in England, 1760–1860.* Baltimore: Johns Hopkins University Press.

"Sir Joseph Banks." (1807) In *Public Characters of 1800–01* (pp. 376–408). London: Printed for R. Phillips.

Smellie, William. (1790) *The Philosophy of Natural History*, vol. 1. Edinburgh: Printed for the Heirs of Charles Elliot.

Smellie, William. (1799) *The Philosophy of Natural History*, vol. 2. Edinburgh: Printed for Bell & Bradfute.

Smith, Charlotte. (1807/1993) *Beachy Head. The Poems of Charlotte Smith*, ed. Stuart Curran (pp. 217–47). Oxford: Oxford University Press.

Smith, Sir James Edward. (1788) *Discourse on the Rise and Progress of Natural History, Read at the Opening of the Linnæan Society, April 8, 1788*. In *Tracts Relating to Natural History* (pp. 60–174). London: Printed for the Author.

Snip, Simon [pseudonym]. (1663/1785) *The Philosophical Puppet Show, or, Snip's Inauguration to the President's Chair*. London.

Spary, E. C. (2000) *Utopia's Garden: French Natural History from Old Regime to Revolution*. Chicago: University of Chicago Press.

Tobin, Beth Fowkes. (2005) *Colonizing Nature: The Tropics in British Arts and Letters, 1760–1820*. Philadelphia: University of Pennsylvania Press.

Wallace, Anne D. (2002) "Picturesque Fossils, Sublime Geology? The Crisis of Authority in Charlotte Smith's *Beachy Head*," *European Romantic Review* 13: 77–93.

Webster, Thomas. (1814) "On the Freshwater Formations in the Isle of Wight, with Some Observations on the Strata over the Chalk in the South-East Part of England," *Transactions of the Geological Society* 2: 161–254.

White, Gilbert. (1789/1853) *The Natural History and Antiquities of Selborne*, ed. Sir William Jardine. London: Nathaniel Cooke.

Yeo, Richard. (1999) "Natural Philosophy (Science)," in Iain McCalman (ed.), *An Oxford Companion to the Romantic Age: British Culture, 1776–1832* (pp. 320–8). Oxford: Oxford University Press.

Yeo, Richard. (2001) *Encyclopaedic Visions: Scientific Dictionaries and Enlightenment Culture*. Cambridge, UK: Cambridge University Press.

Ziter, Edward. (2003) *The Orient on the Victorian Stage*. Cambridge, UK: Cambridge University Press.

Chapter 8
Romantic Sciences: British and Continental Thresholds

Frederick Burwick

Just as not all literature of the late eighteenth and early nineteenth centuries can be properly designated Romantic literature, so too not all science in the Romantic period is congruent with Romantic science. In "The Rise of Modern Science and the Genesis of Romanticism" (1982), Hans Eichner argued that Romanticism was "a desperate rearguard action against the spirit and the implications of modern science" (Eichner 1982: 8). Although Eichner perceived an irreconcilable opposition between Romanticism and science, scientists of the age were directed by the very precepts endorsed by Romantic poets and artists, in Britain no less than on the Continent. Just as literature and art underwent a shift from mimetic form to subjective expression, philosophy from materialism to idealism, politics from monarchical authority to democratic individualism, religion from ecclesiastic dogma to intuitive faith, the sciences witnessed a shift from matter-based physics to energy-based physics. Many scientists conducted experiments on themselves, testing their own response to physical and chemical stimuli. Scientists found allies among the poets and philosophers in challenging traditionally held beliefs.

To be sure, interest in the interconnections between science and literature have evolved considerably since Eichner's seminal essay. Because historians of the sciences have re-examined the "scientific revolution" of the seventeenth century in terms of the revisions and new typologies of the Enlightenment and the "second scientific revolution" of the early nineteenth century, critical studies have become informed by an increased awareness of communication across the cultural and scientific discourses (Cunningham and Jardine 1990). That awareness has been greatly assisted by the effort to regain access to the actual texts of the period, as in Tim Fulford's five-volume collection of primary works, *Romanticism and the Sciences* (2002). These new developments have also led to a greater appreciation of the shared relevance of developments within each of the scientific disciplines. The Romantic period witnessed an extensive increase in the exchange of ideas across national boundaries. Because international dialogue became crucial in the sciences, it is informative to examine in the broader European context those sciences that progressed as modern scientific disciplines.

Geology

The account of creation as given in the Bible was subjected to assault by discoveries in the natural sciences. Long before Charles Darwin, in *On the Origin of Species* (1859), derived from his observations on the Galapagos Islands a theory of evolution that opposed the biblical account of creation in Genesis, geologists were already confronting evidence of dynamic processes of change. Thomas Burnet's *Sacred Theory of the Earth* (1681) reworked René Descartes's speculations to fit the biblical account. In his conception the antediluvian Earth was a smooth ovoid. Over time the surface dried out and the abyssal waters were heated. Eventually the surface cracked, releasing the waters of Noah's flood. John Woodward's *An Essay Toward a Natural History of the Earth* (1695) found Bishop Burnet's account far too scientific: the flood was an act of God that could not be explained by normal physical processes. The evidence, however, continued to demand scientific explanation. John Whitehurst's *An Inquiry into the Original State of the Earth* (1778) observed that the relentless tidal action of the moon exercised an obvious shaping influence on coastal bluffs and caves. Horace-Benedict de Saussure, in *Voyages dans les Alpes* (1779), documented how curved strata, originally laid down as horizontal sheets, were later deformed by forces of upheaval. Abraham Werner, in *Kurze Klassification und Beschreibung der verschiedener Gebirgsarten* (1787), promoted the Neptunist theory for the layers of the Earth as deposits created by the successive advance and retreat of oceans. The contrasting argument that rocks were formed in fire, the Vulcanist theory, was elaborated by Abbé Anton Moro of Venice in his study of volcanic islands (1740). Moro attributed all stratification and upheaval to volcanic activity. This alternative to Werner's ideas was taken up by James Hutton, in *Theory of the Earth; or, an investigation of the laws observable in the composition, dissolution and restoration of land upon the globe* (1785). Combining Neptunist and Vulcanist theories, Hutton advocated a view that the surface of the earth was subject to two basic processes: rocks were worn away by weathering and erosion, and then they were reformed and uplifted by heat and pressure. Asserting that the Earth was far older than the 6,000 years estimated by those who relied on the history in Genesis, Hutton argued that the earth's layers revealed cycles of change through slow processes. The last sentence of Hutton's work was widely quoted: "*The result, therefore, of our present enquiry is, that we find no vestige of a beginning – no prospect of an end*" (Hutton 1785/1970: 12, emphasis in original).

Although many scientists continued the effort to reconcile geological evidence with Scripture, it had become clear that Earth had a long and varied history at odds with the biblical account. Following Burnet, Georges Cuvier, in *Discours sur les Revolutions du Globe* (1812), described the strata of the Paris basin, postulating a series of global catastrophes to explain the Wernerian evidence of successive ocean deposits. The scriptural geologist William Buckland, in *Vindiciae Geologicae* (1820), supported Cuvier's theory with the discovery of the Kirkdale Caves in Yorkshire, which contained the bones of many extinct animals which had apparently died in a sudden flood: "had we never heard of such an event [Noah's Flood] from scripture . . . Geology of itself must have called in the assistance of some such catastrophe to explain the phenomenon" (Buckland 1820: 14). Assuming a Deistic interpretation in his *Principles of Geology* (1830), Charles Lyell, like Hutton, held that the history of Earth was marked not by catastrophes but by slow relatively uniform changes. In the course of the later nineteenth century, it was recognized that the arguments of the uniformists and catastrophists, like those of the Neptunists and Vulcanists, were not either/or but both/and.

Developments in geological science had a profound influence on the literature of the period, as in the subterranean sublime of Coleridge's "Kubla Khan" (1816), the mystical revelations in the underground caverns of Novalis's *Heinrich von Ofterdingen* (1802), or the variation on the Tannhäuser legend in E. T. A. Hoffmann's "The Mines of Falun" ("Die Bergwerke zu Falun," 1820). In his "System of the Heavens" (1846), a review of John Pringle Nichol's *System of the World* (1846), De Quincey also summarized the century-long struggle to reconcile the advances in geology and astronomy with the biblical account of the creation. In this essay, De Quincey revised two earlier pieces: his translation of Immanuel Kant's 1754 work "Age of the Earth" (De Quincey 1833/2000-3, vol. 9: 111-12), and his translation from the 1820 work by Jean Paul (Johann Paul Richter) "Dream upon the Universe" (De Quincey 1824/2000-3, vol. 3: 146). The apparent failure to reconcile Scripture and science, De Quincey argued, was due in large part to the myopia of a literalist interpretation of biblical text. As in his refutation of Hume's "Of Miracles," De Quincey insisted that science, no less than religious faith, explored the boundaries of the unknown constrained by the persisting limitations of human knowledge. In this context De Quincey repeated Jean Paul's "Dream upon the Universe," in which the dreamer is guided by an angel across the vast expanses of space until, overwhelmed by "the persecutions of the infinite," he cries out his despair that "end ... there is none," whereupon "the angel threw up his glorious hands to the heaven of heavens; saying, 'End is there none to the universe of God? Lo! also there is no Beginning'" (De Quincey 1846/2000-3, vol. 15: 236, emphasis in original). In Jean Paul's narrative this moment simply presents the paradox of God's infinitude, an Alpha and Omega. De Quincey transformed it into a more terrifying psychological crisis for human understanding, and he did so with the profound irony of his echo from Hutton, "*we find no vestige of a beginning – no prospect of an end*" (Hutton 1785/1970: 12, emphasis in original).

German Romantic writers, as Ted Ziolkowski has documented, were responsive to the new geology introduced by Werner at the mining school at Freiberg. Friedrich von Hardenberg studied at Freiberg before he adapted the mining metaphor, as Novalis, in *Heinrich von Ofterdingen* (1802). The pious miner becomes a significant character in Achim von Arnim's *Die Kronenwächter* (1817), and young students of mining are featured in the tales of Henrik Steffens's *Die Vier Norweger* (1828). German Romanticism reveals a fascination with subterranean spelunking not merely in metaphor, but also in plot and setting (Ziolkowski 1991: 18-63). In cross-referencing developments in British and Continental geography, Noah Heringman acknowledges a "geological modesty" among women writers, yet he nevertheless observes elaborate geological detail in the poetry of Charlotte Smith and the accuracy of description in Ann Radcliffe's German travels of 1794. He also provides a sound defense of Maria Calcott's account of the earthquake in Chile, which had also been the topic of a tale by Heinrich von Kleist. Drawing from scientific texts (Whitehurst,

Hutton, Davy, Smith) as well as travel accounts and topographical descriptions, Heringman describes the flux of ideas about the earth's formation, and he finds awareness of those ideas in William Wordsworth's "Resolution and Independence," in Percy Bysshe Shelley's "Mont Blanc," in Charlotte Smith's *Beachy Head*, and in William Blake's *Jerusalem* (Heringman 2003).

Astronomy

As Jean Paul's and De Quincey's references to the immensity of the universe in 1846 suggests, there was a major connection perceived between geology and astronomy. The starry heavens were needed to interpret the earth and vice versa (Gaull 1990). Both disciplines seemed to challenge the biblical account of creation. The earth was older, the universe vaster, than any previous generation had imagined; the more the sciences developed and progressed, the older and vaster their subjects became. In presenting his concept of the mathematical sublime in the *Kritik der Urteilskraft* (1791), Immanuel Kant found the readiest example in the recent measurements of the Milky Way and observations on distant nebulae. Modern astronomy commenced with Sir Isaac Newton's theory of universal gravitation in the work *Philosophiae Naturalis Principia Mathematica* (1687). The ensuing century brought the discovery of new planets and their moons, and the tracking of comets. Using Newton's theory of gravitation, Edmund Halley determined that the bright comets of 1531, 1607, and 1682 had almost the same orbits. When he accounted for the gravitational pull from Jupiter and Saturn, he concluded that these were different appearances of the same comet. With these gravitational calculations, he predicted in 1705 that this comet had a 76-year orbit and would return in 1758. Unfortunately, Halley died in 1742, not living to see his prediction come true when the comet returned on Christmas Eve 1758. Halley's Comet put on its next bright display in 1835.

In 1766 Joseph-Louis Lagrange published his observations on the orbits of Jupiter's moons. While looking for comets in 1758, Charles Messier observed other previously unexplained objects – galaxies, nebula and star clusters – and prepared a *Catalog of Nebulae and Star Clusters* (1771). Like other comet hunters, Messier often mistook nebulae for comets. He compiled a list of 103 nebulae as an aid to other comet hunters. This was the first list of nebulae. Messier's list was supplemented by Nicholas Louis de Lacaille, who published his

Catalog of Nebulae of the Southern Sky (1781). In that same year, 1781, a new planet was discovered by William Herschel. While measuring the direction and brightness of stars, Herschel found a fuzzy spot that moved among the stars. This was Uranus, the first planet that was not known to the ancients. In 1783 John Goodricke discovered the eclipses of Algol, the Head of Medusa in the constellation Perseus. Observing the periodic dimming of Algol for a few hours on every third day, Goodricke proposed that the changes in brightness were due to eclipses by a binary companion. Also in 1783, Herschel calculated the speed and direction of the Sun's motion. By analyzing the motions of seven bright stars, he showed that part of their observed motion was due to the motion of the Sun through space. In 1785, Herschel used star counts to map the Milky Way. Herschel assumed that the galaxy extended farther in directions in which he could see more stars. He found the galaxy to be flattened with the Sun near the middle. Completing the construction of a giant optical reflecting telescope in 1789, Herschel discovered two new moons of Saturn: Enceladus and Mimas. Meanwhile, the theory of Black Holes was introduced by Pierre Simon Laplace in 1790. Laplace reasoned that a star might become so compact that its escape velocity would exceed the speed of light, making it impossible for light to escape from the star. Laplace published his "nebular hypothesis" on the origin of the Universe in 1796.

Following Goodricke's documentation of the binary orbits of Algol, Herschel went on to catalogue over 800 binary stars. While the defining characteristic of binaries is that they move around a common center and are held together by reciprocal gravitation, Herschel also observed that their distance from their common center may vary over time as a result of their orbital motion. On January 1, 1801, Giuseppe Piazzi discovered Ceres, the first known asteroid. One year later Pallas, discovered by Wilhelm Olbers, became the second known asteroid. Because of the proximity of these asteroids in a region between Mars and Jupiter, Olbers put forth his hypothesis that asteroids are the fragments of an exploded planet. Olbers's hypothesis prompted a search for more fragments, leading to the discovery of Juno by Karl Ludwig Harding in 1804, and Vesta by Olbers in 1807. Although Lars Regner had effectively disproved the possibility of a "planetary explosion" in 1806, the continuing discovery of new asteroids sustained the popularity of the Olbers hypothesis throughout the first half of the century.

Testing Newton's experiments with prismatic refraction, Herschel discovered "invisible rays of the Sun." At the Royal Society of London, he presented his paper, "Investigation of the Powers of the Prismatic Colours to Heat and Illuminate Objects" (1800). Casting the prismatic spectrum onto photosensitive plates coated with silver salts, he discovered that the red end became hotter, but was hottest just beyond the visible range. Responding immediately to Herschel's discovery, Johann Ritter in Germany was convinced that something must also occur at the opposite end of the spectrum. The reason for Ritter's conviction was the widespread notion that light, like electricity and magnetism, had its poles. Newton, after all, had introduced the concept of polarized light to explain double refraction. The polarity hypothesis may have been wrong, but it nevertheless led Ritter to observe the evidence of "invisible light" beyond the violet end of the spectrum. The metal plate became hottest beyond the red end of the visible spectrum, and the silver nitrate coating became darkest beyond the violet end. At Jena, Ritter presented his paper, "Observations on Herschel's recent Investigation of Light" (1801), describing his discovery of ultraviolet rays. These discoveries of previously unknown properties of light prompted other scientists to give closer scrutiny to prismatic refraction. In 1802 William Wollaston observed dark lines in the solar spectrum. Passing sunlight through a prism, he reported on numerous dark bands and lines in the spectrum. In 1817 Joseph von Fraunhofer, unaware of Wollaston's earlier observations of the dark lines, provided mathematical calculations of the distances between the lines, thus launching the era of solar physics and solar spectroscopy.

On April 26, 1803, over two thousand meteorites fell at L'Aigle in France. Local residents who gathered some of the fragments reported that they were still warm. In his account of the event, Jean Baptiste Biot emphasized that this was indisputable evidence that solid bodies fell to Earth from outer space. There was, inevitably, a degree of fear concerning the size of meteors. If meteors struck the Earth, might not comets? That possibility gave rise to both wonder and panic at the appearance of the Great Comets of 1807 and 1811. The former was declared to be the marvel of the century, until an even grander comet appeared four years later. The Great Comet of 1811 was visible to the naked eye for 260 days. In October 1811, at its brightest, its light was equal to Vega, the North Star, and its coma was easily visible. In December one length of the double tail extended over 60 degrees across the sky. Because it had an extremely large and active nucleus, it became spectacular without passing particularly close to either the Earth or the Sun. First observed on March 25, 1811, by Honoré Flaugergues, its appearance was confirmed in April by Jean-Louis Pons and Franz

Xaver, Baron Von Zach. The sightings continued until June when it was lost to solar glare. It became visible again in August, brightening as it approached perihelion in September and its closest distance to Earth. The nucleus was estimated at 30–40 km in diameter and the orbital period was calculated at 3,757 years (later adjusted to 3,065 years). It remained visible to the naked eye for nine months, a record it held until the appearance of Hale-Bopp, the Great Comet of 1997.

Not surprisingly, many poets and artists of the period gave their impressions of the Great Comet of 1811 (Pasachoff and Olson 1995). In England, superstitious rumors linked the comet to the insanity of George III and the advent of the Regency. While Napoleon declared that it predicted the success of his planned invasion of Eastern Europe and Russia in 1812, others considered it a sign of God's anger at Napoleon's conquest. One newspaper reported: "The present comet must be deemed ominous to Bonaparte from the length of time that it will be visible; no comet ever continued longer except that which appeared in the reign of the monster Nero" (*General Evening Post* 1811). Achim von Arnim wrote two poems, "The Comet" and "Again," and there are references to the 1531 appearance of Halley's Comet in "Isabella of Egypt" (1812) and in the historical drama, "Die Gleichen" (1819). Clemens Brentano also described the ominous portent of the comet in his fragmentary novel, *Shipwrecked Galley Slaves on the Dead Sea* (1811). Other literary responses are Coleridge's "The Comet, 1811," and Isabella Lickbarrow's "Lines on the Comet," published in her *Poetical Effusions* (1814). In addition to "The Comet" (1811), Thomas Rowlandson painted several scenes depicting the popular reaction. Half a century later, in *War and Peace* (1865–9), Leo Tolstoy described the character Pierre observing the Great Comet.

A more extensive literary account of astronomy was the calendar series by Johann Peter Hebel originally published in the *Rheinländischen Hausfreundes* (1808–19) and then collected in his *Schatzkästlein des rheinischen Hausfreundes* (1819). The installments on astronomy included 10 essays: "The Planets" (1808, 1809), "The Comets" (1810, 1811), "The Stationary Stars" (1810, 1811), "General Observations on the Universe" (1812), "The Earth and the Sun" (1812, 1813), and "The Moon" (1814). Hebel provided his readers with a summary of the recent advances in astronomy and account of the discoveries of Herschel and other prominent scientists. The physicist and astronomer Georg Christoph Lichtenberg in his *Sudelbüchern* often posed conundrums and paradoxes derived from late eighteenth-century investigations in astronomy.

Georg Forster, best known as the naturalist who accompanied Captain James Cook on his voyage around the world (1772–5), joined Alexander von Humboldt in 1790 on a journey from Mainz north on the Rhine to Holland, and then on to England, returning through France. His impressions appeared in separate essays between 1791 and 1794, and were collected posthumously into a three-volume work. In England Forster visited William Herschel and wrote a detailed account of his telescope and his exploration of space. Forster marveled at the capacity of Herschel's intellect "to determine the size and distance of the stars, to discover new planets and comets hidden beyond the range of the unassisted eye, yet nevertheless calculate their orbit or course as if they were visible" (Forster 1794, vol. 3: 88).

As already noted, Jean Paul was among the German writers who, like Kant in formulating the mathematical sublime, found suitable analogy for the littleness of human endeavor in the astronomer's evidence for the vastness of space (Dorries 1990). Examples recur in *Dr. Katzenberger's Journey to the Baths* (1809) and *The Comet* (1820–2). From *The Comet*, as also mentioned, De Quincey adapted Jean Paul's "Dream upon the Universe" as finale to his "System of the Heavens" (1846), a review of Nichol's *System of the World* (1846). Later Romantics, like De Quincey in England and Edgar Allan Poe in the United States, turned to writings of John Herschel who extended the work of his father and led the current advances in astronomy. They also read Nichol, who found himself in debate with the younger Herschel over the nature of nebulae. A turning point was the publication of Laplace's *Mécanique Céleste* (1825), summarizing his lifelong work on gravitation, equinoxes, Saturn's rings, and related fields. The new era was made possible through the construction of improved telescopes. In 1844 the first American observatory was constructed at Harvard. In that same year, William Parsons, the third Earl of Rosse, completed the building of this 1.8-meter reflecting telescope in Ireland, the world's largest telescope until 1917 when the 2.5-meter Hooker telescope was built at Mount Wilson. By means of his new telescope, Lord Rosse identified new features of the nebulae, and discovered a spiral-shaped nebula, Messier 51, now known as the Whirlpool Galaxy. This discovery gave rise to a major debate, for the younger Herschel followed his father's contention that the nebulae were, as their name implies, luminous clouds composed of dust and hydrogen. With the improved resolution of his telescope, Lord Rosse claimed that the clouds were revealed to be star clusters. If the nebulae were actually galaxies, they were larger and more distant than the Herschels had assumed. Nichol came to the support of Lord Rosse. In his review of Nichol's work, De Quincey used Jean Paul's vision of the universe to register the fatigue of mind and spirit in attempting to grapple with the concept of infinite space.

Physics

The shift from matter-based to energy-based physics was driven primarily by the new discoveries in chemical, or current, electricity in the 1790s. Experimentation with electricity earlier in the eighteenth century had dealt with static electricity. The fact that amber, when rubbed, would lift a feather or bits of straw was known in ancient Greece, as reported by Thales in 600 BCE and Theophrastus in 321 BCE (in Greek the word *electron* means amber). A variety of experiments with static electricity were reported throughout the intervening centuries, but it was not until 1729 that Stephen Grey discovered that this power of attraction could be transferred from one object to another. The distinction between a conductor and an insulator was provided in 1736 by Jean Theophile Desaguliers, a demonstrator for the Royal Society whose Huguenot parents had found refuge in England. Desaguliers listed amber, glass, and hard rubber as good insulators, and he observed that all metals were good conductors. In 1745 Pieter van Musschenbroek developed a device, the Leyden jar, in which electrical charges could be collected and stored. To account for the transference of charges, William Watson in 1746 distinguished between two sorts of electrical charges: resinous and vitreous. Benjamin Franklin studied the Leyden jar to confirm his contention that its coating held equal resinous and vitreous charges, and that the one was always sufficient to neutralize the other.

During the latter half of the century Franz Aepinus and Henry Cavendish supplied mathematical means to measure the force between electrical charges and their transference. The power of attraction or repulsion provided the means for measuring an electric charge. In 1766 Horace-Bénédict de Saussure suspended pith balls from strings within an inverted glass jar and added a printed scale so that the distance or angle between the balls could be measured. Saussure determined that the distance between the balls was not linearly related to the amount of charge. Upon meeting Franklin in London in 1766, Joseph Priestly became interested in electrical phenomena. One year later he published *The History and Present State of Electricity*

(1767), formulating the law of electrical repulsion. Correcting Priestley's law, Charles-Augustin de Coulomb developed the law of electrostatic attraction in 1781. With an apparatus he devised to measure the electrical forces involved in Priestley's law, Coulomb established the inverse square law of attraction and repulsion of like and unlike magnetic poles. Coulomb's law then became the basis for the mathematical theory of magnetic forces developed by Siméon-Denis Poisson. In the seven treatises on electricity and magnetism submitted to the Académie des Sciences between 1785 and 1791, Coulomb developed a theory of attraction and repulsion between bodies of the same and opposite electrical charge. He demonstrated an inverse square law for such forces and went on to examine the possibility of perfect conductors and dielectrics. In 1789 Franz Aepinus developed a device with the properties of a condenser (now known as a capacitor), The Aepinus condenser was the first condenser developed after the Leyden jar and was used to demonstrate conductive and inductive electricity. The device was constructed so that the space between the plates can be adjusted and the glass dielectric (insulating plate between them) can be removed or replaced with other materials. Instruments of this type became popular in the second half of the eighteenth century and were the subject of experiments and interpretation by Franklin, Alessandro Volta, and other electrical physicists.

With the evidence published by Luigi Galvani in *De Viribus Electricitatis in Motu Musculari Commentarius* (*Commentary on the Effect of Electricity on Muscular Motion*, 1791), the study of electrical phenomena attracted the interest of the medical and biological sciences. Galvani's experiments seemed to demonstrate that animal tissue contained an innate, vital force, which he termed "animal electricity." That animals were capable of generating electricity was known to the Greeks and Romans, who would use the charge of the electric eel and torpedo ray for medical purposes. The torpedo ray would be applied to the patient's foot, temples, or sexual organs to treat gout, headaches, or infertility. Galvani argued that this electricity was not a rare phenomenon exclusive to only a few living creatures, but was a vital force in all living beings. His experiments with frogs' legs showed that even the muscles in a dead animal could be reanimated when the nerve endings were spanned by metal probes. This new force was a form of electricity that was "natural," in contrast to the "artificial" electricity produced by friction (i.e., static electricity). Galvani considered the brain to be the most important organ for the secretion of this "electric fluid"; the nerves served as conductors of the fluid to the muscles and sensory organs.

Galvani's experiments excited widespread interest, but Volta was not convinced. He argued that the frog's legs were a physically responsive conductor, and that the application of the metal probes was the true source of the electrical current. He further argued that, if two dissimilar metals in contact both touched a muscle, agitation would also occur and increase with the dissimilarity of the metals. Rejecting the idea of an "animal electric fluid," Volta went on to construct his electrical "pile," a stack of zinc and copper coins separated by bits of blotting paper soaked in salt water. This device was the first electrical battery and, depending on the size of the "piles," could generate powerful electrical current. Galvani, however, refuted Volta's contention by showing muscular action was stimulated when using two probes of the same metal. The controversy persisted throughout the ensuing decades.

Friedrich Schelling, in his *Zeitschrift für speculative Physik* (1800), argued that energy rather than matter was the pervasive and constitutive force of nature, permeating all things in its three manifestations: electricity, magnetism, and galvanism. When news spread of the chemical generation of electricity through the Voltaic pile, Schelling renamed the third manifestation "chemical process" rather than "galvanism" to avoid the implication that it arose as a life force. But others continued to experiment with the effects of electricity on human and animal organs, living and dead. In Göttingen, for example, Friedrich Blumenbach constructed a huge Voltaic pile (by recent estimates, each of its 10 units were capable of producing up to 20 volts, with a total of 200 volts when all were connected). Achim von Arnim was among the students who applied the electrodes to his tongue, nose, eye, and ear to test the effect of the electricity on the sensory organs. When he subjected his entire body to the full current, he found that he temporarily lost control of his muscles after brief exposure. Arnim published accounts of his experiments in the *Annalen der Physik* (1799–1802). After he turned from the physical sciences to pursue his literary career, he continued to describe electrical and magnetic influences in such tales as *Hollin's Love Life* (1802), *The Marriage Smiths* (1818), and in his novel *Countess Dolores* (1811). When Mary Shelley began her tale of *Frankenstein* (1818), she wrote: "I saw the pale student of the unhallowed arts kneeling beside the thing he had put together. I saw the hideous phantasm of a man stretched out, and then, on the working of some powerful engine, show signs of life, and stir with an uneasy, half vital motion" (Shelley 1818/1974: 228). From Galvani's reanimation of the frog legs, Mary Shelley derived her narrative of Victor Frankenstein's reanimating human body parts in the charnel crypt of Ingolstadt (Burwick 1986: 241, 1987: 266–73).

Chemistry

The physicist's experiments in electricity and magnetism were directly related to the chemist's discoveries in atomic weight and periodicity, and to the rapidly expanding list of known elements. In his novel *Elective Affinities* (1809), Johann Wolfgang Goethe made metaphorical use of one of the most compelling concepts of the age. In studying the polarity of electricity and magnetism, physicists observed that metals were not the only elements that exhibited attraction and repulsion. The phenomenon of "elective affinity" described those elements that readily combined to form compounds. The identification of separate elements and the account of their combinations were a major enterprise. In 1778 Carl Wilhelm Scheele and Antoine Lavoisier determined that air is mostly composed of two elements, nitrogen and oxygen. In 1780 Johann Dobereine observed similarities between elements, thus providing the first indication of periodic relationship. In 1787 Claude Berthollet put forward a systematic plan for naming the elements. And in 1789 Antoine Lavoisier published the first list of chemical elements.

The first clear evidence that "elective affinity" might involve an inherent electrical charge within an element came in 1800. In the preceding section on Physics an account was given of Volta's discovery that electricity could be generated by a "pile" of zinc and copper plates. Volta sent a report of his discovery to Sir Joseph Banks, President of the Royal Society of London, entitled "On the electricity excited by the mere contact of conducting substances of different kinds" (March 20, 1800). Banks commissioned William Nicholson and Anthony Carlisle to construct the device and communicate the results to the Royal Society. The device worked, but a serendipitous laboratory accident led to yet another discovery: electrolysis. Wires attached to the zinc and copper end-poles of the Voltaic pile were left dangling in a vat of water. Nicholson and Carlisle returned the next morning to find that bubbles had gathered on the wires: by means of electricity water had been decomposed into hydrogen and oxygen. As soon as the report was out, Ritter in Germany replicated Nicholson and Carlisle's electrochemical experiments, and the techniques of electrolysis were born. Humphry Davy's *On Some Chemical Agencies of Electricity* (1806) was among the foundational guides to electrochemistry. The following year Davy discovered that the alkalis and alkaline earths are compound substances formed by oxygen united with metallic bases. He used electrolysis to discover new metals such as potassium, sodium, barium, strontium, calcium, and magnesium.

Because gases too could be isolated by electrolysis, the behavior of gases also came under new scrutiny. John Dalton and J. W. Henry questioned whether gases combined in the same way as solids. In 1801 Dalton formulated his Law of Partial Pressure: "The pressure of a mixture of gases is equal to the sum of the pressures of all of the constituent gases alone" (Dalton 1801: 535). Gases dissolve in liquids to form solutions. This dissolution is an equilibrium process for which an equilibrium constant can be written. For example, the equilibrium between oxygen gas and dissolved oxygen in water is $O_2(aq) \leftrightarrow O_2(g)$. The form of the equilibrium constant shows that "the concentration of a solute gas in a solution is directly proportional to the partial pressure of that gas above the solution" (p. 538). This statement, known as Henry's law, was proposed as an empirical law well before the development of modern ideas of chemical equilibrium. In 1803 Dalton noted that oxygen and carbon combined to make two compounds: carbon monoxide and carbon dioxide. Each had its own particular weight ratio of oxygen to carbon (33: 1, 66: 1), but also, for the same amount of carbon, one had exactly twice as much oxygen as the other (Dalton 1803; 1808, vol. 1: 56). This led Dalton to propose the Law of Simple Multiple Proportions, subsequently verified by the Swedish chemist Jöns Jakob Berzelius.

To explain how and why elements would combine with one another in fixed ratios and sometimes also in multiples of those ratios, Dalton formulated his atomic theory of ratios. The constancy of ratios was further demonstrated when Joseph Louis Gay-Lussac showed that water is composed of two parts hydrogen to one part oxygen by volume. From his experiments in 1801–2 Gay-Lussac concluded that equal volumes of all gases expand equally with the same increase in temperature. This conclusion is usually called "Charles's law" in honor of Jacques Charles, who had arrived at nearly the same conclusion 15 years earlier but could devise no experiment to provide an exact proof. In 1804 Gay-Lussac put his experiments with gases to a very different use: he ascended over seven thousand meters above sea level in hydrogen-filled balloons. This experiment was a means for other experiments. He gathered samples of air, and conducted magnetic, pressure, temperature, and humidity measurements at various altitudes. In 1808 Gay-Lussac announced his "Law of Combining Volumes": "The compounds of gaseous substances with each other are always formed in very simple ratios by volume" (Gay-Lussac 1808/1811, vol. 1: 38). Gases at constant temperature and pressure combine in very simple numerical proportions by volume; the resulting product or products also bear a simple proportion by volume to the volumes of the reactants. In that same year the first formulation of modern atomic theory, together with a table of atomic weights, was put forward by John Dalton in *A New System of Chemical Philosophy* (1808). The chemistry of atomic weights and periodicity became firmly established in the ensuing decade. In July 1811, Amedeo Avogadro published his work on the molecular content of gases. In 1813 Berzelius modified Lavoisier's list of elements in order to develop a system of chemical symbols and formulae, a system still used today. In 1818 Berzelius published the molecular weights of more than 2,000 compounds.

Medicine

The parallels and overlapping interests of the scientific disciplines are especially prominent in the medical and physiological sciences. In an age that was preoccupied with the individual and with subjective experience, it seems natural that this would also be the period that gave rise to psychology and mental pathology as disciplines, that described for the first time the efferent/afferent nervous system, explored the regions and functions of the brain, and ushered in new experimentation in sensory experience. Medical practice during the latter eighteenth and early nineteenth century was influenced by the Albrecht von Haller's monograph, *On the Irritable and Sensible Parts of the Body* (1752). The muscular fibers were irritable, the nervous fibers sensible. Because fevers and trauma could disrupt the normal functions of the body, medical treatment involved relieving exacerbated condition of the muscles or the nerves. The major elaboration of Hallerian physiology was introduced by John Brown. In Brown's application, illnesses were caused by an excess (sthenia) or depletion (asthenia) of a body's natural excitability, and were to be countered by measures to restore balance. Brown's *Elements of Medicine* was originally published in Latin in 1780; the English text was published in 1788. When Brown treated himself for gout in 1788, he died from an overdose of alcohol and opium. A second, posthumous, edition of the *Elements* was prepared, with a biographical preface, by Thomas Beddoes in 1795.

Although a practitioner of Brunonian medicine, Beddoes was dubious about the reliance on alcohol and opium, for both affected the patients variously as stimulants and soporifics, exciting when calming was needed and vice versa. Beddoes turned rather to a systematic application of Joseph Priestley's "factitious airs," or gases, to treat consumptive patients. In 1772 Priestley had first produced nitrous oxide gas, and in 1776 he published his findings on the effects of nitrous oxide and other gases in *Experiments and Observations on Different Kinds of Air*. In the 1790s Beddoes established the Pneumatic Institute in Bristol and hired young Humphry Davy as his assistant. It was here in 1799 that Davy produced nitrous oxide and experimented with its physiological effects when inhaled. The frequent fits of hilarity among those who joined in the experiments prompted him to call it "laughing gas." Volunteers in Davy's experiment included Coleridge, Robert Southey, Josiah Wedgwood, and Peter Mark Roget (compiler of the thesaurus). Accounts of their experience are recorded in Davy's book, *Researches, Chemical and Philosophical: Chiefly Concerning Nitrous Oxide* (1800). The anesthetic effect of nitrous oxide was not utilized for another 45 years.

An eminent School of Anatomy was founded in 1770 by William Hunter on Great Windmill Street, London. Author of the *Anatomy of the Human Gravid Uterus* (1774), Hunter trained doctors and midwives in new technique for prenatal care and delivery. Upon Hunter's death in 1783, his sister Dorothea Hunter Baillie and her daughters Joanna and Agnes, who had been living in the Hunter family home at Long Calderwood in Scotland, moved to Great Windmill Street. Hunter's nephew, Matthew Baillie, commenced teaching at the school, served as physician at St George's Hospital in 1787, completed his doctorate in medicine in 1789, became a fellow of the Royal College of Physicians, and was elected to the Royal Society in 1790. Matthew Baillie delivered his Gulstonian Lectures at the Royal College of Physicians in May 1794 on nervous afflictions and pathological conditions of the brain. He also wrote his *Morbid Anatomy* (1793). Joanna Baillie was fully conversant with her brother's symptomologies of brain disease when she commenced her literary career while living in Great Windmill Street (Burwick 2004: 48–68). The first two volumes of *A Series of Plays* she dedicated to Matthew Baillie, "for the unwearied zeal and brotherly partiality which have supported me in the course of this work" (Baillie 1798: iii).

As a method of inducing a trance, and supposedly altering the flow of bodily fluids, animal magnetism was introduced into medical practice in 1775 by Franz Anton Mesmer. Mesmer completed his medical studies at Vienna in 1776. His theory of animal magnetism, stemming from his belief that magnetic influence could alter the flow of cranial fluid, influenced the subsequent history of hypnotism, the name given to the practice by James Braid in 1841 (Pattie 1994). Mesmer at first used magnets, electrodes, and other devices, but preferred to utilize his hands. At the séances several patients sat around a *batique* (a vat with rusting iron filings) while grasping iron bars protruding from the solution. In 1777 an 18-year-old, blind, female pianist, singer, and composer, Maria-Theresa von Paradies, was brought to Mesmer. Although no physician had been able to find anything wrong with her eyes, the girl had been blind since the age of three. She recovered her sight after treatment by Mesmer despite the fact that she had been under the care of Europe's leading eye specialist for 10 years without improvement. This cure, although only temporary, gained international attention and contributed to the adoption of Mesmer's work in the subsequent use of hypnotism in psychotherapy as practiced by Jean-Martin Charcot and Sigmund Freud. While it is doubtlessly true that Edward Jenner's introduction of smallpox vaccination in 1796 was the event that saved more lives, Mesmer's animal magnetism had a far greater impact on Romantic literature than any other discovery in the medical history of the period (Tatar 1978, Winter 1998).

Mesmer moved to Paris in February 1778. With an ever-increasing throng of patients testifying to their cures, Mesmer alienated his rivals on the Faculty of Medicine of the University of Paris, the Royal Society of Medicine, and the Academy of Sciences. The medical faculty took offense at what the public found most appealing about mesmerism – not its theory but its extravagant practices. Instead of bleeding and applying purgatives, the mesmerists ran their fingers over their patients' bodies, searching out "poles" through which they infused mesmeric fluid. This magnetic "touch" was denounced as sexual manipulation. Mesmer reasoned that his own body acted as an animal type of magnet, reinforcing the fluid in the bodies of his patients. Disease caused an obstacle to the flow of the fluid. Mesmerizing broke through the obstacle by producing a "crisis," often signaled by convulsions, and then restoring "harmony," a state in which the body responded to the salubrious flow of fluid through all of nature. Mesmer authored two pamphlets: *Mémoire sur la découverte du magnétisme animal* (1779) and *Précis historique des faits relatifs au magnétisme animal* (1781). A more elaborate account of his system was published by Nicolas Bergasse (1750–1832) in *Considérations sur le magnetisme animal*

(1784). The disciples also formed the Société de l'harmonie universelle, which developed affiliates in France's major cities. The spread of the new medicine alarmed not only the old doctors but also the government, and in 1784 a commission of the French Academy of Sciences was established to evaluate his practice. The commission was composed of distinguished doctors and academicians, including Benjamin Franklin. The report of the commission concluded that Mesmer's fluid did not exist and that his cures were the patients' fantasy. Forced to leave Paris in 1785, Mesmer traveled through England, Austria, Germany, and Italy, before settling in Switzerland, where he spent most of the last 30 years of his life.

Similar hostility arose in response to the medical theories of Franz Joseph Gall, who in the early 1790s introduced his system of organology and brain anatomy in Vienna. Collecting skulls, plaster casts, and wax molds of brains, Gall sought to relate cranial contours with the characteristic behaviors of the persons whose skulls he acquired for his collection. He noted the deaths of striking individuals – whether soldier or thief – in order to add to his collection, which became so extensive that by 1802 he possessed 300 human skulls and 120 plaster casts. Although Gall's pronouncements on the physiology of the brain were linked to his notion of behavioral indications in the shape, he was nevertheless a skilled and innovative brain anatomist. He focused his attention on the structure of the cerebral cortex. In 1796, the same year that Gall began to lecture on his system, Samuel Thomas Soemmerring published an anatomical study of the brain entitled *On the Organ of the Soul*. While Soemmerring attempted to designate a specific anatomical residence for the soul within the brain, Gall ignored the old conundrums on the relation of soul and mind and addressed instead the possibility that sensory and psychological phenomena take place in specific regions of the cerebral cortex. Gall described the nervous system as composed of a multitude of independent nervous centers. His assignation of specific psychological functions to otherwise undifferentiated regions of cortex and the cerebellum is the modern starting point for brain-mapping and cerebral localization. Responding to an outcry from the medical profession, the Austrian Emperor Francis II issued a decree in December 1801, forbidding Gall to publish or lecture on his theories. In Paris, assisted by Johann Gasper Spurzheim in the preparation of the first two volumes, Gall published his *Anatomie et physiologie du système nerveux en général, et du cerveau en particulier* (1810–19).

An even more important pioneer in brain-mapping was Johann Christian Reill. His contributions to the *Archiv für die Physiologie*

(1795–1811), the medical journal of which he was the founding editor, included anatomical studies on the relationship of the nervous system to the brain, the ganglion system to the cerebral system, and the cerebrum to the cerebellum. He also published critiques on the works of Gall and Soemmering. In the history of psychiatric medicine he is known for his *Rhapsodies on the Application of Psychic Cures to Mental Disturbances* (1803). Another foundational study was Charles Bell's *Idea of a New Anatomy of the Brain* (1811), which for the first time distinguished between the efferent and afferent nervous system. François Magendie subsequently provided an anatomical demonstration confirming Bell's theory on the motor function of anterior roots and the sensory function of dorsal roots of spinal nerves ("the Bell-Magendie law").

Developments in science during the period had radically altered the sense of the human presence in the cosmos, in the physical dwelling-place of the planet, and indeed within body and mind. With the shift in understanding of the natural and human world, there was a consequent shift in values, attitudes, and sensibilities. Processes of governance and social structure changed along with the status of science in the cultural community. Modes of acting in the world had been transformed.

References and Further Reading

Bailey, M. E., C. J. Butler, and J. McFarland. (2005) "Unwinding the Discovery of Spiral Galaxies," *A&G* 46, 2: 26–8.

Baillie, Joanna. (1798) *A Series of Plays: In Which It Is Attempted to Delineate the Stronger Passions of the Mind. Each Passion Being Subject of a Tragedy and a Comedy*, vol. 1. London: printed for T. Cadell, jun. and W. Davies.

Buckland, William. (1820) *Vindiciae Geologicae: Or the Connexion of Geology with Religion*. Oxford: Oxford University Press.

Burwick, Frederick. (1986) *The Damnation of Newton: Goethe's Color Theory and Romantic Perception*. Berlin and New York: De Gruyter.

Burwick, Frederick. (1987) *The Haunted Eye: Perception and the Grotesque in English and German Romanticism*. Heidelberg: Carl Winter Universitätsverlag.

Burwick, Frederick. (1992) "Sir Charles Bell and the Vitalist Controversy in the Early Nineteenth Century," in Frederick Burwick and Paul Douglass (eds), *The Crisis in Modernism: Bergson and the Vitalist Controversy* (pp. 109–30). Cambridge, UK: Cambridge University Press.

Burwick, Frederick. (2004) "Joanna Baillie, Matthew Baillie, and the Pathology of the Passions," in Tom Crochunis (ed.), *Joanna Baillie: Romantic Dramatist* (pp. 48–68). London: Routledge.

Cunningham, Andrew and Nicholas Jardine (eds). (1990) *Romanticism and the Sciences*. Cambridge, UK: Cambridge University Press.

Cunningham, Clifford. (2004) "The Discovery of Juno and its Effect on Olbers' Asteroid Explosion Hypothesis." *Journal of Astronomical History and Heritage* 7, 2: 116–17.

Dalton, John. (1801) "Experimental Essays on the Constitution of Mixed Gases," in *Memoirs of the Literary and Philosophical Society, Manchester*, vol. 5. Warrington: Printed by W. Eyres, for T. Cadell, London.

Dalton, John. (1803) "On the Tendency of Elastic Fluids to Diffusion Through Each Other," in *Memoirs of the Literary and Philosophical Society, Manchester*, 2nd series, vol 1. London: T. Cadell.

Dalton, John. (1808–10) *A New System of Chemical Philosophy*, 2 vols. Manchester: Printed by S. Russell for R. Bickerstaff, London.

Davy, Humphrey. (1806/1839) "On Some Chemical Agencies of Electricity," in *The Collected Works of Sir Humphry Davy*, ed. John Davy, vol. V. London: Smith, Elder and Co.

De Quincey, Thomas. (2000–3) "Analects from Richter" (1824); "Immanuel Kant's 'Age of the Earth'" (1833); "System of the Heavens" (1846). In *The Works of Thomas De Quincey*, 21 vols, general ed. Grevil Lindop. London: Pickering and Chatto.

Dorries, Matthias. (1990) "Ent-Setzter Apotheker: Ein Naturwissenschaftler als Metapher in Jean Pauls *Komet*," *Jahrbuch der Jean-Paul-Gesellschaft* 25: 61–73.

Eichner, Hans. (1982) "The Rise of Modern Science and the Genesis of Romanticism," *PMLA* 97: 8–30.

Forster, Georg. (1791, 1794) *Ansichten vom Niederrhein, von Brabant, Flandern, Holland, England, und Frankreich, im Jahre 1790*, 3 vols. Berlin: Voss.

Fulford, Tim (ed.). (2002) *Romanticism and Science, 1773–1833*, 5 vols. New York: Routledge.

Fulford, Tim, Debbie Lee, and Peter J. Kitson. (2004) *Literature, Science and Exploration in the Romantic Era: Bodies of Knowledge*. Cambridge, UK: Cambridge University Press.

Gaull, Marilyn. (1990) "Under Romantic Skies: Astronomy and the Poets," *The Wordsworth Circle* 21, 1: 34–41.

Gay-Lussac, Joseph Louis. (1808/1811) *Recherches physico-chemiques*, 2 vols. Paris: Deterville.

General Evening Post. (1811) "The Comet's Portent," September 21–4, p. 1.

Golinski, Jan. (1992) *Science as Public Culture: Chemistry and Enlightenment in Britain, 1760–1820*. Cambridge, UK: Cambridge University Press.

Heringman, Noah (ed.). (2003) *Romantic Science. The Literary Forms of Natural History*. Albany, NY: SUNY Press.

Heringman, Noah. (2004) *Romantic Rocks, Aesthetic Geology*. Ithaca, NY: Cornell University Press.

Hutton, James. (1785/1970) *Theory of the Earth; or, an Investigation of the Laws Observable in the Composition, Dissolution and Restoration of Land upon the Globe*.

Edinburgh: Transactions of the Royal Society Edinburgh; facsimile rpt. with commentary, Victor Ambrose Eyles. Darien CT: Hafner.

Kipperman, Mark. (1998) "Coleridge, Shelley, Davy, and Science's Millennium." *Criticism: A Quarterly for Literature and the Arts* 40: 409–36.

Pasachoff, Jay M. and Roberta J. M. Olson. (1995) "Comets and Meteors in Eighteenth and Nineteenth Century British Art and Science," *Physics Education* 30, 3: 156–62.

Pattie, Frank A. (1994) *Mesmer and Animal Magnetism: A Chapter in the History of Medicine*. Hamilton, NY: Edmonston.

Rieger, James (ed.). (1974) *Mary Wollstonecraft Shelley, Frankenstein or The Modern Prometheus (The 1818 Text)*, ed. James Rieger. New York: Bobbs-Merrill.

Richardson, Alan. (2001) *British Romanticism and the Science of the Mind*. Cambridge, UK: Cambridge University Press.

Shaffer, Elinor S. (ed.). (1998) *The Third Culture: Literature and Science. European Cultures*. Berlin: de Gruyter.

Shelley, Mary. (1818/1974) *Frankenstein, or the Modern Prometheus*, ed. James Reiger. Indianapolis, Bobbs-Merrill.

Tatar, Maria. (1978) *Spellbound: Studies on Mesmerism and Literature*. Princeton, NJ: Princeton University Press.

Wiegand, Dometa. (2004) "On All Sides Infinity: Coleridge and Astronomy." Paper presented at the Coleridge Summer Conference, Cannington, UK, 22–8 July.

Winter, Alison. (1998) *Mesmerized: Powers of Mind in Victorian Britain*. Chicago: University of Chicago Press.

Ziolkowski, Ted. (1991) *German Romanticism and its Institutions*. Princeton, NJ: Princeton University Press.

Chapter 9

Consumer Culture: Getting and Spending in the Romantic Age

Nicholas Mason

During the early decades of the nineteenth century, foreign visitors to London regularly marveled at much of what they saw, but perhaps nothing proved as consistently astonishing as the scope and opulence of the city's shopping scene. Even travelers from prosperous North American and Continental cities found London's shops and markets absolutely unparalleled in their experience. In the 1814 travelogue *Letters from Albion*, for instance, an anonymous German author recounts:

> The uninterrupted range of shops that line both sides of the street, prevents you indeed from looking upwards, for here you discover wealth and magnificence that you would in vain look elsewhere for. All that Peru and the mines of Golconda can afford, all that refinement and luxury can invent, all treasures that the four quarters of the globe possess, – are here heaped up. It is impossible not to be astonished in seeing these riches displayed. (*Letters* 1814, vol. 1: 79)

Four years later, Richard Rush, an American diplomat making his first visit to Britain, was similarly awe-struck at the enormous volume of goods flowing in and out of the city each day. "The accumulation of things is amazing," he recorded in his journal entry for January 7, 1818. "It would seem impossible that there can be purchasers for them all, until you consider what multitudes there are to buy" (Rush 1833/ 1987: 28). All of this consumer activity, by his account, left the city perpetually on the brink of gridlock, with even the Thames being "choked up with vessels and boats of every description, much after the manner that I beheld Cheapside and Fleet Street to be choked with vehicles that move on land" (p. 29).

By nearly every measure, both anecdotal and statistical, the scale of Britain's retail economy in the late eighteenth and early nineteenth centuries was unprecedented in world history. That Britain was indeed, as Napoleon allegedly scoffed, "a nation of shopkeepers" is borne out in governmental figures. In 1759, several decades before the nation's consumer economy hit full stride, there was one shop per 43 inhabitants in England and Wales and one per 30 in London (Mui and Mui 1989: 40). To maintain a steady stream of customers for these shops, British retailers developed sophisticated new marketing methods and flooded the nation's newspapers with advertisements for their wares. Perhaps nothing better underscores the growth of Britain's retail economy than the enormous proliferation of advertisements that occurred over the course of the eighteenth century. According to governmental figures, 18,220 advertisements were taxed in 1713, the first full year after the introduction of the advertisement duty. By 1750 this number had risen to 125,000, and by 1800 it surpassed 500,000, marking a 25-fold increase in the annual number of taxed advertisements during an 87-year span (Bruttini 1982: 21, Nevett 1982: 26–7, Mason 2002: 416).

Not surprisingly, Britain's artistic canon bears full testament to these shifts in retailing practices and the masses' newfound obsession with commodities. In contrast with earlier writers and painters, whose works pay little notice to shopping or the accumulation of household goods, Hogarth, Dickens, and others who lived through the consumer boom of the eighteenth and nineteenth centuries fill their works with allusions to brand-name products, favorite shops, and the daily rituals of a commercial society. Until recently, though, scholars in the humanities have paid relatively little attention to the histories of consumption offered in artistic texts, leaving the study of consumerism almost exclusively to economists and sociologists. And, thus, while consumerist classics like Thorstien Veblen's *The Theory of the Leisure Class* (1899), Max Weber's *The Protestant Ethic and the Spirit of Capitalism* (1904–5), and John Kenneth Galbraith's *The Affluent Society* (1958) have long been required reading in introductory courses in the social sciences, students in the humanities have traditionally had little sense of the enormous impact changes in consumer behaviors and attitudes have had on the artistic products of the past three centuries.

New Views of Historical Consumerism

Starting in the 1980s, many scholars in the humanities began to recognize how developing a better understanding of consumerism could produce significant new insights into their fields of study. Leading the way in this new interdisciplinary pursuit were the historians Neil McKendrick, John Brewer, and J. H. Plumb, whose collaborative essay collection, *The Birth of a Consumer Society* (1982), compellingly argued that, amid all the research on the Industrial Revolution, scholars had overlooked the simple fact that so dramatic a surge in production could never have occurred without an accompanying surge in consumer demand. McKendrick was particularly forceful in arguing that the late eighteenth century witnessed a "consumer revolution," in which "more men and women than ever before in human history enjoyed the experience of acquiring material possessions" (McKendrick et al. 1982: 1). Drawing heavily upon Veblen's theories of conspicuous consumption, McKendrick suggested that most of the energy behind Britain's consumer revolution came from its newly affluent middle classes, whose growing preoccupation with social status and respectability led to obsessive efforts to emulate aristocratic fashions and tastes. Manufacturers in industries ranging from textiles to china to shaving products were quick to recognize and exploit this shift in consumer attitudes, aggressively advertising their products as the "must-have" items of the season. Under the spell of marketing geniuses like the china manufacturer Josiah Wedgwood – the tradesman who, above all others, emerges as the hero of McKendrick's tale – Britain's grocers, bank clerks, and attorneys, not to mention their wives, developed insatiable desires for the newest "Queensware" table settings or Chippendale chairs.

As might be expected, McKendrick's iconoclastic claim that the eighteenth and nineteenth centuries were shaped as dramatically by a consumer revolution as an industrial one sparked a wave of scholarship devoted to applying, expanding, revising, and debunking his thesis. Inspired by the consumer revolution hypothesis, social historians began scouring wills, ledgers, and insurance claims for evidence of shifting trends in the ownership of pewter, jewelry, and linens (Weatherill 1988, Nenadic 1994); art historians began paying as much attention to the tea sets and brocades as to the human subjects in portraiture (Bermingham and Brewer 1995, Sofaer 2007); and literary critics began noting the impact of consumerist mentalities on even such "antimaterialist" writers as Wordsworth and Keats (Morton 2000, Anderson 2002). Adding a theoretical component to their studies, scholars from across the humanities came to recognize how the insights of cultural theorists such as Roland Barthes, Jean Baudrillard, and Pierre Bourdieu on the illusory, symbolic value of consumer goods might be as fruitfully applied to the past as to the present.

Perhaps the liveliest set of debates in McKendrick's wake has centered on whether the eighteenth century was indeed the moment when a consumer society was "born" in Britain. On the one side are scholars of the early modern period who insist that the same consumer behaviors McKendrick associates with eighteenth-century Britain were already widely manifest in the sixteenth and seventeenth centuries in not only the British Isles but in several Continental commercial centers as well (de Vries 1993). At the other end of the spectrum are those who suggest that McKendrick overstates the extent to which a consumerist mentality had become common in the eighteenth century. According to this school of thought, Britain's retail economy remained, on the whole, rather primitive until at least 1850, and it was only with the late nineteenth and early twentieth-century rise of assembly-line production and colossal department stores that the age of mass consumption truly commenced (Richards 1990, Benson and Ugolini 2006).

To a large extent, such debates over origins hinge upon how liberally one defines the notion of a consumer "culture" or "society." At the most basic level, as the sociologist Don Slater has suggested, "The notion of 'consumer culture' implies that, in the modern world, core social practices and cultural values, ideas, aspirations and identities are defined and oriented in relation to consumption rather than to other social dimensions such as work or citizenship, religious cosmology or military role" (Slater 1997: 24). To state the case more dramatically, the coming of consumer society might be said to mark a new stage in human evolution, the emergence of *homo edens* (man, or woman, the consumer) or *homo gulosus* (man, or woman, the glutton) (Brewer and Porter 1993: 3). Where things get tricky, however, is in deciding how universally shared a consumerist mentality must be in a particular society for it to truly qualify as a "consumer culture." In the case of early nineteenth-century Britain, for instance, we have numerous accounts such as those cited at the beginning of this essay of unprecedented luxury and acquisitiveness amongst the middle and upper classes. Yet we also have abundant evidence that a large percentage of the populace, both in agricultural communities and newly industrialized towns, lived at or near subsistence wages. If most of the commodities pouring in and out of Britain's shops – their muslins and necklaces, their carriages and chocolates – lay well outside the purchasing power of a majority of the population, is it not overstating the case to suggest this was a full-fledged "consumer society"?

Even more fundamental questions about McKendrick's claims have been raised by social scientists. Among economists the most persistent skeptic has been Ben Fine, who in several essays has attempted to dismantle the principal pillars of the consumer revolution thesis. To begin with, Fine charges, McKendrick and his followers' triumphalist tales of Britain's proud consumer heritage "depend upon a scarcely concealed projection from an idealised celebration of twentieth-century standards and mores" (Fine 2002: 157). Pushing this idea even farther, Fine suggests that it seems hardly coincidental that a new scholarly subfield devoted at once to downplaying the significance of industrial labor and heralding the world-historical role of bourgeois shoppers should emerge at a time when Thatcherism reigned supreme in Britain and Reaganomics in America. Ideological motivations aside, an even more fundamental flaw in McKendrick's analysis, Fine suggests, comes in his heavy reliance upon atypical individuals and events. In concentrating, for instance, on goods such as Wedgwood china and high-end clothing, which collectively accounted for a small percentage of the nation's retail spending, it is easy to portray a nation-wide economic dynamic in which social emulation fueled consumer demand, which in turn sparked industrial production. But if we focus instead on, say, coal – a much more economically critical commodity that also experienced a huge increase in demand during the eighteenth century – the narrative looks quite different. As Fine points out, "it would be far-fetched to view the rise in coal consumption as originating out of the emulative behaviour of the lower classes (with fashion emanating from London as the major domestic market)" (Fine 2002: 164). Instead, a coal-centered narrative takes us back to the more traditional "industrial revolution" model, where shifts in productive capacities rather than consumer demands serve as the principal catalyst for socioeconomic change.

In the wake of such objections, scholars have grown increasingly reluctant to pinpoint consumer *revolutions* or even consumer *societies* in world history. If anything, less grand narratives are now in vogue, such as those found in recent histories of the "product revolution," the "commercial revolution," and the "consumer evolution" (Berg 2005:

3–4, Slater 1997: 20, Copeland 1995: 7). A more profitable approach altogether, however, might be studying historical consumerism without feeling compelled to reach for such all-encompassing labels. Some scholars, for instance, have suggested that the sixteenth and seventeenth centuries are all the more interesting because they witnessed widespread shifts in consumer behaviors *without* any accompanying society-wide adoption of a consumerist mindset. And, as if to herald the beginning of a second wave of consumer studies in the humanities, John Brewer – one of the pioneers in the field – has recently expressed weariness over the obsessive debates surrounding the origins of consumer society. After proposing several more profitable avenues of enquiry, Brewer quips: "It's always fashionable to be post-something. I just hope we are post-consumer society" (Brewer 2004: 10).

Consumerism and Romantic Poems

If, as Brewer suggests, the moment for heatedly debating the temporal and geographic origins of European consumerism has passed, there nevertheless remains ample need for applying the insights of consumer theory and history in literary criticism. Inspired by recent histories of consumption, critics are still discovering important new insights into texts that long ago seemed to have yielded up all their secrets. What happens to our readings of *The Rape of the Lock* or *Oliver Twist*, they have asked, when we tease out the signification of previously overlooked commodities such as Belinda's cosmetics or the Artful Dodger's stolen snuffbox? And how do our metanarratives of nineteenth-century British literature shift when we consider fictional accounts of shopping trips to be just as "representative of their times" and "historically authentic" as a character's descent into a textile mill or a coal mine?

For the study of Romantic-era literature, consumerist approaches have proven particularly fruitful, largely because of the frequency with which the age's authors address – at times disparagingly, at others enthusiastically – the material splendor of their times. At the head of the anticonsumerist branch of Romanticism was William Wordsworth, whose poems repeatedly urge readers to reject the din of the commercial world for the serenity and spiritual harmony of nature. Wordsworth's best known sermon on the subject comes in the 1807 sonnet in which he laments,

> The world is too much with us; late and soon,
> Getting and spending, we lay waste our powers:
> Little we see in Nature that is ours;
> We have given our hearts away, a sordid boon!
> (Wordsworth, "The World is Too Much With Us," ll. 1–4)

So disoriented has society become in its all-consuming rituals of "getting and spending" that the poet comes to contemplate the comparative advantages of a pagan world, where deity is to be found not in filthy lucre but in natural forces such as the sea. As he exclaims in the poem's concluding sestet,

> Great God! I'd rather be
> A Pagan suckled in a creed outworn;
> So might I, standing on this pleasant lea,
> Have glimpses that would make me less forlorn;
> Have sight of Proteus rising from the sea;
> Or hear old Triton blow his wreathed horn. (ll. 9–14)

Not surprisingly, Wordsworth's close friend and sometimes collaborator, Samuel Taylor Coleridge, articulated similar anxieties over the steady creep of consumerism. In his 1798 poem "Fears in Solitude," for instance, Coleridge attributes the prospect of England's being invaded by French armies to the nation's sins, not the least of which is its obsession with luxury. "We have drunk up," he laments, "demure as at a grace, / Pollutions from the brimming cup of wealth; / Contemptuous of all honourable rule, / Yet bartering freedom and the poor man's life / For gold, as at a market!" (Coleridge, "Fears in Solitude," ll. 59–62). A generation later, in the fifth canto of *Don Juan* (1821), another Romantic poet, Lord Byron, would extend this notion to suggest that modern consumerism turns all human beings – not just slaves and paupers – into objects for sale. Digressing from a scene in which the poem's imprisoned hero is being ogled at a Turkish slave auction, Byron muses:

> 'Tis pleasant purchasing our fellow-creatures;
> And all are to be sold, if you consider
> Their passions, and are dext'rous; some by features
> Are brought up, others by a warlike leader,
> Some by a place – as tend their years or natures:
> The most by ready cash – but all have prices,
> From crowns to kicks, according to their vices.
> (Byron, *Don Juan*, V. xxvii, ll. 2–8)

Perhaps the most impassioned Romantic-era polemic against society's fetishization of the commodity, however, comes in Book V of Percy Bysshe Shelley's *Queen Mab* (1813). For Shelley, modern commerce is every bit as inimical to the "harmony and happiness of man" (l. 79) as his poem's other targets (monarchy, war, and religion), and he devotes nearly two hundred lines to detailing its abuses. Beneath commerce's "poison-breathing shade," he complains,

> No solitary virtue dares to spring,
> But poverty and wealth with equal hand
> Scatter their withering curses, and unfold
> The doors of premature and violent death
> To pining famine and full-fed disease,
> To all that shares the lot of human life,
> Which, poisoned body and soul, scarce drags the chain
> That lengthens as it goes and clanks behind.
> (Shelley, *Queen* Mab, V, ll. 45–52)

Deceived by empty promises of consumer bliss, men and women not only fritter away their livelihoods but also sign away their souls. So ravenous is the demon Commerce, in fact, that it will not rest until even the purest human emotions and experiences have been commodified:

> All things are sold: the very light of heaven
> Is venal; earth's unsparing gifts of love,
> The smallest and most despicable things
> That lurk in the abysses of the deep,
> All objects of our life, even life itself,
> And the poor pittance which the laws allow
> Of liberty, the fellowship of man,
> Those duties which his heart of human love
> Should urge him to perform instinctively,
> Are bought and sold as in a public mart. (V, ll. 177–86)

Such unrelenting attacks as Shelley's, Wordsworth's, Coleridge's, and Byron's have led many to propose that anticonsumerism is more than just a personal hobbyhorse of select authors, and is in fact a core doctrine of the Romantic creed. Stana Nenadic, for instance, defines Romanticism as "a movement that opposed modern consumerism and evoked a spirit of restraint" (Nenadic 1999: 209). Ann Bermingham goes a step farther in suggesting that so powerful was the antimaterialist ideology of Romanticism that "By the second decade of the nineteenth century, 'art' and 'culture' [had] come to refer to an exclusive realm of refinement and creative genius free from the taint of commerce. It is at this time too that they [took] on their decided anti-bourgeois stance" (Bermingham 1995: 4). This latter assertion, that Romanticism is by its very nature "anti-bourgeois," echoes one of the more provocative and systematic explorations of the movement in recent decades, Michael Löwy and Robert Sayre's *Romanticism Against the Tide of Modernity*. Drawing heavily upon the Marxist tradition, Löwy and Sayre claim that the single feature uniting all the "Romanticisms" that sprung up across Europe and the Americas during the eighteenth and nineteenth centuries was their shared opposition to the "way of life in capitalist societies" (Löwy and Sayre 1992: 17). Far from a passing fad in Western history that began with the French Revolution and had exhausted its energies by 1850, Löwy and Sayre's Romanticism is coeval with capitalism, originating in the mid-eighteenth century as capitalism established its hegemony in Western societies and surviving as a vibrant mode of resistance wherever capitalism remains entrenched today.

However compelling, this approach is far from universally accepted. In fact, many scholars have concluded much the opposite, claiming that, in reality, the Romantic worldview has historically enabled rather than checked the spread of consumer capitalism. The most elaborate exposition of this school of thought comes in the sociologist Colin Campbell's *The Romantic Ethic and the Spirit of Modern Consumerism* (1987). As his title suggests – with its overt allusion to Max Weber's *The Protestant Ethic and the Spirit of Capitalism* – Campbell seeks to update the Weberian theory that the rise of Protestantism, with its emphasis on personal accountability and a gospel of work, laid the foundations for European society's transition from feudalism to capitalism. Equally central to Campbell's project is revising McKendrick's claims that middle-class emulation of the aristocracy fueled Britain's late eighteenth-century consumer revolution. Using Weber and McKendrick as his starting points, Campbell seeks to develop a better understanding of the sociological shifts that prompted so many late eighteenth-century Britons to display such dramatically different consumer instincts than had their forebears.

His answer comes via a detailed survey of how the asceticism of early Protestantism gradually gave way to its mirror image, what he calls the hedonism of Romanticism. At the heart of the Romantic project, Campbell explains, are two interconnected impulses: to seek pleasure and to imagine future pleasures. Not surprisingly, then, when Romanticism gained cultural preeminence in the late eighteenth and early nineteenth centuries, heeding these impulses became increasingly socially acceptable, nowhere more so than in the marketplace. What resulted was "a distinctively modern form of pleasure-seeking," a sort of "autonomous, self-illusory hedonism." In contrast to traditional hedonism, which turns to material goods to alleviate life's discomforts, modern Romantic hedonism produces an endless series of imagined desires, none of which once attained offers more than fleeting pleasure. Hence, the modern consumer-cum-hedonist "is continually withdrawing from reality as fast as he encounters it, ever-casting his day-dreams forward in time, attaching them to objects of desire, and then subsequently 'unhooking' them from these objects as and when they are attained and experienced" (Campbell 1987: 86–7). Viewed from this perspective, it was not through – as McKendrick would have it – the instinctual desire to emulate one's social betters or the individual's helplessness in the face of the modern advertising machine that eighteenth- and nineteenth-century consumerism came to be; rather it was through the ascendance of a Romantic ideology that trapped consumers in a cycle of constantly imagining that their next purchase would finally be the one that delivered the long-anticipated gratification.

Obviously so ambitious a thesis as Campbell's invites skepticism. From a literary perspective, a natural inclination is to ask how extensively he has actually read the Romantics, for it seems doubtful that a movement out of which Wordsworth and Shelley emerged as leading spokesmen could actually bolster consumerism. Campbell anticipates this objection, however, explaining, "although the Romantics certainly did intend both to provide pleasure and to promote day-dreaming, they cannot be regarded as having sought an outcome in which these combined to facilitate the restless pursuit of goods and services" (p. 209). Herein, he suggests, lies one of history's great ironies, namely that a group of writers and thinkers who might very well have been the original cultural critics of mass consumerism actually provided "both the legitimation and motivation necessary for modern consumer behaviour to become prevalent throughout the contemporary industrial world" (p. 206).

A case in point of what Campbell describes here is Keats's "The Eve of St. Agnes" (1820), a poem which, as Timothy Morton has shown, at once celebrates the world of goods and "parodies the rhetoric of the commodity" (Morton 2000: 170). Central to Morton's analysis is the memorable moment in the poem when the amorous hero, Porphyro, slips into the virgin Madeline's bed-chamber and gazes upon her slumbering form. Despite the tumult rising from the celebrations below, Madeline sleeps on:

> And still she slept an azure-lidded sleep,
> In blanched linen, smooth, and lavender'd,
> While he from forth the closet brought a heap
> Of candied apple, quince, and plum, and gourd;
> With jellies soother than the creamy curd,
> And lucent syrops, tinct with cinnamon;
> Manna and dates, in argosy transferr'd
> From Fez, and spiced dainties, every one,
> From silken Samarcand to cedar'd Lebanon.
>   (Keats, "The Eve of St. Agnes," ll. 262–70)

That, even in our hyperconsumptive, globalized age, so many of these commodities remain foreign to the average reader's experience speaks to just how excessively luxuriant Keats's images are. While Keats might very well be parodying rather than celebrating the modern commodity fetish, one ultimate – if possibly unintended – effect of the passage is to summon up Romantic imagination and desire in the service of the modern world's insatiable appetite for luxury. As Campbell would suggest, Keats's "blanched linen," "candied apple," and "lucent syrops" become the imaginary pathways to personal and sexual fulfillment and thereby function as clear symbols of an emergent Romantic hedonism.

Jane Austen as Chronicler of Consumerism

Of course, as critics have increasingly come to recognize, it is logically suspect, if not outright foolhardy, to characterize the entirety of Romantic-era discourse by the writings of a select group of male poets, many of whom were well outside the mainstream of contemporary thought. If, for instance, instead of turning to the era's poets, one were to survey its most influential periodical, the *Edinburgh Review*, one might come away believing the age's intelligentsia generally lined up in support of the new consumerism. For, although they recognized many of the social costs of the still-emerging capitalist system, the Scottish Whigs behind the *Edinburgh Review* firmly believed, as Biancamaria Fontana has shown, that commercial society had "a greater capacity than any other form of social organisation to provide general welfare" (Fontana 1985: 172). Overall, then, when gauging literature's wide-ranging and complex responses to the spread of consumer mentalities, it is essential to also consider how women, novelists, and those less inclined to wholeheartedly embrace the core principles of Romanticism reacted to a society in which the acquisition of nonessential goods had come to demand a significant portion of the average middle- and upper-class Briton's energies. How did a political conservative such as Hannah More, a young mother such as Felicia Hemans, or a provincial spinster such as Jane Austen respond to a brave new world where the acquisition of goods could dominate large portions of a life? Austen's works, in particular, seem ripe for such analysis, not only because of their enduring popularity but also because of Austen's penchant for meticulously chronicling the material pursuits of her characters. In fact, as I will suggest in this final section of this essay, it is entirely possible to read Austen's six completed novels as conduct books on proper consumer behavior and to consider Austen herself the great historian of consumerism in late eighteenth- and early nineteenth-century Britain.

Until fairly recently to label Austen a historian of any sort would have raised eyebrows in many quarters. As Christopher Kent has shown in an insightful study of Austen and consumer history, partisans of what Walter Scott called the "big Bow-wow" school of political and military history have long dismissed the historical accuracy of Austen's world. The Victorian-era scholar Richard Simpson, for instance, said of Austen: "Of organized society she manifests no idea. She had no interest for the great social and political problems which were being debated with so much blood in her day. The social combinations which taxed the calculating powers of Adam Smith or Jeremy Bentham were above her powers." Nearly a century later, one of the twentieth century's preeminent literary critics, Lionel Trilling, concurred, contending that "the impulse to believe that the world of Jane Austen really did exist leads to notable error" and that "any serious history will make it sufficiently clear that the real England was not the England of her novels" (quoted in Kent 1981: 89–91).

The problem with claims such as these, as Kent points out, is their tendency to view the totality of late eighteenth- and early nineteenth-century British history as issuing forth from the two "great" revolutions of the age: the French and the Industrial. Yet if we look at the lived experience of a significant portion of the population, especially middle-class and upper-class women, the French and Industrial Revolutions paled in comparison to what McKendrick and others have called the Consumer Revolution (Kent 1981: 95–6). And while few Romantic-era women wrote extensively about the storming of the

Bastille, Wellington's tactical genius at Waterloo, or the socioeconomic ramifications of the fledgling factory system, no one better captured the pleasures, anxieties, and neuroses of a society fixated upon the pursuit of luxury goods than writers such as Austen, Fanny Burney, and Maria Edgeworth.

Given their upbringing, it is wholly understandable that these women would demonstrate such a fascination with the world of goods. Quite simply, by virtue of growing up female in the privileged ranks of a commercial society, they were trained experts in negotiating with shopkeepers and identifying a fashionable china pattern or ballroom gown. The extent to which Austen herself passed her time "day-dreaming" (as Colin Campbell would phrase it) of impending purchases is documented in her surviving letters. Especially when writing to her sister, Cassandra, Austen speaks compulsively of gourmet foods, tableware, and, most particularly, clothes. Part of this can be explained by the fact that many of her letters were written while away on shopping trips to London or Bath. Yet she herself frequently confesses, often in an attitude of self-mockery, how obsessed she has become with material goods. For instance, in a letter to Cassandra dated October 27, 1798, the 22-year-old Austen reports: "I ... next week shall begin my operations on my hat, on which You know my principal hopes of happiness depend. – I am very grand indeed" (Austen 1995: 16). Seven months later, writing home from Bath, she carefully sketches a lace pattern for her sister before melodramatically proclaiming, "This is what I have been looking for these three years" (p. 42). Such admissions of her weakness for fine clothing remain a staple of Austen's letters into her final years. In an April 1811 letter from London, for instance, she divulges to Cassandra,

> I am sorry to tell you that I am getting very extravagant & spending all my Money; & what is worse for *you*, I have been spending all yours too; for in a Linendraper's shop to which I went for check'd Muslin, & for which I was obliged to give seven shillings a yard, I was tempted by a pretty coloured muslin. (Austen 1995: 179)

Later in the same letter she returns to her obsession with hats: "Miss Burton has made me a very pretty little Bonnet – & now nothing can satisfy me but I must have a straw hat, of the riding hat shape. . . . I am really very shocking" (p. 180).

When back home in Hampshire, most of Austen's purchases would likely have been much more utilitarian. As a single woman living with her mother and older sister, she would not have had primary responsibility for household economy; but as a proper woman of her time, she would still have been trained to consider "responsible consumer spending . . . one of the first female virtues" (Copeland 1986: 77). For women of the middle classes and the lower gentry, one of the principal sociological consequences of the eighteenth-century consumer boom was an increased emphasis on the roles of thrift and restraint in the conception of femininity. Conduct books, sermons, and novels geared toward women stressed just how essential proper household management was to a woman's character (Copeland 1995: 68–71, Kowaleski-Wallace 1997: 6–7). Typical of the times is Hannah More's best-selling religious novel *Cœlebs in Search of a Wife*, which features a succession of homilies on the spiritual and intellectual pitfalls of modern luxury. Accordingly, the inculcation of domestic economy becomes paramount in the upbringing of young women. So crucial, in fact, is economic self-control in the shaping of women's character that Mr Stanley, the tale's moral exemplar, insists, "there is no surer test both of integrity and judgment, than a well-proportioned expenditure" (More 1808/2007: 292).

Although Austen never puts it so bluntly, this basic philosophy is on regular display in her novels. Not surprisingly, given Austen's own predilection for occasional indulgence, her heroes and heroines appreciate the comforts – and even many of the luxuries – of modern life. Yet one of the features that almost invariably distinguishes them from the various braggarts, fops, and fools who fill in the edges of her tales is a proper sense of consumer restraint. In *Sense and Sensibility*, for instance, Austen contrasts the financially straitened Dashwood sisters with the showily extravagant Robert Ferrars. Like other Austen heroines, Elinor and Marianne Dashwood take genuine pleasure in certain nonessential goods, particularly sheet music, books, and fashionable clothes. But, as properly trained women of the lower gentry, they are more inclined to disdain than to emulate the conspicuous consumption of the truly wealthy. Nowhere is this more clearly displayed than when Elinor and Marianne visit the fashionable shop of the real-life London jeweler Thomas Gray. Unlike the typical visitor to Gray's, whose mission was to acquire ever more gaudy rings, bracelets, and brooches, Elinor goes to negotiate "the exchange of a few old-fashioned jewels of her mother" (Austen 1811/2006: 250). This minor errand, however, comes to fill a significant portion of the sisters' morning when they find themselves stuck in a queue behind a gentleman of fashion, later identified as Robert Ferrars, who is ordering, of all things, a jewel-encrusted toothpick case. Oblivious to those lined up behind him, the dandified Robert insists on inspecting every last case in Gray's collection before custom-ordering one more to his liking. At long last,

> The ivory, the gold, and the pearls, all received their appointment, and the gentleman having named the last day on which his existence could be continued without the possession of the toothpick-case, drew on his gloves with leisurely care, and bestowing another glance on the Miss Dashwoods, but such a one as seemed rather to demand than express admiration, walked off with an happy air of real conceit and affected indifference. (p. 251)

In typical fashion, Austen refuses to wax didactic on this scene, yet it is hard to miss her strictures against allowing the tireless pursuit of fashion to trump basic human courtesy.

In other novels, Austen regularly returns to this theme. Her first completed novel, *Northanger Abbey*, features brilliant satirical portraits of the "car-guy" John Thorpe, who tires all within earshot with unrelenting descriptions of the "seat, trunk, sword-case, splashing-board, lamps, silver moulding . . . [and] iron-work" of his horse-drawn gig (Austen 1818a/2006: 41), and the showily acquisitive General Tilney, who bemoans that his two-year-old, high-end tea set is quite out of fashion (p. 179). *Pride and Prejudice* contrasts Darcy's thoughtful, tasteful purchases, such as the piano he buys for his sister, with extravagant and self-centered ones such as the £800 chimney-piece Lady Catherine commissions for Rosings (Austen 1813/2006: 84). And the entire plot of the first volume of *Persuasion* hinges upon the economic disaster that befalls the Elliot family when, following Lady Elliot's death, "method, moderation, and economy" give way to the unchecked spending of Sir Walter and his eldest daughter, Elizabeth. Neither of these spendthrifts, we learn, is "able to devise any means of lessening their expenses without compromising their dignity, or relinquishing their comforts in a way not to be borne" (Austen 1818b/2006: 9–10).

Nowhere, however, is Austen's commentary on the sociology of shopping and the signification of consumer goods sharper than in *Emma*. Whereas other Austen novels feature occasional trips to generic milliners' shops and haberdasheries, *Emma* not only names the village clothing store, but situates it at the epicenter of Highbury society. Ford's, we learn early on, is the town's "principal woollen-draper, linen-draper, and haberdasher's shop united; the shop first in size and fashion" (Austen 1815/2006: 190–1). In a witty exchange midway through the novel, the newcomer Frank Churchill tells Emma that, by all accounts, he won't be a "true citizen of Highbury" until he has bought something at Ford's. Emma responds, only partially in jest, "You were very popular before you came, because you were Mr. Weston's son – but lay out half-a-guinea at Ford's, and your popularity will stand upon your own virtues" (p. 215). Just as important in the world of Highbury as one's choice of stores, however, is the taste with which one displays the items bought there. Several purchases, including such expensive ones as Mrs Weston's carriage, the Coles's new dining room furniture, and Mr Elton's complete home makeover, receive tacit narratorial approval, as they are made without incurring debt and properly reflect the purchaser's newfound social status. Other, showier purchases, however, such as Mrs Elton's gaudy pearls and Frank's (seemingly) dearly bought haircut, are widely perceived to violate basic rules of consumer propriety.

Where Austen truly excels as a historian of consumerism is in her depictions of how in a consumer society certain goods take on such powerful symbolic and ideological resonances that they come to shape their owners' identities. A perfect case in point comes in the strategic deployment of pianos and piano playing in her novels. Far from a simple, nonsignifying household object, the piano was quite possibly the single most ideologically charged product of the Romantic age. Unlike traditional luxury products, whose significations had been established generations earlier, the piano remained relatively obscure into the 1770s and consequently remained unencumbered by a web of meanings. This changed dramatically, however, in the 1780s and 1790s, the period of Austen's youth and young adulthood, when John Broadwood and a host of imitators developed the ability to mass produce high-quality, relatively inexpensive instruments and were thus able for the first time to make pianos widely available (Ehrlich 1990: 16–18).

Equally significant as the industrial processes whereby they increased production are the modern marketing methods these manufacturers employed to invest pianos with cultural meaning. Drawing upon a range of newly developed advertising strategies, these manufacturers were in a relatively short time able to make pianos must-have items even in families where £20 – the price of a low-end Broadwood – represented several months' income. In an early case of product placement, for instance, Broadwood attempted to link his instruments with genius and virtuosity by presenting a gift piano to no less a figure than Ludwig van Beethoven (Burgan 1986: 56). A much more common approach, however, was to tap into the anxieties of socially liminal groups, particularly the upper middle class and the lower gentry, depicting piano ownership as the gateway to gentility. A case in point is the *Piano-Forte Magazine*, a two-shilling and sixpence weekly which targeted middle-income families by promising those who maintained a subscription for five years a free, "exquisite, Brilliant-toned, and Elegant PIANO FORTE, far superior to many Instruments Sold for TWENTY-FIVE GUINEAS each" (*Prospectus* 1796: 3). Unfortunately for loyal subscribers, the magazine ceased operations just prior to its fifth anniversary, leaving, no doubt, a host of long-term readers infuriated that they would never see their promised piano.

Even more important than the class-based meanings attached to pianos during this era were those linking the instrument to the ideals of femininity. The piano, parents of young daughters were told, represented an essential investment in the "finishing" of girls as they prepared to "come out" into the world of courtship and marriage. To begin with, virtuosity at the piano signaled that a young woman hailed from a family sufficiently prosperous to afford both the instrument itself and the leisure needed to refine her skill. Beyond this, the accomplished female pianist was held up as a paragon of grace, sensibility, virtue, and self-discipline, all the requisite features of prescribed femininity (Burgan 1986: 51–61, Nenadic 1994: 153–4). That Austen herself was steeped in this tradition is manifest in one of her earliest surviving letters, written at the highly marriageable age of 20, where she insists, "I practise every day as much as I can" (Austen 1995: 7). Even in her thirties, when her marital eligibility had all but run out, Austen kept up her piano playing, if for no other reason than to accompany the dances of her nephews and nieces (pp. 161, 294).

However active a participant Austen may have been in the piano-buying and playing craze of her age, she was nevertheless critically aware of how this single commodity had come to have an enormous impact on the social construction of individuals. Accordingly, in each of her novels, she uses proficiency or lack thereof at the piano as a major characterization device. Several of her female characters, including Marianne Dashwood in *Sense and Sensibility* and Anne Elliot in *Persuasion*, derive much of their passion or strength of character from their virtuosity at the keyboard. In other cases, such as with Elizabeth Bennet in *Pride and Prejudice*, mere passing competency at the piano is preferable, as it signals balance and self-assurance. Throughout her novels, Austen steadfastly refuses to treat skill at the piano as the be-all and end-all of a young woman's character. In her early story

Lady Susan, for instance, one manifestation of the title character's tyranny is her insistence that her daughter spend long hours at the piano each day. More famously, in *Pride and Prejudice* the excesses of a piano-obsessed culture are on full display in Mary Bennet's bombastic public performances and Lady Catherine's astonishment over the fact that only two of the five Bennet sisters play.

Once again, however, it is in *Emma* that Austen offers her most sustained depiction of how consumer goods in general – and the piano in particular – have come to shape personal identities and govern social relations. When the upwardly mobile Cole family, for example, invests in an expensive grand piano, Austen reveals it has much less to do with their love of music than their desire to host high-end musical gatherings that include the likes of Emma, Knightley, and other members of the local elite. Another socially marginal character who takes advantage of the piano's cultural significations to secure her place in high society is Jane Fairfax, whose brilliant, passionate playing has a siren-like effect upon a series of men, including Mr Dixon, Knightley, and Frank Churchill. So bewitched by her playing, in fact, is Churchill that he completely disregards her lack of fortune and status and proposes marriage. Even the generally self-assured Emma is so taken with the power the piano invests in the otherwise powerless Jane that, the morning after hearing her long-time rival perform, Emma "did most heartily grieve over the idleness of her childhood – and sat down and practised vigorously an hour and a half" (Austen 1815/2006: 249).

Austen's critical awareness of the symbolic capital attached to goods is further manifest when she crafts one of the novel's major plotlines around the piano an anonymous admirer mysteriously bestows upon Jane Fairfax. Far from just any ordinary instrument, Jane's piano is a Broadwood. This level of specificity is noteworthy not only because of the Broadwood company's standing as England's premier piano maker, but because it demonstrates Austen's awareness of the workings of an entirely new type of commodity – the brand-name product. Prior to the late eighteenth century, almost all British goods were packaged and sold generically, coming with little information about where they were made or by whom. One of the side effects of the industrial revolution and the concomitant consumer boom was to put manufacturers across the nation in direct competition with one another, which required marketing their goods as distinctive and investing them with the symbolic value that comes with branding. Hence, by the time Austen began writing *Emma* in 1814, brand-name products such as Packwood's razor strops and Warren's blacking shoe polish were increasingly the norm (Mason 2002). Therefore, to identify Jane's piano as a Broadwood was to recognize an added layer of commercial signification on top of the generic social values already attached to pianos and piano playing. As the ultimately unmasked purchaser of an upscale Broadwood piano, Frank Churchill appears even more spontaneous, financially reckless, and hopelessly passionate. And when seated at her instrument, Jane Fairfax acquires all of the symbolic grace, class, and virtuosity the Broadwood company had labored so tirelessly to attach to their product over a 30-year period.

In *Emma* and elsewhere, then, Austen proves a remarkably astute observer of an increasingly complex and intrusive consumer society. More than just make-believe stories of a hopelessly polite and leisured world that never really existed, Austen's novels offer a richly detailed history of a culture that had become obsessed, as Wordsworth put it, with "getting and spending." Of course, in the decades following Austen's 1817 death, Britain's consumer obsessions would only intensify and spread to lower income groups. And thus, by the time Dickens came on the scene in the late 1830s, literature increasingly reflected a world where factories worked round the clock satisfying consumer demand for brand-name boot blacking, and society took its bearings as much from the neighborhood haberdashery as the local parish church. In the waning days of the Romantic age, as he navigated London streets filled with sandwich-board advertisements, ubiquitous handbills for quack remedies, and "a great Hat seven-feet high" pointing pedestrians toward a new clothing shop, the bewildered Thomas Carlyle declared: "The Quack has become God. . . . To me this all-deafening blast of Puffery, of poor Falsehood grown necessitous, or poor Heart-Atheism fallen now into Enchanted Workhouses, sounds too surely like a Doom's-blast!" (Carlyle 1843/1947: 136).

In many respects, consumerism offers the same dilemmas in today's society as it did in Carlyle's and Austen's. On the one hand, the retail world, then as now, was, in Venetia Murray's words, a "shopping paradise, full of unexpected markets and arcades, an Aladdin's cave of beautiful and costly treasures" (Murray 2000: 94). Even if the pleasures of the marketplace are fleeting and illusory, they are, as Austen's letters remind us, still pleasures. At the same time, though, as many Romantic poets feared, commercial obsessions can dull the natural passions and distract humans from the most meaningful aspects of life. In this respect, far from being voices from an alien time and place, the writers of the Romantic age are still very much our contemporaries. As we struggle to make sense of our own modern consumer society, then, it seems only natural that we would look to its roots. And nowhere are those roots more easily accessed than in the literature of Romantic-era Britain.

References and Further Reading

Agnew, Jean-Christophe. (1993) "Coming Up for Air: Consumer Culture in Historical Perspective," in John Brewer and Roy Porter (eds), *Consumption and the World of Goods* (pp. 19–39). London and New York: Routledge.

Anderson, Robert. (2002) "'Enjoyments of a ... More Exquisite Nature': Wordsworth and Commodity Culture," *Romanticism on the Net* 26. Available online at <www.erudit.org/revue/ron/2002/v/n26/005697ar.html>.

Austen, Jane. (1811/2006) *Sense and Sensibility*, ed. Edward Copeland. Cambridge, UK: Cambridge University Press.

Austen, Jane. (1813/2006) *Pride and Prejudice*, ed. Pat Rogers. Cambridge, UK: Cambridge University Press.

Austen, Jane. (1815/2006) *Emma*, ed. Richard Cronin and Dorothy McMillan. Cambridge, UK: Cambridge University Press.

Austen, Jane. (1818a/2006) *Northanger Abbey*, ed. Barbara Benedict and Deirdre Le Faye. Cambridge, UK: Cambridge University Press.

Austen, Jane. (1818b/2006) *Persuasion*, ed. Janet Todd and Antje Blank. Cambridge, UK: Cambridge University Press.

Austen, Jane. (1995) *Jane Austen's Letters*, ed. Deirdre Le Faye. Oxford: Oxford University Press.

Barthes, Roland. (1974) *S/Z*, trans. Richard Miller. New York: Hill and Wang.

Baudrillard, Jean. (1970/1998) *The Consumer Society: Myths and Structures*. London: Sage.

Benson, John and Laura Ugolini (eds). (2006) *Cultures of Selling: Perspectives on Consumption and Society Since 1700*. Aldershot, UK: Ashgate.

Berg, Maxine. (2005) *Luxury and Pleasure in Eighteenth-Century England*. Oxford: Oxford University Press.

Bermingham, Ann. (1995) "Introduction. The Consumption of Culture: Image, Object, Text," in Ann Bermingham and John Brewer (eds), *The Consumption of Culture 1600–1800* (pp. 1–20).

Bermingham, Ann and John Brewer (eds). (1995) *The Consumption of Culture 1600–1800: Image, Object, Text*. London and New York: Routledge.

Blank, G. Kim. (2006) "The 'Degrading Thirst After Outrageous Stimulation': Wordsworth as Cultural Critic," *Journal of Popular Culture* 39: 365–82.

Bourdieu, Pierre. (1984/2007) *Distinction: A Social Critique of the Judgment of Taste*, trans. Richard Nice. Cambridge, MA: Harvard University Press.

Brewer, John. (1995) "'The Most Polite Age and the Most Vicious': Attitudes Towards Culture as a Commodity, 1660–1800," in Ann Bermingham and John Brewer (eds), *The Consumption of Culture 1600–1800* (pp. 341–61). London and New York: Routledge.

Brewer, John. (2004) "The Error of Our Ways: Historians and the Birth of Consumer Society." *Cultures of Consumption*. Available online at <www.consume.bbk.ac.uk/working_papers/Brewer%20talk.doc>.

Brewer, John and Roy Porter (eds). (1993) *Consumption and the World of Goods*. London and New York: Routledge.

Bruttini, Adriano. (1982) "Advertising and Socio-economic Transformations in England, 1720–1760," *Journal of Advertising History* 5: 8–26.

Burgan, Mary. (1986) "Heroines at the Piano: Women and Music in Nineteenth-Century Fiction," *Victorian Studies* 30: 51–76.

Campbell, Colin. (1987) *The Romantic Ethic and the Spirit of Modern Consumerism*. Oxford: Basil Blackwell.

Campbell, Colin. (1993) "Understanding Traditional and Modern Patterns of Consumption in Eighteenth-Century England: A Character-Action Approach," in John Brewer and Roy Porter (eds), *Consumption and the World of Goods* (pp. 40–57). London and New York: Routledge.

Carlyle, Thomas. (1843/1947) *Past and Present*. London: J. M. Dent.

Christensen, Jerome. (1993) *Lord Byron's Strength: Romantic Writing and Commercial Society*. Baltimore: Johns Hopkins University Press.

Copeland, Edward. (1986) "Jane Austen and the Consumer Revolution," in J. D. Grey (ed.), *The Jane Austen Companion* (pp. 77–92). New York: Macmillan.

Copeland, Edward. (1995) *Women Writing About Money*. Cambridge, UK: Cambridge University Press.

de Vries, Jan. (1993) "Between Purchasing Power and the World of Goods: Understanding the Household Economy in Early Modern Europe," in John Brewer and Roy Porter (eds), *Consumption and the World of Goods* (pp. 85–132). London and New York: Routledge.

Ehrlich, Cyril. (1990) *The Piano: A History*, 2nd edn. Oxford: Clarendon.

Fine, Ben. (2002) *The World of Consumption: The Material and Cultural Revisited*. London and New York: Routledge.

Fontana, Biancamaria. (1985) *Rethinking the Politics of Commercial Society: The Edinburgh Review 1802–1832*. Cambridge, UK: Cambridge University Press.

Fox, Celina (ed.). (1992) *London – World City, 1800–1840*. New Haven, CT and London: Yale University Press.

Galbraith, John Kenneth. (1958/1998) *The Affluent Society*. New York: Houghton Mifflin.

Kent, Christopher. (1981) "'Real Solemn History' and Social History," in D. Monaghan (ed.) *Jane Austen in a Social Context* (pp. 86–104). Totowa, NJ: Barnes and Noble.

Kowaleski-Wallace, Elizabeth. (1997) *Consuming Subjects: Women, Shopping, and Business in the Eighteenth Century*. New York: Columbia University Press.

Letters from Albion to a Friend on the Continent (1814). 2 vols. London: Gale, Curtis, and Fenner.

Löwy, Michael and Robert Sayre. (1992/2001) *Romanticism Against the Tide of Modernity*, trans. Catherine Porter. Durham, NC: Duke University Press.

Lynch, Deidre. (1998) *The Economy of Character: Novels, Market Culture, and the Business of Inner Meaning*. Chicago: University of Chicago Press.

Mason, Nicholas. (2002) "Building Brand Byron: Early-Nineteenth-Century Advertising and the Marketing of *Childe Harold's Pilgrimage*," *Modern Language Quarterly* 63: 411–40.

McKendrick, Neil, John Brewer, J. H. Plumb (eds). (1982) *The Birth of a Consumer Society: The Commercialization of Eighteenth-Century England*. Bloomington: Indiana University Press.

Michie, Elena. (2000) "Austen's Powers: Engaging with Adam Smith in Debates about Wealth and Virtue," *Novel: A Forum for Fiction* 34: 5–27.

More, Hannah. (1808/2007) *Cœlebs in Search of a Wife*. Peterborough, ON: Broadview.

Morton, Timothy. (2000) *The Poetics of Spice: Romantic Consumerism and the Exotic*. Cambridge, UK: Cambridge University Press.

Mui, Hoh-Cheung and Lorna Mui. (1989) *Shops and Shopkeeping in Eighteenth-Century England*. Kingston, Montreal, and London: McGill-Queen's University Press.

Murray, Venetia. (2000) *An Elegant Madness: High Society in Regency England*. New York: Penguin.

Nenadic, Stana. (1994) "Middle-Rank Consumers and Domestic Culture in Edinburgh and Glasgow, 1720–1840," *Past and Present* 145: 122–56.

Nenadic, Stana. (1999) "Romanticism and the Urge to Consume in the First Half of the Nineteenth Century," in Maxine Berg and Helen Clifford (eds), *Consumers and Luxury: Consumer Culture in Europe 1650–1850* (pp. 208–27). Manchester and New York: Manchester University Press.

Nevett, Terence R. (1982) *Advertising in Britain: A History*. London and North Pomfret, VT: William Heinemann.

Porter, Roy. (1992) "Pre-modernism and the Art of Shopping," *Critical Quarterly* 34: 3–14.

Prospectus for the Piano-Forte Magazine; *with Elegant Piano-Fortes (Gratis)*. (1796) London: Harrison.

Richards, Thomas. (1990) *The Commodity Culture of Victorian England: Advertising and Spectacle, 1851–1914*. Stanford, CA: Stanford University Press.

Rush, Richard. (1833/1987) *A Residence at the Court of London*, ed. Philip Ziegler. London: Century.

Selwyn, David. (2005) "Consumer Goods," in Janet Todd (ed.), *Jane Austen in Context* (pp. 215–24). Cambridge, UK: Cambridge University Press.

Slater, Don. (1997) *Consumer Culture and Modernity*. Cambridge, UK: Polity Press.

Sofaer, Joanna. (2007) *Material Identities*. Malden, MA and Oxford: Blackwell.

Stearns, P. N. (2006) *Consumerism in World History*, 2nd edn. New York and London: Routledge.
Trentmann, Frank. (2004) "Beyond Consumerism: New Historical Perspectives on Consumption," *Journal of Contemporary History* 39: 373–401.
Trentmann, Frank. (2006) *Making the Consumer: Knowledge, Power, and Identity in the Modern World*. Oxford and New York: Berg.
Veblen, Thorstein. (1899/2001) *The Theory of the Leisure Class*. New York: Modern Library.
Weatherill, Laura. (1988/1996) *Consumer Behaviour and Material Culture in Britain 1660–1760*, 2nd edn. London and New York: Routledge.
Weber, Max. (1904–5/2001) *The Protestant Ethic and the Spirit of Capitalism*. London: Routledge.
Whitlock, Tammy C. (2005) *Crime, Gender, and Consumer Culture in Nineteenth-Century England*. Aldershot, UK: Ashgate.

Chapter 10

The Romantic-Era Book Trade

Lee Erickson

The book trade formed a small but far-reaching part of Britain's industrializing economy in the late eighteenth and early nineteenth centuries. The paper in books was made from linen and cotton rags, so as the textile industries industrialized, as cheaper cloth and clothes became more available, and as people discarded old cloth and clothes more rapidly and more often, the raw materials for an increased scale of book production in the late eighteenth century were created. During the Napoleonic Wars, when the importation of rags from France and the Continent was curtailed, the prices of paper and books rose sharply, which created economic incentives for inventing the Fourdrinier paper-making machine, perfecting the process of stereotyping, and finally harnessing steam to create the power press. Power presses immediately transformed newspaper production, but did not affect book production, which continued to rely on hand-powered presses until Robert Cadell bought and installed some steam-powered presses in 1830 at the Ballantyne Press to bring out a cheap edition of Scott's novels. At the period's beginning intaglio and copperplate engraving made illustrated books more attractive, and at its end in the 1820s the new process of steel engraving made them even more popular.

Paper production was affected by the industrialization of textile manufacturing and by the greater use of paper in a rapidly growing economy. So by the 1790s the richest men in the Stationers' Company became the paper wholesalers who also owned shares in paper mills. Their interests shifted away from publishing books, just as the business of wholesale bookselling had already become differentiated significantly from printing and retail bookselling, both of which still required apprenticeships. By the 1770s a wholesaling bookseller needed sufficient capital, good judgment, and sound business sense rather than a long apprenticeship in book production. Of the 46 booksellers who brought out Samuel Johnson's *Works* in 1792, most were not liveried members of the Stationers' Company. The economic pressures to specialize were intensified when profitable backlists were opened to any reprinter by the copyright decision in *Donaldson v. Beckett* in 1774. The decision especially helped the Scottish book trade. Although one might have expected many competitive editions of Shakespeare, Milton, Addison, and Pope to appear, few did. The major London booksellers continued to share in and profit from publishing relatively small and expensive editions of the trade's backlist. They limited outside competitors by refusing them credit and trade discounts, and forced London reprinters without trade shares to develop alternative distribution outlets. After the Irish booksellers were barred in 1801 from the unauthorized reprinting of new London imprints for the Irish and export markets, the dominance of the London trade was greater than ever. In the inflationary, book-hungry period from 1800 to the end of the Napoleonic Wars in 1815, books became even more high-priced luxury goods than they had been in the early 1770s and so enforced a consolidation of the trade through bankruptcies and takeovers into a smaller number of better-capitalized firms. In bad years publishers would reduce the number of new titles and increase the percentage of reprinted titles, and, as the technological advances in paper making and stereotyping took hold after 1815, publishers had to respond more flexibly to market demand and to financial conditions, or, like Archibald Constable in 1826, they would quickly go bankrupt. Specialty publishers with distributional advantages, like William Lane of the Minerva Press, acquired a large percentage of their particular market. Even though the publishing and market conditions had been created after 1815 for the great expansion in cheap book publishing to a wide audience that would mark the Victorian period, Romantic publishers remained dedicated to selling high-priced editions to a wealthy readership.

Copyright Law and Book Trade Practices

The Romantic-era book trade began in 1774 with the House of Lords decision in *Donaldson v. Beckett* that affirmed the limitation of copyright duration established by the parliamentary Act of 1710. This was soon followed in 1775 by the decision in *Stationers' Company v. Carnan* that declared the Stationers had no legal monopoly in publishing almanacs. The Scottish booksellers were the real winners in *Donaldson v. Beckett*, since they had pursued the Lords' judgment to resolve contradictory copyright decisions in the Scottish and English courts, and had successfully secured their rights to reprint new editions of the long-lived works that had sustained the English book trade. Alexander Donaldson marked his legal victory in 1774 by publishing a four-volume duodecimo edition of James Thomson's works in Edinburgh and by selling the copies in both his Edinburgh and London shops. The Scottish booksellers could develop their regional market and, because of their lower distribution costs, could extend their trade south into northern England. Above all, the Scottish booksellers had not suffered any prospective loss of capital because of the decisions against the London book trade and the Stationers' Company. Further, they could take advantage of their long experience in dealing with the London trade, and so business arrangements between London and Edinburgh booksellers became increasingly important. The improved finances and new confidence of Scottish booksellers also helped them to publish and promote the authors of the Scottish Enlightenment. Although the universities and colleges soon got Parliament to reverse the copyright decision for their copyrights, the London booksellers and the Stationers were unsuccessful. In addition, until 1801 Dublin printers and booksellers were freely republishing copyrighted books as long as they did not export their books to England or Scotland. So it seemed that free market competition in book publishing would soon flourish.

However, despite much theoretical discussion before and after, the copyright decision in 1774 just slightly rearranged relations in the British book trade, and its effects were chiefly psychological. A few apprehensive London booksellers sold their trade shares to others who recognized that the Lords' decision had not essentially changed the publishing market. As long as competing editions were not published, the most dependably profitable books were still fine new editions of popular authors whose works were no longer in copyright. Throughout the Romantic period, the book trade acted as if perpetual copyright existed and conducted trade sales of shares in expired copyrights. Sharing copyrights and publication among themselves restrained competition from those most likely to produce rival editions and also reduced the financial risk that any individual bookseller would undertake.

Few works were in fact copyrighted. For example, of the more than one thousand publications of the first John Murray, only about 15 percent were entered in the Stationers' register. For most books a bookseller had no reason to secure copyright, since they were unlikely to sell well or would be difficult for London reprinters to reproduce. If Murray felt dangerous competition would arise, the business difficulty was solved by offering a potential competitor a share of a joint publication. When Joseph Johnson told Murray that he was planning to bring out a rival translation of Johann Lavater's *Essays on Physiognomy* in 1787, Murray convinced Johnson to share the costs and risks to be sure of their profits. Such partnerships were usual. Fully 40 percent of Murray's publications were produced jointly, and, since he specialized in medical books, many of them had Edinburgh partners. A bookseller could always issue his publications alone, but prudence dictated that he seek others to share large financial risks.

To move from being a retail bookseller to a publishing wholesale bookseller in the last quarter of the eighteenth century required substantial working capital. For example, the first John Murray became a wholesaling bookseller in 1775 after having inherited over £2,000 in 1774. If one had shares of proven sellers such as Shakespeare, Pope, Addison, Swift, Fielding, Sterne, or Johnson, or if one owned part of a successful periodical such as the *Gentleman's Magazine*, the *Critical Review*, or the *Monthly Review*, then one would need less capital and a less diversified list. In general, however, booksellers needed to bring out at least 20 titles a year to limit their risks and – because of the distinct fall and spring publishing seasons connected to Parliament's sessions – booksellers needed to be able to issue a fall list while waiting for the bills received from the spring list to be paid. Publishers also required reserve capital to weather a financial crisis or an indifferent publishing season.

The book trade was linked together by a system of discounts and credits. Samuel Johnson explained this in a 1776 letter to Nathan Wetherall, Vice-Chancellor of Oxford University, who wanted a London bookseller to distribute the university press's books. Johnson calculated that a book's trade price for the press's London agent was about 70 percent of the retail price. The agent would sell at 75 percent of the retail price to a wholesaler, who in turn would give the retail bookseller a discount of 17 to 20 percent on the retail price, depending on the length of offered credit. The London agent and the wholesaler would expect to pay with three- to six-month bills. London retailers would expect to pay with six-month bills, while country booksellers would expect to pay with bills at nine months to a year in length, and overseas retailers could demand even longer credit. Deeper discounts would be expected for shorter bills or cash. In addition, sellers paid for all shipping and handling charges. Even steeper discounting was done by London wholesaling booksellers who had shares in the syndicate editions of backlist titles: to guarantee their profits they regularly sold their copies to distributing wholesalers like Charles Dilly at 50 or 60 percent of the retail price, and often never saw or sold a single retail copy of an edition.

Booksellers carefully limited their exposure to others' financial difficulties. Because the trade was extremely sensitive to credit conditions, bankruptcies would increase sharply in financial crises, as in 1793 and again in 1825–6. Any large publisher who went bankrupt left others with substantial losses, and so one firm's failure easily led to other bankruptcies. For instance, John Murray II was saved in 1826 because he had not accepted any of Archibald Constable's bills. Warehouse and printing house fires also presented significant trade risks, and required booksellers to be insured and to have a capital reserve sufficient to remain in business while waiting for an insurer to pay.

Even with the surviving books and numbers in front of one, making sense of a bookseller's ledgers has always required advanced forensic accounting. As Byron said in an 1822 letter to Douglas Kinnaird, "It is a difficult piece of Antiquarianism to decypher the Hieroglyphic of a publisher's balance – pro–con – or otherwise – or anywise." Booksellers kept records for individual titles of their receipts from sales and of their payments for copyrights, paper, and printing, but they typically entered amounts in their ledgers during the month they occurred, so determining whether a title made an aggregate profit or loss requires an examination of every year a book was in stock. The costs for warehousing, shipping, handling, and insurance should have been shared out to each title, but instead were treated as overhead and generally do not appear in accounts. Records of net interest gain or expense are altogether absent. Throughout the era, discounts for cash were about 10 percent over and above any regular trade arrangement, and were often handled directly to avoid financial third parties.

An additional difficulty in determining profits and losses stems from the publishers' treatment of advertising expenses. To promote individual titles the London wholesaling booksellers demanded contributions from provincial publishing partners and from authors who were sharing publication risks. However, booksellers purchased advertising in bulk from newspapers and periodicals to promote all of their current publications and so did not usually itemize advertising costs for individual titles. Even when they did, existing evidence suggests that publishers charged authors retail rather than trade or proprietary advertising rates. Advertising was important, since a publisher had to bring a book to the attention of the trade, and once advertising ceased so did the sale of most books. Regular advertising also softened the reviews, and, more important, guaranteed that reviews would appear. For aggressive London publishers such as Longman, advertising is said to have amounted to between 20 and 30 percent of a book's publishing costs. Advertising was especially important for novels publishers, who marketed their books to circulating libraries and so needed to create indirect demand for them. William Lane promoted his fiction in his newspaper, the *Star*, and later Henry Colburn puffed his novels in his weekly *Literary Gazette*. Further, since publishing was tied to the parliamentary and social seasons, a fall advertising campaign was often followed by one in the spring, and, after Parliament rose in May or June, publishers sensibly reduced their promotions. After English officers brought back the German custom of Christmas gift-giving from the Napoleonic Wars, booksellers in the 1820s soon found that November was the best month to bring out new books, especially gift books such as poetry and literary annuals. However, they would then date volumes with the following year so that a title's shelf life would be prolonged.

The strongest booksellers had periodical publications that provided a reliable income and that could serve as an advertising vehicle for their books. At times the periodicals seemed to dominate the book trade, especially after the advent in 1802 of the *Edinburgh Review*, which was the mainstay of Archibald Constable's firm. When Grenville's Whig administration came to power briefly from 1806 to 1807, the *Edinburgh Review* achieved national recognition and its circulation rose to 7,000 copies an issue. Constable then reprinted back issues to satisfy his new London subscribers and so profited further. In opposition to the *Edinburgh Review* and with the Treasury's help, John Murray established the *Quarterly Review* in 1809. The Rivingtons ran the *British Critic*; later William Blackwood created *Blackwood's Magazine*, John Taylor and James Hessey were proprietors of the *London Magazine*, and Henry Colburn had *Colburn's New Monthly Magazine*. A successful periodical would usually contribute a substantial portion of a firm's profits. When the *Edinburgh* and *Quarterly* reviews achieved regular sales above 10,000 copies an issue in the 1810s, they further focused the reading public's attention and so assisted the sale of the small number of titles that they reviewed. As a result, except for a few bestsellers, the London booksellers considered books subsidiary to periodicals from 1810 to the period's end.

The high price of paper during the Napoleonic Wars made books extremely expensive and attracted both readers and publishers to poetry. The price of paper tripled from its lows in the financial depression of 1793 and reached its peak in 1810, when about two-thirds of a book's publishing cost was the price of its paper. As their prices rose, books became even greater luxuries than they had been before, and so a premium was placed upon literature that could stand up to rereading. For this reason poetry became highly fashionable. Sir Walter Scott's *Lady of the Lake* (1810) sold over 20,000 copies in its first six months, even though in its quarto first edition the volume cost a full two guineas (two pounds and two shillings) and in subsequent octavo editions a still expensive 12 shillings. To translate these amounts into today's terms, one should remember that a pound was equivalent to a quarter of an ounce of gold, and so at the current value of $800 for an ounce of gold, a pound then would be worth about $200 or £100 now. Since the standard of living was then much lower, books were even more expensive than the gold-standard equivalents indicate; nonetheless, the figures do suggest how extraordinary the social fashion for the conspicuous consumption of books was in the first two decades of the nineteenth century. Byron set a sales record with his *Corsair* (1814), which sold 10,000 copies on its first day and 20,000 copies in its first two weeks. It appeared in octavo and cost a comparatively reasonable five shillings and sixpence. Even though *Corsair* was less profitable than Scott's most popular work, John Murray II was almost coining money in publishing the volume and rushed more copies into print to meet the great demand. George Crabbe, who emerged from poetic retirement with his 1807 *Poems*, was immediately popular, and so in 1819 Murray paid Crabbe £3,000 for *Tales of the Hall* and *Poems*. And Thomas Moore received £3,000 from Longman for *Lalla Rookh* (1817). It helped publishers to have the copyright prices on readers' lips, because the amounts seemed to justify the purchase of such luxury items.

The high price of paper also provided an incentive for technological improvements in printing. Printers had long wanted to duplicate set type without resetting it and had experimented with methods of doing so. In the 1790s Firmin Didot in Paris made papier-mâché molds of set type and then cast type in those molds, a process which he named stereotyping. Didot had printed a few works using such type, but could not make the technique commercially feasible. Under the direction of Lord Stanhope, Alexander Wilson perfected the process by 1804, and was employed by Oxford University Press in 1805 to print Bibles and prayer books using stereotyping. Cambridge University Press was licensed to use stereotyping in 1809, and by 1820 12 London printing firms used the process. Stereotyping reduced both printing and publishing costs. Printers saved money on type wear and also did not have to keep type set in frames in case a book required immediate reprinting. Publishers benefited by not having to worry about underestimating the size of an initial print run and so could reduce their capital risks. Also responding to the high price of paper, the Fourdrinier brothers developed a mechanical paper-making machine that was producing paper by 1807. As the process improved, the machine reduced waste and improved paper quality. By 1822 mechanical paper making was producing over half of all paper for printing. As a result, despite the increasing demand for paper, the Fourdrinier paper-making machine contributed to a drop of a third in the price of paper from 1810 to the end of the period and thus to lower prices for most books.

Reprinting, Reselling, and Collecting Books

In 1775 the book trade seemed a poor business to enter. The London booksellers appeared to have suffered a large capital loss because they were now vulnerable to cheap reprints of their valuable trade shares, and because the most profitable part of the English Stock, the monopoly on publishing of almanacs, had been taken from the Stationers' Company. The Stationers, however, regained effective control over the almanac market by selling almanacs below cost for several years to prevent new entrants from establishing themselves in the market. They then persuaded Lord North's government to pass a two shilling stamp tax in 1779 on cheap sheet almanacs, and later bought Carnan's almanac titles from his estate after his death in 1788. This effectively kept the almanac monopoly for the Stationers' Company until the tax on sheet almanacs was abolished in 1831. The struggle to restore their almanac monopoly, however, absorbed the Stationers' publishing energies and left London booksellers on their own.

The book trade had suddenly become much riskier and more competitive in 1774, so even wealthy booksellers refrained from acquiring many new copyrights and had little incentive to pay high prices for them. It took another generation for the literary market to recover from the decision in *Donaldson v. Beckett*. Authors like Crabbe, who seemed to have promising writing careers ahead, retreated into patronage positions rather than face the unpromising literary market of the 1780s. Similarly, William Blake, who published his own expensive illustrated *Songs of Innocence* (1789) and *Songs of Innocence and Experience* (1794), soon complained in *The Four Zoas* (1797) that "Wisdom is sold in the desolate market where none come to buy." Blake discovered that new authors and their publishers were now competing with more and cheaper reprints of established literature. So even though the decade saw great industrial growth, an enormous rise in the production of paper, and a corresponding increase in all kinds of printed materials, the 1780s have long been recognized as a literary wasteland. Booksellers, printers, and stationers continued to make money, but few authors did.

The general economic growth created new readers and buyers of books, and especially of cheaper ones. John Bell, the most aggressive of the early London reprinters, published an edition of Shakespeare (1774) in nine volumes, more drama with *The British Theatre* (1776–8) in sixpenny weekly numbers later collected in 21 volumes, and then *The Poets of Great Britain Complete from Chaucer to Churchill* (1777–83), which he issued in 109 18mo volumes. Buoyed by his first successes, Bell printed *The Poets of Great Britain* in an initial edition of 3,000 copies of each volume. Although he advertised each volume in sewn sheets ready for binding at the price of one shilling and sixpence and eight guineas for the complete set, modern bookbinding scholars believe Bell sold most individual copies bound in calf at two shillings and three-pence each and 12 guineas for the sets. A few readers were probably satisfied to read their poetry in unbound sewn sheets or to find their own binders; but most would have selected from the trade bindings Bell offered, which cost up to £33 for sets bound in morocco. Indeed, the chief competitive attraction of Bell's series almost certainly was its availability for purchase in individual volumes. In response to Bell's collection of reprinted plays, the London booksellers had already issued *The New English Theatre* (1776–7) in 12 volumes, and were especially alarmed by the threat to their long-lived trade shares in poetry. After Bell had advertised his new edition of 50 poets, they decided to publish collectively the works of the poets whose legally expired copyrights they thought had any remaining value, and they employed Samuel Johnson to write prefaces for 53 poets in *The Works of the English Poets* (1779–80), which appeared in 60 small octavo volumes of 1,000 copies each. Although we should be grateful for the booksellers' panic, which gave rise to Johnson's *Lives of the Poets*, the limiting of the duration of copyright did not really threaten their preeminence in the trade. Bell's small 18mo pocket volumes in clear but very small type were not cheap at two shillings and threepence each bound in calf; in contrast, the London booksellers' edition cost two shillings and sixpence per volume in boards and was sold as a complete set for seven pounds and 10 shillings.

Because of its small size and type, Bell's more tasteful edition, which included Chaucer, Spenser, Donne, and Churchill, was aimed at younger and more scholarly readers. The London publishing syndicate, on the other hand, was publishing an ill-assorted selection of reprints but had the advantages of better financing and Johnson's prefaces. The London booksellers were seeking to protect the size of their profits and not to increase the number of their customers, and so did not really compete with Bell's edition by allowing their edition to be retailed in individual volumes and then reprinting the more popular ones to meet demand. Instead, the large London booksellers refused to give Bell credit or to allow him trade discounts on their books, forced other retail booksellers to refuse his publications, induced newspapers to refuse his advertisements, and sought to discredit the quality of his series. Bell was forced to distribute his books through his retail shop, his circulating library, and the dealers of his newspaper, the *Morning Post*. He was systematically isolated, a tactic which the London trade found to be effective against all but the most resourceful and determined reprinters like Bell and, much later, William Pickering. As one of the London trade's largest and most efficient bookbinders, Bell was attempting to leverage his bookbinding business through his reprinted series and to create a more vertically integrated publishing firm with independent distribution channels outside the London trade. Fortunately, Bell had issued popular poets at first and so had a profit from the series before a printing house fire forced a long suspension of its production. Bell proved that a somewhat larger book-buying public existed than the London publishers were serving, but he barely survived financially since he operated on a much thinner profit margin, and he later went bankrupt in 1793 and again in 1797. Without reducing their prices to attract the purchasers who bought Bell's edition, the large London publishers had made more money more quickly than Bell had done, and they had also developed another valuable property in Johnson's *Lives of the Poets*, which was later issued in separate editions in 1781, 1783, 1790–1, and 1794.

Bell's *Poets of Great Britain* highlights the importance of bindings for the book trade. The era saw a gradual change from books published in unbound sheets with untrimmed edges ready for binding, to being bound in cheap labeled boards, and then to trade cloth bindings. Booksellers had traditionally allowed purchasers to choose among trade bindings or to order bespoke ones. At the beginning of the period, books were offered in sheets to wholesale and retail booksellers, who would have them bound for customers. In the 1770s and 1780s, as animal skins for binding became much more expensive, titles started to appear in cheap millboards. For many purchasers, this just provided a preliminary state; consequently, copies surviving in original boards are very rare. Around 1825 inexpensive cloth bindings were developed for William Pickering by Archibald Leighton. As common readers became more important than wealthy ones after the Romantic period, and as binding technology advanced, most books later came to be published with cheap cloth bindings.

In the face of competition from reprints, many new publications went unsold and were remaindered to specialized dealers. James Lackington, the largest of them, made a fortune in the remainder trade during the 1780s by buying the stock of bankrupt and overextended publishers for a shilling or two in the pound and then selling the books for a shilling or two more. Unlike almost all other booksellers, Lackington dealt solely in cash. This reflected his experience with poor book buyers and the cash-strapped country retail bookselling trade. As a man who had ready money to offer for the misfortunes of booksellers, Lackington was loathed by others in the trade, all the more so for trumpeting his success and piety in his *Memoirs* (1791) and *The Confessions of J. Lackington* (1804). The center of Lackington's enterprise was the period's largest bookstore, The Temple of the Muses, which he built on Finsbury Square in north London. Lackington was remarkable for his self-promotion, and famous for inscribing on his carriage his slogan, "Small profits do great things." He shamelessly flaunted his working-class origins and brought the entrepreneurial flash of a used-car salesman to a trade that catered primarily to the wealthy readers who bought most new books.

Although now commonly considered a branch of the used book trade, the antiquarian book trade and book auctions that Thomas Frognall Dibdin celebrated in *The Bibliographical Decameron* (1817) required specialized showrooms and catalogues. Because they catered to wealthy readers, booksellers occasionally offered antiquarian book search services, but found that acquiring individual rarities took much time and offered small profits. The salesrooms and catalogues of the Langfords, Leigh and Sotheby, Robert Hardy Evans, and Hodgsons appreciated books and manuscripts for their rarity, beauty, and provenance. The greatest collector of the period was King George III, whose extensive library at Buckingham House (later Buckingham Palace) was open to scholars. The King's interest in book collecting contributed to the fashion of creating large private libraries, especially by buying at the sales of other famous collections. The auction sale of the Duke of Roxburghe's books and manuscripts in 1812 at Evans's salesroom in Pall Mall occurred at a time of great social interest in rare and expensive books, and is remembered as the peak of the period's antiquarian book trade by Dibdin, who was Lord Spencer's librarian at Althorp. The auction was highlighted by the sale of the Valdarfer Boccaccio (1471) for £2,260 to the Marquess of Blandford, later the fifth Duke of Marlborough. Lord Blandford's extravagance, however, soon forced him to sell his library in 1819 at auction. The Valdarfer Boccaccio then fetched only a little more than £918 and indicated how the aristocratic craze for collecting antiquarian books was fading after the end of the Napoleonic Wars. When George IV contributed his father's collection of 67,000 books to the British Library in 1823, the Romantic fashion for the conspicuous collection of books had symbolically come to an end.

Publishing Judgment and Trends

The long-term success of booksellers depended on their judgment. Joseph Johnson and John Murray I both served as their author's editors, knowing that their reputations as booksellers depended on the quality of the works they published. In order to be successful they needed to have good taste in addition to sound business sense. Eventually, however, booksellers grew too large to allow a single person to make every copyright acquisition and publishing decision and so they had to hire editors. This seems to have happened first at Longman's house, which is estimated to have published a little more than 10 percent of all the period's new titles. The house seems to have grown primarily through strategic acquisitions and mergers, the best known of which was Longman's purchase of Joseph Cottle's firm, which had on its backlist Wordsworth and Coleridge's *Lyrical Ballads* (1798). John Murray II compensated for his lack of editors by often soliciting the opinion of other authors regarding manuscripts to help him decide whether to publish a work. For instance, Murray cautiously asked others for advice regarding the publication of Samuel Rogers's *Italy* in 1823, even though Rogers had best-selling titles such as *The Pleasures of Memory* (1792) and *Human Life* (1819) that were still in print. Murray was right to hesitate, however, since *Italy* did not sell at first. The work only became popular after Rogers revised it and in 1830 at considerable expense had the work republished by Edward Moxon with engravings after Turner and Stothard. The exquisite engravings and production carried the poetry, which had attracted little attention by itself, and so finally made *Italy* a publishing triumph that transcended the fashionable style of the literary annuals.

Good taste and business sense were not always combined. For example, Charles and James Ollier published Keats and Shelley but quickly went bankrupt; and Archibald Constable, who had succeeded with Sir Walter Scott's poetry and fiction, saw his firm collapse in 1826 under debt that totaled more than five times his assets. Romantic publishing history offers many such cautionary tales that emphasize the importance of a publisher's judgment, particularly when most books had a selling life of six months and could be counted as losses after that. Most books were printed in first editions that had 1,000 copies, and, if a bookseller thought the audience for a work was limited, often had only 500 or 750 copies. Even for the most popular authors, editions larger than 3,000 copies were rare. If booksellers were doubtful about a manuscript's prospects for success, they could ask an author to underwrite its publication or to solicit subscribers for money in advance and so guarantee a book's sale. Poetry and scientific books were those most commonly published by subscription because of their limited audiences. Such publications were, however, generally unattractive to booksellers because they used time and capital that could be much more profitably employed elsewhere.

The Sunday School movement, which began in 1780, contributed greatly to increased literacy and made the Bible the first book that most people read or owned. Most book buyers in the Romantic period wanted religious publications, and so religious books of all kinds sold well. Indeed, the chief impetus for making stereotyping a commercial printing practice stemmed from the desire of Oxford University Press to reduce its costs in printing Bibles and hymnals. Joseph Johnson, who published Thomas Paine, William Godwin, and Mary Wollstonecraft, was a devout Unitarian, whose religious titles make up more than half of his list. One of his most popular publications was John Newton and William Cowper's *Olney Hymns* (1779), which went through at least 29 editions by the end of the period. The Rivingtons had long been associated with publishing theology and were the appointed publishers to the Society for Promoting Christian Knowledge throughout the era. The firm was closely associated with Alexander Cruden's *Biblical Concordance* (1737, revised edn 1769), which it acquired after Cruden's death in 1770 and continued to reprint long after the copyright had expired. The firm also established the High Church *British Critic* with Pitt's aid in 1793 and was later to publish *Tracts for the Times* from the inception of the series in 1833. Nonetheless, the Romantic period's sermons, theology, and biblical commentary remain uncharted by scholars of book culture.

Latin and Greek classics in translation and standard classical dictionaries were a staple of the Romantic book trade, as were popular histories. Topographical and travel books always had a ready market, as William Gilpin's continuing popularity suggests. Wordsworth's *A Guide Through the District of the Lakes for the Use of Tourists and Residents* went through five editions by 1835. Travel books were especially in demand after 1815, when the wealthy could freely tour the Continent again. As fashionable taste in books shifted, John Murray II began to refuse most poetry manuscripts and to focus instead on travel publications after the success of Mariana Starke's *Travels on the Continent* (1820), which went through many editions under various titles and inaugurated a long and profitable series of travel handbooks that later became synonymous with the publishing house.

The new steel engravings of the 1820s contributed to the demand for travel books and for many other kinds of illustrated books. The publishers of the fashion magazines like *La Belle Assemblé* were soon producing the literary annuals, the most notable of which was *The Keepsake*. These expensive illustrated volumes with attractive trade bindings dominated the Christmas book-giving market from 1825 to the period's end. Rudolf Ackermann published the first of them, the *Forget Me Not* for 1823. These volumes required elaborate preparation and special arrangements for engravings. And since the engravings cost much more than the literary work and required a longer lead time, publishers and editors soon found it more profitable to have authors write about the pictures than to have the engravers illustrate the literature. So, while *The Keepsake* for 1829 memorably had Scott, Wordsworth, Coleridge, Southey, and – posthumously – Shelley as contributors, most other literary annuals offered writing that had cost little or nothing.

Fiction remained almost entirely a circulating library commodity throughout the period. Most novels were read only once and so readers preferred to borrow rather than buy them. For this reason only the most popular novels were purchased by individuals and so made much money for their publishers and authors. By 1800 there were estimated to be a thousand circulating libraries in Britain. The small ones primarily stocked fiction and were often supplied by William Lane, who specialized in novel publishing at his Minerva Press, which he established in 1790 and which was best known for publishing the thrilling gothic romances that so bewitch Isabella Thorpe and Catherine Morland in *Northanger Abbey*. At its peak in the first decade of the nineteenth century the Minerva Press brought out 30 percent of all new novels. Lane traveled to the country's circulating libraries to sell his publications, distributed the trade's novels to the libraries, and offered to supply new circulating libraries with stock chiefly from his own press. Indeed, the surviving catalogues of circulating libraries show that roughly 70 percent of a small library's stock was fiction. In the 1810s and 1820s, Henry Colburn similarly moved from owning a circulating library and the weekly *Literary Gazette* to becoming London's largest and most colorful publisher of novels.

Although Sir Walter Scott's Waverley novels transcended the circulating libraries and were bought by individual readers, his fiction perversely reinforced the circulating library character of novels by establishing with *Kenilworth* (1821) the extraordinarily high price of 31 shillings and sixpence for a three-volume novel. Even though Scott's novels had enormous sales, most readers still could not afford them, and so continued to borrow them from the circulating libraries to which they subscribed. The high price of Scott's fiction made the proprietors of circulating libraries happy because it guaranteed them a captive market and increased the demand for library subscriptions. However, such high prices severely limited the sales of all but the most popular novels, and so most novelists were not as fortunate as Scott in having their fiction bought by readers instead of libraries. For example, John Murray II published 2,000 copies of Jane Austen's *Emma* in 1816 and had sold 1,461 copies by 1820 when it was remaindered, and so the novel was confined primarily to the libraries during her life. Because of the small chance of publishing a novel that many individuals would buy, most booksellers issued few novels and left the field to the specialists like Lane and Colburn who concentrated their effort on advertising and distributing their fiction to the libraries.

The traditional picture of the bookseller as a tradesman who had a retail shop on the ground floor, operated a press in a back room, and lived upstairs from his shop was outmoded in most respects by the Romantic period. Bookselling had become differentiated into retail and wholesale firms. Printing had become a specialized business that was still primarily tied to the production of books, but was becoming more and more devoted to the production of newspapers and periodicals. Wholesale booksellers acquired manuscripts, engaged printing firms to publish them, bought paper from stationers, hired engravers, warehoused the copies, and sold them to retailers. The wholesalers usually had shops that operated as showrooms for their latest publications. In addition, above or behind the showrooms they had offices and meeting rooms that provided comfortable surroundings to discuss business and books. By the late eighteenth century the Paternoster Row and St Paul's Churchyard area was becoming commercial storefront on the ground floor and office or warehouse space above and behind. Thomas Longman II, for example, moved in 1792 from above his shop to a house in Hampstead and then commuted to work, something which gradually became the pattern for all the major London booksellers. There was also a movement of the more fashionable booksellers' shops and offices westward, especially to addresses around St James's Square and on Pall Mall, where some book shops became unofficial political clubs.

The increasing scale and consolidation of publishing during the Romantic period made booksellers richer and more powerful. They became respected and influential figures, even if they had not become the gentlemen with country houses that their heirs would be. The first John Murray, Joseph Johnson, James Lackington, and William Lane all died with estates worth between eight and twenty thousand pounds. On the scale of fortunes made during the first phase of England's industrialization, they were small figures, who belonged to a trade that served a small but growing audience of wealthy book buyers rather than common readers. Even with secure copyrights, bookselling offered only limited opportunities to make monopoly profits, since every title published competed in some sense with every other one available for sale. The period's book trade depended not on its wealth but on what it published for its long-term cultural importance. Even if only one title in a thousand that it published is remembered today, those surviving titles belong to the living British cultural memory and preserve the publishers' and printers' names.

Book Trade Scholarship and Subjects for Further Research

From a Romanticist's point of view 1800 has all too often been used as a terminal date in book trade studies, so that much more is known about the trade before 1800 than between 1800 and 1830. Most studies have understandably focused on the surviving records of successful publishers, and so have continued to celebrate the marriage of business and literary success that marked late nineteenth-century publishing house histories like Samuel Smiles's *A Publisher and His Friends* (1891), which portrayed the bookselling triumphs of John Murray II. Most publishing history has drawn upon correspondence and ledgers to describe the relations between famous authors and publishers, and has investigated those authors and publications important to literary history. A few early studies of individual publishers connected the book trade to popular culture, in particular, Stanley Morison's *John Bell* (1930) and Dorothy Blakey's *Minerva Press* (1939). Both Morison and Blakey, however, saw their booksellers as harbingers of the triumphant expansion of Victorian publishing that Richard D. Altick surveyed in *The English Common Reader 1800–1900* (1957).

Much post-World War II scholarly energy has been devoted to reconstructing historical maps of the book trade and to compensating for the German incendiary bombing in January 1941 of the Paternoster Row and St Paul's Churchyard area that sent so much book history and memory up in smoke. The trade precincts of Paternoster Row and St Paul's Churchyard are being mapped from surviving tax and rental records, and the emerging cartographical picture has recovered much for us. Robin Myers and others have edited essay collections in the Publishing Pathways series (1981–), which cover many aspects of book trade history. And James Raven has framed bibliographical study within a larger cultural history of the book in *Judging New Wealth* (1992), *The English Novel 1770–1829* (Garside, Raven, and Schöwerling 2000), and *The Business of Books* (2007). Much probably remains to be learned by examining the surviving Chancery records of the period's printers and booksellers who went bankrupt. Geoffrey Keynes (1969) has studied the records connected to William Pickering's bankruptcy, but other such cases concerning many members of the book trade have yet to be examined. In particular, the court records connected to Archibald Constable's collapse in 1826 need detailed examination, instead of the mere summary we now have of how many shillings and pence in the pound were paid out to the creditors.

Since it has long been subordinated to the history of ideas and to the modern revaluations of literary history and criticism, the full history of the Romantic-era book trade has yet to be written, and much detailed historical archeology remains to be done. A modern, comprehensive study of Longman's records and archives, many of which are available on microfilm, is sorely needed. As the period's largest firm, its organization, finances, and methods need to be understood much better than they are now. It would also be helpful to have a study of William Darton and his firm Darton and Harvey, which followed the Newberys and John Marshall as the period's most important publisher for children, and, more generally, to have a bibliographical study of the period's educational and children's literature. The best recent study of one of the period's booksellers is *The First John Murray* (1998) by William Zachs, which has illuminated much about the book trade in the late eighteenth century. But many other such studies are needed to arrive at a full understanding. Most of those now at work in the field are either bibliographers or literary historians, who are often faced with puzzling ledgers, and so need a better grasp of the trade's finances and of Britain's economic history. We have not yet understood how the complex cultural phenomena that collectively go under the name of Romanticism were often the effects of, or meditations upon, the great changes in both social and cultural scale created by industrialization. The age viewed booksellers ambivalently, because they put a price on the books that embodied its wishes to transcend itself. Nevertheless, the period's books and its book trade mirrored the diverse tastes and views of a wealthy, expanding elite, and were as much resisting as reflecting the economic and political forces of democratization implicit within Britain's industrialization. The emerging study of book culture promises to see Romanticism more clearly by integrating an economic and structural analysis of the book trade with a knowledge of the works it printed and with a psychology of the readers it instructed, inspired, and amused.

References and Further Reading

Altick, Richard D. (1957) *The English Common Reader: A Social History of the Mass Reading Public, 1800–1900*. Chicago: University of Chicago Press.

Bennett, Stuart. (2004) *Trade Bookbinding in the British Isles 1660–1800*. London: The British Library.
Besterman, Theodore. (1938) *The Publishing Firm of Cadell and Davies: Select Correspondence and Accounts, 1793–1836*. London: Oxford University Press.
Blagden, Cyprian. (1960) *The Stationers' Company: A History, 1403–1959*. London: Allen and Unwin.
Blakey, Dorothy. (1939) *The Minerva Press, 1790–1820*. London: Oxford University Press.
Bonnell, Thomas F. (1987) "John Bell's *Poets of Great Britain*: The 'Little Trifling Edition' Revisited," *Modern Philology* 85: 128–52.
British Publishers' Archives on Microfilm. (1973–82) Cambridge, UK: Chadwyck-Healey.
Chard, Leslie F. (1977) "Bookseller to Publisher: Joseph Johnson and the English Book Trade, 1760 to 1810," *The Library*, 5th ser., 32: 138–54.
Chilcott, Tim. (1972) *A Publisher and His Circle: The Life and Work of John Taylor, Keats's Publisher*. London: Routledge and Kegan Paul.
Coleman, D. C. (1958) *The British Paper Industry, 1495–1860*. Oxford: Clarendon Press.
Curwen, Henry. (1873) *A History of Booksellers: The Old and the New*. London: Chatto and Windus.
Dyson, Anthony. (1984) *Pictures to Print: The Nineteenth-Century Engraving Trade*. London: Farrand.
Erickson, Lee. (1996) *The Economy of Literary Form: English Literature and the Industrialization of Publishing, 1800–1850*. Baltimore: Johns Hopkins University Press.
Feather, John. (1989) *The Provincial Book Trade in Eighteenth Century England*. Cambridge, UK: Cambridge University Press.
Feather, John. (1994) *Publishing, Piracy and Politics: An Historical Study of Copyright in Britain*. London: Mansell.
Garside, Peter, James Raven, and Rainer Schöwerling. (2000) *The English Novel 1770–1829: A Bibliographical Survey of Prose Fiction Published in the British Isles*, 2 vols. Oxford: Oxford University Press.
Herrmann, Frank. (1980) *Sotheby's: Portrait of an Auction House*. London: Chatto and Windus.
Jackson, J. R. de J. (1985) *Annals of English Verse, 1770–1835: A Preliminary Survey of the Volumes Published*. New York: Garland Press.
Jackson, J. R. de J. (1993) *Romantic Poetry by Women: A Bibliography, 1770–1835*. Oxford: Clarendon Press.
Kaufman, Paul. (1967) "The Community Library: A Chapter in English Social History," *Transactions of the American Philosophical Society*, new series, 57, part 7.
Keynes, Geoffrey. (1969) *William Pickering, Publisher: A Memoir and a Check-List of His Publications*, revised edn. London: Galahad Press.
Lackington, James. (1794) *Memoirs of the First Forty-Five Years of the Life of James Lackington*, 7th edn. London: James Lackington.

Maxted, Ian. (1977) *The London Book Trades 1775–1800: A Preliminary Checklist of Members*. Folkestone, UK: Dawson.

Morison, Stanley. (1930) *John Bell, 1745–1831: Bookseller, Printer, Publisher, Typefounder, Journalist, &c.* Cambridge, UK: Cambridge University Press.

Pollard, Graham. (1978) "The English Market for Printed Books," *Publishing History* 4, 7–48.

Pollard, Mary (Paul). (1989) *Dublin's Trade in Books, 1550–1800*. Oxford: Clarendon Press.

Potter, Esther. (1993) "The London Bookbinding Trade: From Craft to Industry," *The Library*, 6th ser., 14, 259–280.

Raven, James. (1992) *Judging New Wealth: Popular Publishing and Responses to Commerce in England, 1750–1800*. Oxford: Clarendon Press.

Raven, James. (2007) *The Business of Books: Booksellers and the English Book Trade 1450–1800*. New Haven, CT: Yale University Press.

Renier, Anne. (1964) *Friendship's Offering: An Essay on the Annuals and Gift Books of the 19th Century*. London: Private Libraries Association.

Roper, Derek. (1978) *Reviewing before the Edinburgh, 1788–1802*. Newark: University of Delaware Press.

St Clair, William. (2004) *The Reading Nation in the Romantic Period*. Cambridge, UK: Cambridge University Press.

Saunders, J. W. (1964) *The Profession of English Letters*. London: Routledge and Kegan Paul.

Sher, Richard B. (2006) *The Enlightenment and the Book: Scottish Authors and Their Publishers in Eighteenth-Century Britain, Ireland, and America*. Chicago: University of Chicago Press.

Twyman, Michael. (1970) *Printing, 1770–1970: An Illustrated History of its Development and Uses in England*. London: Eyre and Spottiswoode.

Tyson, Gerald P. (1979) *Joseph Johnson: A Liberal Publisher*. Iowa City: Iowa University Press.

Zachs, William. (1998) *The First John Murray and the Late Eighteenth-Century London Book Trade with a Checklist of His Publications*. Oxford: Oxford University Press for The British Academy.

Chapter 11
Visual Pleasures, Visionary States: Art, Entertainment, and the Nation

Gillen D'Arcy Wood

Victorian novelists identified the domestic sphere as a place of sanctuary for middle-class sensibilities in an urban mass culture, but in the Romantic age, the modern distinction between private and public, between the inner life and the theatrical, social self, was not yet clearly articulated. Thus we find, in the rapid expansion of visual arts and entertainments in the period, multiple signs of Romanticism's hybrid nature: as at one time a language of private feeling *and* a mode of charismatic public performance. It is the problematic crossing Jane Austen addresses in her debut novel, *Sense and Sensibility* (1811), in which the heroine Marianne Dashwood is unable to distinguish between true sensibility and the mere performance of it in Willoughby, the lover who exploits her uncritical embrace of Romantic feeling.

Marianne must travel from picturesque Devonshire to London for her scene of disillusionment, and this essay will follow in her steps. I begin with the emergence of modern English landscape painting in the late eighteenth century as a visual language of the newly imagined private sphere, in which the ideal of an inviolable inner life resides first with women, both as subjects of the glamorous new genre of landscape portraiture, and as principal consumers in the booming amateur art and landscape tourism markets. My focus then shifts to the headquarters of the new visual-cultural marketplace in London. In addition to adapting the fashionable iconography of the picturesque to its pleasure gardens and panoramas, London offered a stunning range of urban visual entertainments – theaters, circuses, exhibitions of all kinds, even parliament – at which the idea of a modern public sphere was to a great extent enacted. Here in the city, the high–low divide line between Romantic visual art and popular entertainment was most palpable. Ambitious painters mostly fled the teeming city for the countryside – in imagination if not in reality – while documentation of modern city life was left to a host of spectacles and ephemera that can now be reconstructed only through newspaper and diary accounts and popular prints.

The most powerful and problematic figure for the new public sphere was the British nation, the subject of the final part of the essay. The "official" art of the Romantic period – to be viewed at the newly founded Royal Academy and British Museum – was devoted to the creation of a national school of painting, the deep desire for which was expressed in innumerable pamphlets and newspaper articles. The fact that most British academic art of the period is now forgotten should not be construed as a failure of this nationalist agenda. As we shall see, the increasing institutionalization of art in the Romantic period galvanized a remarkable generation of now definitive British artists determined to preserve their independence, and with it the ideal of a private and autonomous Romantic imagination, against the dictates of the various "publics" – commercial and national – that modern art was designated to serve.

Sensibility and the Picturesque

Thomas Gainsborough's 1787 portrait of the Bath singer and celebrity Elizabeth Linley (see Figure 2) is a visual document of sensibility, the predominant literary fashion of the 1780s. Popular women poets like Anna Seward routinely imagined themselves alone in a retired setting, where images of nature blended with a pathetic narrative of memory and desire:

> Slow, thro' the faded Grove, past pleasures glide,
> Or sadly linger by the fountain's side . . .
> Tho' vernal flowr's this bank no more adorn,
> Nor Summer's wild rose blushes in its thorn,
> Yet shelter'd, mossy, dry, and warm, it draws
> The heedless, roving step, to quiet pause.
>   (Seward 1784: 3–4)

Figure 2 Mrs. Richard Brinsley Sheridan, c.1785–87 (oil on canvas) by Thomas Gainsborough (1727–88) ©Mellon Coll., Nat. Gallery of Art, Washington DC, USA/ The Bridgeman Art Library Nationality / copyright status: English / out of copyright

Because of the popularity of such poetry, Gainsborough does not feel compelled to explain his subject's situation, alone and finely dressed in a "faded Grove." Like Seward's Louisa, whose "sensibilities, heightened and refined in the bosom of Retirement, know no bounds" (p. i), Linley has sought out this secluded spot for private reasons of mental sanctuary, for "quiet pause." For both Seward and Gainsborough, the female subject's *inner* life – precisely that which is not visible – is the painting's true theme. "Bold was the happy hand, and unconfin'd, / That shew'd the features of the latent mind," wrote one lyric admirer of Gainsborough's style in the *Bath and Bristol Chronicle* in 1759 (Sloman 2002: 96). Gainsborough blends Linley's unbound hair with the tossing branches of the sheltering tree, while her diaphanous dress merges with the brushstrokes used to convey the waving grass at her feet. Storm clouds churn in the distance. The singer's mood, made visible by its correspondence to the landscape, is unsettled and redolent with passion, suggestive, to a contemporary viewer's mind, of Elizabeth Linley's personal history: her elopement to France with the playwright Richard Brinsley Sheridan was one of the popular romantic narratives of the age, minutely recorded in newspapers and celebrated on the London stage.

That such a scene of pensive solitary retirement was also, in this sense, a form of public performance, both by Gainsborough and Linley, shows the historical task Romantic art shared with Romantic poetry: namely, to sustain the ideal of a rich, autonomous private life in an increasingly commercial, urbanizing, "public" age. The success of artists such as Gainsborough, and the extraordinary growth in visual media in the Romantic period in general, depended on the rapid expansion of an urban-based cultural marketplace and mass audience, while its aesthetic content – dominated by portraiture, landscape, and the sensibility ideal – served as a compensatory, even defensive assertion of individual liberty and self-determination. "Thy subtle essence," wrote Hannah More of sensibility, "still eludes / the chains of Definition" (More 1782: 5–6). In the Linley portrait, the visual language of sensibility holds out just such a promise: that a Georgian woman's "essence" lay beyond the claims (or "chains") of class, commerce, and duties both domestic and public.

The stakes for painters such as Gainsborough were likewise high in the aestheticizing of sentiment. Before the late eighteenth century, English visual artists were largely considered artisans, mere "mechanical" copiers of faces and scenes. With the reinvention of landscape and portraiture as visual lexicons of feeling and individual liberty,

Gainsborough could make implicit claims for painting as a genuine liberal art on a level with poetry, and thereby elevate his own status from tradesman to modern professional and privileged citizen of the republic of taste. The landscape-portrait of Elizabeth Linley was not painted on commission – according to the traditional patronal contract between artist and subject – but for display in Gainsborough's studio, to attract business. The painting is, in this sense, literally theatrical, an urban showpiece, and embodies the tense relationship, in both the literary and visual cultures of the Romantic age, between the commercial demands of the city and a compensatory fantasy of commerce's absence in the wilds of nature.

Women were almost entirely excluded from the profession in which Gainsborough earned his fame, but they dominated the private, amateur sphere of artistic production. For women of the leisure classes – after 1770 this increasingly extended beyond the traditional gentry to the daughters of successful tradesmen and merchants – drawing was an important article of their education, an "accomplishment" vital to their class status and, supposedly, their marriage prospects. The first thing Mr Bingley in *Pride and Prejudice* (1813) hears of any young woman is that she is accomplished, a sign of his own high target value in the marriage market. Conversely, Emma's lazy attitude to drawing is a symptom of her general lack of interest in marriage while, in *Sense and Sensibility*, the competition between Elinor Dashwood and Miss Morton for Mrs Ferrars's approval is played out in a nasty dispute over painted "screens."

An entire industry of art supplies, sketching manuals, and collectible prints emerged to service the artistic development of young British women of the kind we meet in Austen's novels. Just as important as these material accoutrements was an appealing aesthetic theory, which offered landscape subjects and guides to their proper pictorial realization. The setting of Gainsborough's portrait of Elizabeth Linley not only exemplifies this fashionable "picturesque" ideal – a wild, varied natural scene inhabited by gypsies, cottagers, and sentimental wanderers – but is, to a significant extent, its actual source. Uvedale Price, whose *Essay on the Picturesque* (1794) was a bible of amateur art theory, accompanied Gainsborough in his sketching trips around Bath and spent time in his studio. Price evokes Gainsborough in his evocation of the picturesque ideal: "all the beautiful varieties of form, tint, and light and shade; every deep recess – every bold projection – the fantastic roots of trees – the winding paths of sheep . . . what time only, and a thousand lucky accidents can mature, so as to become the admiration and study of a Ruisdael or a Gainsborough" (Price 1794: 29). Price's historical imagining – his appreciation of the marks of time and human culture upon a landscape – invests modern English landscape painting with a nobility and seriousness conventionally reserved for academic painting with its "historical" subjects drawn from antiquity and the Bible.

The picturesque, like any fashion, ultimately became the butt of popular humor. William Gilpin, its most famous proselytizer, was parodied by William Combe and the caricaturist Thomas Rowlandson as the bumbling Dr Syntax, dragging his young family through the pouring rain to make his fortune in the landscape market:

> I'll ride and write, and sketch and print,
> And thus create a real mint;
> I'll prose it here, I'll verse it there,
> And picturesque it everywhere.
> (Combe and Rowlandson 1813: 7)

In Austen's *Northanger Abbey*, set in the 1790s, the Tilneys treat Gilpin's technical language of "side-screen and perspectives – lights and shades" (Austen 1818/1990: 87) seriously, but by the publication of *Sense and Sensibility* in 1811, even that most uncritical Romantic enthusiast, Marianne Dashwood, acknowledges that Gilpin's theory has become a "mere jargon" (Austen 1811/1990: 83). Wordsworth's critique was more serious still: in *The Prelude* he remembers his youthful encounter with Gilpin's system as the "infection of the age," a "tyranny" of the eye he came to disavow. In his signature landscape poems, such as "Tintern Abbey" (1798), the picturesque details of the landscape recede the better to dramatize the poet's mental life – his "half-extinguished thought . . . the picture of the mind" (ll. 58, 61). In "Ode: Intimations of Immortality" (1807), Wordsworth takes his antipicturesque poetics further by setting the poem within a placeless interiority, and reducing nature to a set of generic signifiers: a rainbow, the moon, "land and sea," a "pansy at my feet" (ll. 30, 54).

For all the Romantic reaction against it, however, picturesque theory in the two decades between Price's *Essay* and *Sense and Sensibility* effectively popularized the idea of landscape appreciation, and with it engineered the birth of modern tourism. Owing to almost continuous warfare on the Continent, the customary tourist routes of the British elite were closed. Possibilities for leisured travel thus turned to the domestic beauties of Wales, Derbyshire, and the Lake District, which

Gilpin and other writers celebrated for their indigenous wildness and variety, distinct from the academic landscape ideal of the Italian *campagna*. Most important was the relative accessibility of these places. While the aristocrats of the eighteenth century spent years, and small fortunes, on their Grand Tours of Europe, a middle-class family such as the Gardiners in *Pride and Prejudice* could feasibly escape the city for a few weeks at a time to explore the regional sights. The picturesque was particularly useful to this new tourist class because it combined the prestige of theory with a host of practical applications. Not yet equipped with cameras, these day-trip Romantics relied on their sketching skills to preserve memories of their experiences.

The possibilities for women opened by picturesque tourism and its companion industries of landscape sketching and topographical verse were vital to the feminization of culture in the Romantic period. The poet Charlotte Smith was typical of educated women in her ability to draw well in various genres, and in the auxiliary knowledge she gained in natural science. The vivid pictoriality of her poetry – its self-conscious theatrics of spectatorship – marks a lyric crossing between visual and verbal media characteristic of women's Romantic verse:

> Ah! Hills so early loved! In fancy still
> I breathe your pure keen air; and still behold
> Those widely spreading views, mocking alike
> The poet and the painter's utmost art.
> And still, observing objects more minute,
> Wondering remark the strange and foreign forms
> Of sea-shells . . . (Smith 1807: ll. 368–74)

Denied access to the formal training of painting academies, or the opportunity to establish professional studios like Gainsborough's, amateur women artists eagerly accepted Gilpin's antiacademic notion that the most vital, modern school of art was nature itself, and women its most teachable students.

The picturesque, itself so fashionable, originated as a reaction against another eighteenth-century fashion, in landscape design. The social elite of Georgian England spent their winters in resort towns like Gainsborough's Bath, then moved to London for the spring "season." In high summer and autumn, they retreated to their country estates, to grand houses of the kind that populate Austen's novels. Increasingly, the wealthy gentry brought their city sensibilities with them, and rural life in England was overthrown by a spirit of "improvement."

The guru of fashionable landscape design was "Capability" Brown, whose signature open lawns bound by clusters of trees have come in fact to define "traditional" English landscape. But in the Romantic period, his style was controversial. A contemporary of Seward and Smith, William Cowper, decried the modern frenzy for improvement in his highly influential poem *The Task* (1785):

> Lo! he comes –
> The omnipotent magician Brown appears . . .
> He speaks. The lake in front becomes a lawn,
> Woods vanish, hills subside, and vallies rise,
> And streams as if created for his use,
> Pursue the track of his directing wand.
> (Cowper 1785/1994: Book 3, ll. 765–6, 774–7)

In Austen's *Mansfield Park* (1814), Fanny Price quotes Cowper in deploring Mr Rushworth's intention to "improve" his estate. The impromptu council of landscape enthusiasts on the lawn at Sotherton, led by the dangerous Henry Crawford, marks the moment the young people of the novel definitively escape the supervision of their elders, and illuminates the political subtext of Romantic landscape theory. Debates over estate improvement raged through the 1790s, a time when all subjects were colored by the recent overthrow of the French monarchy and the bloody introduction of a new and supposedly improved political model for Europe. Austen's depiction of the Sotherton "improvers" in *Mansfield Park* as a rebellious band responsible for the familial chaos, libertinism, and misery in the novel places her, alongside Edmund Burke, in the sphere of conservative reaction against the French experiment. Austen's politics of landscape is later made explicit in *Emma* (1816), where the heroine makes a direct sentimental connection between the picturesque view of Knightley's estate and "English culture" (Austen 1816/1998: 325). With picturesque theory, Britain declared its aesthetic independence from Europe. Austen mocked its fashionability in her novels, but not the core picturesque principle Emma's sentiment implies: that England's unique and blessed condition was available for viewing in its landscape.

The Spectacles of London

Cowper's *The Task* exemplifies the Romantic poetics of rural solitude we see embodied in Gainsborough's portrait of Elizabeth Linley. As a

Art, Entertainment, and the Nation

celebrator of country life, Cowper finds his nemesis in the negligent modern landowner who abandons his country estate for the fashionable attractions of Bath and London:

> Mansions once
> Knew their own masters, and laborious hinds
> That had surviv'd the father, serv'd the son.
> Now the legitimate and rightful Lord
> Is but a transient guest . . .
> Estates are landscapes, gaz'd upon awhile,
> Then advertis'd, and auctioneer'd away.
> (Cowper 1785/1994: Book 3, ll. 746–50, 755–6)

The principal London attraction was the theater. "The theatre engrossed the minds of men to such a degree," wrote the actor Garrick's biographer, "that there existed in England a fourth estate, King, Lords, Commons and Drury Lane Playhouse" (Murphy 1801: 381). The Drury Lane Theatre was dominated in the Romantic period by Elizabeth Linley's husband, Richard Sheridan, and his retinue of star actors: the "sublime" tragedienne Sarah Siddons, her brother John Philip Kemble, and the comedienne Dorothy Jordan. Under the management of the scholarly Kemble, Drury Lane, and its rival house Covent Garden, engineered a Shakespearean revival, to which we owe the Romantic period's rich abundance of Shakespeare criticism from Coleridge, Hazlitt, Lamb and others. That said, the would-be Shakespeares of the period were frustrated by Kemble's lack of interest in new plays, and his increasing emphasis on visual spectacle in his productions. After a devastating fire, Drury Lane reopened in 1794 on a scale far greater than any theater London had seen, "a wilderness of a place," as Sarah Siddons described it. Its audience capacity almost doubled to 3,600, Drury Lane became, according to the playwright Richard Cumberland, a "theatre . . . for spectators rather than a playhouse for hearers . . . the splendour of the scenes and the ingenuity of the machinist . . . now in a great degree supersede the labours of the poet" (Cumberland 1807/2002, vol. 2: 201). Kemble blamed his audience: "our world in London [is] at present mad for splendid sights at the Theatre and the most impossible extravagances" (quoted in Kelly 1980: 198). Whoever was responsible, the *visual* experience of the Romantic theater was enhanced, by increasingly sophisticated technological means, at the expense of its literary possibilities. Kemble revived Shakespeare, but at precisely the historical moment when the emergence of a legitimate and longed-for successor to the national bard became materially impossible.

The writer's loss was the actor's gain. As the importance of literary originality on the London stage diminished, attention turned to innovations in stage performance and the actors' interpretation of well-known roles. Kemble weighed each line for new and sometimes controversial emphases, while Siddons "prepared" her roles in what has become the standard modern sense: with an emphasis on rich psychological texture, and a naturalistic relation between word and gesture. In that sense, Siddons announced the arrival of Romantic sensibility and the sublime onto the stage. In Hazlitt's famous account:

> she seemed to command every source of terror and pity . . . Her person was made to contain her spirit; her soul to fill and animate her person . . . [she] touched all the chords of passion; they thrilled through her, and yet she preserved an elevation of thought and character above them, like the tall cliff round which the tempest roars, but its head reposes in the blue serene! (Hazlitt 1828/1933: 408)

As in Gainsborough's portrait of Elizabeth Linley, Siddons's performances – as the sentimental heroines Jane Shore and Isabella, as Shakespeare's Katherine and Lady Macbeth – married the ideal of authentic, private feeling to a theatrical, "public" aesthetic. The modes of the inner life – passion, thought, character – were made visible by Siddons through a modern, naturalized vocabulary of gesture and voice, but also through the intangible measure of "presence" or natural charisma, which Romantic audiences identified in performers such as Siddons and Linley, and which is the phenomenal basis of modern celebrity culture. To see Siddons act, said Hazlitt, "was an epoch in every one's life" (Hazlitt 1814: 198). No surprise then, that actors were the most sought-after and celebrated portrait subjects of the Romantic age. Gainsborough glamorized Siddons as a fashionable society woman, but his rival, Sir Joshua Reynolds, most successfully captured the public imagination with his allegorical portrait of her as the "Tragic Muse."

Frances Burney's best-selling novel *Evelina* (1778) relates the adventures of a young woman from the country brought into the whirl, glamour, and danger of the new London entertainment culture. The novel shows why the rural gentry were tempted to neglect their estates for the pleasures of the city, and also why Kemble felt compelled to maximize the spectacular aspects of his theatrical productions.

Evelina attends Drury Lane three times to see Garrick in various signature roles, but the variety of her experiences in London demonstrates just how intense the competition was for the attention, and purses, of a London public voracious for visual-cultural novelties. The entertainment venues Evelina visits, or hears of, make for a tantalizingly long and varied list: the circus at Sadler's Wells; Don Saltero's tea house, where patrons might tour an extensive cabinet of curiosities; St Paul's and the Tower of London; Cox's Museum, an emporium of luxury clocks and music-boxes; Christie's auction house in Pall Mall; the King's Theatre opera house; and the Pantheon, a luxurious concert venue for people-watching among the fashionable elite. Even Bedlam, the insane asylum, was open to the public for viewing of the inmates (where, it was said, Garrick might be found preparing for his performance of Lear).

Evelina's experience is typical of 1770s and 1780s London in that she spends at least as much of her leisure time outdoors as in. Attendance at public parks and pleasure gardens was a staple of late eighteenth-century life. One of Gainsborough's most popular paintings depicts fashionable women abroad in St James's Park, an unofficial morning parade of the London elite which Evelina wonderingly joins. More stylized yet were the suburban tea-rooms and pleasure gardens, which imported the picturesque delights of the country into the city. The most famous of these gardens, Vauxhall, featured tree-lined groves, a picturesque rural cottage and, at designated showtimes, a spectacular "cascade." Coleridge draws upon the cultural memory of these gardens in his description of the "pleasure-dome" in his 1817 poem "Kubla Khan":

> And there were gardens bright with sinuous rills,
> Where blossomed many an incense-bearing tree;
> And here were forests ancient as the hills,
> Enfolding sunny spots of greenery.
> (Coleridge, "Kubla Khan," ll. 8–11)

That Coleridge's pleasure-dome appears to meet its destruction in a "tumult" of figurative sexual violence is certainly faithful to Evelina's experience at the London pleasure-gardens, where she is beset by a pack of predatory young men in the darkness and, on a later occasion, adopted by prostitutes for their amusement. In Burney's follow-up novel, *Cecilia* (1782), a socialite with money troubles kills himself at Vauxhall before a horrified crowd. In a popular print drawing from

1784, Rowlandson depicts a Vauxhall crowd listening to a singer perform at the famous Rotunda while, in the foreground, a second group of men circles about a pair of attractive, well-dressed women. It is a scene of well-regulated pleasure, the Addisonian ideal, but there is just a suggestion of menace in the men's admiration and, by the end of the century, the Vauxhall era was mostly over. London had become more crowded and more violent – in the words of Thomas De Quincey, "harsh, cruel, and repulsive" – and the experience of class intermingling in the public gardens more threatening than thrilling (De Quincey 1821/1888: 17).

The shows of London that Wordsworth visited in 1802, with the notable exception of Bartholomew Fair, were thus "Spectacles / Within doors." In Book Seven of his autobiographical epic, *The Prelude* (1805, 1850), Wordsworth describes a kind of optical fatigue after visits to Sadler's Wells circus, the famous animal menagerie at the Exeter Exchange, and a popular new pictorial wonder, Barker's Panorama in Leicester Square. The Panorama, a rotunda-shaped building designed to house enormous circular paintings, signified the modern marriage of visual art and technology. Patrons of the panorama entered from the street into darkness, then ascended a circular stairway to a central platform, where they encountered a vast, lifelike, exotic scene of a famous city or battlefield, rendered with strict topographical accuracy. For Wordsworth, the Panorama represented the tyranny of the picturesque eye in its most pernicious form, "a lifelike mockery" (Book 7, l. 263) that offered, like the modern urban experience in general, a "perpetual flow/Of trivial objects" (ll. 702–3) unredeemed by imagination. The second-generation Romantics – Hazlitt, Hunt, Keats – were Londoners accustomed to its visual wonders, and mostly celebrators of its theaters, museums, and public life, but in Wordsworth's response to the "unmanageable sights" of the modern city, we find an important strain of Romantic reaction against the rapid advance of visual media and technology. The pose Wordsworth strikes, of an embattled literary sensibility under visual assault from modern commercial culture, is strikingly familiar to our own age.

Charles Lamb, by contrast, took delight in the nonstop theater of the streets of London. In a letter to the skeptical Wordsworth, he described the city as a perpetual "pantomime and masquerade" (Lamb 1935: 687). The political life of the city, for instance, was infused with theatricality. The major statesmen of the day – Pitt, Burke, Fox, and Sheridan – were all devotees of the theater (Sheridan, of course, was a theater professional) and brought their deep knowledge of dramatic texts and effects to the floor of Parliament. The opposition leader, Fox, was said to know hundreds of dramatic speeches by heart, and drew on them liberally in his speeches. The most famous example of the theatricalization of politics was the 1788 impeachment trial of Warren Hastings, the first Governor-General of British India, for which hundreds of people – including Sarah Siddons and Frances Burney – bought tickets to the parliamentary gallery to witness Sheridan's six-hour-long denunciation of the defendant. Sheridan prepared his speech meticulously, like a script, and, when done at last, sank exhausted into his fellow prosecutor's arms, as if playing Hamlet to Burke's Horatio. As one satirical witness wrote,

> The gallery folk, who, misled by the sport,
> Conceived 'twas a Play-House, instead of a Court;
> And thinking the Actor uncommonly good,
> They clapp'd, and cry'd "Bravo!" as loud as they could.
> (Broome 1791: 67)

When Sheridan later came to write his popular political melodrama, *Pizarro* (1800), which he filled with martial speeches decrying colonial oppression and upholding the sacred cause of liberty, Prime Minister Pitt, when asked his opinion of the play, declared that he had heard it all years before, in Sheridan's speech at the Hastings trial (Rhodes 1933: 181).

Plays in the Romantic age were full of such politics – revolutionary narratives and the expanding empire featured prominently – but more significant, perhaps, was the political culture of each theater, its Whig, Tory, or radical constituency. George III shunned Drury Lane on account of Sheridan's oppositional politics, preferring Covent Garden, which was considered friendly to the Pitt government. The aristocrats of the West End, in turn, held greatest power at the King's Theatre, the most important Italian opera house outside Milan. There, the very construction of the theater – with a King's Side, a Prince's Side, and a Crown Gallery filled with politically connected patrons – mirrored the triangulated political divisions of George III's reign with its divided court and unstable ministry. Patrons were required to wear court dress, while the operas themselves were constructed around the vocal splendor of a single imported star singer, who served as symbolic regent of music. Opera-lover Leigh Hunt's *Examiner* was the first liberal periodical to produce regular reviews of King's Theatre productions, and it treated the issue of opera reform with the same passion it brought to overhaul of the Parliamentary system and defense of young "liberal" poets such as Keats and Shelley. Hunt championed the operas of Mozart, whose emphasis on complex ensemble singing and the dramatic role of the orchestra challenged the diva-driven tradition and, by extension, the entire aristocratic regime at the King's Theatre (Wood 2005). The triumphant London debut of *Don Giovanni* in 1817, hailed as a "red letter day" in the history of English theater, brought modern psychological realism and vocal democracy to the opera stage, while Mozart himself was sanctified by the liberal metropolitan press as an honorary literary genius on the scale of Homer and Shakespeare. With the Romantic canonization of Mozart, Italian opera, like landscape painting and stage acting, had joined poetry in the ranks of the progressive, modern liberal arts.

Art and the Nation

For all George III's animus toward the Whig management of Drury Lane, he did attend *Pizarro* to hear Kemble deliver speeches that gave voice to the national defiance of Napoleon:

> My brave associates . . . Your generous spirit has compared as mine has, the motives, which, in a war like this, can animate *their* minds and ours. – They, by a strange frenzy driven, fight for power, for plunder, and extended rule – We, for our country, our altars, and our homes. – They follow an Adventurer whom they fear – and obey a power which they hate – we serve a Monarch whom we love – a God whom we adore. (Sheridan 1800/1973, vol. 2: 669)

An atmosphere of militant patriotism, from which the king naturally benefited, provided common ground between Whig and Tory during the Napoleonic Wars, refiguring the divisive party politics of the 1780s. Rolla, the Peruvian hero of *Pizarro*, was one of Kemble's most popular roles – he was duly immortalized by the portraitist Thomas Lawrence in the act of delivering the famous speech – and Kemble's traffic in patriotic themes and imagery extended to his Shakespeare productions. Stagings of *Henry V*, in particular, doubled as propaganda rallies for the war against France.

Painters, too, found both inspiration and a good trade in patriotic subjects. Perhaps the best-known British painting of the eighteenth century was Benjamin West's "Death of General Wolfe," (1770) which depicted the British hero's death at the moment of victory at the Battle of Quebec in 1759. The picture is composed with neo-classical balance: Wolfe lies in Christ-like repose surrounded by a grieving retinue of officers and a Native American whose respectful genuflection offers, as a kind of feel-good propaganda bonus, an implicit blessing of British imperialism in the Americas. Exhibition of the "Death of General Wolfe" created a sensation, and prints of the painting made in excess of 15,000 pounds. The managers of the Vauxhall Gardens, grasping the commercial possibilities of patriotic art, erected a gallery in the grounds for the exhibition of military paintings by Francis Hayman. At the conclusion of the long-running wars with France, David Wilkie's painting of the news of victory at Waterloo being delivered to a streetside group of veterans was so popular it had to be roped off from its clamoring public. Wilkie's "Chelsea Pensioners" (1822) was Britain's most celebrated nationalist painting until Turner's "The Fighting Temeraire" (1839), which, at the end of the Romantic era, pictured British naval glory in the form of a noble ghost ship being tugged to its final port by a little black steamer. The image both eulogized those victories that had secured the nation – the Temeraire had distinguished herself at Trafalgar – and certified the technological obsolescence of that once world-dominant fleet in the new steam era. Turner pictures the age of Nelson's navy, so lovingly depicted in Austen's *Persuasion* (1818), passing into a refulgent twilight.

Nationalism was an essential means of dignifying visual culture, otherwise tainted by its association with commerce and the vanities of display. The "official" visual language of British nationalism in the early Romantic period was borrowed principally from Rome and the neoclassical revival. Kemble, for example, was routinely likened to Roman statues, and his portraits most often portrayed him in classical garb. Painting likewise sought the legitimating power of classicism, adapted to a nationalist agenda. Sir Joshua Reynolds looms large over the Romantic period as the first President of the Royal Academy of Art (founded 1768), the patriotic goal of which was to provide Britain with "an ornament ... suitable to its greatness" (Reynolds 1791/1997: 13). Though Reynolds himself was a brilliantly successful portraitist active in the modern art marketplace, his Academy curriculum and annual exhibitions promoted history painting – the so-called "grand style" of the Italian Renaissance artists Raphael and Michelangelo – at the expense of British art's strong commercial traffic in portraiture and landscape. Reynolds considered history painting the most literary, intellectual genre of painting, and thus most likely to promote those neoclassical civic virtues – courage, piety, self-denial – that would identify painting with a nationalist project in the arts. His famous *Discourses on Art* (1791) thus denounced topicality and fashion, anything that would tie art to its lowly artisanal origins. Even West's General Wolfe, Reynolds insisted, should have worn a toga (Galt 1820, vol. 2: 46).

As a modern, nationalist institution that promoted a Renaissance, cosmopolitan ideal of painting, the Royal Academy struggled to transcend its own contradictions. The Romantic artists and critics in the generation after Reynolds thus defined themselves in often hostile opposition to its ideology. "This man," wrote William Blake in the margins of his copy of Reynolds's *Discourses*, "was hired to depress art" (Blake 1808?/1997: 284). The Romantic reaction against the neoclassicism of the Royal Academy took multiple brilliant, progressive forms. Blake eked out a living at the margins of the art marketplace as an engraver. But the privately published illustrated books that were his life's work adapted his academic training to an entirely idiosyncratic pictorial cosmology, where the static, statuesque forms of a thousand academic life-drawing seminars are infused with light and arching, vortical motion. Likewise, Turner was an Academy prodigy, whose early work drew dutifully on the landscapes and mythology of Ancient Italy. But already in those works, Turner's classically columned buildings and robed figures seemed on the point of dissolving into the atmosphere, the true Turnerian subject. The late works on which Turner's enormous reputation rests rejected the neoclassical landscape formula – with a foreground of bucolic persons framed by trees, a bridge or town in the middle distance leading gently to a geometric conclusion of mountains and sky – for painterly evocation of the dynamic and destructive powers of Nature. More than any other British paintings, Turner's images of an avalanche in the Alps, storms at sea, the Parliament buildings on fire, and a steam train seeming to burst from the canvas in a cloud of its own fiery light, have come to define the Romantic sublime in British art, icons of a "golden age" when painters embraced experimentation and proposed influential new visual languages for the modern age. This art-historical account of Turner's influence on modern European painting – both Impressionism and twentieth-century Abstract Expressionism – is true only retrospectively. At the time, Turner's late style was viewed with suspicion. Like Blake, he was thought to be mad.

No less "modern," though less obviously so in his techniques, was the landscapist John Constable. Constable's radicalism, like Wordsworth's, lay in his personalization of landscape. In his 1826 painting

Figure 3 "The Cornfield" by John Constable (1776–1837). Presented by subscribers, including Wordsworth, Faraday and Sir William Beechey, 1837 / Credit: © The National Gallery, London.

"The Cornfield" (Figure 3), he employs landscape to embody complex orders of time, the inversions of memory by which "The Child is Father of the Man." The backward-looking reaper near the cornfield gate literalizes the retrospective act of the poet of "Tintern Abbey," contemplating a former version of himself, a boy absorbed in the unselfconscious delight of drinking from a stream. As in Wordsworth's poem, the "aching joys" of the drinking boy are irrecoverable, while the "abundant recompense" for their loss is the work of lyric art itself. Constable has detailed the botanical peculiarity of the foreground trees with exacting care. On the rising ground at their base, dancing wildflowers and grasses form a spontaneous counterpoint to the agricultural order of the cornfield. These virtuosic painterly effects create a sense of "nowness," or historicity, in the image that complements the painting's longitudinal temporal structure concluding in the distant church spire. The scene is a *locus amoenus* of Constable's boyhood: it imagines the lane he walked as a boy from his home in East Bergholt to school at Dedham. As such, the painting suggests the distillation of memory as a "serene mood," an aesthetic dividend of life contemplatively lived. Constable's landscape thus transcends picturesque formulae or mere topographical description; it is as powerful a Romantic autobiography as "Tintern Abbey," the perfect product of a Wordsworthian "philosophic mind."

That said, such a powerful visual statement as "The Cornfield" could never issue from mere satisfaction. Like Wordsworth's anxious, reiterated directions to Dorothy at the conclusion of "Tintern Abbey" not to forget him, Constable idealizes his own boyhood at a specific historical moment when Britain's agricultural way of life stood at the brink of industrialization and radical change. So-called "Constable country" has since been nationalized: Constable's intensely personal "Cornfield" now holds an iconic status in the British cultural imagination as memorial to a distinctive agricultural rhythm of national life that has been lost. The Royal Academicians who devoted themselves in vain to the foundation of a national school of painting perennially ignored Constable's claims for membership, mostly from a disregard for the landscape genre. They simply could not see the powerful elegiac nationalism in the paintings, just as we are unable to look at "The Cornfield" without an instinctive sense, however uncritical, of its profound Englishness. Though never truly popular in his time, Constable, like Wordsworth, succeeded where the academic artists of the period did not, in creating the taste by which he was to be enjoyed.

Like Blake and Constable, James Gillray and Thomas Rowlandson were students of the Royal Academy who forged a distinctively British art form by adapting the Academy's visual language to their new medium, but otherwise rejecting all it stood for. These artists of modern life eschewed institutionality for a critical, often iconoclastic commentary on the state of the nation. William Hogarth had pioneered the popular print with his satirical series, including "The Rake's

Progress" (1735) and "Marriage à la Mode" (1745), which, like Burney's novels, exposed the morally pernicious luxuries of London life in the new commercial age. Rather than creating multiframe morality tales, Gillray's interests were topical and political, and found expression in an entirely modern visual language of caricature: exaggerated but recognizable figures engaged in some pictorial allegory of the political moment. One famous print – "The Plumb-pudding in Danger; or State Epicures taking a Petit Souper" (1805) – shows the elongated, abstemious figure of the Prime Minister, Pitt, at a dinner table with Napoleon, whose small physical stature is exaggerated into dwarf-like squatness. Together they are engaged in carving up the globe set before them on a platter. The moral content of the image is realized in formal rather than narrative terms, in the deviations of the individual portraits from natural likeness – Pitt is a prig, and Napoleon manic-eyed and belligerent – and by the depiction of symbolic, theatricalized acts. The comic mode is bathos: the world-historical gravity of the Napoleonic Wars is reduced to an unsavory competition over a pudding. Gainsborough was famous for his gift of capturing a likeness, and his humanizing of landscape. Gillray inverts that approach, by marrying likeness to the grotesque, and stylizing his subjects' environment as a theatrical arrangement of political references. Gillray's "Voluptuary under the Horrors of Digestion" (1792) depicts the Prince of Wales as a jaded gourmand with a whale-like belly, as careless of his luxuries as of the unpaid bills scattered on the floor. The image captures both the Regent's moral repulsiveness and its consequences – a waste of the public purse – while the title mockingly contrasts the true horrors currently suffered by the French nobility with the Regent's self-inflicted dyspepsia. In such cartoons, Gillray's achievement was to *visualize* the political life of the nation outside of court ritual and the self-serving theatrics of Parliament. His greatest immediate influence was not on other artists – his postwar imitators were far tamer – but on the political writers of the 1810s, both Tory and radical, who trafficked in literary caricatures of their political opponents, exploiting single pathological traits – dementia, impotency, obesity, libidinousness – as synecdoches of corruption.

As a social commentator, rather than political satirist, Rowlandson is the more direct heir to Hogarth. Like Gillray, he uses his visual medium for irreverence and subversion, a profoundly anti-institutional artistic practice. His "Exhibition Stare Case" (Figure 4) gleefully actualizes his antiacademic position in fantasizing a rude comic disaster at

Gillen D'Arcy Wood

Figure 4 "The Exhibition Stare Case," c.1800 (engraving) by Thomas Rowlandson (1756–1827)/British Museum, London, UK/ The Bridgeman Art Library Nationality / copyright status: English / out of copyright

the annual Royal Academy exhibition. A small dog has precipitated a fleshly pile-up of patrons on the stairs. Dresses fly up, and the chubby bottoms and thighs of the fashionable female art-lovers are exposed to a leering crowd. As in the Vauxhall Gardens print, the opportunity for male voyeurism and general salaciousness in the public spaces of London is the principal subject. But it is also a satire of the Academy itself, at which Rowlandson once studied. Reynolds attempted to regulate the crowds at the Academy exhibitions by instituting a hefty admission fee. Rowlandson is having none of such posturing, and shows us the natural vulgarity of Reynolds's elite class of connoisseurs. As the pun in the title suggests, the Academy's idealized rituals of spectatorship are literally crushed beneath the libidinal energies of the urban crowd. The perfectly posed neoclassical nudes of the Exhibition, visible in the background, find themselves upstaged by the bawdy spectacle of their own audience. Rowlandson exploits the pretensions of each – both marble flesh and academic contemplation of that flesh – as a theatrical folly, as just another urban entertainment.

Next to the Royal Academy, the most important national institution of art in the Romantic period was the British Museum. Founded in 1753 from the bequeathed collections of wealthy connoisseurs, the Museum gradually expanded its premises and its access to the general public to the point where, in the post-Waterloo period, an ordinary Londoner such as John Keats was able to view its collections. The most important role the Museum played in the evolution of Romantic aesthetics was in its ever-growing collections of antiquities. The early galleries, such as that devoted to Lord Townley's collection, suggested the visual remainders of an aristocratic Grand Tour, and featured Roman sculpture exclusively. But with the controversial acquisition of Lord Elgin's Parthenon marbles in 1816, London museum-goers were exposed to Greek art in its original, albeit crumbling form. Painter Benjamin Haydon's account of his first sight of the Marbles takes the rhetorical shape of an epiphany, a spontaneous Romantic historiography in which the past is troped as future, the old as shock of the new:

> I felt the future, I foretold that they would . . . overturn the false beau-ideal, where nature was nothing, and would establish the true beau-ideal, of which nature alone is the basis. I shall never forget the horses' heads – the feet in the metopes! I felt as if a divine truth had blazed inwardly upon my mind and I knew that they would at last rouse the art of Europe from its slumber in the darkness. (Haydon 1853/1926, vol. 2: 67)

Haydon and Hazlitt saw in the naturalism and anatomical precision of the Elgin Marbles a decisive blow against the neoclassical aesthetic regime of Reynolds's *Discourses*, with its "fashionable and fastidious theory of the ideal" (Hazlitt 1822: 147). Similarly, their friend Keats's museum poems abandon the connoisseur language of Reynoldsian idealism entirely in favor of a self-conscious, *historical* response to the facticity of ancient art, as "sculpture builded up upon the grave / Of their own power" ("The Fall of Hyperion," Canto I: ll. 383–4). In his sonnets on the marbles, Odes on a Grecian Urn and Psyche, and "Fall of Hyperion," Keats inaugurates a modern brand of agonized sentimentality, in which the poet plays the role of the modern British subject confounded by the palpable but ambiguous legacy of ancient European civilization.

That Lord Elgin could not afford to keep his marbles, but gave them up for purchase by the government for display in a public museum is emblematic of a radical change in the British cultural order in the early nineteenth century, with the visual arts at the vanguard. The parliamentary showdown between partisans of Elgin's collection and representatives of the traditional connoisseur elite (the Society of Dilettanti derided the marbles) was won by professional artists and critics from the same metropolitan middle class that, the following year, scored a victory over the aristocratic managers of the King's Theatre with the staging of Mozart's *Don Giovanni*. The middle class is forever rising, but Romantic visual culture traces the growing bourgeois ascendancy in many such episodes. The foundation of the National Gallery of Art in 1824, to which many of the great private eighteenth-century art collections were donated, was the culminating institutional union of art and the bourgeois nation in the Romantic period. Thereafter, the wealthy elite represented their connoisseurship and love for the arts in maintenance of public institutions of culture. Art was no longer a matter for private delectation but a national property, and the education of public taste came increasingly to be seen as a civic responsibility to be shared by government and a connoisseur class which discovered, in the new public galleries and museums, venues in which to reassert their cultural leadership in the modern age.

Neither John Keats nor Elizabeth Linley, however, were born into this privileged class. Their notable participation in the visual culture of the Romantic age thus exemplifies its principal trajectory: a media revolution that was commercial in its operations and "democratic" in its effects. Romantic writers responded variously to this explosion in the volume and variety of visual arts and entertainments: Smith, Lamb, Keats and Hunt with (mixed) delight; Austen, Wordsworth, Coleridge, and Shelley with (mixed) loathing and distrust. Even the progressive Hazlitt worried about the indiscriminate appetites of a new urban, leisured class disposed to see themselves as patrons of culture. Both Gainsborough's portrait of Elizabeth Linley and Keats's British Museum poems offer Romantic figures for art's reception in the new age: rather than describing the Greek sculptures themselves, Keats dramatizes his own response to them, while Linley luminously models for us, her viewers, the shape and expression of our own wished-for Romantic sensibility. It is an emphatic sign of the cultural modernity of late Georgian Britain that its art, and the literary response to that art, acknowledged the desires of the viewing audience – the self-conscious act of visual consumption – as both its condition of possibility and its subject.

References and Further Reading

Altick, Richard. (1978) *The Shows of London*. Cambridge, MA: Harvard University Press.
Andrews, Malcolm. (1989) *The Search for the Picturesque: Landscape, Aesthetics, and Tourism in Britain, 1760–1800*. Aldershot, UK: Scholar Press.
Austen, Jane. *Sense and Sensibility* (1811/1990) Oxford: Oxford University Press.
Austen, Jane. *Emma* (1816/1998) Oxford: Oxford University Press.
Austen, Jane. *Northanger Abbey* (1818/1990) Oxford: Oxford University Press.
Barrell, John. (1986) *The Political Theory of Painting from Reynolds to Hazlitt*. New Haven, CT: Yale University Press.
Blake, William. (1808?/1997) "Annotations to Reynolds," in Joshua Reynolds, *Discourses on Art*, ed. Robert Wark (pp. 284–319). New Haven, CT: Yale University Press.
Brewer, John. (1997) *The Pleasures of the Imagination: English Culture in the Eighteenth Century*. New York: Farrar, Straus, Giroux.
Broome, Ralph. (1791) *The Letters of Simpkin the Second, Poetic Recorder of All the Proceedings Upon the Trial of Warren Hastings*. London: Printed for John Stockdale.
Combe, William and Thomas Rowlandson. (1813) *The Tour of Dr. Syntax in Search of the Picturesque*. London: R. Ackermann.
Cowper, William. (1785/1994) *The Task, and Selected Other Poems*, ed. James Sambrook. London: Longman.
Cumberland, Richard. (1807/2002) *The Memoirs of Richard Cumberland*, ed. Richard J. Dircks (2 vols in 1). New York: AMS Press.

De Quincey, Thomas. (1821/1888) *Confessions of an English Opium Eater.* London: W. Scott.

Eaves, Morris. (1992) *The Counter-Arts Conspiracy: Art and Industry in the Age of Blake.* Ithaca, NY: Cornell University Press.

Everett, Nigel. (1994) *The Tory View of Landscape.* New Haven, CT: Yale University Press.

Galt, John. (1820) *The Life, Studies, and Works of Benjamin West,* 2 vols. London: Cadell.

Gidal, Eric. (2001) *Poetic Exhibitions: Romantic Aesthetics and the Pleasures of the British Museum.* Lewisburg, PA: Bucknell University Press.

Haydon, Benjamin. (1853/1926) *Autobiography and Memoirs,* ed. Tom Taylor, 2 vols. London: Peter Davies.

Hazlitt, William. (1814/1933) "Miss O'Neill's Juliet," in *The Complete Works of William Hazlitt,* ed. P. P. Howe, 21 vols (vol. 5, pp. 198–200). New York: J. M. Dent.

Hazlitt, William. (1822/1933) "On the Elgin Marbles," in *Complete Works,* ed. P. P. Howe (vol. 18, pp. 145–66).

Hazlitt, William. (1828/1933) "Mrs. Siddons," in *Complete Works,* ed. P. P. Howe (vol. 18, pp. 406–10).

Kelly, Linda. (1980) *The Kemble Era.* London: Bodley Head.

Kroeber, Karl. (1975) *Romantic Landscape Vision.* Madison: University of Wisconsin Press.

Lamb, Charles. (1935) *The Complete Works and Letters of Charles Lamb,* ed. E. V. Lucas. New York: Modern Library.

More, Hannah. (1782) *Sacred Dramas, to Which Are Added, Sensibility, a Poem.* London: T. Cadell.

Murphy, Arthur. (1801) *The Life of David Garrick.* Dublin: B. Smith.

Oettermann, Stephan. (1997) *The Panorama: History of a Mass Medium,* trans. Deborah Lucas Schneider. New York: Zone Books.

Paulson, Ronald. (1982) *Literary Landscapes: Turner and Constable.* New Haven, CT: Yale University Press.

Pointon, Marcia. (1993) *Hanging the Head: Portraiture and Social Formation in Eighteenth-Century England.* New Haven, CT: Yale University Press.

Price, Uvedale. (1794) *Essay on the Picturesque.* London: Printed for J. Robson.

Reynolds, Sir Joshua. (1791/1997) *Discourses on Art,* ed. Robert R. Wark. New Haven, CT: Yale University Press.

Rhodes, R. Crompton. (1933) *Harlequin Sheridan: The Man and His Legends.* Oxford: Basil Blackwell.

Russell, Gillian. (1995) *The Theatres of War: Performance, Politics, and Society, 1793–1815.* Oxford: Clarendon Press.

Scott, Grant. (1994) *The Sculpted Word: Keats, Ekphrasis, and the Visual Arts.* Hanover, NH: University Press of New England.

Seward, Anna. (1784) *Louisa, a Poetical Novel, in Four Epistles.* Lichfield, UK: J. Jackson.

Sha, Richard. (1998) *The Visual and Verbal Sketch in British Romanticism*. Philadelphia: University of Pennsylvania Press.

Sheridan, Richard Brinsley. (1973) *Dramatic Works*, ed. Cecil Price, 2 vols. Oxford: Oxford University Press.

Sloman, Susan. (2002) *Gainsborough in Bath*. New Haven, CT: Yale University Press.

Vaughan, William. (1999) *British Painting: The Golden Age from Hogarth to Turner*. London: Thames and Hudson.

Smith, Charlotte. (1807) *Beachy Head with Other Poems*. London: J. Johnson.

Thomas, Sophie. (2007) *Romantic Visualities: Fragments, History, Spectacle*. New York: Routledge.

West, Shearer. (1991) *The Image of the Actor: Verbal and Visual Representation in the Age of Garrick and Kemble*. New York: St. Martin's Press.

Wood, Gillen D'Arcy. (2001) *The Shock of the Real: Romanticism and Visual Culture, 1760–1860*. New York: Palgrave/Macmillan.

Wood, Gillen D'Arcy. (2005) "Cockney Mozart: The Hunt Circle, the King's Theatre, and *Don Giovanni*," *Studies in Romanticism* 44: 367–97.

Chapter 12

What's at Stake? Kantian Aesthetics, Romantic and Modern Poetics, Sociopolitical Commitment

Robert Kaufman

Why – in a world that condemns untold millions to poverty, exploitation, and oppression, and that often appears more inclined to blow itself up than to address potentially catastrophic social conflicts humanely and constructively – are you bothering to read this? More to the point, why – when your attention, energy, and commitment would seem indispensable to hands-on political and ethical actions that could help engage the problems confronting us – do you waste time on art, aesthetic experience and, in particular and perhaps most inexplicably, imaginative literature?

Before even beginning to approach these questions substantively, you may sense, given the context of this volume of essays, the suggestion of a formally parallel or allegorical relation between the Romantic moment and our own. But the suggested comparison goes deeper than mere parallelism or allegory, for Romanticism actually inaugurates the modern status of the very questions posed above. Indeed, what has come to be called High Romanticism has come also to be understood as the point of departure for the question of "aesthetics and politics," the notion that in modernity the artistic-aesthetic and the sociopolitical, in a push–pull dance-tension of retreat and involvement, somehow help shed light on or perhaps constitute – even as they paradoxically may seem also to compete with or negate – one another.

Of course the problem of art's (or poetry's, or, in classical terms, *imitation*'s) relation to knowledge of objective reality (and to action based thereon) long predates Romanticism; via Aristotle's response to Plato's Socrates, it virtually shapes Western philosophy from the beginning as a debate over whether artistic imitation (*mimesis*) contributes to, or is parasitic on, our attempts to understand, and effectively to act in and on, reality. But in its emergence from the Enlightenment's burgeoning secularism, Romanticism sets a modern literary-aesthetic stage on which age-old markers of tradition – like hereditary monarchy and established religion, along with their apparent guarantees of relatively secure grounds for knowledge – have gone missing, or seem greatly diminished in their authority (evidenced most dramatically in events like the American and French revolutions of 1776 and 1789). In this new dispensation, aesthetics and literature – above all in Kantian and related philosophy and in High Romantic poetry – seem insistently to claim priority vis-à-vis acts of knowing and doing. And Romanticism appears insistently to literalize this claim of priority by making artistic or aesthetic thought-experience come *prior to* objective knowledge or concrete action, in a sequencing-logic that seems to continue to insist on the separation or alienation of aspects of cognition from one another, and then on the separation of cognition as a whole from action.

Kantian-Romantic Aesthetics and Left Critique

Perhaps Romanticism insists too much? Romantic aesthetics and poetics (and their profound if complicated influence on modern art and criticism) have been pilloried in a basically left-wing critique already articulated during the Romantic era, but whose voice gains strength later in the nineteenth century, speaks strategically within important strains of modernism, and has often seemed to predominate in art and criticism since the late 1960s. They are denounced not only for putting the cart of impractical, "useless" or "purposeless" imaginative thought and subjective experience before the horse of purposeful, integrated, objective knowledge and ethical-sociopolitical action, but for permanently corralling the horse itself. How, the critique demands, can one intellectually, ethically, or politically justify – much less celebrate

– the separation, alienation, *segregation*, of thought from action, poetry from life, art from politics and society? Who has the time, leisure, or inclination for such an approach – and, intentions aside, who benefits from these divisions?

In recent decades, this powerful and popular line of Left critique has generally been known as the "Critique of Aesthetic (or Romantic, or Modernist) Ideology" (McGann 1983, 1989, Lloyd 1985, 1989, Eagleton 1990). This critique has taken much of its vocabulary and concepts from classical Marxism and from a cluster of related literary-critical and cultural-studies methodologies that emerged, in the 1960s and after, from structuralism and poststructuralism. It puts the systemic case in more or less the following manner: at a foundational moment for modern-bourgeois, desocialized, individualist, merely "representationalist" ideologies of aesthetics, ethics, and politics, Kant's 1790 aesthetic treatise *Critique of Judgment* (often called the Third Critique) and the Romantic art contemporaneous with it established an essentialist or transcendental theory of cultural value, a theory based on the uniqueness – and hence the *autonomy* from material, sociopolitical life – of literature and the other arts, of the aesthetic realm, of literary or aesthetic imaginative *form* over against life's or society's real *content*. This theory's rebellious Other, from Romanticism through the twentieth century, will therefore be the material, the social, and the historical, all of which are erased by or made subservient to artistic-philosophical form. Thus a historically emergent, historically bourgeois commitment to aesthetic form – to formalism – ideologically *de*forms material, sociohistorical reality, turning it first into art and then into art theory. Attention to larger social content – the larger substance of life that would include or emphasize and thus affect the status of the subjugated populations (the working class, women, people of color) who together constitute a majority – is strategically arrested by the emphasis on the autonomy of imaginative thought and its expression in and as artistic-aesthetic form, perhaps above all in and as that most ephemeral, most removed-from-social-bustle art, lyric poetry.

What does such insistence on poetic-aesthetic autonomy – such autonomous art – look or sound like? In the British context, one very famous instance goes like this:

> Imagination – here the Power so called
> Through sad incompetence of human speech,
> That awful Power rose from the mind's abyss
> Like an unfathered vapour that enwraps,

> At once, some lonely traveller. I was lost;
> Halted without an effort to break through;
> But to my conscious mind I now can say –
> "I recognize thy glory": in such strength
> Of usurpation, when the light of sense
> Goes out, but with a flash that has revealed
> The invisible world, does greatness make abode,
> There harbours whether we be young or old.
> Our destiny, our being's heart and home,
> Is with infinitude, and only there:
> With hope it is, hope that can never die,
> Effort, and expectation, and desire,
> And something evermore about to be.
> Under such banners militant, the soul
> Seeks for no trophies, struggles for no spoils
> That may attest her prowess, blest in thoughts
> That are their own perfection and reward,
> Strong in herself and in beatitude
> That hides her . . .
>
> (Wordsworth, *Prelude*, Book 6, ll. 592–614)

Or, with perhaps more recognition of a world outside the self and its imaginative consciousness, but still taking direction or impetus from them:

> O! the one Life within us and abroad,
> Which meets all motion and becomes its soul,
> A light in sound, a sound-like power in light,
> Rhythm in all thought, and joyance every where –
>
> (Coleridge, "The Eolian Harp," ll. 26–9)

The first passage, from Wordsworth's *Prelude* (1850), quickly became and has since stood as one of modern Anglo-American poetry's signal dramatizations of strong imaginative and aesthetic assertion, of an assertion that aims not only to privilege imagination and self-reflective consciousness but to let them seem virtually to eliminate external sources of determination (and to do so despite the rich ambiguities built into such passages concerning, for example, whether "the light of sense / goes out" indicates an extension or an extinguishing). The second passage, rather less severely – indeed, joyously – shows Coleridge in "The Eolian Harp" (1795) likewise constructing an interfusion of mind and nature, consciousness, and the real, in which mind, soul, consciousness, or imagination undeniably strikes the poem's animating note (even – especially! – where, as here, the poem's plot and ostensible subject matter purport to move in the opposite direction, since, apparently, the point was to have been that *nature's* breezes initially caress or tickle human consciousness into movement).

As for the informing theory or philosophy, the Kantian description of what takes place in aesthetic experience – particularly in the experience-judgment of beauty – involves a foundational substitution of image or illusion for objective, empirical, reality. Indeed, this substitution is frankly theorized as the momentary misrecognition or mistaking of a subjective experience for a conceptual-objective reality; the subject operates in *semblance*, under (and ultimately – crucially – *in awareness of*) the *illusion* that the thought-experience of aesthetic judgment is already objectively, that is, universally, operative. Another way to put this Kantian notion is that aesthetic illusion works a double movement of fictive construction-projection that is first undertaken/enjoyed, and then recognized as having really taken place, but as the real experience of a fiction. Again, for Kant, the source of this doubleness is the generative illusion in which the subject thinks in the *form* of conceptuality, but without an extant, substantive, determinant concept really being involved. Synonymous – if not causal – with this illusion is the aesthetic's "uselessness," "lack of purpose," its Kantian "purposiveness without purpose." In aesthetic experience-judgment, what exists genuinely is the *feeling* of imaginative activity undertaken with the intensity of goal or purpose, but with the proviso that the feeling winds up being the whole story, for it has created the semblance or illusion of purpose or objectivity, an "as if" experience of the latter, where the subject's actual subjective experience is independent of – thus autonomous from – determination by objective-empirical reality (Kant 1790/1987: 45–6, 53–4, 60, 79–84, 399–404).

Though one might view skeptically Kant's or the Romantic poets' attempts at a theoretical description or practical enactment of what they deem to occur in aesthetic experience, it's interesting that the poetic instances from Wordsworth and Coleridge have often seemed to incite more – and more heated – condemnation than the philosopher-theoretician's. This may be largely due to the historical trajectory of the two canonical, enormously influential British poets who wrote the lines quoted above. Notoriously, both Wordsworth and Coleridge, liberal or even radical adherents of revolutionary politics in their youthful, early period of poetic fame, subsequently turned against the

French Revolution and British progressivism or reform. For the Critique of Aesthetic Ideology, this turn – this retreat from activist sociopolitical and ethical behavior (or at least impulse) to political quietism and then downright Conservatism or Reaction – is understood to have originated in poetic theory and practice themselves: aesthetic autonomy, the decoupling of imaginative experience from protocols of use, purpose, and objectivity, prepares the way for or is itself the depoliticization of art and literature.

But thorny questions arise. If Wordsworth and Coleridge were politically progressive during the early years of their adult poetic careers, why should we not regard their literary output of those years as similarly progressive, rather than the seed of forthcoming defection? Or we could perhaps more rigorously ask what justifies inferences or assumptions of *causality* between the poetry and the politics – as opposed to seeing these relations as contingent. Moreover, vocabulary and rhetorical style aside, it can be shown without difficulty that the Left Romantic poets – above all, Blake and Shelley – who started off and remained significantly more radical than Wordsworth and Coleridge had ever been, largely share Wordsworth's and Coleridge's fealty to literary-aesthetic autonomy, and indeed argue for the revolutionary (rather than quietist) character of such autonomy, such resistance to the external conceptual determination of thought or consciousness. Furthermore, given the Critique of Aesthetic Ideology's reliance on key concepts taken from Marx and Engels, and then from the Left modernist critics belonging to the Frankfurt School (particularly Theodor Adorno and Walter Benjamin), we might feel compelled to ask why those figures all regard Romantic poets like Shelley, Byron, Keats, Heine, Hölderlin, and others with great admiration, and indeed praise them precisely for the politically progressive character of their art.

In other words, what may be at stake in the debates over Kantian aesthetics, Romantic poetics, and sociopolitical or ethical commitment – not only in terms of the Romantic era and the later nineteenth century themselves, but also for Romanticism's extraordinary influence on key strains of modernist and postmodernist art and criticism – is something that cannot be conceived so one-sidedly after all. For if the key figures in both nineteenth- and twentieth-century Left and Marxian criticism have such positive things to say about poets quite clearly committed to an inescapably Kantian aesthetics and High Romantic poetics, how can we avoid inquiring whether that praise comes not despite but because of such formalist literary commitments?

To push the point further: what if first Marx and Engels themselves, and then today's much-relied-upon-by-the-Left Frankfurters, all effectively adopt Percy Shelley's own militant defense of a complicated but necessary commitment to literary and aesthetic formalism – to aesthetic autonomy – precisely in order to contribute towards human beings' abilities to develop versions of a subjectivity and critical agency that, in a complex, difficult modernity, can help us exercise the faculties necessary for significant ethical and sociopolitical engagement in the first place?

Shelley's *Defence of Poetry* (1821) indeed emphasizes that, having learned how formally to derive critical thought from poetry and the aesthetic, one need not limit the field to the writings of self-consciously revolutionary artists. The final passages of the *Defence* attest to the importance of certain unnamed poets, Wordsworth undoubtedly chief among them. These poets may have "little apparent correspondence with the spirit of good of which they are the ministers"; nonetheless – and without any argument for the simple *reversal* of the manifest meaning of their words – Shelley asserts that "it is impossible to read the compositions" those poets have produced "without being startled with the electric life which burns within their words" (Shelley 1821/2002: 535). Again, the suspension of interest in the manifest content permits the reader to understand that such poets express "the spirit of the age," even if the poets themselves "express what they understand not." Hence the strong Shelleyan claim (adopted almost verbatim by Brecht and other twentieth-century militantly Left poets and critics) about such autonomous aesthetic form: the latter's dynamic is such that its contributions towards critical agency can stem from artists and works that are apolitical, or that have become or perhaps always were undeniably conservative. As noted above, the precise term for this problem so ruminated upon by Marx, Engels, Brecht, Benjamin, and Adorno is, in Shelley's vocabulary, *Wordsworth*.

All this is to reiterate that there is – with terrible unintended irony for the Critique of Aesthetic Ideology's reliance on Marx and the Frankfurt School for the Critique's stigmatization of High Romantic aesthetics and poetics – a very significant reliance in classical Left theory and criticism on the resources of Romantic aesthetics and poetics. And in ways that may but perhaps shouldn't be surprising, a great deal of this stems from the fact that the Romantic era gave birth not only to the art and theory under consideration here, but also, quite inescapably, to the wild, earth-shaking socioeconomic developments that would be taken up in a barely post-Romantic text called *Das Kapital*.

Marx and the Persistence of Romanticism

It's therefore worth bringing right into the heart of our discussion the final movement in *Capital*'s historical critique of exchange value and commodity form. For *Capital* (1867) initially makes Enlightenment economist David Ricardo the virtual hero of its commodity story, emphasizing the progressive character of Ricardo's demonstration in *On the Principles of Political Economy and Taxation* (1817) that what defines the commodity is not use-value but production for and as exchange value. (Ricardo showed why the commodity is not based on the inextricable relation of particularity to use, but rather on a universalizable abstraction of labor time. Hence, value is derived vis-à-vis an abstraction of the labor time necessary for each product produced over against all other products within the market). Marx then steps past Ricardo, and past what by the mid-nineteenth century has already begun to identify itself as Left-Ricardian, labor-theory-of-value socialism. Marx notes that the commodity's value derives not only from the conceptual abstraction of labor time but also, crucially, from an ongoing, sociohistorical, and now contestable judgment that this abstraction of labor time must or should be the final basis for all value whatsoever. Instead of this permanent grip of the conceptual abstraction of labor time on determining value, Marx outlines a judgment process that's capable of holding that the abstraction of labor time should be a significant, but not necessarily the ruling or determining, basis for valuation, so that value finally would not need to remain determined by, but would be free to transcend – to *not* be determined by – labor time.

Marx shows that this ability to transcend the conceptual abstraction of labor time as the ultimate determinant of value would break open – initially, via Kantian aesthetic judgment! – exactly what Kantian aesthetic judgment by definition offers the *form* or *semblance* but not the *substance* of: an already extant, determined, determining *concept*. In this breaking open, stretching past, or sidestepping of existing, substantive-objective conceptual determination (i.e., a definite concept that should direct the judgment at hand), subjects feel and experience their semblance-play with conceptual form as if this "play" already *were* a clear and definite idea (or in philosophical terms, a substantive-determinative-objective conceptuality). Such a conceptuality would somehow feel freely chosen rather than determinatively compelled. In the Kantian terms discussed above – as well as in Friedrich Schiller's account of "play" in *On the Aesthetic Education of Man* (1795)

– aesthetic judgment thus begins to enact, in form or semblance, the experience and process of forming or constructing something that is not conceptually predetermined. Marx's historical critique of Ricardo stresses ultimately that it has been and continues to be capital's decision – not labor's – to make the conceptual abstraction of labor time the final, untranscendable basis, limit, or horizon of socioeconomic value. In doing so, capital ideologically proclaims the concept of exchange value (along with exchange value's embodiment in/as commodity form and its enactment in/as mechanical reproduction) to be a matter of natural or scientific determinate judgment. Similarly, and again in a quite Kantian analysis that grasps semblance-experience as what enables thought to stretch past existing conceptual determination, Marx reiterates the need to break open this seemingly already adequately conceptualized question of value when he insists that any kind of socioeconomic valuation should be subject to ongoing judgment – "reflective" or "aesthetic" judgment rather than conceptual predetermination. This is why, from *The Poverty of Philosophy* (1847) through *Critique of the Gotha Programme* (1875) and beyond, Marx remains adamant that labor socialism's goal of simply expropriating, nationalizing, or "socializing" exchange value and commodity production is woefully inadequate to labor's own most pressing sociocultural, let alone socioeconomic, needs – starting with labor's need to make, and then to take action to realize, valuations arrived at through reflective – not already conceptually determined – judgments (Marx 1867/1965: 81–6, 1875).

Humming just beneath this analysis is something about exchange value, commodity form, and conceptualization that might otherwise go unheard. Marx argues that economic modernization has largely involved the emancipation of exchange value, which has made central not just the concept and practice of exchange value, but also the socioeconomic takeoff or initial triumph of determinate conceptualization itself. For the first time in history, Marx emphasizes, neither an unpredictable (because particular) individual use nor an unpredictable (because powerfully arbitrary) feudal or authoritarian diktat or set of directives, but rather a single predetermined conceptual operation – the abstraction of labor time (predictable in its operational formula if not in the yield of its case-by-case data) – has a major, if not *the* major say in determining socioeconomic value. This holds enormously generative possibilities for socioeconomic productive capacity. But even while the new mode of production tends, in an era of emancipatory and egalitarian discourse, greatly to expand the social character of production and amount of goods produced, it simultaneously intensifies the disparities of wealth and resource-distribution, meanwhile causing an increasing disappearance of particularity as well. This waning of particularity is related to, if not wholly caused by, the disappearance of *use* as a determinant of value. The loss-of-particularity theme, already developed by Marx and Engels, famously becomes in Benjamin's and then Adorno's writings "the crisis of experience." In this crisis, subjectivity, reflective judgment, and critical agency confront a felt evisceration of the capacity for provisionally spontaneous, not already conceptually determined experience. This is the experience presupposed in the ability to project "aesthetic" or more-than-mechanistic relations between the individual and the collective, the particular and the potentially universal. Two further conditions are of great significance. First is the close if not synonymous relationship between conceptual thought and exchange-value abstraction; for when abstract exchange-value embodies itself in commodity form, it tends to appear as the apotheosis of conceptuality and conceptual determinacy themselves. There is *then* the way language is deemed (certainly by Marx and Engels and then by the Frankfurters) the key medium for significantly communicable conceptuality. This complex situation leads first Marx and Engels and then the Frankfurters to intensify a High Romantic theme (rooted deeper still in classical poetics and aesthetics): lyric poetry bears a special, radical relationship to conceptuality as such and, in modernity, to the way determinate conceptuality manifests its socioeconomic identity as exchange value and the commodity.

Romantic art and theory thus begin to take, as subject matter, modernity's problematic apotheosis of determinate conceptuality – and Romanticism likewise indicates that both its apotheoses of natural beauty and its tortured explorations of the dangers of experience-denying modern determinism register an abiding threat in contemporary reality. This threat is what can be called the *non*experience of human beings for whom judgment is by definition becoming – by the very definition of exchange value and the commodity – an already conceptualized, predetermined affair external to them and to any version of their subjectivity emphasizing their capacity for reflective judgment and critical agency (and the concomitant importance of these latter in making socioeconomic judgments). Romanticism consequently begins to wager about whether, starting if not concluding with sheerly formal artistic-aesthetic dynamics, a significant modern lyric poetry can emerge just when the experiential preconditions for it are starting to seem as though they've gone missing. Likewise Romanticism starts wagering that such a poetry might *have* to inculcate critique of socio-economic modernity's concept of concepts, the superconcept of *exchange value*. For wouldn't such artistic-aesthetic activity likewise constitute, enable, or begin to enact a sensed recognition of renewed possibilities for conceptually undetermined experience and judgment?

Aesthetic Semblance-Illusion vs. Commodity Delusion

Art or semblance, the argument goes (as it moves from Kant's aesthetics and High Romantic poetics through significant strains in Left modernist art and critical theory), is critical precisely in its formal character of aesthetic *illusion*, as opposed to an unknowing aesthetic*ist* *de*lusion. Art critically marks itself as illusion by offering the form rather than substance of conceptuality, or what Kant calls the generative "misattribution" or "misrecognition" of an "as-if" objectivity to subjective judgment experience. As it thus advertises its *aesthetic-* or *il*lusion-character to its audience, art signals the interaction and interdependence of, as well as the difference between, itself and the world. (Aesthetic*ist de*lusion, on the other hand, tends toward the collapse of the different identities – at times under the pressure of good-faith, radically intended assumptions of responsibility for sociopolitical or ethical engagement, for changing the world – and can thus contribute unwittingly toward an inability to distinguish between artwork and world.) Critical aesthetic illusion thus pivots on a formal dynamic or dialectic of *charged distance*, to paraphrase Benjamin: the artist's, artwork's, and audience's intense engagement and correspondence with – amidst an awareness of difference from – the empirical, sociohistorical and political, Real (Benjamin 1939/1969: 188).

The audience that participates in the semblance character at the core of Kantian-Romantic (and often Kantian-modernist) aesthetics and poetics provisionally treats the semblance – the formal artwork or our aesthetic experience of it – as if it were real or had the dignity of the real. Or, what amounts to the same thing, the audience judges it as such and feels it can cognitively make such a judgment, that it can experience or know the feeling of this judging agency. On the other hand, and virtually at the same moment, the audience also knows – indeed, the dynamic, constructivist semblance we call "form" *demands* that the audience know – that this is only an as-if, fiction-generated experience. This awareness comes because, despite the real subjective feelings of agency engendered, nothing (or at least nothing much) has yet been done to the empirical world. In other words, the formal or protocritical dynamic of art's semblance-character constructs the true fiction whereby one feels the capacity for cognizing, and then for acting on and changing, the world, while, at the same time, aesthetic semblance-character negatively, in its *anti*aesthetic*ist* vocation, reminds the subject that however much it might seem or feel otherwise, this capacity has yet to be practically applied and realized.

In the quite explicitly Romantic-Kantian traditions of poetics and aesthetics that Marx and then the Frankfurt School inherit, lyric's special role derives not from its being better, nobler, or more right on than other kinds of literature, art, or cultural works, but from the otherwise almost unremarkable fact that, as a formal matter, lyric maintains a special relationship to the presumptive medium for significantly communicable conceptuality: language. Each art has its own unique character; lyric's is to take language, the presumably bottom-line medium of objectivity (in the Frankfurters' and others' philosophical-theoretical vocabulary for the attempt to cognize reality, of *conceptuality*) and, first, to subjectivize it, affectively to stretch conceptuality's bounds in order to make something that seems formally like a concept but that does something that ordinary, "objective" concepts generally do not do – sing. For lyric song to reach and give pleasure to a significant audience, it must then construct its own form of objectivity or coherence, though the logic is that of art – here especially involving poetic art's relationship to musicality – rather than strictly mathematical-conceptual logic. Each of the arts has its mode or modes of semblance. In lyric, semblance primarily involves making speech acts appear as if their very logic has compelled them somehow to burst – naturally, justifiably, as it were – into song, which suddenly seems necessary but certainly hadn't yet felt predetermined, and which in its bursting the formal contours of extant conceptuality (in a manner inseparable from pleasure), allows for a renewed sense of capacity or agency vis-à-vis *materials* that can eventually be grasped as reconceived or newly conceived sociopolitical, historical, and/or ethical *content* within the newly stretched form or formal capacity (Adorno 1957).

In ways that the Romantics fully anticipate, twentieth-century Left artists and critics theorize that the age of art's technological reproducibility ("mechanical reproduction") is characterized not by the aesthetic aura (or the semblance character, illusion character, or appearance character [*Scheincharakter*]) that, as discussed above, operates through charged distance, suspension, or negation. Rather, technological reproducibility or mechanical reproduction operates by way of the commodity form's version of aura or semblance, wherein a privileged concept – the superconcept called exchange value – pretends (by means of what Benjamin initially and influentially thinks of as phony aura) that it *isn't* the already determined and determining concept (exchange value) that has already conceptualized the way to arrive at the value of anything and everything socioeconomically significant. It thus pretends, among other things, that its allegedly particular instantiations are free, are not already predetermined and conceptually subsumed. Commodity aura is thus the photo-negative of aesthetic aura's genuinely distanced-yet-charged (because openly acknowledged) semblance character. (And lyric poetry is especially relevant here because of the ways that lyric's linguistic character leads it by definition to stretch conceptuality's linguistic medium towards the aura of songfulness.) The specially charged distance of recognized or admitted aesthetic semblance is to be grasped as a critical (though only formal) negation of exchange-value or commodity-value. The charged distance of aesthetic judgment provides a provisional negation or suspension emerging from the process in which the experience of aesthetic thought phenomenally takes the form of conceptual thought. But of course, as Kant's aesthetics maintained, it takes only the "form," and is thus only the "semblance," of a determinant, substantive-objective concept.

The commodity, on the other hand, attempts positively to sell or serve up its apparently auratic luminosity as genuine, free immediacy, and the commodity does not wish to admit that its seeming freedom from conceptual determination is illusory. That is, commodity form does not present aura, or illusion, either in or as charged distance. Hence the commodity form does not really proffer its aura through the aesthetic's thought-and-felt *as-if*, where semblance is simultaneously engaged as if it were reality, while also being marked consciously as mere aesthetic semblance, inherently distant from reality. Rather, the commodity presents aura through aestheti*cization* (where the audience is meant to lose sight of the status or character of illusion, and thus to have the illusion fully meld into identity and immediacy with reality). Moreover, the commodity does this work in lockstep with aestheticization's march towards its own logical endpoint: the collapse into pure immediacy of the "as-if"'s constitutive tension of charged distance. In such collapse, semblance or illusion is no longer critically, simultaneously enjoyed and also recognized *as* illusion, but instead produces the *de*lusion of literal, immediate, particularized presence that supposedly never was illusion, or that has somehow left illusion, semblance, mimesis, and judgment-play behind. This collapse of charged aesthetic illusion into delusion leads to – or is in itself – the concomitant collapse of the experiential preconditions for reflective judgment and critical agency.

It is, then, for the Kantian-Romantic and Left modernist aesthetics outlined above, by offering a seeming, apparent, or merely formal or semblance version of substantive-objective conceptuality that the aesthetic becomes effectively *quasi*conceptual. Through what appears as an affective experience of conceptuality – *feeling* rather than intellectually understanding a seemingly objective concept – aesthetic experience permits and can even propel new thought or the eventual expansion of objective conceptuality. The semblance-character of art and aesthetic experience underwrites their relative lack of responsibility to – or their relative freedom from determination by – already established concepts. It is important to point out that this does not mean freedom from the sociohistorical or political; it means freedom from determination by extant governing (or, for that matter, oppositional) *concepts* of the sociohistorical or political. The crucial difference between sociohistorical/political determination and conceptual determination has consistently been collapsed in variants of Marxian, neo-Marxian, and post-Marxian Left critique. But the difference is what makes Marx possible – what makes a human subject, conditioned by the sociohistorical and subjected to reigning concepts and ideologies, nonetheless capable of thinking through and past existing concepts and ideologies – in the first place (Benjamin 1931, Adorno and Benjamin 1999: 104, 280, 298, 304).

Semblance character's freedom from substantive conceptual domination allows the aesthetic's inherently experimental stretching – its stretching past those already known, determined, and determining concepts that it is not bound by – to feel not like dutiful work but rather, to a highly significant degree, like play. Aesthetic work with conceptual form literally becomes play-work, the mere form or semblance of conceptually determined intellectual operations. From the very beginning, one plays around with, and is free to recombine, stretch, or extend the conceptual materials, in ways not usually sanctioned where an already determined conceptual content necessarily delimits the acceptable range of results. (One thinks, among other famous Romantic instances, of Shelley's articulation of poetic or aesthetic "pleasure" as a mode of play-work that produces "a thousand unapprehended combinations of thought," 1821/2002: 517). All of which helps explain why there is, not only in Romanticism, but also among classic Left and Marxian artists and critics, a kind of art and aesthetic experience distinct from aestheticization but also from thematized political interventionism that is highly, maybe even supremely, valued. It is valued for its ability to provide a provisional, formal suspension or negation of extant ruling concepts, and thus for its ability to stimulate the type of imaginative and affective experience that can allow for the emergence, into our fields of apprehension, of materials that can eventually provide a basis for the postaesthetic construction of new concepts and the new social dispensations that would correspond to them (Adorno 1970).

And so one could perhaps claim that what lyric semblance and other kinds of artistic semblance effect, in their semblance-character, is proto-critical illusion: their aesthetic *"as if"* announces and identifies itself *as* illusion or semblance, so that both the semblance, and the reality it relates to but differs from, are simultaneously registered. Again, this aesthetic experience is to be distinguished from aestheti*cization*, where illusion and reality are not simultaneously registered but collapsed, so that what was once aesthetic illusion, now no longer asking to be seen in tandem with the reality it differs from, ceases to be the critical or protocritical phenomenon of aesthetic illusion and instead becomes the sociopolitical or ethical delusion that art or criticism has already counted as, or towards, real-world commitment or engagement, has already counted as an *action* in and on the world.

From Romanticism onward, what advanced art, criticism, and, especially, lyric continuously remake and rediscover is *how* art (poetry above all) discovers critical (not consolatory or redemptive, but probing) formal means to wrest a sense of aura from aura's absence. They discover how to particularize particularity's disappearance, how to invest the seeming unavailability of reflective experience with the charge and force *of* reflective experience (so that one might be enabled to reflect, for starters, on what it means to appear to have lost reflective capacity itself). In short, high Romantic and post-Romantic poetry discover how – in, as, *lyric* (and therefore suffused with lyric's history of constructing and presenting the semblance of a singular, particularized voice that, emerging from play with language's ostensibly determined-objective-universal character, offers the possibility of others' hearing that voice as theirs and their voices as the poem's) – to sing song's impossibility (Benjamin 1939, Adorno 1957, 1970).

Romantic Poetics in Modernism and After

Perhaps the later-Modernist American figure who most profoundly inherits the traditions, strains, and materials in question is Robert Duncan (1919–88).[1] Like a number of the so-called Objectivist poets, but even more so, Duncan refused to follow blindly the presumably advanced view that Romanticism was precisely what experimental Modernism needed to overcome. Greatly attracted to Modernism's astonishing formal achievements, Duncan nonetheless showed – brilliantly and painstakingly, in his poetry and criticism – how deeply inflected with and shaped by Romantic poetics Modernist poetry really was. With others, he demonstrated, *pace* Pound, Eliot, et al., how only genuine insight into and extension of the Romantic legacy *within* Modernist poetics would be able to articulate the ways that Modernist experimentalism could (not least through the construction of distilled, often atonal or dissonant poetic afterlives for Romantic musicality and sympathy), play an important role in enlarging the scope of the reflective capacity (and its lifeblood of imagination) that, across almost all liberal and Left traditions of consequence, underwrite the possibility of critical agency.

This was true at cultural and political levels of analysis, but it usually began for Duncan at the poetic bone and in its marrow, with demonstrations that, for instance, it was often the daring examples in Romantic metrical practice that led Modernist poetry into the search for metrical constructions that, far from eschewing meter and rhythm, demanded instead a renewed rigorous conception of them as it sought the Poundian desideratum of "composition by musical phrase" achieved by leading the ear with the vowel tones that sculpt cadential structure.

Of decisive consequence was Duncan's and others' understanding that, in and after the 1950s, generations of Americans – particularly younger Americans – were successively attracted to the allure and excitement of experimental Modernist poetry, and, in even greater numbers of course, to so much of the more popular forms of art that were and continued to be inconceivable without poetry's founding examples and ongoing influence. Duncan enunciated the Romantic entailments inside the Modernist departures taking place, and, crucially, how those departures could – in translated terms able to preserve and develop Modernist precision and impersonality together with Romantic imagination – again provide the basis for an at once affective and intellectual knowledge process able critically to register the sources of social crisis and to generate a sense of agency about the possibility of transforming them.

Although poets and critics have for decades been aware of Duncan's unique abilities in this regard (even among fellow Black Mountain poets and members of the San Francisco Renaissance), the 2004 publication of Duncan's correspondence with poet Denise Levertov, and the forthcoming publication of the complete, accurately edited version of Duncan's literary-critical and literary-historical meditation *The H.D. Book* (sections of which have for decades lived a subterranean life in small poetry and poetics journals) are even more radically reconfiguring this terrain of understanding. Together with Duncan's poetry, the *Letters* show in terrific detail how constantly and extraordinarily Duncan returns to meditate on, and work with various issues, materials, and problems, for purposes of extending Modernist poetic art in ways that, he believes, will make the art true to itself and to the exigencies of American and international politics. These concerns include Coleridgean treatments of imagination and fancy as they appear and complicate themselves in mid-to-late twentieth-century poetry; notions of organic form and their Modernist descendants (here Duncan finds four or five different *kinds* of organic, or rather organic-constructivist, form that had emerged by the early 1960s); Wordsworthian-derived strangeness as a still-signifying sign of English language lyric's efforts to reclaim historical memory; Blakean prophetic modalities, but with renewed attention (as had too often been lacking) to the rhythmic and syntactic precision and tautness in Blake's prophetic works, should poets and readers really look and listen closely (Duncan 2004: 404–9 and passim).

Here are lines from "Up Rising: Passages 25," one of Duncan's many poems whose materials stem from US intervention in Indochina; first published in poetry journals in the 1960s, the piece was made famous by its inclusion in Duncan's 1968 volume *Bending the Bow*. (The *Passages* was an ongoing, never-finished series of poems extending across a number of Duncan's published volumes of poetry.)

> Now Johnson would go up to join the great simulacra of men,
>   Hitler and Stalin, to work his fame
>   with planes roaring out from Guam over Asia
> all America become a sea of toiling men
>   stirrd at this will, which would be a bloated thing,
>   drawing from the underbelly of the nation
>   such blood and dreams as swell the idiot psyche

>   out of its courses into an elemental thing
>   until his name stinks with burning meat and heapt honors
>
>   And men wake to see that they are used like things
>   spent in a great potlatch, this Texas barbecue
>   of Asia, Africa, and all the Americas . . .
>
>   [. . .]
>
>   But the mania, the ravening eagle of America
>   as Lawrence saw him "bird of men that are masters,
>   lifting the rabbit-blood of the myriads up into . . ."
>   into something terrible, gone beyond bounds, or
>   As Blake saw America in figures of fire and blood raging,
>   . . . in what image? the ominous roar in the air,
>   the omnipotent wings, the all-American boy in the cockpit
>   loosing his flow of napalm, below in the jungles
>   "any life at all or sign of life" his target, drawing now
>   not with crayons in his secret room (Duncan 1968)

Among the things that astounded Duncan's contemporaries and, perhaps more important for our purposes today, what astounded Duncan's younger audiences (including those who have in their turn become today's veteran poets and who have asked, in their art and criticism, just what poetry, the other arts, and culture might mean in our current situation) was the way that the Duncan who already had clearly and powerfully synthesized his readings of Poundian poetics with a keen, sympathetic sense of the subtle tone-and-beat shifts suffusing the hauntings of Wordsworth, Coleridge, Keats, Shelley, the French Symbolists and Surrealists, had *now* shown that there was something far more ambitious that one could do with Blake than the Beats (and Ginsberg above all, in Duncan's view) had been able to do.

That is, Duncan in this instance shows and demands an ability to *rant* with no holds barred and yet simultaneously to build or formally construct every phrase – indeed, virtually every syllable – with a music whose starts and stops, shifts, turns, and circlings are little short of remarkable. As the rest of Duncan's poem makes evident (not least when we see, late in the poem, Duncan's virtuosic, momentary eruption – or fall – into and then out of prose poem, in a manner at once unsettling and formally justified, which is to say, emerging from form-process and revelatory of the content itself), we have here one of Modernist and later-Modernist poetry's greatest reimaginings of Blake, most specifically, Blake's "America: A Prophecy." The importance of Blake in this Vietnam War poem, and of Blake's "America" in particular, cannot be gainsaid. It's as if Duncan had, among other things, set himself the task artistically, but also with an inherent cultural-political logic, of following through on his often-voiced critical analysis that, for all his admirable strengths and attractiveness, Ginsberg had far too frequently come to rely on a spirit-poetics that had the inherent tendency to turn simply into a rebellious attitudism and a Left-shtick, into a mode *not* fundamentally inimical to what was problematic in and about contemporary American culture, precisely because the poetic at hand increasingly came to forego what Duncan tended to call (in yet another insistence, again virtually singular in the American, though not the German context, for this sort of formulation of Romantic-Modernist affinity) "the organic-constructivist" poem (over against the Ginsbergian afflatus-chant).

Duncan identifies Blake as an ultimate test case and proving-ground for how American poetry might make manifest that artistic construction is never to be foregone, that for full and fully critical aesthetic experience the poem must, in instances like "Up Rising: Passages 25," meld the most seemingly natural and songful expression (or, alternately, the most naturally urgent and impelled ranting) with a kind of formally attentive and rigorous constructivism. What's being constructed is expression or expressive capacity itself, the affective-intellectual capacity to begin to know the not-yet-settled in human history and above all, as Adorno might put it, the history of human suffering. The construction, singing, and active reception of such a poetry depends on and can further stimulate a kind of agency that had too often been assumed to have been divorced from the noted impersonality of Modernist poetics (precisely parallel to the ways that Blake was thought – wrongly, as Duncan establishes – to have had nothing to do with the kind of later twentieth-century poetic line that Duncan here reels out and reels in, indicating how Blake and later Modernism in the right hands can be – rhythmically, syntactically, tonally, and in terms of address and content – brought together).

This very Blakean poem is not an endpoint for Duncan, nor does it imply that for Duncan Blake stands higher than other Romantic poets when it comes to saving American Modernist poetry and later-twentieth-century America. But Blake's utter lack of value in terms of how T. S. Eliot understood what could and couldn't be built on from the poetry of the recent past helps make this Duncan poem very instructive, because it's clear that Duncan finds Eliot's judgment to have been pronounced not only on radical Blakean form and not only radical Blakean agency but on their inseparability. The desire to maintain that fusion and nurture its development belongs to the story of how British Romanticism helped save Modernist American poetry and America itself, so that Blake's "America" could, via "Up Rising: Passages 25" gesture toward a new chapter, a new dispensation that we might think of without italics as Blake's America, something that may have begun in poetry but that, as will be recalled, worked its way rather dramatically into other areas of American culture and politics (and that in poetry itself spoke volumes to figures like Robert Creeley, Denise Levertov, Diane DiPrima, Nathaniel Mackey, Michael Palmer, and many others). One might look, for one measure of possibilities Duncan helped create, to Michael Palmer's "Seven Poems With a Matrix for War," written in the aftermath of what we now call the First Gulf War, first published in the largest-distribution poetry journal in the US, *American Poetry Review*, and then in Palmer's 1995 book *At Passages*, a book whose very title conjures intertexts that include Duncan's "Passages" and Walter Benjamin's *Passagenwerk* or *Arcades Project* (Palmer 1995, 1997). Duncan exhibits an acute awareness of why it had become urgent to reconsider those aspects of Modernism – aspects associated precisely with the latter's anti-Romantic, anti-democratic strains – that had seemed to make critical agency, and indeed reflection itself, beside the point (e.g., Eliot's and related salvos against the Hamletian sublime, against, in fact, interpretation *tout court* as inimical to poetic and aesthetic experience). It may well be that this overarching story – of poetry, critical agency, and the political situation within and outside the United States – has additional chapters waiting to be written. If that proves to be in the first place a hoped-for possibility, Duncan's point had already been that the critical thought of hope itself is given to us historically, and not least by British Romanticism's continued presence in American poetry and poetics, criticism, and culture.

It bears returning to an earlier, pre-Vietnam Duncan, but one at least as influenced by Romanticism, the Duncan just becoming famous in 1960:

> "Often I am Permitted to Return to a Meadow"
>
> as if it were a scene made-up by the mind,
> that is not mine, but is a made place,
>
> that is mine, it is so near to the heart,
> an eternal pasture folded in all thought
> so that there is a hall therein
>
> that is a made place, . . .

> Often I am permitted to return to a meadow
> as if it were a given property of the mind
> that certain bounds hold against chaos,
>
> that is a place of first permission,
> everlasting omen of what is. (Duncan 1960)

The jointure and tension here cross-connect the made-up and the really-made, the mind and what is or is not the subject's own, his or her "mine" configured in the play of field and force, a sphere beyond the already determined. Duncan instantiates a sense of how the poem's rubbing its elements together, including the crossing or collision of its lines and sounds, is finally what constitutes the form meant to bring everything – unresolved and unreconciled, but fully present – together, in a manner that can make the imagined inseparable from the truly made. In the language Duncan shares with fellow poets and the Frankfurt School, we could say that lyric's constellative or constellating activity, in its ability to make the constructive and the expressive feel united, likewise makes the previously undetermined come to seem objectively real, true, as the breath and stress beats give the feel to the line, the line to the syntax, the syntax to the sentence.

In Duncan's eyes, the only apparently formalist, imaginative-aesthetic enclosure underwrites the ability to create the more explicitly engaged Vietnam poem. In a related vein, Duncan knows – at least as well as any other Modernist or later-Modernist poet – the importance of Romantically constellating such ongoing defense and development of imagination with explorations aiming to grasp the experience of modern labor: alienation. I've discussed elsewhere at some length Duncan's remarkable poem "Answering" – remarkable not least for its powerful, dynamic creation of force fields between the Romantic and Modernist (Kaufman 2005). Limits of space prevent me from quoting more than a few lines and offering the briefest of comments as a way to conclude this essay.

> "Answering" (after "Claritas" by Denise Levertov)
>
> A burst
> of confidence. Confiding
>
> a treasured thing
>
> kept inside,
> as if it were a burden,

worrying about money
or were pride
and ambition struggling –

sings out.

It was a song I did not sing.

The men are working in the street.
The sound

of pick and pneumatic drill
punctuates
the chirrup a bird makes

[. . .]
They are making a living
Where I take my life.

[. . .]
With no more earnest skill
than this working song

sings
– as if the heart's full

responsibility
were in the rise of words

as momentarily
that bird's notes he concentrates

above the swaying bough,
the fluttering wings.
[. . .]

For joy
breaks thru

insensible to our human want.
Were we birds too

upon some blowing crown of seeds
it would be so,

we'd sing as we do.

The song's a work of the natural will.
The song's a work of the natural will.

(Duncan 1964)

Quoting the entire poem would make even clearer how scored with multiple voicings the seemingly simple, pared-down poem "Answering" actually is. The multiplicity is inextricable from its weaving together, on the farther side of later Modernism if not postmodernism itself, of Romantic and Modernist currents. Already something like a string quartet on the way towards orchestral transcription, it's hardly accidental that this poem's voice seems to come from some impossible location of style and diction. While there's a strong feeling of now-archaic Romanticism, it's a weirdly after-Modernism Romanticism that sounds nothing like mid-to-late twentieth-century, anti-Modernist neo-Romanticism. Rather, it folds into itself chronologically Modernist materials (most obviously, the pick and pneumatic drill) and distilled, taut phrasing (with debts to Williams but also to a Romantic and post-Romantic manner of working with irregular rhyme) as part of the poem's central poesis of both the conflict, and the possibly generative interaction, between creative-animating and mechanical-deadening labor. Sustained treatment would allow us to consider how the poem works up Duncan's own wage-labor experience as a clerk-typist, his experiences of a stark difference and also some complex interactions between creative-meaningful and for-survival work (the various connotations of "making a living" and "taking my life"), and Duncan's sense that it is Wordsworth who hums the undersong of "Answering"'s complexly, anachronistically Romantic revivification of modern socioeconomic problems and Modernist-with-a-difference poetics.

The very protestations within "Answering," that something external (the literal birdsong, the workers' sounds, Denise Levertov's previous birdsong poem above all) must break through a modern-mechanical dullness and depression of self that has no small source in the socioeconomic, are not so much belied as powerfully accompanied by a rhythm, a lineation, and an overall sculpting in sound-movement that causes one to pause before pretending that the critic's commentary can really add much to Duncan's poem-answer to "Claritas." Yet it might be observed that the closing of "Answering" – the poem's singing, doubled assertion that its song is a song of the natural will – has something not just wonderful but also strange about it. That "natural" will has many sources, even within Wordsworth himself. But whether in Wordsworth or, for example, Blake, Romantic plottings of mutually sustaining relationships between nature and a desire-spurred human consciousness almost always owe part of their force, ironically enough, to their being rendered (or sneakily seeming as if they should have been rendered) in the conditional, subjunctive, or even imperative, and with an appropriately gauged, compressed energy of concern or anxiety about thought or behavior that, being "natural," would presumably come easily and without effort or artifice.

Back of Duncan's lines stand Wordsworth's lines "The Child is father of the Man; / And I could wish my days to be / Bound each to each by natural piety." (The famous doubling in Wordsworth is that the lines – the final three of "My Heart Leaps Up When I Behold" – are doubled or repeated when the poet decides to use his own lines as epigraph to the "Ode: Intimations of Immortality from Recollections of Early Childhood.") The point is that one's days are not necessarily or automatically bound to each other, nor to or by a piety that stems from, or returns to, nature. Alternatively, if one's days (and nature and piety) are so bound – or if something far more congenial to many twenty-first-century liberal and Left ears is substituted for "natural piety," say, transformative agency vis-à-vis the social – the rub is that this natural or social is made in part from, or in a bidirectional feedback loop that includes, the conditional and its desire-energized acts of thought and agency. With marked affinities not only to the Romantic poets, and not only if somewhat more surprisingly to important strains of Modernist poetry, but equally to those Left figures in art, philosophy, and criticism often far too hastily considered hostile to Romanticism, Duncan's poem shows what's been at stake in later engagements with and commitments to Romanticism, to aesthetic and lyric experience: a capacity crucial for a searching subjectivity and for the development of critical agency, namely, an ability to hear (and see, think, feel) more than what's already been determined to be apprehendable and – somehow synonymously – an indispensable responsive capacity to answer.

Note

1 Some of the material in my discussion of Duncan previously appeared in the online article "Lyric's Constellation, Poetry's Radical Privilege" (Kaufman 2005).

References and Further Reading

Adorno, Theodor W. (1957/1991) "On Lyric Poetry and Society," trans. Sherry Weber Nicholsen. In *Notes to Literature*, ed. Rolf Tiedemann (vol. 1, pp. 37–54). New York: Columbia University Press.

Adorno, Theodor W. (1970/1997) *Aesthetic Theory*, ed and trans. Robert Hullot-Kentor. Minneapolis: University of Minnesota Press.

Adorno, Theodor W. and Walter Benjamin. (1999) *The Complete Correspondence, 1928–1940*, ed. Henri Lonitz, trans. Nicholas Walker. Cambridge, MA: Harvard University Press.

Benjamin, Walter. (1935/1969) "The Work of Art in the Age of Mechanical Reproduction," in *Illuminations*, ed. Hannah Arendt, trans. Harry Zohn. New York: Schocken.

Benjamin, Walter. (1939/1969) "On Some Motifs in Baudelaire" (1939), in *Illuminations* (pp. 155–200).

Benjamin, Walter. (1938/1973) "The Paris of the Second Empire in Baudelaire," in *Charles Baudelaire: A Lyric Poet in the Era of High Capitalism*, trans. Harry Zohn (pp. 9–106). London: New Left Books.

Benjamin, Walter. (1931/1999) "A Little History of Photography," in *Selected Writings*, ed. Michael W. Jennings, Howard Eiland, and Gary Smith, trans. Rodney Livingstone, vol. 2 (pp. 507–30). Cambridge, MA: Belknap-Harvard University Press.

Caygill, Howard. (1989) *Art of Judgment*. Oxford: Blackwell.

Duncan, Robert. (1960) "Often I Am Permitted to Return to a Meadow," in *The Opening of the Field* (p. 7). New York: New Directions.

Duncan, Robert. (1964) "Answering," in *Roots and Branches* (pp. 124–6). New York: Charles Scribners Sons.

Duncan, Robert. (1968) "Up Rising: Passages 25," in *Bending the Bow* (pp. 81–3). New York: New Directions.

Duncan, Robert. (2004) *The Letters of Robert Duncan and Denise Levertov*, ed. Robert J. Bertholf and Albert Gelpi. Stanford, CA: Stanford University Press.

Eagleton, Terry. (1990) *The Ideology of the Aesthetic*. Oxford: Blackwell.

Hanssen, Beatrice and Andrew Benjamin. (2002) *Walter Benjamin and Romanticism*. New York: Continuum.

Kant, Immanuel. (1790/1987) *Critique of Judgment*, trans. Werner S. Pluhar. Indianapolis: Hackett.

Kaufman, Robert. (2005) "Lyric's Constellation, Poetry's Radical Privilege," *Modernist Cultures* 1: 209–34.

Kaufman, Robert. (2008) "Lyric Commodity Critique, Benjamin Adorno Marx, Baudelaire Baudelaire Baudelaire," *PMLA* 123,1 (January: 207–15.

Lloyd, David. (1985) "Arnold, Ferguson, Schiller: Aesthetic Culture and the Politics of Aesthetics," *Cultural Critique* 2: 137–69.

Lloyd, David. (1989) "Kant's Examples," *Representations* 28: 34–54.

Marx, Karl. (1867/1965) *Capital: A Critique of Political Economy*. New York: International.

Marx, Karl. (1875/1890–91/1970) *Critique of the Gotha Programme*. In *Marx/Engels Selected Works*, vol. 3. Moscow: Progress.

McGann, Jerome. (1983) *The Romantic Ideology*. Chicago: University of Chicago Press.

McGann, Jerome. (1989) *Towards a Literature of Knowledge*. Chicago: University of Chicago Press.

Palmer, Michael. (1997) "Robert Duncan and Romantic Synthesis," available online at <http://www.poets.org/viewmedia.php/prmMID/15949>.

Palmer, Michael. (1995) "Seven Poems Within a Matrix for War," in *At Passages* (pp. 15–26). New York: New Directions.

Ricardo, David. (1817/1971) *On the Principles of Political Economy and Taxation*, ed. R. M. Hartwell. Harmondsworth, UK: Penguin.

Shelley, Percy Bysshe. (1821/2002) *A Defence of Poetry*. In *Shelley's Poetry and Prose*, ed. Donald H. Reiman and Neil Freistat. New York: Norton.

Index

Note: page references in italics indicate illustrations

Abrams, M. H., *The Mirror and the Lamp*, 3, 30, 58
   Natural Supernaturalism, 3
Abstract Expressionism, 247
Académie des Sciences, 178
Ackermann, Rudolf, 225
Addison, Joseph, 49, 99–100, 104, 116, 213, 215
   The Spectator, 99
Admiralty court, 121
Adorno, Theodor, 262–3, 266, 275
advertising, 190–1, 198, 204, 207, 220–1, 216–17, 221, 226
Aepinus, Franz, 177–8
aesthetics, 2, 24, 28, 30, 42, 47–8, 53, 69, 101, 111, 122–3, 125, 127, 129, 132–3, 235, 258, 266, 268, 277
   and experience, 261, 270–1, 276, 280
   as ideology 259, 263
   illusion and semblance, 267–71
   judgment, 261, 264–5, 269
   and nationalism, 84
   and neo-classicism, 253
   in painting, 235–6, 249
   and politics, 259, 262
   in theatre, 241
   and uselessness, 261
agnosticism, 18
agriculture, 64, 80
alienation, 277
Altick, Richard D., *The English Common Reader 1800–1900*, 228
American Poetry Review, 276
American Revolution, 90, 123, 258
Analytical Review, 101–2, 111
Anderson, Benedict, 81, 85–6
   Imagined Communities, 77
Anglicanism, 15–18, 21, 23, 29
   Book of Common Prayer, 16
Anglo-Saxons, 53, 128
Anstey, Christopher, 126
anthropology, 154
antiquarianism, 92–3, 160–1, 163, 216
antiquities, 152, 154, 156, 252

Index

Antoinette, Marie, 133
Arabian Nights, 36, 41
Archiv für die Physiologie, 185–6
Arians, *see* Unitarianism
Aristotle, 146, 258
Arnim, Achim von, 171, 175, 179
Ascham, Roger, 53
Ashford v. Thornton, 125
astronomy, 10, 47, 145, 151, 171–7
atheism, 14, 17, 18, 29, 31
Atiyah, P. S., 135
Austen, Jane, 2, 10–11, 16–18, 37, 137, 201–8, 226, 232, 236, 238–9, 254
   Emma, 86, 203–4, 206–7, 226, 239
   Lady Susan, 206
   Mansfield Park, 126, 239
   Persuasion, 203, 205, 246
   Pride and Prejudice, 134, 203, 205–6, 236, 238
   Northanger Abbey, 85, 203, 226, 237
   Sense and Sensibility, 134, 202, 205, 232, 236–7
authorship, 123
Avogadro, Amedeo, 182

Baillie, Joanna
   Plays upon the Passions, 29
   Series of Plays, 183
Ballantyne Press, 212
Ballie, Agnes, 183
Ballie, Dorothea Hunter, 183
Ballie, Matthew, 183
   Morbid Anatomy, 183
Banim, John, 94
Banim, Michael, 94
Banks, Sir Joseph, 2, 142–3, 146–7, 149–50, 153–6, 163, 180
Baptists, 18
   Anabaptists, 18
Barker, Robert, 156
Barker's Panorama, 243

Barthes, Roland, 192
Bath and Bristol Chronicle, 235
Baudrillard, Jean, 192
Beat poets, 274
Beddoes, Thomas, 182–3
Bell, Charles, *Idea of a New Anatomy of the Brain*, 186
Bell, John, 220–2
Belle Assemblé, La, 225
belles-lettres, 60
Benjamin, Walter, 66, 262, 267, 269
   Arcades Project, 276
Bentham, Jeremy, 30–1, 106, 200
Bentinck, Margaret, Duchess of Portland, 142
Bergasse, Nicolas, 184
Bermingham, Ann, 196
Berthollet, Claude, 180
Berzelius, Jöns Jakob, 181–2
Bewell, Alan, 157
Bhagavad-Gita, 40, 42
Bible, 17–18, 49, 169–71, 219, 224
   Genesis, 169–70
Bildungsroman, 130
biogeography, 154
biology *see* botany, natural history, medicine
Biot, Jean Baptiste, 174
Black Dwarf, 112
Black Mountain poets, 273
Blackstone, William, 128, 131
   Commentaries on the Laws of England, 8–9, 113
Blackwood, William, 65, 68, 217
Blackwood's Edinburgh Magazine, 60–3, 67, 70–3, 111, 217
Blair, Hugh, 89
   Lectures on Rhetoric and Belles Lettres, 88
Blake, William, 2, 6, 12, 17, 20–2, 26–7, 29, 37–9, 45, 49, 220, 247, 249, 262, 273–5, 279
   "America: A Prophecy," 274, 276
   The Book of Thel, 143

The Book of Urizen, 26
The Four Zoas, 220
Jerusalem, 172
The Marriage of Heaven and Hell, 26, 38
"The Mental Traveller," 27
Milton, 20
Songs of Innocence and Experience, 220
Blakey, Dorothy, Minerva Press, 228
Bloom, Harold, *Romanticism and Consciousness*, 3
Blumenbach, J. F., 151, 159, 179
book history (as a field of study), 85–6, 228
book production, 212, 218
　antiquarian trade, 222
　bookbinding, 220–2
　booksellers, 103, 107, 126, 144, 213–20, 223–4, 226–9
　paper making, 212, 219
　steam press, 212
　stereotyping, 212–13, 219, 224
　book trade, 105, 212, 214–15, 219, 222, 227–9
Boswell, James, 122
botany, 143, 153–5, 157–8, 161
　ethnobotany, 155
Bourdieu, Pierre, 192
Bowles, John, *Reflections on the Conclusion of the War*, 108
Braid, James, 184
Brecht, Bertolt, 263
Brentano, *Shipwrecked Galley Slaves on the Dead Sea*, 175
Brewer, John, 194
　The Birth of a Consumer Society, 191
British Association for the Advancement of Science, 150
British Critic, 217, 225
British Museum, 144, 233, 252
British Theatre, The, 220

Britishness, 60, 85–6
Broman, Thomas, 152
Brown, "Capability," 239
Brown, John, 182
　Elements of Medicine, 182
Buckingham House (Palace), 223
Buckland, William, *Vindiciae Geologicae*, 170
Buffon, Comte de, *Histoire naturelle*, 145, 154
Bunyan, John, *The Pilgrim's Progress*, 17–18
Burke, Edmund, 39, 46, 82–5, 106, 108, 110, 127, 134, 239, 243
　Reflections on the Revolution in France, 8, 21, 78–9, 81–2, 102, 104, 110, 133–4
　Tracts Relating to the Popery Laws, 78, 81
Burke, Kenneth, *Rhetoric and Religion*, 32
Burnet, Thomas, *Sacred Theory of the Earth*, 169
Burney, Frances, 2, 201, 244, 250
　Cecilia, 242
　Evelina, 241
Burns, Robert, 62
　"A Cotter's Saturday Night," 29
Burwick, Frederick, 143
Butler, Marilyn, 7, 58, 78
　Romantics, Rebels, and Reactionaries, 4
Byron, George Gordon, Lord, 2, 16, 18, 28, 30, 37, 45, 83, 94, 122, 150, 195, 216, 218, 262
　Childe Harold, 28
　Corsair, 218
　"Darkness," 163
　Don Juan, 122, 195
　Manfred: A Dramatic Poem, 27

Cadell, Robert, 68, 212
Calcott, Maria, 171

285

Index

Calhoun, Craig
   Nationalism, 83, 84–5
   Nations Matter, 84
Calvinism, 15, 20, 26, 29
Cambridge University Press, 219
Camden, William, *Britannia*, 157
Cameron, Charles Hay, 132
Campbell, Colin, 199, 201
   The Romantic Ethic and the Spirit of Modern Consumerism, 197
Carlisle, Anthony, 180
Carlyle, Thomas, 207
   The French Revolution: A History, 21
   Sartor Resartus, 28
Carnan, Thomas, 219
Catholic Defender movement, 95
Catholicism, 14, 16, 18–19, 21, 28, 94
Cavendish, Henry, 177
Celtic Tiger, 92
Chakrabarty, Dipesh, 66
   Provincializing Europe, 74
chancery, 121, 123, 228
Chandler, James, 5, 59, 63, 65–6, 101
   England in 1819, 58
Charcot, Jean-Martin, 184
Charles I, 14
Charles, Jacques, 181
Chaucer, Geoffrey, 221
chemistry, 145, 151, 180–2
"Church" and "chapel," 14, 16–17, 19–20
Churchill, Charles, 221
chemistry, 145, 151, 180–2
Chippendale chairs, 191
circuses, 233, 243
Clare, John, 157
class, 18, 83, 106–7, 114, 129, 132, 147, 197, 252, 259
   middle class, 18, 89, 112, 192, 197, 200, 202, 232, 238
   working class, 85, 106, 259

classicism, 30, 37, 246
   see also neo-classicism
Cobbett, William, 2, 18, 22, 84, 111–13, 123
   Political Register, 111, 114
   Rural Rides, 17
Cockburn, Henry, 100
coffee-houses, 99
Colburn, Henry, 217, 226
Colburn's New Monthly Magazine, 217
Coleridge, Samuel Taylor, 15, 18–20, 22–3, 26, 28–31, 57, 110, 114–15, 125, 146, 150–1, 156, 183, 195–6, 223, 225, 240, 242, 254, 261–2, 273–4
   Biographia Literaria, 30
   "The Comet," 175
   "The Eolian Harp," 25, 260
   "Fears in Solitude," 195
   "Kubla Khan," 170, 242
   Rime of the Ancient Mariner, 23
Cohn, Bernard, 42
Colley, Linda, 87–90
   Britons: Forging the Nation, 85
Colman, George, 124
colonialism, 39–40, 60, 65, 73, 95, 154, 156–7, 160, 162–3
Combe, William, 237
   "The Catchpole," 119
commercial culture, 38, 61, 64, 87, 90, 108–10
   see also consumer culture
Congo, 65
Conrad, Joseph, *Heart of Darkness*, 65
conservatives, 103, 106–7, 128, 200
Constable, Archibald, 69, 109, 213, 216–17, 224, 228
Constable, John, 247–9
   "The Cornfield" 248

consumer culture, 189–208
　anticonsumerism, 192, 194, 196
　consumer revolution, 191, 193, 197, 200
　and economics, 190, 192
Cook, Captain James, 144, 154, 176
Copernicus, 146
copyright, 120, 123, 126, 129, 213–16, 218, 220, 223, 225, 227
　see also Donaldson v. Beckett
Cornwallis, Charles Lord, 51
cosmopolitanism, 82–4, 91, 95, 109, 247
Cottle, Joseph, 223
Coulomb, Charles–Augustin de, 178
Covent Garden, 240, 244
Cowper, William
　Olney Hymns, 29, 225, 240
　The Task, 239
Crabbe, George
　Poems, 218
　Tales of the Hall, 218
Crawford, Robert, 88–9
　Devolving English Literature, 87
Creeley, Robert, 276
Critical Journal, 108
Critical Review, 109, 215
Cruden, Alexander, Biblical Concordance, 225
cultural capital, 59
cultural production, 80, 84, 86, 91
Cumberland, Richard, 240
Curtis, William, Botanical Magazine, 151
Cuvier, Georges, 151–2, 159, 162–3, 170
　Discours sur les Revolutions du Globe, 170
　"Memoir upon Fossil and Living Elephants," 152

Dacre, Charlotte, 37
Dalton, John, 181
　A New System of Chemical Philosophy, 182
Darnton, Robert, 103
Darton, William, 229
Darwin, Charles, On the Origin of Species, 29, 169
Darwin, Erasmus, 144
　The Botanical Garden, 9, 143, 153
　The Loves of the Plants, 153
　Plan for the Conduct of Female Education, 153
Davy, Humphry, 151, 160, 180–1, 183
　Researches, Chemical and Philosophical, 183
　On Some Chemical Agencies of Electricity, 180
De Quincey, Thomas, 32, 50, 124, 127, 170–2, 177, 243
　Suspiria de Profundis, 32
　"System of the Heavens," 170, 176
deconstruction, 3
Defoe, Daniel, The Adventures of Robinson Crusoe, 18
deism, 14, 19–20, 170
Deluc, Jean-André, 160
depression, economic, 111–12
Derham, William, 157
Desaguliers, Jean Theophile, 177
Descartes, René, 23, 169
determinism, 270
Devine, T. M., Scotland's Empire, 89
d'Herbelot, Barthélemy, Bibliothéque orientale, 41
Dibdin, Thomas Frognall, The Bibliographical Decameron, 222
Dickens, Charles, 190, 207
　Oliver Twist, 194
　A Tale of Two Cities, 21
Didot, Firmin, 218
Dilly, Charles, 216

Index

DiPrima, Diane, 276
D'Israeli, Isaac, 85
  Curiosities of Literature, 102
Dissensions of 1783–84, 147, 149
dissent and dissenters, 6, 16–19, 21–2, 81, 94
divorce, 121
Dobereine, Johann, 180
domestic sphere, 232
Donaldson v. Beckett, 213–14, 220
Donne, John, 221
Drennan, William, 95
Drury Lane Theatre, 240, 242, 244–5
dueling, 122, 132
Dumezil, Georges, 32
Duncan, Ian, 63, 108–9, 111
  Scott's Shadow, 58, 80, 88
Duncan, Robert, 12, 272–80
  "Answering," 277–9
  Bending the Bow, 273
  "Claritas," 279
  H. D. Book, 273
  Letters, 273
  Passages, 273
  "Up Rising: Passages 25," 273, 275–6
Dundas, Henry, 61
Durkheim, Emile, 32–3
Dyer, Gary, 125

Eagleton, Terry, 125
East India Company, 36, 41–2, 52
  education policy of, 36
Edgeworth, Maria, 201
  Belinda, 68
  Castle Rackrent, 68, 131–3
  Patronage, 124
  "Moral Tales for Young People," 68
  "Tales of Fashionable Life," 68
Edinburgh Monthly Magazine, 68
Edinburgh Review, 45, 60–3, 66, 69, 100, 108–11, 199, 217

Edinburgh Speculative Society, 63
education, 78, 107, 142, 236
Eichner, Hans, "The Rise of Modern Science and the Genesis of Romanticism," 168
Eldon, John Scott, Lord, 122–3, 128
  Anecdote Book, 128
electricity, 177–80
Elgin, Lord, 252–3
Elgin Marbles, 252–3
Eliade, Mircea, 32
Eliot, George, translations, *The Life of Jesus*, 29
Eliot, T. S., 16, 272, 275–6
  Christianity and Culture, 33
empire, 36–7, 39, 43, 85, 146–7, 157
empiricism, 59
Encyclopaedia Britannica, 143, 150–1
Endeavour, voyage of, 144–5, 147, 152, 154–5
Engels, Friedrich, 262–3, 266
Englishness, 79, 90, 249
Enlightenment, 4, 6–8, 57–9, 61–6, 69, 71, 73–4, 80, 110–11, 114–16, 151, 168, 258, 264
  Counter-Enlightenment, 8
  Scottish Enlightenment, 59–61, 64, 66, 70–1, 73, 109
Erdman, David, *Blake: Prophet Against Empire*, 3
eroticism, 44, 149
Erskine, Thomas, 104, 130–1
ethnography, 154–5
evangelicalism, 15, 106
Evans, Robert Hardy, 223
Evans v. Evans, 136
evolution, 169
Examiner, The, 244
exchange value, 265–7
exhibitions, 161, 233, 246, 252
exploration, 144

Ferguson, Adam, 109, 154
Ferris, Ina, 94
feudalism, 135, 197
Fielding, Henry, 215
Fine, Ben, 193
First Gulf War, 276
Flaugergues, Honoré, 174
Fontana, Biancamaria, 199
Forget Me Not, 225
formalism, 259, 263, 277
Forster, Georg, 176
fossils, 141, 143–4, 152, 158–60, 163, 170
Foucault, Michel, 162
Fox, Charles James, 243–4
Francis II, Austrian Emperor, 185
Frankfurt School, 262–3, 266, 268, 277
Franklin, Benjamin, 20, 177–8, 185, 263, 266
Fraunhofer, Joseph von, 174
freedom of the press, 104, 128
  freedom of speech, 104
  political freedom, 110
French Academy of Sciences, 185
French Revolution, 14, 18, 21–3, 25, 31, 33, 72, 84, 100–1, 107–8, 110–11, 123, 153, 197, 200, 258, 262
Freud, Sigmund, 184
Fulford, Tim, *Romanticism and the Sciences*, 168

Gaelic language, 89
Gagging Acts, 112, 115
Gainsborough, Thomas, 233, 235–9, 241–2, 250
  "Mrs. Richard Brinsley Sheridan," 233, *234*, 235–7
Galapagos Islands, 169
Galbraith, John Kenneth, *The Affluent Society*, 190

Gall, Franz Joseph, 185–6
  Anatomie et physiologie du systéme nerveux, 185
Galland, Antoine, *Les mille et une nuits*, 41
Galt, John, 2, 7, 66–74
  Annals of the Parish, 67, 70–3
  Autobiography, 70
  "The Ayrshire Legatees," 70, 72
  Life of Cardinal Wolsey, 70
  Literary Life, 70–1
  "The Pastor," 69
  "The Steam-Boat," 70, 72
  "Tales of the West," 70
Galvani, Luigi, 179
  De Viribus Electricitatis in Motu Musculari Commentarius, 178
Garrick, David, 242
Garside, Peter, 67
Gay-Lussac, Joseph Louis, 181–2
Gellner, Ernest, 81
  Nations and Nationalism, 80
genius, 38, 42, 45, 49, 63
Gentleman's Magazine and Historical Chronicle, 103, 107, 122, 128, 215
geography, 47
Geological Society, 158–9, 161
geology, 10, 152, 153, 158–62, 169–72
George III, King of England, 72, 103, 124, 142–3, 147–8, 175, 223, 244–5
George IV, King of England, 88, 124, 223
Germany, 152
Gide, André, *Journals*, 24
Gillray, James, 79, 249–50
  "The Plumb-pudding in Danger," 250
  "Voluptuary under the Horrors of Digestion," 250
Gilmartin, Kevin, 106
  Print Politics, 114

289

Index

Gilpin, William, 237–8
Ginsberg, Allen, 274–5
globalization, 95–6, 157
Godwin, William, 84, 224
  Caleb Williams, 124–5
  Political Justice, 79
Goethe, Johann Wolfgang, *Elective Affinities*, 180
Goldsmith, Oliver
  The Deserted Village, 38
  History of the Earth and Animated Nature, 145
Goodricke, John, 173
Gordon Riots, 72
Gorgon, The, 114–15
Gould, Stephen Jay, 146
Grand Tours of Europe, 238, 252
Grant, Charles, 49, 52
Gray, Thomas, *Elegy in a Country Churchyard*, 24
Gray, Thomas (jeweler), 202–3
Grey, Stephen, 177
Grimm, Jakob, 32
Grimm, Wilhelm, 32

habeas corpus, 112, 134
  Suspension of Habeas Corpus Act, 116
Habermas, Jürgen, *Structural Transformation of the Public Sphere*, 84
Hadfield, James, 127, 131
Halhed, Nathaniel Brassey, *Gentoo Laws*, 42
Haller, Albrecht von, *On the Irritable and Sensible Parts of the Body*, 182
Halley, Edmund, 172
Hamilton, Elizabeth, 37
Harding, Karl Ludwig, 173
Hartman, Geoffrey, *Wordsworth's Poetry*, 3
Hastings, Warren, 40–1, 44, 50, 244
Hatfield, John, 125

Haydon, Benjamin, 252–3
Hayman, Francis, 246
Hazlitt, William, 15, 22, 63, 84, 114–15, 240–1, 243, 253
  "What is the People?" 115
Hebel, Johann Peter
  Rheinländischen Hausfreundes, 175
  Schatzkästlein des rheinischen Hausfreundes, 175
hedonism, 197–9
Hegel, G. W. F., 59, 65, 151
  Encyclopedia, 151
hegemony, 136, 154, 197
Heine, Heinrich, 262
Hemans, Felicia, 200
Hendrickson, Susan, 144
Henry, J. W., 181
Herder, Johann Gottfried, 66, 71, 73
Heringman, Noah, 171
Herschel, William, 173–4, 176
  "Investigation of the Powers of the Prismatic Colours to Heat and Illuminate Objects," 174
Hessey, James, 217
historicism, 4, 7, 58–9, 66, 69, 71, 73–4, 77
  conjectural history, 60, 71
  cultural history, 78, 82, 150, 158
  historical novel, 58–9, 71, 73
  new historicism, 58
  philosophical history, 61
  stadial history, 7, 65
  "theoretical history," 70–1
Hobsbawm, Eric, 81
  The Invention of Tradition, 77
  Nations and Nationalism since 1780, 79
Hoffmann, E. T. A., "The Mines of Falun," 170
Hogarth, William, 190, 249–50
  "Marriage à la Mode," 250
  "The Rake's Progress," 249–50

Hogg, James, 68–9
  Confessions of a Justified Sinner, 128
  The Spy, 68
  "Tales and Anecdotes of the Pastoral Life," 68
  Winter Evening Tales, 68–9
Hölderlin, Friedrich, 262
Homer, 124, 245
Hone, William, 112, 129
Horace, *Ars Poetica*, 133–4
Howard, John, *State of the Prisons*, 125
Hudson, Nicholas, 79
Hulme, T. E., 29
Humboldt, Alexander von, 150, 176
Hume, David, 7, 19, 59, 61, 65, 70–1, 73, 109, 127
  "Of Miracles," 171
Hunt, John, 112, 115
  see also Yellow Dwarf
Hunt, Leigh, 111–12, 115, 243–5, 254
Hunter, William, *Anatomy of the Human Gravid Uterus*, 183
Hutchison, Francis, 109
Hutton, James, 172
  Theory of the Earth, 170
hypnotism, 184

idealism, 124, 146, 150, 168
imagination, 4, 6, 85, 102, 124
  in aesthetics and politics, 259–60, 272–3
  and imperialism, 53–4, 58
  and religion, 23–5, 31–2
  and the visual arts, 233, 243, 249
imperialism, 5–6, 36–7, 39–45, 49, 54–5, 90, 149, 154, 246
impressionism, 247
improvement, 38–40, 49, 73, 156, 238
India, 39, 244

individualism, 120–1, 134, 168, 259
industrialization, 11, 16, 38, 71, 73, 80, 227, 229
  and consumer society, 191, 193, 200
Insurrection of 1745, 64
Irish Uprising, 72
Irving, Washington, 68
Islam, 7, 49–50

Jacob, Margaret, 95
Jacobites, 64, 69, 83, 106, 125, 131, 136
Jarrells, Anthony, 7–8
Jeffrey, Francis, 2, 9, 57, 61–3, 67, 71, 74, 109, 122
  "Secondary Scottish Novels," 66, 70
  see also Edinburgh Review
Jenner, Edward, 184
Johnson, Joseph, 101, 215, 223–4, 227
Johnson, Nancy, 125–6
Johnson, Samuel, 215, 220
  Lives of the Poets, 221
Jones, Sir William, 6, 39, 43–4, 49
  "Essay on the Poetry of the Eastern Nations," 36
  Grammar of the Persian Language, 42
Jordan, Dorothy, 240
Judaism, 16–17
justice, 5, 8, 21, 101, 123–6, 129–30, 134, 137
  aesthetics of, 126
  and cosmopolitanism, 84
  see also poetic justice

Kant, Immanuel, 22, 176, 258–9, 261–2, 264, 266, 268–9
  "Age of the Earth," 171
  Critique of Judgment, 172, 259
Kaufmann, David, 134

291

Index

Keats, John, 16, 19, 28, 192, 224, 243, 245, 252, 254, 262, 274
 "The Eve of St. Agnes," 198–9
 "Fall of Hyperion," 253
 "Ode to a Grecian Urn," 253
 "Ode to Psyche," 253
Keble, John, *Christian Year*, 29
Keepsake, The, 225
Kelley, Theresa, 157, 159, 162
Kemble, John Philip, 240–1, 245
Kent, Christopher, 200
Keynes, Geoffrey, 228
Kidd, Colin, 63
King's Theatre, 244–5, 253
Kinnaird, Douglas, 216
Klancher, Jon, 103, 121
Kleist, Heinrich von, 171
knowledge, 37, 40–3, 49, 57, 95, 99, 127, 141, 146, 151–2, 154, 272
Koran, 49
Korobkin, Laura, 130

Lacaille, Nicholas Louis de, 172
 Catalog of Nebulae of the Southern Sky, 173
Lackington, James, 222, 227
 The Confessions of J. Lackington, 222
 Memoirs, 222
Lagrange, Joseph-Louis, 172
Lamb, Charles, 11, 15–16, 243, 254
Lamont, Claire, 68
Landor, Walter Savage, 37, 51
Lane, William, 213, 217, 226–7
Langford, Leigh, 223
Langford, Sotheby, 223
Laplace, Pierre Simon, 173
 Mécanique Céleste, 176
Larson, Peter, 144
Latour, Bruno, 157
Lavater, Johann, *Essays on Physiognomy*, 215
Lavoisier, Antoine, 180, 182

law, 5, 119, 124, 132, 134
 and authors, 121–2
 common law, 123, 126
 contract law, 135–6
 and individuals, 126, 134
 and lawyers, 130–1
 and legal aesthetics, 125, 128
 and marriage, 135–6
 natural law, 125
 and subjectivity, 120
 and theatricality, 131
Law, Edward, Lord Ellenborough, 129
lecturing, 114, 145
Leerssen, Joep, 92
Leighton, Archibald, 222
Letters from Albion, 189
Levertov, Denise, 273, 276, 279
Lévi-Strauss, Claude, 101
libel, 112–13, 126, 129–30, 136
libraries, circulating, 107, 217, 221, 226
 public libraries, 43, 223
Lichtenberg, Georg Christoph, *Sudelbüchern*, 175
Lickbarrow, Isabella
 "Lines on the Comet," 175
 Poetical Effusions, 175
Linley, Elizabeth, 233, 235–6, 239–41, 253
Linnaean Society, 143, 145
Linnaeus, Carolus, 141, 149–50, 153, 155, 162–3
 System of Nature, 141–2
Literary Gazette, 217, 226
Literary Journal, 99
Locke, John, 19–21, 63, 120
 An Essay Concerning Human Understanding, 19
 Essay on Toleration, 19
 Two Treatises of Government, 80
Lockhart, John Gibson, 2, 61–7, 69, 74
 Adam Blair, 67
 Peter's Letters to his Kinfolk, 60–1

Index

London Corresponding Society, 95, 123, 125
London Magazine, 217
Longman, Thomas, 227
Longman Publishing Group, 217–18, 223, 228
Löwy, Michael, *Romanticism Against the Tide of Modernity,* 197
loyalists, 101, 106
Lukács, Georg, 63
  The Historical Novel, 59
Lyell, Charles, *Principles of Geology,* 170

Macaulay, Thomas, 6–7, 29–31, 39–40, 46–8, 52–5
  "Minute on Indian Education," 36, 45, 47, 52–3
  review of *Life of Byron* by Thomas Moore, 29
Macdonald, Archibald, Sir, 104–5
Mackey, Nathaniel, 276
Macpherson, James, 59
magazines, 59, 68, 107, 112–14
Magendie, François, 186
Majeed, Javed, 41
Makdisi, Saree, 63, 65–6, 156
Malthus, Thomas, 17
Manderson, Desmond, 126–7
Mansfield, William Murray, Lord, 122–3, 126–7
Marshall, John, 229
Marx, Karl, 12, 262–6, 270
  Critique of the Gotha Programme, 265
  Das Kapital, 263–4
  The Poverty of Philosophy, 265
Marxism, 4, 32, 197, 259
  Marxist literary criticism, 262, 270–1
Maturin, Charles Robert, 94
  The Wild Irish Boy, 91
Maturin, Thomas, 8

McGann, Jerome, 58, 127
  The Romantic Ideology, 4, 77
McKendrick, Neil, 192–3, 197–8, 200
  The Birth of a Consumer Society, 191
media revolution, 253
medicine, 10, 145, 182–6
Mee, Jon, 107–8
Menely, Tobias, 157
Merian, Maria Sibylla, 156
  Insects of Surinam, 156
Mesmer, Franz Anton, 183–5
  Mémoire sur la découverte du magnétisme animal, 184
  Précis historique des faits relatifs au magnétisme animal, 184
Messier, Charles, 172
  Catalog of Nebulae and Star Clusters, 172
Methodism, 5, 15, 18, 26
Michelangelo, 246
Mill, James, 49
Mill, John Stuart, 30–2
  Autobiography, 30
Millar, John, 58, 61, 64
Milton, John, 124, 157, 213
  Paradise Lost, 27
mineralogy, 143, 153, 158
Minerva Press, 213, 225
Mitford, Mary Russell, 68
modernism, 4–5, 12, 258, 262, 267, 270–1, 273–7, 279–80
modernity, 6, 8, 38, 60, 74, 102, 120, 266
modes of production, 80
monarchy, 85, 168
Montaigne, Michel de, 19, 154
Monthly Review, 99, 101, 109, 116, 215
Moore, Thomas, 37, 218
  Lalla Rookh, 218
  Life of Byron, 29

Index

More, Hannah, 2, 16, 18, 106–7, 200, 235
　Cheap Repository Tracts, 106
　Cœlebs in Search of a Wife, 202
More, Thomas, 46, 50, 53
Morison, Stanley, *John Bell*, 228
Morning Post, 113, 221
Moro, Abbé Anton, 169–70
Morton, Timothy, 198
Mournier, Jean Joseph, 110
　De L'Influence attribuée aux Philosophes, 110
Moxon, Edward, 224
Mozart, Wolfgang Amadeus, 245
　Don Giovanni, 245, 253
Murray, John I, 215, 217, 223, 227
Murray, John II, 216, 218, 223–5, 228
Murray, Lady Charlotte, *The British Garden*, 153
museums, 243, 252–4
　British Museum, 144, 233, 252
　Cox's Museum, 242
　natural history museums, 143–4, 146, 154, 161
Musschenbroek, Pieter van, 177
Myers, Robin, 228

Napoleon, 14, 111, 190, 245, 250
Napoleonic Wars, 152, 212–13, 217–18, 223, 245, 250
nation, 2, 11, 78–82, 83–4, 87, 94–6, 120–1, 131, 134, 153, 233
nationalism, 4–5, 7, 28, 44, 61–5, 74, 77–83, 85–96, 249
　and art, 233, 246–7
　anticolonial nationalisms, 87, 93
　antiquarian nationalism, 92
　national character, 78–79, 82–3, 85, 87
　Scottish nationalism, 62, 87
　United Irish nationalism, 94

natural history, 141–8, 150–1, 153–8, 162–3
　colonial, 153–6
　see also botany, fossils, mineralogy, paleontology, zoology
Natural History of Fishes and of Reptiles, Insects, Waters, Earths, Fossils, Minerals, and Vegetables, A, 152
natural philosophy, 141–2, 145–7, 149–52
naturalists, 142, 144, 156, 163
Nenadic, Stana, 196
neo-classicism, 37, 246–7, 252–3
　see also classicism
New Criticism, 3
New English Theatre, The, 220
Newgate prison, 113
Newman, Gerald, 82–3, 85
　The Rise of English Nationalism, 82
Newton, John, 225
Newton, Sir Isaac, 141, 146–7, 173
　Philosophiae Naturalis Principia Mathematica, 172
Nichol, John Pringle, 176–7
　System of the World, 170, 176
Nichols, Ashton, 162
Nicholson, William, 180
Nietzsche, Friedrich, 27, 33
Nonconformists, 15
　see also dissent and dissenters
North, Frederick, Lord, 219
Northumberland, Hugh Percy, Lord, 122–3
Novalis (Friedrich von Hardenberg), *Heinrich von Ofterdingen*, 170–1
Nugent, George, Lord Grenville, 217

Olbers, Wilhelm, 173
Ollier, Charles, 224
Ollier, James, 224

294

Index

Oriental Renaissance, 36, 42, 50
Orientalism, 2, 6–7, 37, 42–8, 51, 53–5
  as a cultural construction, 44
  eighteenth-century Orientalism, 40–1
  as a field of study, 43
  and Oriental languages, 37, 41–2, 47–8
  Romantic-era Orientalism, 40–1
opera, 244–5
otherness, 37–8, 43–4, 48, 259
Owen, Robert, 106
Owenson, Sidney, 80–1, 94–5
  Florence Macarthy, 80
  Lay of an Irish Harp or Metrical Fragments, 93
  The Wild Irish Girl, 92
Oxford University, 17, 215
Oxford University Press, 215, 224

Paine, Thomas, 17, 82, 84, 100–1, 104–6, 130–1, 224
  The Age of Reason, 19
  "Letter Addressed to the Addresser," 101
  The Rights of Man, 8, 82, 100, 104–5
painting, 2, 11–12, 232, 233–9, 245–7, 249, 252
  and actors, 241
  and imperialism, 246
  landscape painting, 232, 235, 237–9, 247
  and theatricality, 236
paleontology, 152
Palmer, Michael, *At Passages*, 276
  "Seven Poems With a Matrix for War," 276
pamphlets, 17, 21, 82, 87, 103, 107, 113, 125, 147, 150, 233
panoramas, 11, 156, 232, 243
Paradies, Maria-Theresa von, 184
Parkinson, James, 155, 159

Parkinson, Sydney, 154–5, 162, 164
  Journal, 156, 164
Parsons, William, Earl of Rosse, 176–7
Pascal, Blaise, 24
patriotism, 108, 245
Paul, Jean (Johann Paul Richter), 172, 176–7
  The Comet, 176
  Dr. Katzenberger's Journey to the Baths, 176
  "Dream upon the Universe," 171, 176
Peace of Amiens, 108
Peacock, Thomas Love, 120, 122–3
  Nightmare Abbey, 123
Pennant, Thomas, 142, 144, 147, 157
  British Zoology, 152
Phillips, Mark Salber, 57, 60
Philosophical Magazine, The, 151–3
Philp, Mark, 106
physics, 10, 141, 145, 149, 151, 168, 174, 177–82
Piano-Forte Magazine, 205
Piazzi, Giuseppe, 173
Pickering, William, 221–2, 228
picturesque, 236, 238–9, 242–3
Pitt, William, 111, 225, 243–4, 250
Platonism, 19, 24
  Neo-Platonism, 19
pleasure gardens, 11, 232, 242
Pliny, *Naturalis Historia*, 146
Plot, Ray, 157
Plot, Robert, 157
Plumb, J. H., *The Birth of a Consumer Society*, 191
Pneumatic Institute, 183
poetic justice, 2, 9, 124, 126–7
Poets of Great Britain, The, 220, 222
Poisson, Siméon-Denis, 178
Polanyi, Karl, 8, 120
Polwhele, Richard, *The Unsex'd Females*, 153

295

Index

Polynesia, 144, 154
Pons, Jean-Louis, 174
Pope, Alexander, 124, 213, 215
   The Rape of the Lock, 194
postcolonialism, 4, 73–4
postmodernism, 262, 270
poststructuralism, 3, 259
Pound, Ezra, 272, 274
Presbyterianism, 18, 28
Price, Richard, 82
Price, Uvedale, 237
   Essay on the Picturesque, 236–7
Prickett, Stephen, 29
Priestley, Joseph, 15, 19, 84, 177–8, 183
   Experiments and Observations on Different Kinds of Air, 183
   The History and Present State of Electricity, 178
Prince of Wales, 250
print capitalism, 78, 85–7
print culture, 4–5, 8, 82, 84–6, 88, 95, 100–3, 107, 114, 129, 145, 154
Proclamation of 1792, 103–4
Protestantism, 15, 16, 18, 21, 24, 28, 85, 90, 197
Public Characters, 156
public opinion, 101–2, 106
public sphere, 92, 94, 111, 152, 156, 233
publishing, 2, 5, 10, 99, 103–5, 107–8, 121–2, 129, 143, 212–21, 223–5, 228
   see also book production, book trade

Quakers, 17–18
Quarterly Review, 111, 217

Radcliffe, Ann, 171
Ramsay, Robert, 142, 145
Raphael, 246
rationalism, 19–22, 45, 114, 128–30

Raven, James
   The Business of Books, 228
   The English Novel 1770–1829, 228
   Judging New Wealth, 228
Ray, John, 157
Reaganism, 193
realism, 59
reason, 58, 101, 122
Reflector, 111
Reform Acts of 1832 and 1837, 16
Regner, Lars, 173
Reill, Johann Christian, 185–6
   Rhapsodies on the Application of Psychic Cures to Mental Disturbances, 186
republic of letters, 84, 107, 109–10
   see also public sphere
Reynolds, Sir Joshua, 241, 246, 252
   Discourses on Art, 247, 253
Ricardo, David, 264–5
   On the Principles of Political Economy and Taxation, 264
Ritter, Johann, 174, 180
   "Observations on Herschel's Recent Investigation of Light," 174
Robertson, William, 58, 64, 70–1
   History of the Reign of Charles V, 64
   History of Scotland, 64
Robespierre, Maximilien, 14, 21
Robinson, Mary, 125
   The Natural Daughter, 120
Rogers, Samuel
   Human Life, 224
   Italy, 224
   The Pleasures of Memory, 224
Roget, Peter Mark, 183
Romilly, Samuel, 124
Rose, Mark, 120
Rousseau, Jean-Jacques, 19–21
   Social Contract, 21, 80

Rowlandson, Thomas, 237, 243, 249–52
  "The Comet," 175
  "Exhibition Stare Case," 250, *251*, 252
Roxburghe, Duke of, 223
Royal Academy of Art, 233, 246–7, 252
Royal Botanical Gardens at Kew, 144
Royal Society of London, 143, 145–7, 152, 162, 173, 177, 180, 183
Royal Society of Medicine, 184
Rudwick, Martin, 159
Ruisdal, Jacob von, 237
Rush, Richard, 189
Russell, Bertrand, *History of Western Philosophy*, 28

Said, Edward, 44
San Francisco Renaissance, 273
Saussure, H. B. de, 151, 177
  Voyages dans les Alpes, 169
Sayre, Robert, *Romanticism Against the Tide of Modernity*, 197
Schelling, F. W. L. von, 151
  Zeitschrift für speculative Physik, 179
Schiller, Friedrich, *On the Aesthetic Education of Man*, 264
Schleele, Carl Wilhelm, 180
Schlegel, Friedrich, 65–6, 74
  Lectures on the History of Literature, 65
Schopenhauer, Arthur, 32
Schwab, Raymond, 36–7
sciences, 2, 141–2, 145, 154, 160, 164, 168–88
  see also astronomy, chemistry, geology, medicine, natural history, natural philosophy, physics

Scott, Sir Walter, 2, 28–9, 59–71, 73, 77, 81, 87, 200, 212, 218, 224–6
  Antiquary, The, 8, 80, 89
  Black Dwarf, The, 67
  Bride of Lammermoor, The, 67
  Chronicles of the Canongate, 67–8
  Heart of Midlothian, The, 28, 67, 128
  Ivanhoe, 124–5
  Kenilworth, 226
  Lady of the Lake, 218
  A Legend of Montrose, 67
  Life of Napoleon, 68
  Old Mortality, 67–8
  Waverley, 64, 69
  Waverley novels, 8, 28, 63, 65, 67, 69, 226
  Woodstock, 68
Scott, William, 135–6
séances, 184
Secord, James, 146, 150
secularization, 52
sensibility, 233, 235, 238
Seward, Anna, 2, 233, 235, 239
Shakespeare, William, 114, 213, 215, 220, 240–1, 245
  Henry V, 245
  The Tempest, 37
Shelley, Mary, *Frankenstein*, 128, 179–80
Shelley, Percy, 2, 10, 12, 16–19, 24, 26, 29, 32, 37–9, 50, 198, 224–5, 245, 254, 262–3, 270, 274
  Defense of Poetry, 263
  "Mont Blanc," 172
  The Necessity of Atheism, 17
  "Ozymandias," 115
  Prometheus Unbound, 29
  Queen Mab, 38, 196
Sheridan, Richard Brinsley, 235, 240, 243–4
  Pizarro, 244

Index

Siddons, Sarah, 240–1, 244
Simpson, David, 83
Simpson, Richard, 200
Sinclair, Sir John, *Statistical Account of Scotland*, 73
Slater, Don, 192
slavery, 40, 50, 156, 195
Sloane, Sir Hans, 147
smallpox vaccination, 184
Smellie, William, 142–3, 145, 147, 151, 154
  Philosophy of Natural History, 142–3, 145
Smiles, Samuel, *A Publisher and His Friends*, 228
Smith, Adam, 7, 61, 64–5, 73–4, 109, 200
Smith, Charlotte, 2, 9, 11, 121, 123, 150, 153, 157–62, 171–2, 238–9, 254
  Beachy Head, 9, 143, 145, 150, 153, 157–8, 160–4, 172
  Elegiac Sonnets, 121–2, 157
  The Old Manor House, 121
  Rural Walks, 157
Smith, Sir James Edward, 142, 144, 156
  Discourse on the Rise and Progress of Natural History, 142, 144
Smith, Sydney, 17
Snip, Simon, 149
  "The Natural__ist," 148
  The Philosophical Puppet Show, 148–9, 164
socialism, 264
Société de l'harmonie universelle, 185
Society of Antiquities, 155
Society for the Propagation of Christian Knowledge, 18, 225
Soemmerring, Samuel Thomas, 186
  On the Organ of the Soul, 185
Solander, Daniel, 154

Sorenson, Janet, *The Grammar of Empire in Eighteenth-Century British Writing*, 89
Southey, Robert, 2, 5–7, 21–3, 37–40, 46–54, 57, 156, 183, 225
  Colloquies on the Progress and Prospects of Society, 38, 45–6, 49–50, 53
  The Curse of Kehama, 6, 48
  "On the Means of Improving the People," 49
  "On the Rise and Progress of Popular Disaffection," 49
  Thabala the Destroyer, 6, 48–51
Spencer, George, Lord, 223
Spencer-Churchill, George, Marquess of Blandford, 223
Spenser, Edmund, 221
Spurzheim, Johann Gasper, 185
St Clair, William, 86
  The Reading Nation in the Romantic Period, 85
stamp tax, 114, 219
Stanhope, Charles, Lord, 219
Star, The, 217
Starke, Mariana, *Travels on the Continent*, 225
Stationers' Company, 212–15, 219
Stationer's Company v. Carnan, 213
Steele, Richard, 49
Steffen, Henrik, *Die Vier Norweger*, 171
Sterne, Laurence, 215
Stewart, Dugald, 7, 61, 63, 70, 74
Stokes, Eric, 52
Stothard, Thomas, 224
Strauss, David, *The Life of Jesus*, 29
structuralism, 3, 259
Stuart, Charles Edward, 90
Stuart, John, Third Earl of Bute, 90
sublime, 32, 47, 54–5, 122, 127, 134, 161, 170, 176, 240, 276
Surrealism, 274

Surrey Institution, 114
Swift, Jonathan, 215

Taine, Hippolyte, *History of English Literature*, 57
tales, 67–71, 74
　national tales, 58, 93, 95
　regional tales, 60, 62
taxonomy, 154, 157
Taylor, John, 217
technology, 38–9, 72, 86, 151, 213, 218, 243, 246, 268–9
Temple of the Muses, The, 222
Thames, 65
Thatcherism, 193
theatre, 2, 11–12, 29, 119, 233, 240, 243
　political culture of, 243–5
　theatricality, 243–4
Thompson, E. P., 114
Thomson, James, 214
　"Rule Britannia," 87
　The Seasons, 29
Thornton, Robert, *The Temple of Flora*, 152
Tilloch, Alexander, 151–2
Times, The, 113
toleration, religious, 16
Tolkien, J. R. R., 39
Tolstoy, Leo, *War and Peace*, 175
Tone, Theobald Wolfe, 95
Tories, 17–18, 23, 111, 245
tourism, 150, 225, 232, 237–8
Tower of London, 242
Townley, Lord, 252
Tracts for the Times, 225
travel writing, 109, 155, 172, 225
treason trials, 125, 127–30, 136
Trevor-Roper, Hugh, 84
Trilling, Lionel, 200
Trumpener, Katie, 63
　Bardic Nationalism, 58, 88, 93
Turner, J. M. W., 224, 247
　"The Righting Temeraire," 246

unconscious, the, 24
Unification of Great Britain, 88
　Act of Union of 1707, 88, 90–1
　Union of Ireland with Britain, 94
Unitarianism, 6, 15–16, 18–19, 23, 224
United Irishmen movement, 94–5
United Scotsmen, 95
United States of America, 17, 28
utilitarianism, 30–1

Valdarfer Boccaccio, 223
Vauxhall Gardens, 242–3, 246, 252
Veblen, Thorsten, 191
　The Theory of the Leisure Class, 190
Vietnam War, 274
Volney, Comte de, 51
Volta, Alessandro, 178, 180
　"On the electricity excited by the mere contact of conducting substances of different kinds," 180
Voltaire, 19–20
voyeurism, 252

Wakefield, Priscilla, *An Introduction to Botany*, 152
Wallace, Anne, 161
Watson, William, 177
Weber, Max, *The Protestant Ethic and the Spirit of Capitalism*, 16, 190, 197
Webster, Thomas, 161–2
　Transactions, 161
Wedderburn, Robert, 113
Wedgwood, Josiah, 183, 191
Wedgwood china, 193
Werner, Abraham, 169–71
　Kurze Klassifikation und Beschreibung der verschiedener Gebirgsarten, 169
Wesley, Charles, 15

Index

West, Benjamin, 156, 245–6
  "Death of General Wolfe," 245–6
Westminster Review, 132
Wetherall, Nathan, 215
White, Benjamin, 144, 150
White, Gilbert, 144, 150, 157, 160, 163
  The Natural History of Selborne, 144, 155, 157, 160
Whitehurst, John, 171–2
  An Inquiry into the Original State of the Earth, 169
Wilberforce, William, 52
Wilkes, John, *The North Briton*, 90
Wilkie, David, 246
  "Chelsea Pensioners," 246
Wilkins, Charles, 42
William the Conqueror, 158
Williams, Raymond, 116, 279
  Culture and Society, 3
Wilson, Alexander, 219
Wilson, John, 66–7
Wiltshire, Mary, 136
Wollaston, William, 174
Wollstonecraft, Mary, 16, 82, 84, 101, 106–8, 224
  Vindication of the Rights of Man, 82
  Vindication on the Rights of Woman, 99, 107, 116
  The Wrongs of Woman, 82
women, and authorship, 137
  and consumerism, 200–3
  and domesticity, 29
  and femininity, 202, 205, 238
  and marriage, 17, 134, 136
  and painting, 233–5, 238
  and religion, 18
Wood, Marcus, 129
Woodward, John, *An Essay Toward a Natural History of the Earth*, 169

Wooler, T. J., 112
  see also Black Dwarf
Wordsworth, Dorothy, 145, 249
Wordsworth, William, 2, 6, 10–11, 16, 18, 21–3, 28–31, 39, 57, 62–3, 83, 109, 122, 125, 145, 150, 192, 194–6, 198, 223, 225, 237, 243, 247, 254, 261–3, 273–4, 279–80
  The Excursion, 30
  A Guide Through the District of the Lakes for the Use of Tourists and Residents, 225
  Lyrical Ballads, 38, 44–5, 57–8, 223
  "My Heart Leaps Up," 280
  "Ode: Intimations of Immortality," 237, 280
  Prelude, 125, 237, 243, 260
  "Resolution and Independence," 172
  "Tintern Abbey," 237, 249
Works of English Poets, The, 213, 220

Xaver, Franz, 174–5
xenophobia, 90

Yeats, William Butler, "September 1913," 77
Yellow Dwarf, 8, 100, 112–13, 115
Yeo, Richard, 145
Young, Arthur, 22, 26
  Travels in France during the Years 1787, 1788, and 1789, 25

Zachs, William, *The First John Murray*, 229
Zimmerman, Sarah, 121
Ziolkowski, Ted, 171
zoology, 143, 152